HUMAN MIGRATION

HUMAN MIGRATION

A Guide to Migration Literature in English
1955-1962

J. J. MANGALAM

with the assistance of
CORNELIA MORGAN

University of Kentucky Press
LEXINGTON : 1968

To
H. K. S. and J. S. B.
Fellow students, friends, and mentors

ACKNOWLEDGMENTS

One does not always know to whom all appreciation is due in the production of a volume such as this. Among those to whom the author feels consciously indebted are the following:

James S. Brown and Harry K. Schwarzweller, senior colleagues in the Beech Creek Migration Study;

The National Institute of Mental Health, the Department of Sociology and Rural Sociology of the University of Kentucky, the Kentucky Research Foundation, and the University of Kentucky Research Committee for financial support;

Gladys Ernst, Jeanne Goff, and Kathleen Moran Young for help at the various stages of abstracting and editing and of preparing the subject index;

Robert Chanteloup, Dennis Dedrik, David Krugel, John Seggar, and Robert Whitten, members of a graduate seminar in migration, for checking on the reliability of abstracting;

Nancy Carlson, Joyce Feusner, Dianne Cochran, and Art Gallaher of the Center for Developmental Change for help in typing the manuscript;

Donald J. Bogue, Otis Dudley Duncan, C. Horace Hamilton, Rudolf Heberle, Clarence Senior, Henry S. Shryock, Jr., T. Lynn Smith, Conrad Taeuber, Irene Taeuber, Warren S. Thompson, Rupert Vance, and Charles Westoff, who were consulted in the initial stages of this work and who made useful suggestions.

The Introduction has benefited a great deal from the criticisms and comments made by Harry K. Schwarzweller and Sylvia Mangalam. Frank E. Jones, T. R. Ford and George Hillery also made useful suggestions.

To all these the author is deeply grateful but he alone is responsible for the errors and inadequacies to be found in the work.

It is comfronting to know that Harry-Joseph and Kunjalichi Theadora still love their Daddy, even after his missing a Christmas celebration to prepare this manuscript.

CONTENTS

INTRODUCTION

This work is a byproduct of a systematic search of migration literature during the initial phase of designing the Beech Creek Study, an investigation of social adjustment and personal stability of migrants from an isolated, three-neighborhood area in eastern Kentucky to places in Kentucky and adjoining states. We found that the vast amount of existing literature, empirical and otherwise, was scattered widely in a variety of sources such as scientific journals, dissertations, books, and reports. Furthermore, we found that, in spite of the large number of existing works dealing with migration, only a very few of them ventured any theoretical statements, and most of them did not suggest any theoretical import for their empirical findings. This lack of theoretical statements has resulted, as Hamilton (124) and Beijer (1963: 316)[1] and others have pointed out, in the virtual impossibility of making use of the existing research findings as an analytical tool. Theoretical statements that do exist in the contemporary literature, while useful and adequate for interpreting a specific segment of the migration field or for making sense out of specific data in each instance, largely fail to provide a general framework within which the vast amount of existing facts from different migration studies can be integrated and given meaning.

The task of building a general theoretical framework that can efficiently interpret migration data of diverse kinds and weld them into a single suggestive explanatory system confronts numerous obstacles. Sociologists, for example, are not the only social scientists interested ih the study of migration. On the contrary, migration has been and will continue to be a proper subject for study, for example, by anthropologists, demographers, economists, human geographers, geneticists, political scientists, psychologists, social psychologists, and statisticians. Within each of these disciplines there are differences in orientation to the study of migration and in approaches to specific problems. We propose to demonstrate here, however, that it is possible to begin developing a theoretical approach that is general enough to avoid some of the pitfalls of the specific, segmental approaches that are so characteristic of migration studies in sociology and other behavioral sciences. The ideal of a comprehensive theory of migration is not only a possibility but must be an important concern in the future.

A survey of migration literature will expose the strengths and weaknesses of scholarly writings on the subject during 1955-1962. What beyond the findings of Ravenstein (1885), of Sorokin, Zimmerman, and Galpin (1932), and of Dorothy Thomas (1938) do we know on migration from the studies under review? What major trends in the study of migration are revealed by the present review of literature? What theoretical guidelines have been formulated for future migration studies? These questions are related and need to be answered conjointly in order to provide a balanced view of the current state of migration research preparatory to setting forth a theoretical framework.

After noting the lack of acceptable generalizations about the selectivity of internal migration, Dorothy Thomas added: "That so much of the recent empirical research seems trivial and inept may be attributed partly to the newness of the field, and the lack of adequate data and techniques, and perhaps, also, partly to a reaction of the 'fact finders' against the conflicting and unfounded claims of the speculators that migrants were 'better' than, or 'worse' than, or both better and worse than, or not at all different from non-migrants" (1938: 161). Some triviality does perhaps still exist in the recent empirical research; there are still problems in quality of data and techniques; and "fact finders" continue to be pitched against "speculators." But it is not true any more that the field of migration studies is new with respect to empirical research. Awareness of the importance of migration studies has steadily grown over the years since Thomas' statement. Not only a steady increase in the number of journal articles and monographs dealing with migration but also a sophistication in the techniques of collection and processing of migration data, a diversification of variables used in recent migration studies, and a growing concern with theoretical aspects of the study of migration attest to an increased awareness of the importance of studying migration. This awareness is found not only in the North-Atlantic countries but also in southern Europe, Africa, Asia, and Latin America. Partly, this results from the sheer numerical increase of demographically oriented social scientists.

But this increased awareness has another basis as well. Migration has become recognized not only as a problem-creating phenomenon but also as a problem-solving social process. Whether international or internal, migration is generally assumed to be a response to new and existing opportunities in terms of migrants' unmet wants, both material and nonmaterial. Whereas the processes and effects of internal migration in the United States are not necessarily applicable as such to other nations, it is generally agreed that both in technologically developing and developed nations, migration plays an important part in economic growth. Studies in Egypt (Abu-Lughod, 1) and India (Anderson and Banerji, 6) exemplify this concern with understanding the dynamics of social change and economic growth through an understanding of population changes. It has been shown that even countries like India (Zachariah, 379) in their initial stages of industrialization are confronting the effects, problems, and consequences of internal migration. Humanitarian reasons, a slowly developing international ethics, and a disciplined self-interest on the part of the receiving countries have continued to permit a fair amount of international migration to occur in the post-World War II period.[2] The current state of interest in migration, particularly rural-urban migration in emerging nations, is such that one can safely predict a rapid increase in migration studies in the years ahead of us.

Demographers' recognition of migration as a fundamental dimension in the study of population and its changes, their general orientation to and excellent training in statistics, and the amenability of demographic variables such as age, sex, and distance traveled to statistical manipulation have combined to produce a considerable improvement in the measurement of internal migration as a demographic phenomenon. Granted that there are reasonable voices raised for better methods of analysis (Hamilton, 124) and more adequate data (Tarver, 335; Taeuber, 331), still there is an operational elegance and mathematical neatness to the definitions of terms used in migration analysis and their measurement (Thomlinson, 345). In these days of computer programming and simulation methods, demographic analysis of migration data will very soon become a fast job, with high speed computers handling scores of variables and multivariate analysis in a matter of a few hours or days. Building of mathematical models for migration studies suitable for computer simulation has been underway for some time (Price, 261). These quantitative methods, some direct and others indirect, are generally known (Bogue, 32).

However, improvements in the techniques of demographic analysis have not been matched by sophistication in the methodology of migration analysis. Although Dorothy Thomas as early as 1938 had advocated a combination of case and statistical methods, emphasizing the environmental conditions in the sending and receiving communities (1938: 162-67), migration studies have continued to be largely statistical and occasionally case studies, but seldom, if ever, a combination of both.[3] Thomas did not provide a foolproof methodology or a neat theoretical frame of reference, but following her suggestions would have prevented a great many of the studies since that time from becoming trivial in their research designs and substantive findings.

Another development in the study of migration is the variety of the kinds of variables used for understanding this complex phenomenon. Besides the traditional demographic and sociodemographic variables such as age, sex, distance traveled, ethnic origin, education, occupation, and income, and such psychological variables as intelligence, recent studies show a growing interest in such sociopsychological and social dimensions as attitudes, aspiration, motivation, community identification, and institutional influence. This diversification of variables is the result of a recognition of the complex nature of migration as an aspect of motivated human behavior (Tarver, 336) and parallels the growth of methodology and theory in social sciences in general. This growth has had, and continues to have, its influence on migration studies because of the increasing interest which nondemographers are beginning to take in the study of migration. Also, in these studies and elsewhere there is an increasing, though still small number of statements about the relationships between population changes and social change (Bogue, 32; Taft and Robbins, 624; Taeuber, 1964). The relationship between population and social changes has been almost a virgin field for theoretical and empirical research and has been left practically untouched since the days of Durkheim (1933), although works of Davis (1949, 1951) and more recently statements by Moore (1959) and Hillery (1957) demonstrate sociologists' interest in interrelating sociological and demographic variables. As Thomas has correctly noted, the characteristics of a sociologically lower order of significance (demographic variables such as age, sex, and physical health) should act as control variables for characteristics of a higher order of significance such as motivation and assimilation (1938: 160). This, in turn, would lead to more meaningful statements of truly social organizational significance.

Undoubtedly one of the most important studies of migration ever done from a theoretical point of view is Thomas and Znaniecki's *Polish Peasant in Europe and America* (1927), considered a classic in sociological theory, research, and writing, though little read and still less used by contemporary students of migration theory and methodology. First, these authors say that the study of human behavior cannot afford to overlook

[2]

either of the two concepts, attitudes and values. In their lengthy "Methodological Note" (1958), they have emphasized this point of view in the following words: "The cause of a social or individual phenomenon is never another social or individual phenomenon alone, but always a combination of a social and an individual phenomenon . . . . The cause of a value or of an attitude is never an attitude or a value alone, but always a combination of an attitude and a value." (Vol. I, p. 44). Later in the same "Note," they have argued that the best method for studying migration is to investigate how the values of the migrants act upon their pre-existing attitudes, resulting in their migrating or not migrating. The second major contribution of Thomas and Znaniecki is less explicit than the first one. By actually studying the conditions and characteristics of the social organizations in which the migrants were involved, they have suggested forcefully the need for understanding the migrants and their problems in terms of both their areas of origin and that of their destination——a theme repeated in Dorothy Thomas' research memorandum (1938: 162). In spite of the relevance of these recommendations for research in migration, none of the studies under review reveals explicit benefits from the *Polish Peasant*. Thus a lack of theoretical perspectives in migration studies does not entirely result from a complete absence of a theoretical framework or of important guidelines for the construction of one. Perhaps the reasons for theoretical inadequacy of these studies have to be sought elsewhere.

What kinds of theoretical efforts are revealed by a review of the studies presented here? Nearly a fifth of the studies under review have used some kind of explicit hypotheses to guide their research. Although studies testing hypotheses derived explicitly from a theoretical frame of reference are few, the works of Forman (96), Goldsmith (107), Eisenstadt (439), and Litwak (192) exemplify this kind of study. These researchers did not depend upon census data for their works. But even census data have been shown to be amenable to a certain degree of sociological analysis (Nishiura, 232; Wakeley and Nasrat, 356). Of course, it should be readily granted that studies such as these are exceptions to the general practice of setting up of *ad hoc* hypotheses, which generally imply some theoretical concern but are not derived initially from any body of organized theory. A fuller understanding of the relatively poor level of conceptualization in migration studies can be obtained from a consideration of the kinds of variables used for explaining and predicting various phases of migration.

Let us first consider the variables used to describe the migrants in the theoretically oriented studies. Traditionally, migration selectivity has been generally attributed to physical, biological, biosocial, sociodemographic, and psychological variables, such as age, sex, race, physical health, grades completed, occupational categories, and intelligence.[4] Important as these surely are, there has been a dearth of strictly sociological variables to explain at least part of this complex phenomenon, which has its sociological as well as non-sociological aspects. Whereas a majority of studies under review continue to use these traditional variables, a few praiseworthy attempts to capture the sociological dimension of migration differentials need to be noted. Yaukey (378) has combined age and marital status as an indicator of position in the life cycle, a more truly sociological variable than each of the components taken separately. Another example of lifting nonsociological variables to a sociological level is provided by the works of some rural sociologists (Brown, 46; Martin, 214), where variables such as income and employment on the farm have been subsumed under tenure status. Granted that these innovations are not earthshaking, they surely point toward ways of avoiding reductionistic approaches in the sociological study of selectivity of migrants.

Just as in the case of migration differentials, a few theoretical advances may be noted in the study of the cause of migration. In other words, what factors are responsible for people deciding to move? Also, how is the decision to move arrived at?[5] It cannot be denied that *one* of the strong "push" factors operating to influence people to migrate is economic in nature. However, that "labor moves in the direction of wages" is much too deterministic a formulation to be true, and, like all other deterministic explanations of complex human behavior, much too simplistic an explanation of migration.[6] Bogue (32), Petersen (561), Tarver (336), and others have noted the importance of noneconomic factors in understanding motivations for migration. More important than these for our purpose are the ways in which the economic factor has been incorporated into a social organizational or a sociological framework. The attempts in this area are not many. But Nishiura's (232) use of "occupational role structuring of location migrants" is worth noting. She follows the work of Sarah Smith, whose contribution is within the framework of Parsons and Shills. Unfortunately, Nishiura uses census data in her study, and this understandably limits the application of such a theory of action. Another theoretical advance revealed by the studies under review is the use of community obligations on the part of migrants as actors (Goldsmith, 107) instead of such psychological variables as attitude toward communities, and community satisfactions as found in studies by Bowring and Durgin (40), Eicher (88), and Forman (96). A rather novel way of using demographic data has been formulated and demonstrated in part by Albert F. Anderson (5) and Nasrat (228). Both of them have used a framework built around three concepts, namely cohesion, deprivation, and adaptation to deprivation, to infer indirectly reasons for migration from census data.

It must also be pointed out that there is a slight trend among scholars toward using an institutional framework for understanding the process of making a decision to move. Martin (214), Knowlton (170), and Litwak (193), for example, have noted the influence of family and kinship in the migration process. These insights, if followed through in future studies of reasons for migration and decision-making to migrate, are likely to be fruitful.

With respect to area of destination and its relationships to area of origin of the migrants, the two dominant themes are opportunities and distance. Perhaps the most significant finding related to these two themes has been a convergence or a reconciliation of the hypotheses of Zipf and Stouffer as achieved by Theodore R. Anderson (7). Although studies like those by Paul F. Sharp (299) and Stanislawski (321) have called attention to the similarity between social organizations at the place of origin and the place of destination as a clue to determining the direction of migration, nothing significant by way of research has been done in this area. A limited number of studies such as that by Smith (310) has called attention to the part played by institutions such as family and kinship in determining the destination of the migrants. From this brief review of contemporary migration literature it may be concluded that not much progress has been made in developing significant frames of reference with respect to the destination of the migrants that take into account the behavioral aspects of migration.

Actually, the characteristics of the migrants, the reasons for their special mobility or the factors responsible for migration, the direction of migration, and the description of the areas of destination have received less attention from sociologists and other behavioral scientists than the problems that result from migration. In other words, if we exclude the more strictly demographic studies, social problems have dominated the research scene more than any other aspect of migration; consequently nearly half of the publications with more or less theoretical underpinnings are devoted to one social problem or another. These problems span a wide range, including racial transition of neighborhoods, continuities and discontinuities in denominational loyalty, problems of assimilation of immigrants, migrants' adjustment to city life, social participation of rural migrants in urban setting, changes in the value patterns of migrants, anomie and social class of migrants, psychological and mental health aspects of migration and homelessness, delinquency and crime and migration, migration and socioeconomic status, problems of urban public housing resulting from an influx of rural migrants, family disorganization and migrant labor, educational problems of the migrant children, economic problems of the migrants, and political effects of rural migration.[7] Then there are studies such as those by Zubrzycki (384), Elkholy (90), and Liu (193) suggesting ways of ameliorating the conditions created by migrants. Fewer studies, such as those by Blumberg (30) and Doerflinger (77), concentrate more strictly on the effects of migration on the social structure.

The problem of assimilation of immigrants into the host society is the theme on which more studies of theoretical import have been written than on any other on the basis of the abstracted studies. In a dozen or so studies focused on assimilation, there is none that has formulated an explicitly social organizational frame of reference. Excellent as they are within the limits of their problems and the data, they have generally used sociopsychological frames of reference (e.g., Degroot, 73; Eisenstadt, 439) or set up ad hoc hypotheses on the basis of available knowledge (e.g., Krueger, 174; Hutchinson, 138; Richardson, 265), or a combination of both (e.g., DeFleur and Cho, 72). In the case of sociopsychological frame of reference, the emphasis is on migrants as individuals, and in the case of ad hoc hypotheses, the emphasis is on finding immediate solutions to pressing problems. Such studies are thus limited in their perspectives, although each of them may have something to contribute towards a more general framework. One that comes closest to a sociological point of view is Eisenstadt's study (439) of the absorption of Jewish immigrants into the state of Israel, using a framework based on "the immigrants' basic motivations and role-expectations, as developed throughout the migratory process, and the various demands made upon and facilities offered to them in the country of absorption" (p. 10). Although Eisenstadt was focusing on the absorptive phase of migration, his point of view has a great deal to contribute toward a more general theory of migration. Eisenstadt himself was more concerned about "the sociopsychological nature of the processes of immigration" and thus had a narrower framework than is required to understand a more complete picture of the total migration phenomenon.[8] Jones (154) has reviewed Eisenstadt's study at some length, pointing out the sociopsychological nature of the framework used. He in turn has suggested two related sociological approaches to the study of immigrants' adjustment. One approach is to treat adjustment within the context of socialization, studying "what occurs between socializer and socializee as interaction structured in a system of roles" (p. 45); and the other, "to study the significance of new members to a social system with emphasis on the relation of the system's functional requirements to its methods of dealing with new members" (p. 45). Although Jones' article appeared in 1955, the studies abstracted here do not contain any work that has followed up his suggestions. There are other studies like those by Blumberg (30) and Litwak (192) which have theoretical implications. These are referred to later in the concluding section of this chapter, where some guidelines for developing a general theory of migration are presented. Suffice it to note here that none of these studies provide an overall general theoretical point of view to make sense out of the ever-increasing number of empirical and quasi-empirical studies dealing with the various phases of migration mentioned in the foregoing discussion. As Wilber (367) and others have pointed out, these studies, detached and isolated in conceptual and methodological advances as they are, ought to be treated as an interim phase toward a more comprehensive theory of migration.

The current paucity of generalized theories of migration evident in the foregoing brief summary of contemporary studies demands consideration of the probable reasons for this paucity, for any remedial measures can only follow such an analysis. In our judgment, the major reasons for the absence of a general sociological theory of migration can be summarized under four headings: conception of the nature of migration, nature of the data used in migration studies, disciplinary orientations of the scholars, and a lack of concern by social organizational theorists for the phenomenon. These reasons need to be elaborated further.

Conceptualization of Migration

It is almost a truism to say that the manner in which a phenomenon is abstracted influences considerably its conceptualization and, following that, its investigation.[9] Most of the studies of migration reveal inadequate abstractions of the phenomenon, and these have led to a number of inadequate definitions and treatments.

The notion that migration is a random phenomenon because there is little or no predictability in the selectivity of the migrants still seems to have some currency (Sorokin, 1932: 507; Thomas, 1938: 160; Petersen, 245; Bogue, 34: 348). How much the lingering notion of migration as a random phenomenon has affected interest in developing theoretical schemes for studying it is uncertain. For, if migration is random behavior, then the question of building a scientific theory of migration is pointless. A scientific theory, based on inductive method, can only be built on the basis of recurring

and patterned events. Fortunately, this particular view of migration being a random behavior is not very widely held among contemporary scholars.

A more serious misconception than randomness of migration, although held more implicitly than explicitly, is the widespread influence of what might be called physical and biological reductionism or an attempt to explain and predict direction and volume of migration by physical and biological variables. In his concluding remarks on internal migration, Bogue has said, "For example, some of us have approached human migration as one would approach the study of migration of birds or the dispersion of insects from a common source. Others have likened migration to the fundamental laws of descriptive mechanics, gravitation, or electrostatics" (33: 505). The two outstanding examples of physical reductionism in migration studies are the variables of distance and age. Stouffer's attempt to replace distance with intervening opportunities reflected the awareness of some sociologists concerning this bias. Attempts to replace age, a correlate of time, have been rather limited in the work of sociologists, although some effort has been made to use stage in the life cycle as a sociological substitute for chronological age (Yaukey, 378).

The most prevalent influence of biological reductionism in migration studies is exemplified by the use of sex of the migrant as an explanatory and predictive variable. One seldom, if ever, comes across sex role and its relationships to the migration phenomenon, although a part of sex role in the form of occupational role structuring is reflected in a few studies such as that by Nishiura (232).

The point to be made here is a simple one, namely that some variables such as age and sex can be interpreted physically or biologically or sociologically. But it is a serious error for a sociologist to incorporate a physical or biological observation or variable into sociological theory or interpretation without providing a sociological "sense," which is quite different from its demographic, or biological, or ecological "sense."

Two more misdirecting influences on the efforts to conceptualize migration need to be mentioned. One is the emphasis on the individual in the study of migration. Many of the psychological and sociopsychological studies of migration using such variables as individual attitudes, motives, and aspirations give evidence of a misconception of migration as only an individual behavior, different from interindividual or social behavior. This approach tends to leave out the human interactional element from migration and to concentrate on individual characteristics. Most of the better known studies of migration fall into this category. Our objection to this approach is not that it is wrong, but that it is too truncated a view of migration—a view that takes the heart of the matter away from the phenomenon.

Last, but not the least of the misconceptions of the nature of migration is the treatment of each study of migration as if it were a unique case, by implication if not in explicit formulation. The best evidence in support of this criticism comes from the fact that in so many studies variables are chosen and hypotheses are set up in an *ad hoc* fashion as if the findings of other migration studies had little relevance to the particular case in question. In spite of the efforts by scholars like Heberle (127) and Petersen (243) to set up typologies of migration, very little attention has been paid to using them as conceptual tools. One must conclude from these errors of omission, both in design and generalization, that a misconception of each migration as a unique phenomenon has undoubtedly reinforced or rationalized the lack of effort to formulate a general theory or theories of migration.

Although the four elements discussed above (assumption of randomness, tendency to be reductionistic, emphasis on the individual, and the implicit ascription of uniqueness to each case) have been called misconceptions in the study of migration, it is not suggested that physical, biological, and psychological variables, for example, are not involved in migration. On the contrary, no one can deny that attitudes and aspirations enter into making decisions to move. One can even understand why these factors were employed, explicitly or implicitly, to understand the migration phenomenon. Migration as a social problem needs to be understood in terms of tangible remedial measures, and physical, biological, and psychological variables are more tangible in an immediately practical sense than some of the sociological variables. Some social scientists, in a hurry to help solve social problems, cannot or do not always wait for the sequence of prediction following explanation; prediction becomes an end in itself. The more tangible and easily quantifiable the predictors, the more readily they are accepted. These approaches, seemingly sociological or social organizational, have left out an important aspect of migration, namely its interactional nature. To the extent to which the interactional content of migration has been largely left out, efforts at building a general social organizational theory of migration as a collectivity phenomenon have been minimal. Migrants have been treated largely like inanimate bodies moving through physical space and time.

Nature of the Data Used in Migration

Another important reason for a demonstrated general lack of interest for building theories in the study of migration is the nature of the data used in a large proportion of these studies. Traditionally migration studies have depended heavily on official statistics such as bound volumes of government censuses whenever available. Other important primary data for migration studies have been derived from such secondary sources as medical records, telephone directories, and, in the case of international migration, from such sources as port statistics (Thomas, 340). These statistics vary in degrees of accuracy (Bogue, 32; Hamilton, 124; Taeuber, 331; Tarver, 335). Besides, they cannot and do not touch upon the social processes involved in migration. Students of demography agree almost unanimously that data from more accurate and direct surveys are needed to arrive at reasonable generalizations on migration. If this is the view among established demographers, the need for direct observational data to provide information on the normative structures of the migrants will be felt even more by sociologists and other behavioral scientists.

Disciplinary Orientations of the Scholars

The third reason for the absence of a general theory of migration has to be traced to the disciplinary orientation of the students of migration. It has been pointed out that migration studies have heavily leaned on government statistics such as census data for their source of information. A majority of those who have used this information for the study of migration happen to be basically demographers, with or without training in theory of social organization.

Another important class of students of migration are labor economists, who generally have dealt with labor and labor movement as abstract qualities and not as part of the complex behavior of the migrants in the interactional sense. Thus, in the considerable number of studies one comes across in the two journals of the International Labor Office, for example, there is little to choose from for one who is looking for a behavioral explanation of migration.[10]

The more strictly sociologically oriented students of migration have either dealt with migration from a psychological or sociopsychological point of view as, for example, in the case of The *Polish Peasant* by W. I. Thomas and Florian Znaniecki (1927) and *The Absorption of Immigrants* by Samuel N. Eisenstadt (439), or treated each migration study as an individual case as done in so many studies included in the present volume. The use of sociopsychological frames of reference and variables as in the works of Thomas and Znaniecki, Eisenstadt, and Goldsmith (107), are understandable because of the need to take into account the subjective responses of the individual migrant to his total situation before making the decision to move. But what is disappointing is that a sociopsychological framework has been used almost to the exclusion of a more comprehensive social organizational framework.

Lack of Concern by Sociological Theorists for the Phenomenon

One reason for resorting to sociopsychological variables and frames of reference to study migration has already been mentioned, namely a propensity to treat migration as an individual process. But this does not necessarily explain the apparent rejection of social organizational frames of reference. This rejection seemingly is fostered by a failure on the part of contemporary social organization theorists to concern themselves with population and the three components of its change, namely fertility, mortality, and migration. As a matter of fact little or no major work of theoretical importance has appeared since Emile Durkheim's *On the Division of Labor* (1933) that related population growth and social organization. The major works of such contemporary theorists as Talcott Parsons, Robert K. Merton, Robin M. Williams, Jr., George Homans, and Howard Becker do not concern themselves, except in a passing manner, with the articulation of social theory with one of the major contingent conditions for any society, namely population. One notable exception is found in the works of Kingsley Davis. In his *Human Society* (1949: 588-91) he has indicated some of the problems involved in the study of migration and has provided a typology, which is not intended to be a theoretical framework. In *The Population of India and Pakistan* (1951), he sticks closely to traditional demographic treatment of migration, his data being derived from official Indian censuses. Whereas the existing social theories can contribute to the study of migration, there is little doubt that there has been a lack of explicit interest among leading social organization theorists in the study of migration. For this reason a general theoretical framework for the study of migration has not been developed; instead, a large number of *ad hoc* hypotheses scientifically noncumulative, have been advanced and tested by empirical researchers. As a consequence, our current knowledge of migration tends to be fragmentary and noncumulative.

The need for a general theory as an aid in migration research has been expressed by many scholars in different ways. For example, a general theoretical reorientation with a multidisciplinary emphasis in the study of migration has been advocated by Wilber (367); Hauser (1956) and Vance (1956) have noted a dearth of theory in all aspects of demography, including migration. Attempts to construct typologies of migration (Duncan, 81; Gupta, 113; Heberle, 127; Petersen, 243, 244) add another kind of evidence of scholars reaching out for some kind of organizing principle to make sense out of the steadily accumulating mass of migration data. Efforts at model building to study various aspects of migration on the part of many (Anderson, 5; Folger, 93; Goldsmith, 107; Nishiura, 232; Taft, 332) illustrate a similar need for theoretical guidelines for the study of migration. As Beijer (1963), Tarver (336), and others have noted, migration cannot be understood without understanding the dynamic interplay that exists among demographic, economic, and social factors, and any attempt at formulating theoretical statements on migration ought to take this interplay into consideration.

A social organizational theory of migration that meets these varied and complex demands is not likely to be formulated in the near future. The work of conceptualization, systematization, and verification which must precede the statement of a theory is only beginning. What follows then is offered as guidelines that may suggest future directions.

Migration in this context is basically conceived of as a social phenomenon with some aspects of it within the social system, some within the culture system and some within the personality system of social organization. The framework that is outlined below, then takes into account mainly the collectivity or group aspects of migration, modified by its cultural and personality dimensions insofar as such modification is both meaningful and manageable in a theoretical sense.[11] Developing a basically social organizational framework for the study of any social phenomenon consists of at least four steps. First, that part of the phenomenon which is social (interactional) has to be abstracted from the totality of its dimensions, and then the abstraction must be defined. Second, a general theoretical orientation for the study of society in social organizational terms has to be outlined. Third, the phenomenon under study has to be located within the general theoretical orientation. Fourth, the major questions to be answered concerning the phenomenon within the framework have to be spelled out to demonstrate the usefulness of the approach.

Definition of Migration

Why should migration be defined again when so many definitions already exist? As has been already pointed out, there are a number of misconceptions of migration, and these have led to inadequate conceptualizations of the phenomenon that are partly responsible for the state of the existing studies. Writers have defined migration in the following terms:

> We define migration as the physical transition of an individual, or a group from one society to another. This transition usually involves abandoning one social setting and entering another and different one. (Eisenstadt, 439: 1)

> Henceforth we will use the term migration for the change of residence of an individual from one parish or commune to another. (Hagerstrand, 481: 28)

A migration means, therefore, not merely a shift of a certain number of undifferentiated persons from one place to another, but also a change in the occupational and population structure of both countries or regions. (Petersen, 562: 592)

Migration is defined in this chapter as the movements (involving change of permanent resident) from one country to another which take place through the volition of the individuals or families concerned. (Thomas, 340:510)

Human migration is the changing of the place of abode permanently, or, when temporarily, for an appreciable duration as e.g., in the case of seasonal workers. It is used symbolically in the transition from one surrounding to another in the course of human life. (Weinberg, 663: 265-66)

And who is a migrant?

A migrant is defined as an individual who moves from one area or section of the country to another for the purpose of taking up residence. (Omari, 237: 48)

A migrant is defined here as a person who resides in a place different at the end of a specified period of time from the beginning of the time period. (Thomlinson, 346: 357)

These definitions of migration and migrant are not the only ones found in the literature but are typical of the definitions used by leading students of migration. What do these definitions reveal about the implicit or explicit conceptions of migration held by these writers? Or, more pertinently, what are the conceptual components included in working definitions of migration? First, clearly migration is seen as a physical movement of people through space. Second, more or less permanent change of residence is prerequisite to considering this movement as migration. Third, migration is seen as an individual activity, although none of the definitions necessarily exclude movement of a collectivity. The definitions imply other dimensions as well. Eisenstadt talks about "abandoning one social setting," Hagerstrand about "one parish or commune," Petersen about "change in occupational and population structure," and Weinberg adds a symbolic dimension. Some, like Olson (236), have talked about "movement from one community to another," and others, like Brown and Buck (47), have called attention to improving and resettlement involved in migration. Reviewing the process of international migration Taft and Robbins write: "The emigrant leaving his native land breaks ties with his people, and with the goals and practices of his home culture. The immigrant entering his adopted land establishes new ties, comes to accept new values; yet he contributes something himself to the new culture. And whatever his direction, the migrant is caught up in the larger problems which confront both native and foreigner. These include

population growth, the search for economic satisfaction, racial contacts and conflicts, the development of national loyalties, the establishment of intercultural relations. In short, the migrant is part of, and influenced by, the basic social processes" (624: 634). These statements apply, with necessary modifications, to internal migrants as well. An implied, but not well-incorporated, notion is the interactional dimension of the phenomenon. A still less clearly defined dimension of migration is brought out by Thomas' phrase, "through the volition of the individuals or families concerned." In other words, migration is motivated behavior, not mechanical or involuntary. An act of volition implies decision-making, based on a hierachy of values.

A comprehensive definition of migration, then, should include the interactional dimension and decision-making process that are at best only implied and not made explicit in the above definitions. A hierarchy of values as the selection criterion to choose from available alternate goals of migrating or not migrating should be included also. Although not exhaustive, the following definition is sufficiently inclusive of the phenomenon's major social dimensions and should therefore be more useful. *Migration is a relatively permanent moving away of a collectivity, called migrants, from one geographical location to another, preceded by decision-making on the part of the migrants on the basis of a hierarchically ordered set of values or valued ends and resulting in changes in the interactional system of the migrants.* The characteristics included in this definition set the boundaries for the study of the phenomenon of migration. The identification of instances of migration *in these terms*, excluding others often called migration is a necessary condition for a proper study of migration within a general theory of social organization.

The most frequently stressed aspect of migration is *permanent moving* or change of residence. The permanent moving away of people rules out such cases as commuters, salesmen, and tourists as migrants. However, the period of time implied by the term *permanent* cannot be generalized for all instances of migration, but has to be considered individually in each specific case. Also, geographic mobility can mean moving across the street, from one neighborhood to another within the same community, across county or district lines, or from one country to another and can involve thousands of miles in some instances. The fourth criterion, *changes in the interactional system of the migrants*, sets limits to the time and distance involved before a particular movement can be called migration.

Collectivity is the social organizational, especially the sociological, dimension in the definition of migration. This criterion rules out as part of the migration phenomenon isolated and individual cases of movement of people which, though natural, come under the head of unique and random events; however, events that are seemingly random and unique should not be rejected outright without careful examination. For example, a holder of a university degree permanently leaving his native place for a distant town in search of an occupation appropriate to his training and education might seem to be a unique case. But on further examination, although it might be the only one case in that particular place, it may be seen as one of many similar cases. In other words, this individual, abstracted from his immediate surroundings and conceptualized as an *actor* (a "bundle" of status roles) with certain attributes, can very well be a member of a collectivity, a member of a category of actors within a certain normative system different from that of the home village. In this sense, many of the migration studies within the demographic tradition have taken into account the collectivity dimension, though only accidentally. For, more often than not, little effort is made to delineate the collectivity with respect to its normative system.

The criterion of *decision-making on the basis of a hierarchically ordered set of values or valued ends* is highly important if we are to understand the dynamics of the migration process, the problems that follow the act of migration and their resolution. Migration is not to be treated as a random behavior of those who migrate, not only because random behavior, like an unique event, cannot be scientifically studied, but also because migration in general is not random in the sense that it is an erratic behavior. It is not to be denied that there are found occasionally individuals who "pick up and go without any rhyme or reason." But these cases are very few and are exceptional.

A more or less stable and on-going social organization implies a group of people living with a minimum satisfaction of their needs according to their values. When these minimum needs are not met by the existing conditions within a society or a sector of it, certain members entertain the thought of moving out of it and going to another society altogether or to a different sector of the same society where they perceive conditions more adequate to meet satisfactorily their unmet needs or relative deprivations.

Two things need to be noted concerning these relative deprivations. First, they are *relative*. All people have deprivations of one kind or another. The mere existence of some deprivations does not result in movement from one geographical location to another. One of the devices a given people's social organization develops is a capacity to live with *certain* deprivations, although not with *all* of them. It is important to ask what deprivations at a given time a particular collectivity is willing to endure. It is assumed that the criteria used, whether the members articulate them fully and explicitly or not, are their values, expressed in terms of valued ends. Values are abstract in nature, but they have overt behavioral expressions, such as, for example, children's education, greater income, wanting to live close to friends, and freedom to worship. These overt expressions are called valued ends. These valued ends might represent such values as family life, material comfort, friendship, and religious freedom. These values or the corresponding valued ends are ascribed differential importance in the minds of the members of the collectivity——which results in a hierarchy. The deprivations in the more highly valued ends are more important in the study of migrations. Not only are these deprivations in the more highly valued ends significant in the decision to move, but they are also important factors in the adjustmental phase that follows migration. For, it is legitimate to assume that if the deprivations responsible for the move continue to exist even after migration, the probability of a lack of adjustment after the move is very great. More positively, the greater the extent to which the initial deprivations vanish in the new surroundings after migration, the greater will be the adjustment of the migrants, provided no new deprivations develop.

The second factor to be noted concerning high relative deprivations in some areas (e.g., material comfort) is that a given social organization has more than one way for the realization of its members' values. Thus, not even a high degree of deprivation of some valued ends is sufficient condition for migrating. It is necessary that all or almost all satisfactory or desired means of overcoming existing deprivations are closed for the collectivity in question within the place of origin. Thus, among other things, both the existence of a high degree of deprivation of one or more values of a collectivity *and* the blocking of almost all the satisfactory means normally available to the collectivity to overcome such deprivations are preconditions to a decision to migrate.

It should be emphasized here that a decision to move is a highly subjective act. It is subjective in that a high degree of deprivation in certain values as well as the blocking of all the means for overcoming them need only to be felt by the collectivity, whether or not objective evidence exists for that feeling. In other words, the existence of these preconditions may or may not be related to the objective facts of the situation, but it is very much a function of perception on the part of the members of a collectivity.

The existence in the collective or social perception by the members of a collectivity of both a high degree of deprivations in the upper hierarchy of values and a lack of means to overcome these deprivations would make a given collectivity readier to migrate. However, this readiness to move will not result in actual migration unless some further conducive conditions are present. Chief among these additional conditions are certain characteristics of the locations which are potential destinations for the collectivity. In societies where individuals are reasonably free to locate and relocate themselves territorially whenever they please, they tend to move to places where they see ways to overcome their felt deprivations, but *without* giving up, as far as possible, the satisfactions they were enjoying at the place of their origin. In other words, the collectivity in question tries "to eat its cake and have it too." That may or may not always be possible. Lacking ideal conditions of human existence, the collectivity weighs further the alternative places available for migration. The manner in which the dimensions of social organization of the potential places of destination would be weighed by the intending migrants will be further elaborated under the fourth category of the definition of migration.

To summarize, the decision-making process before migrating has at least the following factors to be considered: a high degree of relative deprivation in some important values, perception of inability to meet these deprivations in the place of origin, perception of better ways of meeting the unmet needs in other places, and the selection of a place from the available ones on the basis of where the social organization most suited to the needs of the collectivity may be found. These decision-making steps may not always be carried out overtly in a hierarchically ordered set of values and in a logically articulated fashion by all potential migrants. But these elements are present in varying degrees in any given case of migration, and their detection and isolation are an important task for the researcher.

Changes in the interactional system of the migrants is included in the range definition of migration in order to emphasize the social system of migration. The decision-making aspect of the definition discussed above reflects to a great extent the subjective, intrapersonal, or psychological dimension of migration; the value factor involved in establishing priorities of choices is part of the culture system aspect of social organization. The change in the interactional or normative system, on the other hand, connotes the on-going social system aspect in this attempt to outline the essential foci for the proper study of migration. Actors do not have to change their interactional system in order to meet their unfulfilled needs. It is a matter of common experience that within an on-going social system, the actors can, and actually do, reorganize both needs and resources to match each other. This reorganization or redefinition of needs and resources to fulfill the ego-alter orientation process results in an adequate level of social adjustment, and under these circumstances no migration occurs.[12]

Migration, following the first criterion, implies geographical movement and a change in residence of the actors. It occurs because the local resources are insufficient to meet the actor's value-related needs, no matter how great an effort is made to match the needs and the resources. However, a change in residence *per se* does not necessarily mean a change in the interactional system of the actors. A group of actors can travel some distance, establish residence in a faraway place, and still be found to participate basically in the same type of interactional system in which they were before. That is, the essential structural elements which define the system remain, by and large, the same. It is this that makes control groups possible in experimental designs. For example, a group of professors moving from one university campus to another, both of which having certain identifiable parameters of action nearly the same, are basically in the same interactional system before and after the move. According to our definition of migration, these professors are not migrants. For, in their occupational roles, community relations, religious participation, and other significant activities, they might not have undergone any significant change. At least such a situation is conceivable. There might be some very temporary changes in their daily routine of life consequent upon the added chores of moving from one place to another and, in many cases, as a result of getting acquainted with new colleagues and making new friends. But soon in a matter of a few days or weeks, life settles down for these professors and their families, following more or less the same routine they used to follow before moving. The social structures of the two places are basically the same. I am not saying that this is so in all cases, but that such cases are conceivable and do actually occur. It must be added here that under such circumstances no real problems of adjustment occur consequent upon moving.[13]

However, there is an error committed by some in assuming that often when rural people move from their villages to cities, they basically retain their original social organization.[14] This is the result of a misconception of social organization. The error committed in this assumption can be easily pointed out by saying that these rural people, when they come to cities, have to earn a living from occupations found in the city, and not by following their earlier rural occupations. This change in occupations alone is sufficient to bring about significant changes in the interactional system of these migrants. Of course, there might be other changes, too, that may be important such as in the educational system, which cannot be avoided in the city altogether because of one's concern for one's children. Recreational activities are still another area in which changes begin to occur relatively soon because of a general lack of availability of the types of recreation rural migrants are used to. Without enumerating the areas in which behavioral changes set in, it is sufficient here to point out that rural people moving to urban areas cannot possibly escape some significant changes in their interactional system. The mistaken notion of migration occurring without significant changes in the interactional system of the migrants is probably the result of a conception of social organization different from the one employed here. The point may be clarified here by spelling out some of the implications of this definitional element, namely changes in the interactional system of the collectivity.

First and foremost, migration is conceived here as a process that links two systems or subsystems of social organization—two systems of intersocietal migration such as international migration, or two sub-systems of intrasocietal migration such as internal migration. A knowledge of both of the systems linked by the migrants is a prerequisite for an adequate understanding of the process of migration. Methodologically, either both of the systems should be delineated by collecting fresh facts, or, in the absence of this ideal possibility, both of the systems should be reconstructed from available facts on the two systems. But dealing with the migrants in terms of one system alone, either the "donor" or the "recipient" one, is invalid because it does not furnish sufficient facts.[15]

An understanding of the problems arising out of migration can be fully reached only by a careful delineation of those sectors of social organization where interactional changes have taken place. For example, consider the problems of social control that are associated with migration. There is no conclusive evidence whether migration is crimogenic or not. One might ask the simple question: Why should migration result in an increase (or decrease) of crime or deviant behavior? There is no inherent reason why the physical movement of people from one location to another should affect the crime rate, unless the type of interaction pattern that had stabilized the deviant behavior rate at some magnitude before migration is somehow upset in the process of migration. This upsetting might be a change in the primary group relations, in the differential association with a new collectivity like the juvenile gang, or a change in amount of anonymity in the new type of interaction.

So, whether it is to decide where a particular collectivity wishes to move or to understand what problems arise as a result of migrating, delineations of the type of social organizations at the place of origin and at the place of destination are important. An axiomatic assumption is that a particular type of social organiza-

tion is the product of a certain complex type of interaction pattern. When changes in the interactional system of a collectivity occur, they necessarily call for reintegration of the collectivity into the new, changed interactional system and reorganization of the entire social system of the place of destination.

A General Theoretical Orientation for the Study of Society

Conceptual elements in a theory of social organization such as cultural system, social system, and personality system have been discussed as if these terms were generally understood. With the terminological confusion in a nascent science like sociology, it is necessary to spell out the main ingredients of such a general and theoretical orientation and to raise some of the important questions to be answered on migration.

What follows is a highly abbreviated form of what is generally known as the functional approach to the study of social organization within an action framework.[16] The major formulations of this action framework are schematized in Figure 1. The symbols used in this schematic representation should be understood as follows:

> Each box represents a collectivity: I, society where the migrants originate; M, migrating collectivity (migrants); II, society where migration terminates.
> S_I, social organization of I in general; $S_I T_1$, social organization of society I at a given time T_1; $S_I T_2$, social organization of I at time T_2.
> $S_I T_1 - S_I T_2$, changes in the social organization of I during a time period, $T_1 - T_2$.
> $S_{II} T_1 - S_{II} T_2$, represents changes in the social organization of II for the period, $T_1 - T_2$; and, $S_M T_1 - S_M T_2$ represents changes in the social organization of the migrating collectivity during $T_1 - T_2$.
> I−M, society I after the migrants have left; II+M, society II after the migrants' arrival.
> S_{I-M}, social organization of I−M; S_{II+M}, social organization of II+M.

A brief explanation of this scheme is as follows: There are four basic conditions that together determine the course of events in an on-going society at any given point in time. These, called *contingent conditions*, are the size and the quality of its population, the natural and man-made environment, the historical time context of the society, and the technological base available to the members to manipulate its resources. Under the given parameters of these four contingent conditions, the members of a particular society interact to produce a particular type of social organization.[17]

The social organization at the place of origin of migrants at a particular time, T_1, is represented in the figure as $S_I T_1$. For analytical purposes the social organization $S_I T_1$ can be seen as composed of three identifiable systems: the culture system, the social system, and the personality system. The culture system represents

Figure 1

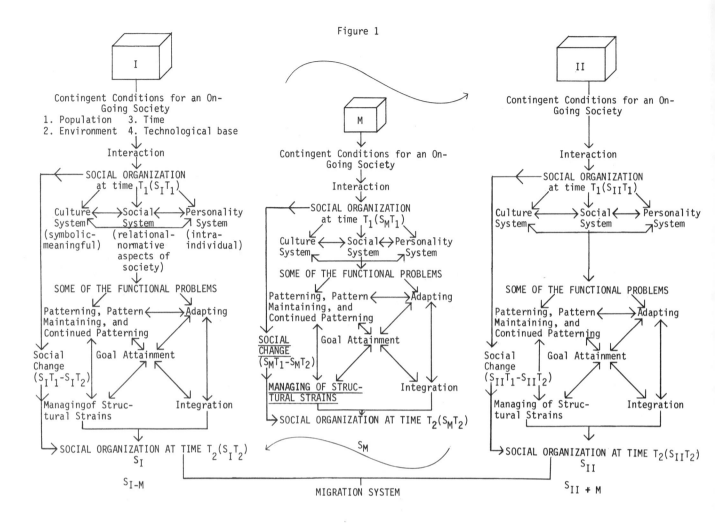

the symbolic-meaningful aspects of a social organization.[18] It is in a sense the total representation of the past of a people. It includes such elements as language, art and architecture, music and folklore, style of life including manner of dressing, culinary skills and tastes, and such other elements that were developed and valued in the past in varying degrees. These values, to the extent to which they are still retained, give direction and guidance to the behavior of the people, without necessarily determining it and serve as selection principles from "available means, modes and ends of action."[19]

The personality system has relevance to immediate action, but largely on an individual level, although in a given society, particularly in a subsector of it (e.g., the middle class) certain personality types can be identified, each one of which has relevance beyond a single individual. But essentially, the personality system concerns itself with an individual or a particular type of individual, and reference points for action are more within the realm of the individual psyche than a collectivity.

The social system is interindividual, and in this sense, relational-normative. That is to say, the reference points for action are more within the realm of the functional problems faced by a collectivity than within any individual personality, and action is governed more by the demands of the normative structure of the collectivity than by individual needs, motives, or aspirations. The essential difference between the social system and the personality system is one of relative emphasis on group or collective pressure versus individually perceived needs. Whereas both the social system and personality system have direct bearing on action systems, the influence of the culture system on human action is indirect (latent) and less pressing.

The functional problems of a social system in the relational-normative sense are many. It is not necessary here to enter into arguments for and against reducing these functional problems to a fixed number on an a priori basis. However, some of these problems within the context of the social system of the social organization of a given society can be listed.[20] These include the problems of *patterning* of the normative structure, its maintenance and continued patterning; *adaptation* or allocation of the scarce means to desired ends; attainment of the *collective goals*, coping with the *structural strains* produced in the on-going social processes; and *integration* of the totality of social processes and actions into a meaningful whole. As shown in Figure 1, all these functions are interrelated in the social system, which in turn is interrelated with both the culture system and the personality system to form the overall social organization, S_1, of the given society at time T_1.

The functioning of this social organization over time results inevitably in a new set of relatively stable relationships, giving rise to a different social organization, S_1T_2, after a lapse of time, T_2-T_1. In a meaningful sense, social change is this difference between social organizations of a given society at two different points in time, comprising changes in any or all the three component systems, namely the culture, social, and personality systems. These changes can occur or be initiated in any part of the social organization.[21]

This bare outline of a general theoretical perspective is a very highly condensed version of what is generally known as a functional theory for the study of society. The concepts norm, status-role, and institution are found to be the most useful in this type of sociological analysis. These are interrelated concepts, made popular through the works of the "structural-functional" theorists.

A norm is a mutually expected behavior in a social situation, which is a recurring group event. A status refers to one's position in the social structure, and one status always implies another. For example, teacher implies student, and husband implies wife. There are obligations and rights associated with each status, obligations of one being the rights of its polar opposite. Thus husband's obligations are wife's rights and vice versa. Whereas the same status may exist in two societies, the corresponding expected behavior or role may not have the same content in the two. It is known that the content of husband role in a patriarchal society is quite different from that in an egalitarian society. Because of this, status and role have been hyphenated to imply that status-role refers to the behavioral content of a particular status in a specific society.[22] A status-role can be conceived as a set of interrelated norms that exhaust the obligations and rights associated with it. An institution is a more complex notion than status-role. Social institutions regulate actions of individuals with regard to a relatively well-delineated function. Socialization of children, for example, is a function that has to do with patterning of behavior. In any given society socialization of children can be seen as a system of status-roles in all of which one polar opposite is con-

stant, namely the child. Socialization in a middle-class, white, Protestant home in the United States can be seen as a complex whole of a set of status-roles such as mother-child, father-child, sibling-sibling, peer-peer, and Sunday school teacher-pupil. An institution is defined here as an interrelated system of appropriate status-roles included in all those groups which fulfill a clearly delineated function.[23]

A major reason for drawing special attention to these three out of a multitude of concepts is their importance for structural-functional analysis of migration within an action framework. The actor in an action situation can be conceived of as a status-role system. If we call the migrant the ego, he has many alters (interaction partners), depending upon the number of status-roles he has. The alter in each case is the polar opposite, while the ego remains the same. Thus, a migrant (ego) who is a son, husband, and physician, has as alters parents, wife, and patient. In the event of ego's migration in this case, the obligations and rights involved in these social relations need to be taken into consideration.

There is another reason to emphasize the above concepts, particularly status-role. It has been noted that social system and personality system bear more directly than culture system on the normative behavior of the migrants. Status-role provides a link between social system and personality system functions, for an actor can be conceived of as a system of status-roles. Though an actor's status-roles do not exhaust his personality, they form a significant sector of it within an action frame of reference. In other words, status-roles are constituents of both social institutions and actors. In the former case, the status-roles involved perform a social function such as socialization; in the latter case, the status-roles involved form part of the personality system of actors. Where social functions are being fulfilled by actors, there is some theoretical advantage in being able to find some common building blocks between institutions that regulate normative action and actors. As has been explained, status-role is a structural link between institution and personality system.

The bare essentials of the suggested action framework can be diagnosed very simply, as follows:[24]

Figure 2

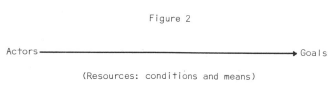

(Resources: conditions and means)

An action situation, as suggested by Figure 2, is a recurring event in which a collectivity is involved in working toward certain specified goals. Members of the collectivity in a specific action situation are generalized into actors, each actor implying a status-role system.

Migration, conceived as motivated action, is directed toward certain goals. The more clearly the goals are defined in the minds of the actor, the greater the efficiency with which he will be able to utilize the resources at his disposal. The resources available to the actor can be divided into two kinds: conditions and means. Conditions are those resources which cannot be changed by the actor's manipulation. Age, sex, and intelligence come under this category, for example. Means are those resources that can be increased or decreased by the actor's effort. Income and certain skills acquired through training exemplify this kind of resources. However, there is nothing absolutely fixed about most resources. What are conditions and what are means for a given actor or set of actors depend upon the particular action situation. But an awareness of the distinction between conditions and means on the part of the researcher is essential for an understanding of the utilization of available resources by the actors. A recognition on the part of the migrants of the means and conditions is likely to increase their own ability to manipulate the environmental conditions within which they have to operate, particularly in the adjustmental phase that follows migration.

The aim here is not to elaborate fully this scheme of social organization but to argue that studies of migration can and should be done within the context of this or a similar theoretical orientation. Placing a middle-range theory or an *ad hoc* hypothesis or a specific research design within the framework of such a general theoretical framework would enable researchers and others to see the dynamics of migration in its proper perspective and beyond the narrow framework of individual studies. Not only would such a procedure, which, of course, should be the *modus operandi* for all research projects that hope to make a theoretical contribution, permit one to see the relationships among migration and other human activities within a larger whole, but also it would facilitate the identification of those substantive areas where information on migration is badly needed. Hypotheses derived from a general orientation such as the one presented here will, it is believed, add analytical clarity and depth in interpretation of the findings and enable the researcher to contribute to the growth of not only a body of migration theory but to the larger body of sociological knowledge.

As noted earlier, two interactional systems or two social organizations are involved in the study of migration: one at the place of origin (S_I) and the other at the destination of the migrants (S_{II}). In trying to understand the migrants one needs to keep the two side by side and to compare differences in them while assessing the various dynamic elements in the process of migration. Differentials can exist in any or, in extreme cases, all of the elements of social organization; but it should be emphatically stated that if no differential exists between two given social organizations, then migration will not have occurred from one to the other. For, the fundamental assumption in this whole argument is that migration will occur from one social organization to another only if the collectivity facing relative deprivations in the former perceives in the latter means to overcome these deprivations without the introduction of any new important deprivations. According to this point of view, all geographic movements of people are not necessarily migrations in the social organizational sense. New deprivations are usually produced as a result of migration, and these new deprivations provide important clues to the identification and solution of the adjustment problems that follow migration. In other words, relative deprivations are inherent in the nature of man no matter where he lives. But the deciding factor in migrating or not migrating is which relative deprivations are members of a collectivity willing and able to put up with or to cope with. Eastern Kentuckians who travel to urban centers in Ohio because of desperate need for employment find that a great deal in their Eastern Kentucky social organizations is missing in their new social organization of urban Ohio. Housing, food, primary group relations, kin-oriented activities, legal demands, and even personal identities of the individual migrants appear to take on new dimensions. The migrants have to cope with the new deprivations as well as overcome the old deprivations that gave rise to the decision to migrate in the first instance.

Locating Migration within the Framework of Social Organization

If the general theoretical orientation presented here for the study of social organization minimally meets the need for a general organizing scheme for the study of migration, there is still the problem of locating the phenomenon within some definite sector of social organization. Because of the very nature of the phenomenon of migration, one has to conceptualize it within the social system component of social organization. From the reasoning that migration is a response to relative deprivations as perceived by a collectivity of individuals or groups, one logical place to locate it is within the functional area of adaptation. In other words, as a collectivity phenomenon, migration is an adaptive process whose major objective is maintaining the dynamic equilibrium of the social organization with a minimum of changes and at the same time providing those members ways to overcome their deprivations. Migration in this sense might be called a system-adapting mechanism for the place of origin of migrants (i.e., community, neighborhood, region, society, etc.). Whereas migration is thus the result of some inadequacies in the functioning of a given social organization, migration of a collectivity from an on-going social organization sets in motion a number of changes in its three systems (culture, social, and personality). Besides, the social organization of the destination of the migrants is forced to make some changes within itself to accommodate the social organization, S_M, that the migrants bring in. Thus, although migration is conceived initially as an adaptive mechanism within a single social organization, a complete understanding of migration demands that it be treated as a phenomenon that floats between and affects two social organizations, one at the place of origin and the other at the place of destination. Thus migration represents a collectivity of actors that in some measure links two social organizations that are different from each other in some distinctly identifiable elements. So it is correct to say that the migrants themselves constitute a third social organization, S_M, somewhere between the two which they "bridge."[25]

The migrants' own social organization is represented in Figure 1 on a reduced scale to emphasize that the size of the collectivity involved in this is generally smaller than the corresponding populations who constitute S_I and S_{II}. However, two elements of S_M deserve to be specially noted in relation to the corresponding elements in S_I and S_{II}. Recall that changes in the contingent condition of population are likely to bring about social change in a given society or in any sector of it. In Figure 1, S_I loses population and S_{II} gains it, resulting in social change in both S_I and S_{II}. This can be of a major or minor order depending upon the quality and size of the migrant group. But the greatest change is to be expected in S_M itself, because it is not only affected by the number and quality of the migrants but by variations in an indefinite number of elements in S_I and S_{II}. This change can sometimes be of an extreme nature. Also, the structural strains involved in S_M as a result of migration are of a crucial nature.[26] These strains can result, and actually do, from changes in practically all areas of functional problems. New ways of patterning, adapting, goal gratification, and integration hit the migrants almost all at once. Because of these considerations these two elements (social change and strain management) of S_M are printed in capital letters in Figure 1.

Figure 1 also represents interchanges between S_I and S_{II} through S_M. Although in some instances of migration (e.g., short-distance, internal migration) migrants move back and forth between the localities of origin and destination, the more basic interchanges we have in mind are of a communicative nature in terms of symbolic influence. Letters and gifts exchanged between migrants and their kin back home are examples of this type of symbolic interchanges between S_I and S_{II}. This influence between S_I and S_{II} is an inevitable occurrence except perhaps in very extreme cases.

Some Suggested Topics for the Study of Migration

The objective has been to propose some guidelines for the study of migration within a holistic frame of reference with special emphasis on the interactional nature of migration. So in what follows there is an attempt to demonstrate the usefulness of the theoretical approach presented here by drawing from it some relevant questions that need to be answered for future understanding of the migration phenomenon. Basically, there are at least four questions that at once come to mind in connection with any given instance of migration:

a. Who are the migrants?
b. Why did they migrate?
c. Where did they migrate?
d. What are the consequences of migration?
These questions need to be answered in terms of the theoretical orientation presented in Figure 1. This will be done in the form of a paradigm, suggesting but not exhausting, the variables and factors that need to be considered in any study of migration.

a. Who are the migrants? Under this heading we are interested in delineating the characteristics of the migrants in terms of the relevant elements of social organization, relevance being determined in terms of the differentials between S_I and S_M. In other words, in a particular case of migration *some* of these differentials take greater importance than others, although it cannot be established *a priori* in which characteristics such differentials would exist. However, from general considerations of the nature of social organization the following kinds of information seem important:
1. Aspects of the contingent conditions:
    a. Population characteristics: age and sex composition
    b. Ecological factors: land resources and climatic conditions; kinds of neighborhood and community relations
    c. Historical time dimension: special features of the historical antecedents of the groups
    d. Technological base: special skills of the collectivity produced by education and training
2. Kinds of interaction: the extent of cooperation and competition; their expressive or instrumental nature; conflict; communication facilities; etc.
3. Overall nature of the collectivity's social organization, S_M: here account needs to be taken of the changes that have occurred in the migrating collectivity along any one of the chosen continua that characterizes S_M as different from S_I. Very often the migrants' social organization, S_M, would

have attained a value different from that of the original one, S_1, along a continuum of, say, rural-urban.

4. Culture system components: food tastes and habits; clothing and other style of life; folklore, art and architecture; ideological commitments (moral ideology); values (cultural); language, its special features with respect to the collectivity's behavior.

5. Personality system components: health; needs; values (individual as distinct from the cultural); aspirations; identity; integrity; role performance in significant statuses.

6. Social system components:

a. Socialization practices: educational system; family and kinship relations; position in the stratification system; reward and punishment system

b. Type of economy: ways of making a living; formal and informal methods of budgeting time; place in the occupational structure

c. Clarity of definition of goals: expressive and instrumental nature of goals; relative emphasis on immediate or remote gratification; symptoms of goal frustrations

d. Kinds of stress in the system: structures under relatively high strain; ways of avoiding or minimizing strain within the system; extent to which migration is perceived as an alternative way to alleviate strain

e. Level of integration: interdependence of the social units; extent of breakup of solidary groups; interactional symbols; etc.

Comment: These points are illustrative of the kinds of information needed for a thorough understanding of the migrating collectivity. As noted earlier, the social organization of the migrating collectivity, S_M, will be found to be somewhat different from that of S_1. Special effort must be made to delineate these differences, "migration differentials," which are leads to answering the next question: Why did they migrate?

It might be added here that one cannot but be impressed by the lack of information in migration literature on a majority of the elements of social organization listed. There is information, though not abstracted in terms of social organization elements, on some of the contingent conditions. Sociodemographic variables are well represented in the literature. Reasonable generalizations can be made on such variables as age, sex, socioeconomic status and occupational categories. Some attention has been paid to such personality variables as attitude, aspiration, and health. Occasionally one encounters concerns with neighborhood relations and community satisfactions. But when it comes to describing the migrating collectivity in terms of differentials

in culture system and social system components, the existing literature is very weak. This weakness is indicative of a lack of effort to study the migration phenomenon from the overall perspectives of an organizing principle like social organization. Obviously, migration is practically a virgin area for those who want to study the phenomenon from a behavioral point of view with emphasis on culture and social systems. And until these systems have been delineated for S_1 and S_M, one cannot answer the next question.

b. Why did they migrate? If the migrants have been characterized in terms of the differentials between S_1 and S_M, this characterization ought to have revealed a number of aspects of social organization in which S_1 and S_M are significantly different, without which differences migration cannot occur.[27] But the mere existence of these differences is not sufficient reason for migration to take place. For example, all societies have some kind of a stratification system, implying the existence of collectivities which differ from each other in some elements of their social organizations. And yet in many of them no extensive migration occurs. The most important factor is how the migrating collectivity has viewed the differences between S_1 and S_M. Some of these differences can be called trivial in the sense no one particularly cares about these differences, and some differences may not be known even to the migrants. In some characteristics, however, the differences take the form of deprivations. These deprivations, following our definition of migration, are hierarchically ordered in terms of their values. In some instances the society may have means to help them overcome some of these deprivations, while others remain unresolved. If and when these differences between S_1 and S_M become deprivations and remain unresolved due to lack of means as perceived by a particular collectivity, they will withdraw from active participation in S_1, either to migrate or to lead a life of sociocultural isolation within the same territorial limits. The migrating collectivity, either as individuals or groups, has sought resources outside the social organization of their place of origin. Thus there are members of a collectivity, called migrants, who have become, in one sense, part of two social organizations, one they grew up in but in which they feel deprived permanently of characteristics they value highly, and the other, S_{11}, known only vaguely to them but one in which they perceive the existence of necessary resources accessible to them for overcoming the deprivations in S_1.

Two points need to be mentioned before concluding this section. First, it should be emphasized that a migrating collectivity is seldom, if ever, able to take cognizance of the new deprivations that might arise at the place of destination. This lack of ability has consequences for the adjustment of the collectivity after migration.

Second, the migrants almost never totally reject their place of origin and its social organization. S_I and S_M are different only in *some* aspects; they have a good many things in common, and these common elements continue to influence the life of the migrants in the new community. The extent of similarity between S_I and S_M is a contributing factor in deciding where the collectivity migrates.

c. Where did they migrate? Perhaps there are two principles that emerge from theoretical considerations and might guide us in finding answers to the above question: First, the migrants seek a destination where their deprivations or unmet wants can be satisfied; second, the migrants go to a place where the social organization is as closely related as possible (in their perception) to the one in their place of origin. In other words, referring to Figure 1, the migrants tend to choose (not necessarily with conscious deliberation) a destination so as to make S_I and S_{II} as far as possible the same. It is immaterial how far the migrants move—whether they are internal migrants, rural-urban migrants, or international migrants—the tendency will be to bring about as little disturbance in their social organization as possible. Obviously, the two social organizations cannot be matched in all aspects. After locating a number of possible places to migrate, selection will then be made in terms of the most important aspects of life in which S_I and S_{I_I} are closely matched. Thus values once again play an important role in determining what elements of S_I can and cannot be sacrificed in making a move.

One can conceive of situations in which the first consideration is met best. For example, a migrating collectivity in search of a living finds a place X where there are plenty of employment opportunities, but where the type of social organization is not the kind the migrants are used to. If no other place of any better approximation to their own social organization is located and if the economic deprivation in their place of origin is of an extreme magnitude, migration will take place to X, at least initially. If the migrants place a very high value on their social organization, they would be aware of the compromise they have made in choosing to go to X. A number of alternative behaviors could then be predicted under different conditions. (1) They may live literally in two worlds, having semipermanent attachment to both the place of origin and that of destination. (2) They may introduce to the social organization of X, their own type of family and kinship relations, their own social organization. (3) They may temporarily settle at X, while looking for another place whose social organization, particularly with regard to family and kinship relations, will approximate their own, while providing job opportunities. (4) They may be forced to return to their earlier state of economic deprivation because of a higher value attached to social organization as compared with economic settlement. (5) They may abruptly break away from their own social organization and accept the one prevalent at place X. In all these, and other possible solutions, each one has its own consequences. For example, in the first case mentioned, one would predict considerable symptoms of mental ill-health, at least initially.

d. What are the consequences of migration? Consistent with the framework, the first thing to be recognized is that there are consequences stemming from migration for all the three social organizations we are dealing with, namely S_I, S_M, and S_{II}. It is obvious that Society I has lost a certain number of persons and Society II has gained them, bringing about changes in the contingent conditions of both. The not so obvious fact is that the migrating collectivity, M, also has changes brought about in its own contingent conditions, except in its population size, which remains the same. It has changed in its ecological conditions, and in its historical time dimension in relation to its past while it was still part of Society I. These changes mean that one will find changes in all the three systems of each one of the social organizations. Of course, some changes may be too small to be visible with the kinds of observational tools one has in the behavioral sciences. Whether these changes are of large or small magnitude, it is fundamental to recognize that changes are possible in the culture, personality, and social systems of the social organizations at the place of origin, S_I, of the migrating collectivity, S_M, and at the place of destination, S_{II}. A list of the potential areas of changes stemming from migration, then, requires an outline, as detailed as possible, of the various elements of the culture, personality, and social systems.

All such changes are not necessarily consequential. Theoretically, changes are taking place in a given social organization constantly, but most of them go unnoticed because of their relative unimportance. So when we talk about consequences of migration, we are focusing our attention on those aspects of changes brought about as a result of migration. And as noted earlier, these changes are in all three social organizations, S_I, S_M, and S_{II}. The consequences can be seen for the originating society, the migrating collectivity, and the society of destination. Figure 3 shows the theoretical possibilities of these consequences in the social organizations for the three collectivities involved. The main purpose of Figure 3 is to emphasize the fact that not only changes in S_M can be consequential to the migrants, but also changes in S_I and S_{II} that migration has brought about. Obviously these changes cannot be detailed here; Figure 3 merely indicates the areas and relationships of the possible changes. Whether or not all of these theoretical pos-

Figure 3

Consequences for Members of	Changes in Social Organization								
	S_I			S_M			S_{II}		
	Culture System	Social System	Personality System	Culture System	Social System	Personality System	Culture System	Social System	Personality System
Society I									
Migrating Collectivity									
Society II									

sibilities become consequential to the life of the migrants depends upon a particular instance of migration. The same thing applies to members of the society of origin and the society of destination. It is in this that S_I, S_M, and S_{II} form one migration system, that after a collectivity of any significant size has migrated from one society to another, the three systems are interactionally related. Interchanges of elements of social organization take place among the three through the medium of the migrants, sometimes by their visiting patterns and at other times by means of communication such as letters. Also, it is not always recognized that exchange of artifacts between the society of origin and that of destination sets in motion changes of far-reaching consequences. At any rate, the notion of migration system comprised of the three social organizations with interlinkages largely operating through the

migrants is an important notion for making any realistic assessment of the consequences of migration.

In its totality of implications, mapping out all of the possible consequences for any particular instance of migration is a colossal problem. Fortunately, important consequences do not occur in *all* aspects of migration system; by the nature of social organization, migration occurs in a manner to endanger the least number of elements in it. However, in any particular research where attention is concentrated on a few selected aspects of migration, an overall view of the *migration system* as presented here will help in locating major areas of theoretical and practical consequences.

In conclusion, one might ask the question: Why is the study of migration so important? One answer is written all through this volume, namely its social consequences. This is not strictly a scientific reason. Of course, study of any recurring phenomenon arouses scientific curiosity. But there is an aspect of the scientific reason that ought to excite social scientists, particularly behavioral scientists, and to make them undertake migration studies: Study of a migrating collectivity provides the behavioral scientists with a natural laboratory situation to observe changes in human behavior under varying conditions. For example, a migrating collectivity contains humans with different potentialities and at different levels of socialization. What happens to the society of origin when the migrants are withdrawn from it? What happens to the society of destination when the migrants are introduced into it? What happens to the migrating collectivity itself? Answers to these questions have a far greater scientific importance than the immediate knowledge concerning migration differentials and consequences of migration *per se*. The theoretical guidelines suggested here will help in the designing of migration researches aimed at a deeper understanding of how a social organization functions.

Notes

1. The numbers from 1 to 681 refer to items in the bibliography. Other references with years of publication after them will be found at the end of these notes.
2. For accounts of international migration in the twentieth century, see Donald R. Taft and Richard Robbins, *International Migrations* (625). Rupert Vance's statement, "Prerequisites to Immigration: Elements of National Policy" (353), points out some social and economic aspects to be taken into account in planned, international migration.
3. One of the strengths of Beech Creek Study ("Social Adjustment and Personal Stability of Kentucky Mountain Migrants") is, we believe, the use of a combination of methods, structured interviewing (data amenable to statistical analysis) and participant observation of three "family groups" (data amenable to case history analysis). For an initial statement of the Beech Creek Study, see Brown, Schwarzweller, and Mangalam (1963).
4. Studies using these variables are too many to enumerate here. See the Subject Index.
5. For a collection of all the relevant abstracts that pertain to this topic, see "Causes of Migration," "Incentives to Migrate," and "Reasons for Migrating," under the Subject Index. Here we are primarily interested in drawing attention to those studies that have used a more than *ad hoc* approach, especially those with a general sociological framework.
6. For a summary of various economic theories of migration, see Brinley Thomas (1954). Even some of the economists see limitations to this economic thesis. For example, many farmers prefer farming to non-farm occupations even when this preference means lower wages (Heneberry, 1960).
7. Examples of each one of these problems resulting from migration can be found in the abstracts.
8. It is no a sociopsychological framework *per se* that is objectionable, but the fact that such an approach seems to exclude equally important aspects of the migration phenomenon. The same criticism can be raised against the *Polish Peasant*.
9. The distinction drawn here between abstraction of a phenomenon

and its conceptualization is a simple but necessary one. Abstraction implies what Lazarsfeld (1959: 48) has called "originating observation." By conceptualization is meant translating this original imagery to communicable words in a workable definition, not necessarily operationalized. This is step one in Lazarsfeld's "translating this imagery into empirical research instruments."

10. These journals are *International Labour Review* and *Industry and Labour*.

11. The term collectivity includes three types: group, category, and aggregate. See Fichter (1957). As used in this discussion the term refers to group and category.

12. Social adjustment is admittedly a difficult notion to conceptualize, although it is relatively easy to develop for oneself an imagery of it. A working definition of this notion will be found in Brown, Schwarzweller, and Mangalam (1963: 67).

13. In cases such as this, usually problems of adjustment arise as a result of new needs, new values, new perceptions, and so on, in the new situations, which are not to be ascribed to migration *per se* but to conditions that could arise even in the absence of migration.

14. An example of this sort of position is found in the statement made by Oscar Lewis during a conference on rural-urban migration. (N.I.M.H., 1964:11).

15. In an earlier statement (Brown, Schwarzweller, Mangalam, 1963: 66) we have used the term "donor sub-system" and "recipient sub-system" to denote the two parts of a single *migration system*. Figure 1 represents this notion of the *migration system*, with slight modification to include the social organization of the migrating collectivity, which acts as the link between the two subsystems. When we talk about the donor system and the recipient system, we are referring to the social systems of the areas of origin and destination respectively before migration occurred.

16. Attack and defense of functionalism, particularly of the variant known as structural-functional analysis, has been going on for some time in the profession. We have no intention to enter this battle on either side, much less to attempt to settle the issue. However, any objective observer is likely to find a considerable amount of common elements in the approaches of such modern theorists as Davis (1949), Levy (1952), Merton (1957), Parsons (1937, 1951, 1954, 1956), Sorokin (1947), and Williams, Jr. (1951). It is this general tradition that I have called

functional approach. And it is to these men that I owe a conscious intellectual debt.

17. The social organization so produced has been characterized in an overall sense by such dichotomies as rural-urban (Sorokin), sacred-secular (Becker), mechanical-organic (Durkheim), gemeinschaft-gesellschaft (Tonnies), folk-urban (Redfield), and community-association (McIver). Each contrasting dichotomy is actually a continuum in the sense that the types as defined by each side of the dichotomy are really ideal states or conditions and are never come across in real life as a pure type. A given social organization at a given time has, for example, some of the secular and some of the sacred elements, although one of them might be present only in a very small measure.

18. The distinction drawn here between culture system and social system follows the recommendations made jointly by Kroeber and Parsons (1958).

19. This is an expression used by Clyde Kluckhohn (1951) while defining values. I feel that not only values in the abstract as Kluckhohn talks about them, but also the valued elements in a culture act as selection principles, acting as prototypes of those which are valuable.

20. Although the functional problems listed here follow more closely Parson's view, other similar lists are available (Davis, 1949; Levy, 1952).

21. One of the major ways in which rapid social change hits a contemporary society is through changes in its contingent conditions, particularly in population and technological base.

22. Another manner in which to look at status and role is by attributing rights to status and duties to role (Johnson, 1960: 16).

23. When we talk about a school as an educational institution in vernacular, we include institution in its sociological sense, plus a part of the role-set of each status-role involved. For an explanation of the role-set, see Merton (1957: 370-77), Johnson (1960: 34-35).

24. See Parsons (1937:43-86) for elaborations on this point.

25. Social organization, S , has to be differentiated from S in some elements. Otherwise, no migration will take place.

26. An example of structural strain can be seen in the incompatibilities in status-role relations between husband and wife in interclass marriages where the two parties derive their normative orientations from two different social subsystems.

27. It should be abundantly clear by now that migration is different from movement. Differentials between S^1 and S are not necessary for *movement*, but they are essential for *migration*.

Bibliographic References

(excluding those included in the book and numbered from 1 to 681)

Beijer, Gunther

   1963   *Rural Migrants in Urban Setting* (The Hague, Martinus Nijhoff), 327 pp.

Brown, James S., Harry K. Schwarzweller, and Joseph J. Mangalam

   1963   "Kentucky Mountain Migration and the Stem Family: An American Variation on a Theme by Le Play," *Rural Sociology*, 28: 48-69 (March).

Davis, Kingsley

   1949   *Human Society*, (New York, Macmillan), 655 pp.

   1951   *The Population of India and Pakistan* (Princeton, Princeton University Press), 263 pp.

Durkheim, Emile

   1933   *On the Division of Labor in Society*, trans. George Simpson (New York, Macmillan), 439 pp. (First French edition, 1893).

Fichter, Joseph H.

   1957   *Sociology* (Chicago, University of Chicago Press), 450 pp.

Hauser, Philip M.

   1956   "Present Status and Prospects of Research in Population," in *Population Theory and Policy*, ed. Joseph J. Spengler and Otis Dudley Duncan (Glencoe, Ill., The Free Press), pp. 70-85.

Heneberry, Bill

   1960   "Why Don't More People Leave Farming," *Michigan Farm Economics*, Department of Agricultural Economics, Michigan State University, Cooperative Extension. Service Series, No. 208, pp. 2-3.

Hillery, George A.

1957 "The Negro in New Orleans: A Functional Analysis of Demographic Data," *American Sociological Review*, 22: 183-88 (April).

Johnson, Harry M.

1960 *Sociology: A Systematic Introduction.* (New York, Harcourt, Brace), 688 pp.

Kluckhohn, Clyde

1952 "Values and Value-Orientations in the Theory of Action: An Exploration in Definition and Classification," in *Toward a Theory of Action,* ed. Talcott Parsons and Edward A. Shils (Cambridge, Harvard University Press), 506 pp.

Kroeber, A. L., and Talcott Parsons

1958 "The Concept of Culture and of Social System," *American Sociological Review*, 23: 582-83 (October).

Lazarsfeld, Paul F.

1959 "Problems in Methodology," in *Sociology Today,* ed. Robert K. Merton, Leonard Broom, and Leonard S. Cottrel, Jr. (New York, Basic Books) pp. 39-78.

Levy, M. J.

1952 *The Structure of Society* (Princeton, Princeton University Press), 584 pp.

Merton, Robert K.

1957 *Social Theory and Social Structure* (Glencoe, Ill., The Free Press), 645 pp.

Moore, Wilbert

1959 "Sociology and Demography," in *The Study of Population,* ed. Philip M. Hauser and Otis Dudley Duncan, (Chicago, The University of Chicago Press), 864 pp.

National Institute of Mental Health

1964 *Proceedings of the Rural-Urban Migration Conference,* (Bethesda, Md.), 89 pp.

Parsons, Talcott

1937 *The Structure of Social Action* (New York, McGraw-Hill); reprinted in 1949 (Glencoe, Ill., The Free Press), 817 pp.

1951 *The Social System* (Glencoe, Ill., The Free Press), 575 pp.

1954 *Essays in Sociological Theory* (Glencoe, Ill., The Free Press), 459 pp.

Parsons, Talcott, with N. J. Smelser

1956 *Economy and Society* (Glencoe, Ill., The Free Press), 322 pp.

Ravenstein, E. G.

1885 "The Laws of Migration," *Journal of the Royal Statistical Society* 48:167-235. (Quoted from Sorokin, Zimmerman and Galpin, 1932, p. 516.)

Sorokin, Pitirim

1947 *Society, Culture and Personality* (New York, Harper), 742 pp.

Sorokin, Pitirim, Carle C. Zimmerman, and Charles J. Galpin

1932 *A Systematic Source Book in Rural Sociology,* Vol. III, Chapter XXII, pp. 458-627 (Minneapolis, University of Minnesota Press), 752 pp.

Taeuber, Irene

1964 "Population and Society," in *Handbook of Modern Sociology,* ed. Robert E. L. Faris (Chicago, Rand McNally), 1088 pp.

Thomas, Brinley

1954 *Migration and Economic Growth* (Cambridge, Cambridge University Press), 362 pp.

Thomas, Dorothy Swaine

1938 *Research Memorandum on Migration Differentials* (New York, Social Science Research Council), 423 pp.

Thomas, W. I., and Florian Znaniecki

1927 *Polish Peasant in Europe and America* (New York, Alfred Knopf; 2nd rev. ed. reprinted in 1958 by Dover Publications, Inc.) Vol. I, 1114 pp.; Vol. II, 1135 pp.

Vance, Rupert B.

1956 "Is Theory for Demographers?" in *Population Theory and Policy,* ed. Joseph J. Spengler and Otis Dudley Duncan (Glencoe, Ill., The Free Press), pp. 88-94.

Williams, Robin M., Jr.

1951 *American Society* (New York, Alfred Knopf), (Revised, 1963), 577 pp.

HUMAN MIGRATION

INTRODUCTORY NOTE

A number of bibliographies on migration literature already exist, but are out of date. Furthermore, most of them contain no annotations, and those that are annotated provide such limited information that they are of little help to prospective researchers in planning their projects. The present work is intended to fill these gaps to some extent. I say "to some extent" advisedly, for I have come to agree with Irene Taeuber's warning, which accompanied her encouragement to undertake this enterprise: "The publications of bibliographies are always difficult. You accomplish a bit by never, never calling it a bibliography." How true!

In the listing which follows items are arranged alphabetically in three sections, although for convenience of reference all items have been numbered consecutively and joint authors and issuing agencies are cross-referenced. The first section includes articles, chapters from books, and dissertations; the second, books and reports. The third contains material included in or listed in *Industry and Labour*, *International Labour Review*, and *Population Index*.

The first two sections include the documents on migration published under signed authorship and found in and through the following sources for the period from 1955 through 1962, which covers the time between the designing of the Beech Creek Study (1962) and a year somewhat arbitrarily set, but beyond which our resources did not permit us to proceed with the work of abstraction. We have reason to feel that the publications during this period are highly representative of the post-World War II studies in migration.

A. *Journals*
   1. *American Journal of Sociology*
   2. *American Sociological Review*
   3. *Human Relations*
   4. *Milbank Memorial Fund Quarterly*
   5. *Population Studies*
   6. *Rural Sociology*
   7. *Social Forces*
   8. *Social Problems*
   9. *Sociology and Social Research*
   10. *Southwestern Social Science Quarterly*

B. *Recent Bibliographic Sources*
   11. Gunther Beijer, *Rural Migrants in Urban Setting* (The Hague: Martinus Nijhoff, 1963), 327 pp. (Bibliographies at the end of each chapter.)
   12. Cornell University, *Bibliography of Researches in Rural Sociology*, Rural Sociology Publications No. 52 (Ithaca, New York: Cornell University Agricultural Experiment Station, August, 1957). (Publications listed under the heading "Migration and Mobility.")

13. Hope T. Elridge, *The Materials of Demography: A Selected and Annotated Bibliography* (New York: Columbia University Press, 1959), 222 pp.
14. Research Group for European Migration Problems. Publications 10, 11, 12.
15. Henry S. Shryock, Jr., "Annotated List of Estimates of Net Migration, 1940-1950, By the Residual Method" *Population Index*, 25: 16-24 (January, 1959).
16. J. J. Spengler and Otis D. Duncan (eds.), *Demographic Analysis: Selected Readings* (Glencoe, Ill.: The Free Press, 1956), 819 pp. (Bibliographies under the headings, "International Distribution of Population and Migration" and "Internal Distribution and Migration.")
17. Brinley Thomas, *International Migration and Economic Development: A Trend Report and Bibliography* (Paris: UNESCO, 1961), 85 pp.
18. U. S. Department of Agriculture (Economic and Statistical Analysis Division, Economic Research Service), *Migration of Farm People: An Annotated Bibliography*, 1946-1960 (Washington, D. C.: U. S. Government Printing Office, Miscellaneous Publication No. 954, October, 1963), 37 pp.
19. George L. Wilber and James S. Bang, *Internal Migration in the U.S., 1940-1957: A List of References*, Sociology and Rural Life, Series No. 10 (State College, Miss.: State University Agricultural Experiment Station, 1958).

C. *Other General Reference Sources*
   20. *Agricultural Index*
   21. *Dissertation Abstracts*
   22. *Education Index*
   23. *International Index*
   24. *Library of Congress Catalog of Books*
   25. Margaret I. King Library, University of Kentucky Card Catalog
   26. *Sociological Abstracts*

All the articles listed in the above sources as well as in the footnotes of the articles themselves that deal with migration and related themes such as migratory labor and residential mobility were abstracted, except for those not easily accessible. Although a number of important journals might seem to be left out, we feel reasonably certain that the majority of the articles published on migration during the period are included in this book.

Books and most reports were not abstracted but simply listed in the second section. Those acquainted with general bibliographic sources for migration literature will notice the omission of *Industry and Labour*, *International Labour Review*, and especially, *Population Index* among the sources listed. We originally intended to exclude the migration entries in these from the present work and to make them available in a separate volume. But later considerations have shown that inclusion of these items would enhance the value of the present work as a reference volume. Hence they are included unannotated in the third section along with materials appearing under state and federal agencies in the United States and the United Nations and its agencies. Asterisks against entries in this section indicate that the original works are not in English, but they include summaries in English. The English title in each case is as given in the original source. Although some of the entries in this section do not seem directly related to the topic of migration, they are included because they are taken from the migration section of the originating documents.

We regret that articles in languages other than English, particularly the ones in the European languages, have not been included. Fortunately, Beijer's *Rural Migrants in Urban Setting* compensates for this. The bibliographies given at the end of each chapter in that volume, although not annotated, are helpful to researchers with facility in European languages.

A brief mention should also be made of the method of abstraction. Initially, the abstracters were instructed to look for the following items: the universe and the sample studied, the general focus of the study, hypotheses tested, the major variables used for analysis, special measures (scales) employed, and the general conclusions of the study. Of course, all studies did not have all these items. An independent check of the reliability of the initial abstracters in locating and abstracting the documents was carried out by assigning the advanced students in a graduate seminar on the sociology of migration to duplicate the work of the initial abstracters on the migration literature to be found during a six-year period (1957-1962) in the following journals: *American Journal of Sociology, American Sociological Review, Human Relations, Rural Sociology,* and *Social Forces.* A comparison between the abstracts done by the initial abstracters and the seminar members reassured us that our abstracts were adequate and that probably no article of importance was being left out.

Each abstract was typed on a 5 x 8 Unisort Analysis Card. Both sides of each card were used where necessary for each abstract. A code key was constructed for the major variables that were judged to be important in the study of migration; the key, based partly on theoretical reasons and partly on empirical evidence, was derived from an initial reading of the first hundred abstracts. Though not a foolproof method, this manner of abstraction helped to produce in the abstracts a certain degree of uniformity and accuracy which would have been otherwise lacking. The fact that a standard 5 x 8 Unisort Card provides only 91 holes limited the number of possible items that could be notched into the card. This necessitated lumping together a few items, which were later separated by hand sorting. Each ab-

stract that appears in this volume has undergone further editing to condense it into two paragraphs. Because of this, some of the abstracts in their printed form may not mention all the variables with which they are credited in the Subject Index. But those variables are dealt with in the original works.

As far as possible, chapters on migration included in books devoted to more general themes have been treated as articles, and their abstracts have been included. Abstracting books and reports posed a formidable problem. The initial decision to list the chapter headings of books on migration and related topics in place of abstracts was abandoned, largely because these headings often did not meet researchers' need to know the actual content of the chapters. Books and these other reports are more readily available than articles scattered in a large number of journals. So it was decided to expand the limited resources of time and money in abstracting the articles and to list the other documents unabstracted.

Some information about our procedure in this study will be helpful. First, we have not drawn any distinction between internal and international migration——a distinction commonly made in bibliographies on migration. The reason for this is theoretical and has been discussed in the Introduction.

Second, each abstract is given in two paragraphs: the first one gives information on the universe and sample, the main focus of the study, any hypothesis tested, and any special measuring devices employed. The second paragraph is devoted to the main conclusions of the study. As far as possible we have retained the authors' own words.

Third, the major variables involved in each abstracted investigation are not listed systematically in the body of the abstract but instead are listed under the subject index. This index provides a ready reference to researchers on the studies dealing with certain variables. Speaking from our own experience, we believe this index will be of value to researchers, especially when new research is being designed.

Fourth, authors are not indexed, but can be located in alphabetical order under the three sections.

Fifth, we have included an appendix of addresses of all original sources for the materials abstracted. This may not be important for researchers in the North-Atlantic countries, especially in the U.S.A., where reference sources are readily available. But in technologically underdeveloped countries, where migration studies are being planned—and where they are sorely needed—researchers may not have easy access to literature sources. Researchers there, we believe, will find this appendix useful. Wherever possible, the addresses were taken from the latest issues of journals; in other cases they were taken from Eileen C. Graves (ed.), *Ulrich's*

Periodicals Directory, New York: R. R. Bowker Company, 1963 (10th edition).

We are certain that for the period covered and even under the stated limitations there must be important items left out. Authors and others should bring such omissions, unintentional as they are, to our notice. A bibliography of this type is like an ever-growing plant. We hope to have less errors and omissions in a later edition of this work, if it proves useful to the researchers in the area of migration.

I. ANNOTATED BIBLIOGRAPHY

Aas, Dagfinn. *See* 249.

Abu-Laban, Baha. *See* 289.

1. Abu-Lughod, Janet

 1961 "Migrant Adjustment to City Life: The Egyptian Case," *American Journal of Sociology*, 67:22-32 (July).

A study of 630,000 migrants to Cairo as shown in the 1947 national census—census data and Social Agency Directory. One of the major cushions in the assimilation of rural migrants is the nature of the subcommunity to which they gravitate. Among the variables used in the study were: type of migrant, kind of adjustment, kind of association, occupational status, and sex.

For the rural migrants, the urban subcommunity provides comforting similarities to the ruralness of their origin.

2. Adler, Dan L.

 1960 "Psychological Problems of the Voluntary Migrant to Australia," in *Uprooting and Resettlement,* Papers of 11th Annual Meeting of the World Federation for Mental Health, Vienna, Austria, August 1958 (London, World Federation for Mental Health), pp. 100-106.

Twelve-year-old children in the state schools of Australia's capital cities. Five hundred migrant children and 700 Australian children were studied in order to compare family life of migrants with that of Australian families in the same social and economic strata.

During the first two years of migrant residence, the autonomous role of the mother was greater for Australians than for migrants. In the Australian group, the mother decided what was to be done and did it herself. Migrants who had been in Australia for seven or more years differed in no significant respect from Australians. Migrant families of different nationalities varied in their rate and pattern of change.

Migrants' influence on the Australian stems from the side-by-side existence of several different cultures in the same community, which discomfited him. What he would prefer is monistic assimilation, one in which he would digest and incorporate the migrant as an indistinguishable unit of the Australian way of life. Thus, for the Australian, the bright hope for resolution of the conflict lay with the children of migrants.

Affleck, Marylin. *See* 83.

3. Allen, John H., Roy C. Buck, and Anna T. Wink

 1955 *Pulling Up Stakes and Breaking Apron Strings: A Study of Mobility Among Pennsylvania's Rural Youth,* Pennsylvania Agricultural Experiment Station Progress Report 136, 20 pp.

A survey of 2,062 students in the sophomore classes of 74 fourth-class high schools in Pennsylvania. Study of mobility among Pennsylvania's rural youth: (1) who leaves home? (2) where do they go? (3) how well do they make out? Personality Adjustment Score.

It was concluded that: (1) The direction of spatial mobility was (1a) generally urbanward (1b) related to IQ. (2) Village, open-country non-farm, and farm represent points along a continuum of origin along which, (2a) there were respectively declining proportions of outward mobility for boys, (2b) the reverse was true for girls, (2c) early (male) entry to the labor force decreased, (2d) the proportion reporting white-collar employment in 1951 decreased, (2e) the proportion of girls classified as housewife in 1951 increased, (2f) the number of job changes, employer changes, months on first job did not vary, (2g) first job pay decreased. (3) Girls were more apt than boys to (3a) be living away from their parental homes, (3b) travel farther, (3c) experience lower first job pay, (3d) have occupation vary with intelligence, (3e) experience decreasing difference in average salary, difference being associated with point of origin in (2). (4) In each 1947 residence category, and for both sexes, lowest first job pay was associated with subsequent changing occupations. (5) By 1951 the occupationally mobile were reporting a little higher salaries than were those who had made no change. (6) No marked relationship was found between personality adjustment scores and occupational mobility or spatial mobility. (7) Religion was not found to be markedly associated with spatial and occupational mobility.

4. Almon, C., Jr.

 1956 "Origins and Relation to Agriculture of Industrial Workers in Kingsport," *Journal of Farm Economics*, 38:828-36 (August).

Data from a sample of 700 workers in two major manufacturing plants in Kingsport, Tennessee. A study of background factors, including farm origin, of industrial workers.

The two Kingsport plants drew a little more than half their workers from farm backgrounds. Eighty-five percent of the workers originated within a 75-mile radius of the plants. The residence of the workers when hired showed marked changes over time in geographical concentration. These changes indicated that the industries drew most heavily on the farm population after they were well established but were still growing rapidly. Men reared on the farm and men reared in town made about equally good workers. Men with previous training in skilled trades or truck driving were more likely to be promoted to the semiskilled level than were the men coming directly from the farms.

5. Anderson, Albert F.

 1962 "Theoretical Considerations in the Analysis of Migration," unpublished doctoral dissertation,

Iowa State University of Science and Technology, 141 pp.

Using the U.S. census, a series of hypotheses were tested within the framework of the following theoretical considerations: "Cohesion, defined as the degree to which the units of a social system accept the roles prescribed by the system, was hypothesized to vary inversely with deprivation which was defined as the degree to which reward expectations exceed achievement actualities. Deprivation was hypothesized to vary directly with ambiquity which was defined as the degree to which roles in a social system remain undefined. Assuming the predominance of an economic value system, poorly defined economic roles were expected to be accompanied by smaller rewards than anticipated. Such deprivation was expected to be related to deviancy from or rejection of the prescribed roles, such deviancy or rejection functioning as an adaptation to deprivation." Answers to two questions were sought: (1) Can the variations in rates of net migration for the 1950-1960 decade among the counties of Iowa be explained and predicted from the theoretical framework? and (2) Do other types of adaptation to deprivation function as alternatives to migration?

"Ten of the hypotheses were supported by significant, consistent correlations within the sets of three variables. Six of those 10 involved net migration as a measure of cohesion. The significant correlations found were generally consistent with the hypotheses." Factor analysis indicated that the migration losses were greatest in areas which exhibited strong rural characteristics. Only variation in income and mental committals failed to relate as hypothesized to the other measures.

6. Anderson, Stig, and D. Banerji

    1962 "Report on a Study of Migration in Four Taluks of Bangalore District," *Population Review* (Madras) 6:69-77 (January).

Thirty-five villages in Channapatna, Devonahalli, Magadi, and Nelamangala Taluks of Bangalore District, India, in February-April, 1960. The purpose of the study was to establish the rate of emigration from the villages, with a view to forecasting the likely loss of study population in a follow-up study. Other demographic characteristics of the population were also studied. The 35 villages surveyed were found to have a population of 13,838 persons at the time of interview. The total number of immigrants was 230, (rate: 17 per 1000). The number of emigrants was 307, (rate: 22 per 1000). Barring unlikely change, it could be estimated that no more than 5 percent of the population would be lost by emigration over a period of two years. About one-third of the emigrants went to the same taluk and two-thirds elsewhere. About a fourth of the emigrants went to Bangalore City. It was clear from the age distribution that a good proportion of the women's emigration was because of marriage, and also that only a small proportion of the emigrants were more than 30 years old. On the basis of this study a fair estimate could be made that 20 percent of the population would migrate out of the study areas during the course of the next two years.

7. Anderson, Theodore R.

    1955 "Intermetropolitan Migration: A Comparison of the Hypotheses of Zipf and Stouffer," *American Sociological Review*, 20:287-91 (June).

Migrants from 54 metropolitan subregions within the Northeast and North Central regions of the U.S. to each of the nearest 30 metropolitan subregions, 1935-40. Census data: Distance, intervening opportunities, and related factors used in determining the relative size of migrant streams. Three formulas were used and four hypotheses were tested.

(1) Number of intervening opportunities does not appear to be a more accurate measure of distance than highway mileage. (2) Population size should be corrected for the extent of unemployment, which makes the numerator in Zipf's formula more in line with the concept of opportunities. (3) State boundaries operate as inhibiting factors, tending to block movement, and, hence, to reduce the accuracy of Zipf's formula. (4) This research suggests an alternative general hypothetical model: the number of extra multiplying variables should be held to a minimum and the powers to which the basic variables are raised should be treated as *variables* from one application to another, rather than as overall constants.

8. Anderson, Theodore R.

    1956 "Intermetropolitan Migration: A Correlation Analysis," *American Journal of Sociology*, 61:459-62 (March).

Migrants between the 54 major metropolises in the North Eastern and North Central regions of the U.S. in 1940. Census data. The variance in the four migration rates (in-migration, out-migration, net migration, and total migratory activity) will be substantially reduced by a linear multiple regression equation involving the following characteristics of the metropolises: percentage of the labor force that is unemployed, mean rent of all dwelling units, log of the population size, and log of the sum of population divided by distance, summed over the ten metropolises nearest the one being considered.

The study concludes that the "net migration can be explained purely in terms of the push-pull theory. The hypothesized variables are sufficient to explain most of the variation in migration rates. Other census data do not, in general, improve the explanation materially."

9. Anderson, Walfred A.

    1958 *The Characteristics of New York State Population*, New York Agricultural Experiment Station Bulletin 925, 72 pp.

People of New York, 1900-1950. Census data.
In Section VII of this publication the following observations were made: (1) New York people were residentially more stable than those of the country as a whole. (2) The proportion of the population changing residence varied from 10 to 15 percent in 44 of the 62 counties of the state. (3) Most movement was within the county. (4) Migrants into the state made up 11 percent of the movers. (5) New Jersey and Pennsylvania contributed most heavily to New York "in-migrants." (6) The rural nonfarm population of New York moved

most; the urban population least. (7) But, New York, with more "out-" than "in-" migrants during this single year, suffered a net loss of 66,955 residents to other states. The farm population contributed only slightly to this loss. (8) In the exchange of residents, New York had a net loss of residents to 39 states and the District of Columbia, a net gain for only 8 states. (9) Institutions, individuals, and families are affected by these residential changes.

Anderson, Walfred A. *See* 262, 263.

10. Appleyard, R. T.

    1962 "The Return Movement of United Kingdom Migrants from Australia," *Population Studies,* 15:214-25 (March).

    United Kingdom migrants from Australia. A 20 percent sample of re-registrants for National Insurance Cards completed by workers who returned to the United Kingdom from Australia during seven months of 1959. The study was aimed at obtaining marital status, age, and occupation of the migrants from Australia to the United Kingdom.
    The annual rates of return have risen from 11.7 percent in 1957 to 19.2 percent in 1960. Eighty-one percent of the workers were under 46 years of age when they returned to Great Britain; 76 percent had occupations in the professional, intermediate, and skilled classes; and 67 percent emigrated to Australia after 1955. Finally, interviews with 100 (or 42.5 percent) of the sampled workers revealed that 33 percent had returned to Great Britain either for visits to their relatives or because of the death or illness of a relative and planned to return to Australia.

11. Auerbach, Frank L.

    1957 "Recent Developments in the Immigration Field," *Department of State Bulletin,* 37(964): 1030-35 (December).

    Review of developments since Refugee Act of 1953, especially the provisions of the Act of September 11, 1957.
    This address was made before the Conference on Immigration, sponsored by the United Community Services of Metropolitan Detroit and the Michigan Commission on Displaced Persons and Refugees at Detroit, Michigan, on December 10, 1957.

Aurback, Herbert B. *see* 125.

B

12. Babow, Irving

    1955 "Types of Immigrant Singing Societies," *Sociology and Social Research,* 39:242-47 (March-April).

    A study of the secular European immigrant singing societies in San Francisco from 1851 to 1953 in an attempt to type them. Four types were identified: the nostalgic (reflecting cherished memories of the homeland), the ceremonious (displaying talent at concerts and ceremonial observances), the cultural indoctrination (teaching the young to use their parents' language and to identify themselves with the national culture of their parents' homeland), and the protest (rebelling against patterns of social experience). Organized singing activity is an important folk art found in most European immigrant groups. "During the early period of immigrant settlement, the immigrant singing society plays a more vital role within its community and in the larger society than in the later period. . . . Some functions of the singing society are unwitting consequences of the organized expressive behavior and were not conscious or deliberate functions for which the chorus was organized. The singing society varies in significance in different immigrant communities. The singing society seems to have a symbolic function in regard to sentiments and morale, especially during a period of crisis in the homeland and the immigrant country."

13. Bachmura, Frank T.

    1956 "Migration and Factor Adjustment in Lower Mississippi Valley Agriculture, 1940-50," *Journal of Farm Economics,* 38:1024-42 (November).

    A 24-country area in the Lower Mississippi Valley. Data from population and agricultural censuses. Hypotheses: "(1) Population change has been selective as to a) income, b) race, c) residential sector, and d) local development in manufacturing industry; (2) Agricultural production has become more a) labor extensive, b) land intensive with respect to labor and extensive with respect to capital, and c) capital intensive with respect to land and to labor and that d)these movements have been 'income corrective' with respect to county income differentials."
    Persistent geographically disparate county incomes relate to rates of migration and population change in a way that equilibrates all-sector county populations, regardless of race. For the areas as a whole, lower income groups tend to have higher rates of out-migration, to ease the low-income problem in the area. The presence of local manufacturing industry tends to attract in-migration or lessen out-migration (except for the nonwhites). Highest agricultural income counties had largest per worker, and per acre investment in capital items, and the best ability to increase these, and to increase harvested land acreage. Geographical equilibration of county incomes calls for still higher rates of population exodus as well as for changes in the amount and form of capital investments in counties of lowest income.

14. Bachmura, Frank T.

    1958 "Small Area Population Response to Full Employment," *Southern Economic Journal,* 25:159-73 (October).

    Study of 24-county area surrounding Memphis. Census data. Emphasis: (1) the relationship between demographic data and the level of economic development, and (2) the relevance of full employment in solving the low-income problem in Southern agriculture.
    "In general the findings vindicate a policy of full employment as an aid both to improving levels of per worker farm income and of contributing little more to average farm income disparities than depression. The role of full employment in accelerating industrial development both locally and nationally introduced a

dynamic quality to income improvement in the area. In the process of stimulating mobility and births, full employment brought out racial, sectoral, and age-sex selectivities not apparent during depression. While local opportunities for nonfarm employment expanded notably during full employment, higher urban birthrates provided an enlarged potential labor pool in nonfarm areas; therefore, a given rate of growth of nonfarm jobs will not be able to absorb so large a proportion of redundant farm labor."

15. Bachmura, Frank T.

1959 "Man-Land Equalization Through Migration," *American Economic Review,* 49:1004-17 (December).

Comparative study of Iowa and a 24-county case-study area around Memphis. Census data. Relative changes that have occurred in the ratio of farm land per farm worker in the two areas between 1940-1950 are considered, with some extrapolations of these results to 1965. The Iowa level of county farm income is used as the criterion for the adequacy of migration from the farm sector of the case-study area. Various policy recommendations are briefly examined.

The study revealed a number of advantages in unsubsidized migration: (1) It rewards directly individual initiative on the part of people whose resources are much too small to permit effective farm reorganization within agriculture or to establish a local non-agricultural business. (2) Changes can be made without delay for governmental action. The magnitude of the ameliorative influence of migration for the low-farm-income problem obtained and obtainable through unsubsidized migration seems to have been considerably neglected. Efforts to encourage local industrialization within the case-study area have achieved results which are evidently far from the magnitude required to absorb natural increase within the area.

Bailey, Wilfrid C. *See* 16.

16. Baird, Andrew W. and Wilfrid C. Bailey

1958 *Farmers Moving Out of Agriculture,* Mississippi Agricultural Experiment Station Bulletin 568, 7 pp.

Farm operators living in six communities in Alcorn County, Mississippi. Data from 161 respondents. Characteristics of the people moving between farm and nonfarm occupations, whether the shift is a sudden one or whether several steps or stages are involved in the process, and what happens to the land formerly operated by people who shift from farm to nonfarm occupations. "The transition from farming to nonfarm employment in Alcorn County has both economic and social implications. From the economic standpoint, part-time farming in this area appears to be a stage in the shift from farming to full time nonfarm employment.... Some look upon their nonfarm employment as temporary and expect to return to farming during periods of high farm prices or unemployment. ... At least three aspects of the occupational changes have social implications. The median age of the rural residents is rising because the younger men are turning to nonfarm occupations and

they are the ones who are most likely to leave the community. The rural communities are losing population as men move to other areas to find employment. Finally, many of those who retire or find nonfarm employment continue to live on the same land but are classified as rural nonfarm. Thus the occupational pattern of the rural community is shifting. These changes are having an impact on the structure of the community and on its role in the lives of its residents."

17. Balmer, D. G.

1961 "Migrant Labor Legislation in Oregon," *Western Political Quarterly,* 14:77-78 (September Supp.).

A description of the individual and group actions which led to the enactment by the 1959 Oregon legislature of five laws to improve the conditions of migrant farm workers.

"The passage of these laws over the opposition of the powerful Oregon Farm Bureau Federation to the last four bills was a significant accomplishment. Credit for this accomplishment can be attributed to organized religious groups, skillful political leadership, and support from administrators of key state agencies. A not unfairly apportioned legislature was also a factor."

Banerji, D. *See* 6.

18. Barley, Delbert

1957 "Refugees in Germany: Relationship Between Refugees and the Indigenous Population of a Rural Black Forest Community," unpublished doctoral dissertation, University of Pennsylvania, 277 pp.

Fifty-three refugees or heads of refugee households and 50 indigenous persons. "West German problem of assimilating its postwar influx of refugees and expellees is examined (1) in its broad statistical, economic and geographic aspects, and (2) in the specific relationships between refugees and the indigenous population of a rural Black Forest community." Interview material supplemented by ten months of participant observation in the community.

Difficulties of adjustment and the clashes of culture center about "(1) general interaction patterns between refugees and indigenous persons, (2) the rural-urban conflict and comparative standards of living, (3) financial difficulties: work opportunities and state support for refugees, and (4) religious differences. ... Refugee assimilation in terms of 'status' is aided more by a similar rural background than by either membership in the community religious group (Roman Catholic) or economic integration (satisfactory occupation, income and housing). ... Satisfactory occupation and income-housing adjustment is much more closely related to the retention of previous occupational status. ... An additional factor in refugee adjustment in the community is the presence of friends and relatives from the former home community. ... The breaking of bonds with the past, and the isolation of refugees from persons who 'know who one is,' is a serious obstacle to adjustment. The indigenous population of the community tends to be frustrated and irritated by the assumed superiority of many refugees, as well as by the heavy taxes enacted for their support. . . . Enough sympathy for the refugee's lot remains to ease potential conflicts and to dissolve (up to the present) much of the predicted political radicalism among refugees."

19. Bauder, Ward W.

1959 "Analysis of Trends in Population, Population Characteristics, and Community Life in Southern Iowa," Seminar on Adjustment and Its Problems in Southern Iowa, CAEA Report 4, Iowa State University College of Agriculture, pp. 113-37.

Nineteen counties in Southern Iowa. Data mostly derived from U. S. censuses. Partly devoted to a study of the effects of heavy out-migration on problems of community adjustment.

Trends in population (numbers and characteristics) of the people 1850 to 1950 were examined to determine adjustments needed in a number of southern Iowa communities. "Out-migration together with changes in birth and death rates have changed rather drastically the age distribution of the population in southern Iowa. . . . The effects of age selectivity in out-migration are most marked in the age group 25-30. The continued heavy out-migration of young adults has reduced the proportion of persons under ten years of age in southern Iowa relative to the state or nation. [It] has reduced the proportion of women of child-bearing age sufficiently to reduce crude birth rates. [It] has apparently caused a reduction in overall fertility rates even though the families remaining in the area may be rather large."

20. Beijer, G.

1959 "Overseas Migration of European Agriculturists, 1918-1940 and 1946-54", in Rural Migration, Papers presented at the 1st Congress of the European Society for Rural Sociology, Brussels-Louvain, September, 1958 (Bonn, privately published), pp. 280-93.

Migrants from Belgium, Germany (Federal Republic), Ireland, Italy, the Netherlands, Norway, Portugal, Spain, Switzerland, and the United Kingdom. Data mostly from census reports and governmental statistical reports.

"On the whole, the trend of the totals of emigrants shows the influence of the drastic restrictions in the 'thirties,' but for the emigrants with agricultural professions from Belgium, Germany, Ireland, the Netherlands, Norway, Switzerland and the United Kingdom the trend is a decreasing one." The paper includes separate discussions of the characteristics of the migrants to Argentina, Australia, New Zealand, Union of South Africa, and the United States.

Bell, Robert R. See 30.

21. Benewitz, Maurice C.

1956 "Migrant and Nonmigrant Occupational Patterns," Industrial and Labor Relations Review, 9:255-406 (January).

Male migrants, 25 years of age and over, St. Paul, Minnesota, 1950. A sample of 278 cases. Hypotheses tested: (1) "Occupations of rural migrants are not significantly different from those of the St. Paul population." (2) "Rural male migrants not in the professional, technical, managerial, and kindred classifications are similarly distributed by occupation to the 73% of the St. Paul male population not in the professional, technical, managerial, and kindred class."

The first hypothesis was rejected, but the second one was supported. "The interurban migrant group contained a higher percentage of professional and skilled persons than the St. Paul male population. These persons seem to move for purposes of economic advancement, and the mobility of professional and managerial persons in particular seems to be high."

22. Bennett, John W., and Robert K. McKnight

1956 "Misunderstandings in Communication Between Japanese Students and Americans," Social Problems, 3:243-56 (April).

A study of 30 male Japanese students in order to understand the genesis of misunderstandings in communication (other than language) between Japanese students and Americans and the way in which "personal response to the interactional situation" helped or impeded actual interaction. Model for analysis of American-Japanese interaction patterns presented.

"Difficulties are founded on contrasting norms and expectancies in the culture of the two societies and are specifically accentuated by images and attitudes based on the historical relations of the two countries over the past 90 years. . . [I]t is hoped that an understanding of the cue-confusions, status-images, and cultural differences involved may lead to an acceleration" of relating in meaningful terms. "Along theoretical lines, it would seem that the study of interpersonal dimensions of cross-cultural relations in the modern world requires deeper penetration into cultural and historical aspects of the social situation than is demanded in comparable studies of interaction within one society. The need is clearly indicated for an integration of sociological and socio-psychological observations on the one hand, and anthropological and historical data on the other."

Bergen, Bernard J. See 99.

23. Bertrand, Alvin Lee

1958 "The Rural Population," in Rural Sociology, by Alvin Lee Bertrand (New York, McGraw-Hill, pp. 51-75.

Rural people of the United States. Data from 1950 U. S. census. Number and distribution, composition and characteristics, the nature of vital processes, and population trends among the rural population of the U. S.

"The data on migration show that the rural-farm population made proportionately fewer moves . . . than did the rural-nonfarm and urban populations. . . . There are several specific migrations involving rural people. . . . Two of these are rural-urban exchanges and movements of seasonal migratory agricultural workers. . . . The persons who leave the farm and move to the city, are for the most part, young people in their late teens or early twenties, and females tend to leave the farms in greater proportionate numbers than males. . . . The number of persons involved in seasonal migratory agricultural work is not definitely known."

24. Beshers, James M., and Eleanor N. Nishiura

1961 "A Theory of Internal Migration Differentials," *Social Forces*, 39:214-18 (March).

Streams of internal migration in Indiana 1935-1940 and 1949-1950. U.S. census data. Hypotheses: "(1) When a change of locale is involved, the amount of migration within the professional category will be greater than the amount of migration within other occupation categories; (2) the amount of migration among farmers and farm managers is less than the amount of migration among most other occupation groups; (3) more migration will occur among young adults than among other age groups; (4) migration among persons 65 and over will be greater than that within the age category immediately preceding theirs except in streams of a rural area of origin; (5) 15-19 year olds will migrate from rural [...] tion in a particular stream is less among those with 6 or fewer years of education than among other education groups; (7) the amount of migration among those who have a college education will be greater than the amount among other education groups in the same stream; (8) in urban-urban and urban—nonadjacent suburban streams proprietors, managers, and officials will migrate more than the majority of occupational groups; (9) in urban—urban and suburban—nonadjacent urban streams, migration of craftsmen and foremen and operatives and kindred workers is less than migration of other occupational groups; and (10) in rural—rural streams, the amount of migration among farm laborers will be much greater than the amount of migration among farmers and farm managers."

Hypotheses were supported in all cases except number one, where, in 1935-1940, the professional category ranked fifth among the six occupational groups in urban—adjacent suburban streams and sixth in the suburban—adjacent urban streams. "The differential streams of migration are regarded as consequences of social and cultural constraints upon the head of a household. . . . Environmental and structural factors will be mediated by the degree of local orientation characterizing various occupations."

25. Beveridge, Ronald Murray

1959 "Subregional Migration Within Illinois, 1935-40," unpublished doctoral dissertation, University of Illinois, 131 pp.

Illinois migrants. Data from unpublished Special Census Tabulations of Migrants provided by the Scripps Foundation for Population Studies. Study emphasis: "To reveal the patterns of gross subregional migration streams within Illinois for the migration interval 1935-40, to analyze these patterns, to find significant correlations of the migration streams with economic and social subregional characteristics, and to discover meaningful generalizations concerning the subregional migration streams." Cartographic analysis.

"The largest movements of in- and out-migration occurred reciprocally, in general, with the same contiguous subregion, and the smallest movements of in- and out-migration occurred reciprocally, in general, with the same noncontiguous subregion. . . . The greater portion, 54.9%, of the total intrastate migration occurred within the subregions of the state. . . . Almost one-third of the total intrastate migration, however, took place within the three metropolitan subregions where such movement was possible. . . . Four times as many migrants moved from the central cities, Chicago and Peoria, to their own rings as moved in the opposite direction. There was a strong positive correlation, (1) between the size of the total out-migrant and in-migrant streams, and (2) between the total resident subregional population and the number of migrants originating in each subregion. The trend of net migration was from south to north. . . . Metropolitan subregions had relatively little attraction for migrants from other metropolitan subregions, while the populations of the metropolitan subregions were being infiltrated chiefly by migrants from nonmetropolitan subregions. . . . The highest rates of net gain were recorded by the metropolitan subregions at the expense of the nonmetropolitan subregions, and the greatest rates of net loss were suffered by the southern nonmetropolitan subregions. The rates of net migration tended to vary directly or inversely with many of the economic and social subregional characteristics. The most significant correlations were: (1) the inverse correlation with the rate of unemployment, (2) the direct correlation with the proportion employed in manufacturing, and (3) the direct correlation with educational attainment of the subregional population."

26. Bevins, Robert Jackson

1962 "A Measurement of Agriculture's Public Investment in the Education of 1940 Decade Farm-Nonfarm Migrants," unpublished doctoral dissertation, Michigan State University, 122 pp.

Migrants, U.S. "An attempt was made to determine the magnitude of the unamortized agriculturally derived public educational investment which resided in off-farm migrants of the 1940 decade." A number of estimating procedures used.

"It appeared that the educational investment made by agriculture in the migrants was about $2.5 billion in 1940 dollars. . . . this drain on agricultural incomes was only a small part of the total drain which resulted from excess population in agriculture. . . . This study clearly indicated that there is a flow of social capital from agriculture to nonagriculture. . . . Should the nonfarm sector become aware of the contribution which it apprears to be receiving from agriculture it is possible that attempts may be made to find ways by which more equitable' participation may be had in the costs of rearing and educating farm people who are destined to make their productive contribution to the nonfarm economy."

27. Bishop, C. E.

1960-61 "Economic Aspects of Migration From Farms," *Farm Policy Forum*, 13(2):14-20.

Migrants from farms and the extent to which migration helps to equalize incomes of farm and nonfarm people. Implications for policy.

"Migration has failed to equalize returns for farm and nonfarm labor because the number of people who are willing to transfer to nonfarm jobs at prevailing rates of return exceeds the number of jobs that are available. . . . Migration increases when jobs become available in spite of the fact that during these periods the return per worker in agriculture increases relative to the return per worker in nonfarm employment. The rate of migration decreases as unemployment increases. . . . The analysis lends support to the idea that a critical level of unemployment in terms of providing motivation for nonfarm migration develops when unemployment reaches 5% of the labor force. . . . When underemployment is the result of lack of knowledge concerning nonfarm employment opportunities, underemployment results from a malfunctioning knowledge market. . . . Underemployment can be removed only if the number of additional nonfarm jobs created exceeds the new entries to the labor force."

28. Blackwood, P. E.

    1957 "Migrants in our Schools", *Educational Leadership*, 14:207-13 (January).

    Migrants in the U.S. Various aspects of the mobile population of the United States are discussed and related to the school needs of children of migratory families. Policy questions.
    At local, state, and national levels there is a genuine concern for improving the welfare of the agricultural migrants. "The phenomenon of mobility or our population, including school-age children, highlights two major questions regarding public education in the United States." First, what curriculum adaptations are needed to assure continuous school progress for all pupils? Second, what is the best way to finance the schools to provide maximum educational opportunity for all children?

29. Blair, Harry E.

    1955 "Human Relations Problems of Migratory Students," *National Association of Secondary School Principals Bulletin* 39:63-70 (March).

    Children of migrants to Kern County, California. Personal and social characteristics of students from migrant families. The importance of the roles of the community, school, and home for their adjustment.
    "Migrant students . . . desire permanence, community ties, and a feeling of belongingness. . . . One survey report shows that approximately 61% of the migrant students surveyed were as well adjusted as others in their classrooms." There is, however, an "extraordinarily high incidence of behavior difficulties among this group of children. . . . The most frequent problem reported was that of timidity and withdrawing from the group; while aggressiveness was the next most frequent problem. Lying, stealing, cheating, sex irregularities, poor health habits, and the inability to concentrate were other problems noted. . . . Dealing with students who don't 'stay put' is fundamentally a problem of attendance and child welfare. . . . [T]he primary need of migrant students is for 'acceptance' which underlies the basic human need for security. Security . . . comes from the interaction of the home,

the school, and the community. The administrator must gain the support of his community and the student's home if he is ever to provide a program for the acceptance of the migrant student. . . . He must adjust his curriculum better to fit the educational needs of the migrant student. Attendance and instruction are interdependent. Better attendance means better learning, and better instruction means better attendance. Both mean better education for the migrant students."

30. Blumberg, Leonard, and Robert R. Bell

    1959 "Urban Migration and Kinship Ties," *Social Problems*, 6:328-33 (Spring).

    Negro migrants into Philadelphia. Based on 133 interviews. An interpretive essay on the theme, "The family and kinship are more important for some population elements in urban community than for others, and hence the dysfunctional rural-to-urban 'adjustment' analysis may be limited in its application."
    Family, kin, and close friendships have much deeper personal roots for migrants into the urban community than might have been anticipated. This seems to be true for recent and older, and for white and Negro migrants. However, if the spatially mobile migrant achieves vertical social mobility, an element in the mobility achievement is to modify, if not drop many of his old family ties. This estrangement is facilitated when vertical social mobility is accompanied by migration. The class-mobile, middle-class migrant breaks kinship ties. The lower-class migrant, especially from the rural South, strives to reinforce them, or to create pseudo-kin relationships.

31. Bogue, Donald J.

    1958 "Economic and Social Implications of Population Changes in the Chicago Metropolitan Area: A Case Study," *Selected Studies of Migration Since World War II*, Proceedings of the 34th Annual Conference of the Milbank Memorial Fund, New York, 1957, Part III, pp. 125-36.

    People of Chicago Standard Metropolitan Area. Most of the data derived from materials prepared for the Population Research and Training Center of the University of Chicago, U.S. census reports, and previous publications by the author. "This is a case study of the Chicago Standard Metropolitan Area, submitted as an example of what is happening in this movement toward a metropolitanization of the population."
    Demographic, economic, and social implications of metropolitanization are discussed. This relatively recent, rapid growth is heavily concentrated in the metropolitan ring outside the central city. Suburban rings are focal points for great net in-migration, preponderantly white. The central city has a very substantial net in-migration of Negroes, and, in some cases, Puerto Ricans, whose patterns of settlement are similar. In the suburbs, there has been an unprecedented building boom, high land values and rentals, increased commercial and manufacturing activities, and a rising standard of living. Within metropolitan areas, the racial barriers confining the Negroes to a small congested sector recently have been broken. Today's emphasis on children and upon more spacious apartments or houses and less ground-

coverage have changed our estimate of what is a desirable neighborhood; and metropolitan populations do not appear to be placing themselves in urban captivity. "By the cross-section approach we tend to see the migrant only as a low-income newcomer, arriving in particular 'ports of entry' to the metropolis and being not too well adjusted to city life. We forget that he graduates from the slums and joins the society at large. We know little of how long he retains his low-economic status, or of the process by which he reaches eventual adjustment."

32. Bogue, Donald J.

1959a "Internal Migration," in *The Study of Population*, ed. Philip Hauser and Otis Dudley Duncan, (Chicago, University of Chicago Press), pp. 486-509.

"This chapter summarizes some methodological lessons of migration research acquired as a part of a long-range program of research in population distribution."

The following subjects are discussed: "Why Should Demographers be Interested in Internal Migration?"; "The Problem of Defining Internal Migration"; "Definitions of Concepts and Terms Used in Migration Analysis"; "Methods of Measuring Migration: Indirect Methods"; "The Direct Measurement of Internal Migration"; "Summary of Existing Knowledge" (under this heading migration-stimulating situations for persons, factors in choosing a destination, and socioeconomic conditions affecting migration are listed and knowledge about migration streams and knowledge about differential migration are discussed); and "Next Steps in Research." A selected bibliography is included.

33. Bogue, Donald J.

1959b "Internal Migration and Residential Mobility," in *The Population of the United States* (Glencoe, Ill., The Free Press), pp. 375-418.

Utilizes the U.S. census of 1950, various reports of the Bureau of the Census, existing researches, and special researches done for projects; emphasizes description and interpretation of internal migration during 1950-1960 and historical trends and changes in recent past.

The major headings are: the extent of internal mobility, the differential mobility of different segments, the effect of internal migration upon the regional distribution of population, interregional migration, migration and metropolitanization, selectivity of internal migration, and factors underlying internal migration.

34. Bogue, Donald J.

1959c "International Migration and National Origins of the Population," in *The Population of the United States* (Glencoe, Ill., The Free Press), pp. 348-74.

Data source and emphasis same as in item 33.

The discussion includes a brief history of United States immigration, characteristics of immigrants, emigration, countries of birth of the foreign-born population, the second generation, and assimilation of immigrants. Differences associated with ethnic origins still exist in the population. "Some of these groups have

managed to attain a socioeconomic level higher than that of the native-born population of native parentage; others are still striving toward equal socioeconomic status." Achieved socioeconomic ranking by members of various ethnic groups, aged 25-44 and residing in urban areas in 1950, is given. "Almost without exception among the various foreign-stock groups, a larger proportion of males were unmarried than were males of native stock, and bachelorhood was even more pronounced among the second generation than among the first. A similar situation exists among second-generation women of almost every nationality. ... This postponement or rejection of marriage by members of the second generation may reflect their ambition to achieve a higher socioeconomic status than that attained by the first generation." The process of assimilation of the second generation seems to involve the clerical occupations as a way of obtaining a foothold in the white-collar occupations, and also a rise from laborer to operative and from operator to craftsman.

35. Borrie, W. D.

1959 "The Growth of the Australian Population with Particular Reference to the Period Since 1947," *Population Studies*, 13:4-17(July).

Australian census data and other published reports. The growth of the Australian population and "what have been the outstanding features of immigration to Australia since World War II; and why has it been possible to sustain the flow at such high levels."

Between January, 1947 and June, 1958, assisted immigration has amounted to more than half the permanent arrivals. "Directly and indirectly through their Australian-born children, immigrants were responsible for approximately half the national growth during the decade. More significant, however, than their quantitative impact has been the role of immigrants in filling gaps in the nation's stock of young manpower and in providing a mobile, adaptable work force without which major developmental projects of the post-war era could not have been undertaken. ... The nation's stock of capital is much more adequately equipped now ... to cope with the demands of a continuing flow of immigrants, but ... the economic absorption of immigrants in the future at the same level as in the past will not be without its difficulties. ... The rate at which immigration will flow will also depend to a large extent upon the attitude of organized labour."

36. Borrie, W. D., and Jerzy Zubrzycki

1958 "Employment of Post-War Immigrants in Australia," *International Labour Review* 16R, 77: 239-53 (March).

Data on 1,200,000 immigrants to Australia since 1945 from records of International Refugee Organization, statements by immigrants on admission, and census data for 1947 and 1954. The distribution by country of origin, industry, occupation, and employment of migrants since 1945 and an examination of the success of the government's policy of planned immigration and of the adjustment of the migrants themselves in their country of adoption.

Data examined show that the government policy of

selecting migrants to fit specific occupations has done much to minimize the problems usually encountered in migration processes; immigrants have been rapidly absorbed into employment and subsequently vertically mobile. The friction which has occurred has been in the employment of immigrants with professional qualifications.

37. Bowles, Gladys K.

1956 *Farm Population ... Net Migration from Rural-Farm Population, 1940-1950,* Agricultural Marketing Service, Statistical Bulletin 176, June, 174 pp.

Those who migrated to or from the rural-farm population, 1940-1950. U.S. census data. Information on the types of persons involved in farm-nonfarm migration— that is, age, sex, and color composition of the persons making up the excess of the migrants. Survival ratios used in estimating net migration.

In the 1940-1950 decade, rates for children and for persons 25-44 were low in most areas; rates for young people, those 10-19 in 1940, were highest in all areas; rates for persons older than 45 were generally intermediate between the rates for the other groups. For persons who were under 20 in 1940, rates for girls and young women were usually higher than were rates for young men; for the ages 20-29, men tended to have higher rates than women; for those over 35, rates for women were higher than those for men. Rates of net out-migration were usually higher for nonwhite persons than for white persons. White females generally had higher rates of net out-migration than white males among most age groups; the same relationship exists between rates for nonwhite males and females. Findings are also reported by geographic regions and state economic areas of the U.S.A.

38. Bowles, Gladys K.

1957 "Migration Patterns of the Rural-Farm Population, Thirteen Economic Regions of the United States, 1940-1950", *Rural Sociology,* 22:1-11 (March).

A concise version of item 37.

39. Bowles, Gladys K.

1958 *Migration of Population in the South: Situation and Prospects,* U.S. Department of Agriculture, Agricultural Marketing Service, 17 pp

Southern migrants in the U.S. census data and related publications. Study of the migration of population in the South, with special emphasis on the movement of young people.

"In recent years a net annual loss through movement to and from farms or through change in classification of residences of over one million persons has occurred in the country as a whole. 60% of this net loss took place in the South." Several findings similar to item 37. "Prospects are that, in the future, migration from the South as a whole will continue for some time. The annual average loss of population as a result of migration may be about 200,000 between the present time and 1970. . . .Since the numbers of men leaving

working ages are likely to be only about half the numbers entering the working ages in the South, a minimum of 50% of the rural-farm young men will be looking for employment opportunities outside of agriculture. And a substantial proportion of these young people will migrate from farms to find such opportunities."

Bowles, Gladys K. *See* 309.

40. Bowring, J. R., and O. B. Durgin

1958 *The Population of New Hampshire. 4. Factors Influencing the Attitudes of Farmers Toward Migration Off Farms,* New Hampshire Agricultural Experiment Station Bulletin 458, 10 pp.

Farm operators in New Hampshire. Interview data from 253 farm operators. Farmers' attitudes toward leaving the farm and factors influencing these attitudes. Seven factors were hypothesized to be related to farmers' attitude toward leaving the farm: age, education, farm improvements, migration of children, community ties, and farm indebtedness.

Hypotheses supported by data. Only 36 of the 253 operators interviewed had considered moving off the farm.

41. Bowring, J. R., M. S. Purington, and O. B. Durgin

1956 *The Population of New Hampshire: Migration and Changes in Composition.* New Hampshire Agricultural Experiment Station Bulletin 425, 22 pp.

People of New Hampshire. Most of the data derived from U.S. censuses. A descriptive study of migration and changes in composition of the population of New Hampshire in age, dependency, fertility, and sex ratios as a result of migration. Methods used in estimating migration, in estimating resident deaths by single years of age for each year, and in assessing the relative weight of natural causes and migration are explained.

"The net migration from New Hampshire between 1940 and 1950 by numbers of persons was small. The major changes resulting from migration were in the age and sex structure of the population. . . . There was a net loss from the state of persons who were 10-24 in 1940. . . . A much smaller loss was apparent in the 45-64 age groups. . . . There was a net gain of females for the state. . . . The dependency ratio . . . increased for the state. The greatest increases were in rural farm-land nonfarm residents. . . . In all counties but one the decline in sex ratio was due more to migration than to natural causes."

42. Bracey, Howard E.

1958 "Some Aspects of Rural Depopulation in the United Kingdom," *Rural Sociology,* 23:385-91 (December).

Rural residents in the United Kingdom. A study of the causes and effects of rural emigration to urban areas.

"Rural emigration has helped to make the United Kingdom the most urbanized nation in the world. . . . It has created two groups of people, an urban majority and a rural minority each with a different outlook on life. Since 1939, new forces have helped to weaken the barriers between the two groups and have also tended to halt or restrain the tide of depopulation. . . . The tide of depopulation has receded with every new bus service and every improvement in communication." "Social Services and Organizations," "Villages with Declining Population," "The Country Emigrant," and "Continuing Depopulation" are discussed.

43. Brantner, John Paterson

   1958 "Homeless Men: A Psychological and Medical Survey," unpublished doctoral dissertation, University of Minnesota, 205 pp.

   Admittees to the Minneapolis Salvation Army Men's Social Service Center. Information from 1,622 case records, 466 medical examinations, and results of 296 Minnesota Multiphasic Personality Inventories. It is a historical survey of vagrancy and homelessness, and a review of the related published work, including literary, religious, sociological, psychiatric and psychological studies.
   "Over one-half of these men obtained scores on the Psychopathic Deviate Scale two standard deviations or more above the normal mean, and nearly one-half had that scale as the highest scale in their profile. . . . MMPI scores and case record data lent further support to the thesis of basic sociopathy in this group. . . . One-half of these men had been in Minneapolis a week or less when they were interviewed. Two-thirds of them had no legal residence or settlement. They tended to drop out of school earlier than the rest of the male population. Their occupational levels were low, and their work was casual and intermittent. One-third were divorced and almost one-half never married. One-half of them had spent some time in penal institutions. . . . They drank excessively, but this appeared to be pathological, non-addictive drinking. . . . Tuberculosis rates and the incidence of venereal disease were significantly high. They did not show medical signs that they are subject to prolonged anxiety. . . . Three-quarters of the sample were physically fit for employment, yet they consistently spent considerable time in idleness."

44. Breazeale, Norma J.

   1958 "Association of Selected Socio-Economic Characteristics with Net Migration from Three Kentucky Economic Areas, 1920-1950," unpublished masters thesis, University of Kentucky, 156 pp.

   Migrants from three Kentucky economic areas (3a, 8 and 9), 1920-1950. Census data. Test of hypothesized relationships between migration flow and four other factors: economic level, level of transportation facilities, level of communication, and strength of locality ties.
   "The dominant association revealed in this analysis . . . was the highly significant negative correlation of economic level with net out-migration. Economic level was found to be highly associated, not only with migration, but also with . . . levels of transportation and communication and strength of locality ties. . . . The findings of high negative correlations between economic level and volume of out-migration offered definite support for an explanation of migration as a response to economic differentials. The theory was further supported by the appearance of higher correlations when economic

differentials were assumed to be greater for the study areas—in periods of agricultural depression coincident with industrial prosperity, and in the decline of the area's leading industry."

45. Brewster, J. M.

   1959 "Impact of Technical Advance and Migration on Agricultural Society and Policy," *Journal of Farm Economics*, 41:1169-84 (December).

   Farm workers in U.S. An interpretive essay discussing migration as a solution to excess agricultural capacity and the low income position of agriculture.
   "(1) Agriculture is a competitive industry in a larger world where less than fully competitive markets are widespread, and where there is normally much less than full employment. (2) Agriculture is also afflicted with a rate of technical advance that expands farm output appreciably faster than the growth of effective demand for farm products. These conditions preclude out-farm migration by itself from providing a long-run solution to the problem of excess capacity and the relatively low income in agriculture."

46. Brown, Claude Harold

   1960 "Personal and Social Characteristics Associated with Migrant Status Among Adult Males from Rural Pennsylvania," unpublished doctoral dissertation, Pennsylvania State University, 121 pp.

   Young adult males from the rural areas of Pennsylvania. A sample of 974 contacted in 1947 when sophomores in rural high schools and reinterviewed in 1957. The purpose of this study was to ascertain the influence of selected factors related to the migration of rural youth.
   (1) An examination of the mobility pattern revealed that nearly three-fourths of the young people remained in rural areas, the rest migrating to urban areas. (2) Intelligence, personality adjustment, rank and types of parental occupations, amount and type of education were not related to migration status. (3) Married people migrated more than single ones.

   Brown, Claude Harold. *See* 55.

47. Brown, Claude Harold, and R. C. Buck

   1961 *Factors Associated with the Migrant Status of Young Adult Males from Rural Pennsylvania*, Pennsylvania Agricultural Experiment Station Bulletin 676, 34 pp. (Based on the senior author's doctoral dissertation. *See* 46.)

48. Brown, James S., and George A. Hillery, Jr.

   1962 "The Great Migration, 1940-1960," in *The Southern Appalachian Region: A Survey*, ed. Thomas R. Ford, (Lexington, University of Kentucky Press), pp. 54-78.

   People of the Southern Appalachian Region. U.S. census data and related publications, including special tabulations. Seeks answers to the following questions: "How many migrants were there? Where did they go? What were they like? Why did they move? What implications does this great migratory movement hold for the Region, for the nation, and for the migrants them-selves?"

"Regardless of the extent to which the Appalachians appear to have been separated from the main stream of American social and cultural development, they have become increasingly integrated, possibly re-integrated, into that stream. In this process of integration, migration has played an important role." An increasing proportion of persons are moving from mining and subsistence agricultural areas where the old social and cultural patterns have been especially persistent. The most apparent reason for Appalachian migration has been economic, but factors such as urbanization, family structure, education and mass communication, have also entered into the picture. Because of depopulation of mining and subsistence agricultural areas, such areas face serious consequences of adjustment: maintenance and support of local governmental services and school systems, reorganization of the total institutional structure, etc. Future composition of the population of cities such as Cincinnati, Columbus, Akron, etc. (systems to which Appalachian areas belong) "will continue to be affected by the composition of their migrant streams." Thus, the training of persons in these feeder-areas is a crucial problem. "The focal points of change within the Region will be the metropolitan areas." Their future growth rate "will be determined to a large extent by the effectiveness with which they compete with the more vigorous urban centers which surround it." Neither the subsistence farming nor mining areas can hope to hold their natural increase so that "a program of guided migration might well be a more realistic solution than an attempt to maintain an economic base compounded chiefly of large numbers in relative poverty."

49. Brown, L. B.

1957 "Applicants for Assisted Migration from the United Kingdom to New Zealand," *Population Studies*, 11:86-91 (July).

Four hundred forms of application for the Assisted Migration Scheme. Information collected in two stages: (1) 150 forms received during March, 1953, and (2) 250 received in July, 1953. A description of general characteristics of the applicants.

"Men predominate among the applicants, and the majority of the applications are from single people, under the age of 30. The applicants seem to have had more formal schooling than the general population, and those from an urban background predominate. These would-be emigrants have a background of previous moves and do not represent a cross-section of occupations. It is of importance to note that these selective characteristics are evident at the time of making application and not only in the process of actual migration. . . . It would seem likely that many people do not consider applying for assistance because they believe that they would not be accepted."

50. Brown, L. B.

1960 "English Migrants to New Zealand: The Decision to Move," *Human Relations*, 13:167-74 (May).

The implicit universe is all English citizens that might possibly move to New Zealand, either as civilians

or as servicemen through government assistance. Information gathered from 100 single men, born in England, seeking assisted passages to New Zealand as either civilians or servicemen during 1952. Also, a control group of 100 comparable people not actively contemplating migration was used. What caused the decision to move?

"There were no differences found between migrants and non-migrants in an expression of their general attitude to England. . . . New Zealand is seen by the migrants as a highly attractive place to go, with other destinations being undervalued. . . . The migrants have been subjected to greater influences from people outside England than have the non-migrants; these influences tend to be concentrated on New Zealand. . . ."

51. Brown, Morgan C.

1962 "Selected Characteristics of Southern Rural Negroes Exchanged to a Southern Urban Center," *Rural Sociology*, 27:63-70 (March).

Rural Negroes who entered Baton Rouge, Louisiana, from farm areas beyond the parish (county) borders. A total of 312 adult Negro migrants. A randomly selected control group of 88 Negro married family heads, born and reared in the central city. A study of selected characteristics of rural Negro migrants.

One hundred and ninety-two males, 61.5%, came from adjoining counties, traveling a median distance of 25 miles. No migrant came from a parish or county in which there was a city of 50,000 population or more. More recent migrants brought their entire family. More recent migrants had a higher educational level at the time of entry. Family units were relatively small on entry. Many family heads entered alone.

52. Brown, Phillips H., and John M. Peterson

1960 "The Exodus from Arkansas," *Arkansas Economist*, 2:10-15 (Winter).

Migrants from Arkansas. Most data derived from 1950 census reports. Study of general facts about out-migrants: How many? Who? Where do they come from? When do they leave? Why do they leave?

"The implied net outmigration over the past eight years amounted to a cumulated total of 371,000. A similar computation for the 1940-1950 decade indicates a net out-migration over that 10-year period of 431,000. . . . Most of the migrants from Arkansas, as elsewhere, have been young adults and very young children. . . . As a consequence of this age-selectivity of migration, as well as of the higher birth rate in the state, Arkansas in 1957 had a greater than average proportion of its population among the dependent youth. . . . Negroes, while a minority of the migrants, accounted for a disproportionate share of Arkansas' net outmigrants during the decade of the 1940's and to a lesser extent in the 1950's. . . . Arkansas' population has not kept pace with the national growth during any decade since 1900 except the 1930's; yet it long has had a faster rate of natural increase. Thus, there has been a continuing flow of net outmigration from Arkansas decade by decade at least since the turn of the century. . . . The reason Arkansas has been losing population is because not enough manufacturing jobs have been created to absorb the large number of people being reared on and leaving Arkansas farms. Furthermore, while recent industrial development efforts in the state have produced noteworthy results in new plants and plant expansions; these gains have been partly offset by declines in some industries."

53. Brunner, Edmund deS.

1957 "Population Research," in *The Growth of a Science: A Half-Century of Rural Sociological Research in the U.S.* (New York, Harper), pp. 42-63.

A digest of research studies in population, illustrating the types of research being done, subject matter covered, methods used, and results achieved.

Findings emerging from practically all studies of migration and population mobility are: "(1) Females leave rural areas, especially farms, in disproportionately larger numbers and at an earlier age than males. (2) The bulk of the rural-urban migration begins at age 16 and is over by age 30. (3) While a majority of migrating youth in their first move settle near their parents' homes, the better educated go farther. (4) The greater the distance a migrant moves, the more likely it is that his destination is a large city. (5) The youth of tenant families are more mobile than those of owner families, but they move shorter distances. (6) Males, though less migratory than females, travel farther. (7) Nearby cities attract disproportionately large proportions of unskilled workers from rural America, more distant and larger cities a higher proportion of more capable and of professional workers. (8) Younger families are more mobile than older, operators of small farms than those with larger holdings. (9) Families with a number of organizational contacts in their community are less mobile than those with few. (10) Rates of migration tend to vary with urban economic conditions."

54. Bryant, E. S., and G. L. Wilber

1961 *Net Migration in Mississippi, 1950-1960*, Mississippi Agricultural Experiment Station Bulletin 632, 14 pp.

Mississippi migrants, 1950-1960. Most of the data derived from U.S. censuses, Mississippi State Board of Health, and U.S. Department of Health, Education and Welfare. Net migration in Mississippi during 1950-1960 is the study emphasis. Residual method.

"A disproportionately large segment of dependent age persons resulted from the combined factors of heavy out-movement of persons in their productive years, in-movement of retirement age persons, and the high rate of natural increase. Also significant has been the increase in ratio of white to nonwhite citizens. . . . The streamlining of farming enterprises plus the expanding of industries in the cities have spurred thousands of Mississippi's surplus rural youth to seek new homes and new occupations in the nation's burgeoning urban areas. Many of the migrating white persons found new residences in Mississippi's own growing cities, but nearly all the nonwhite migrants moved to regions outside the state." If investment and production losses are added together, Mississippi's migration loss during the 1950's cost the state an average of $700 million a year. . . . Industrial expansion in the state has thus far not kept pace with the natural increase in inhabitants."

Buck, Roy C. *See* 3 and 47.

55. Buck, Roy C., and C. Harold Brown

1959 "The Implications of Rural Youth Migration and Occupational Mobility for Agriculture," *Journal of Farm Economics*, 41:1155-68 (December).

Data from 1,042 male sophomores from 74 rural Pennsylvania high schools who provided complete information during a ten-year period, 1947-1957. "The problem was to discover the extent to which place of residence in childhood and early youth was a significant factor contributing to differentiating processes of spatial and occupational mobility as well as certain allied attributes." I.Q. scores and California Test of Personality used.

The evidence redefined the hypothesis of marked differentiation between the socioeconomic futures of farm-reared and rural nonfarm-reared young adults. The factor of residence had varying importance, depending upon the other factors being investigated and the time of investigation during the ten-year period.

56. Burchinal, Lee G.

1960 "Who's Going to Farm," *Iowa Farm Science*, 14:12-15 (April).

A study of 103 high school farm boys in the tenth and twelfth grades in Iowa. "Do the brightest, most able youths tend to leave the farm and rural areas?" "Will rural areas be depleted in future leadership by the migration of youth?"

Sixty-eight percent of the fathers "of the boys who planned to farm (farm oriented) were farm owner-operators. Only 30% of plan-nonfarm-job (nonfarm oriented) boys and of the uncertain boys lived on owner-operated farms. Also, the boys who planned to farm much more frequently reported that a farm was or would be available to them. In all three groups, "boys more often reported their mothers than their fathers as having expressed some opinion about their sons' occupational plans. Boys who had reached a definite decision about their future occupations most often reported discussions with both fathers and mothers about their occupational plans. . . . Mothers more frequently than fathers put emphasis on encouraging their sons to continue education." The boys who planned to farm had lower grades, rated freedom on the job as the most important factor, and rated farming over nonfarm work. They less often consulted teachers or counselors about their occupational plans. They were more satisfied with their present job information and had less often plans for education beyond high school.

57. Burnight, Robert G.

1957 *100 Years of Interstate Migration, 1850-1950*, Connecticut Agricultural Experiment Station Bulletin 330, 15 pp.

Connecticut migrants, 1850-1950. A study of migration of native-born population into and from Connecticut using census data.

"In 1850 there were more Connecticut-born persons living in other states than persons from other states living in Connecticut; from 1900 on, however, this situation was reversed." During 1850-1950 the "vast majority of migrants came from nearby states but that during this period more and more migrants were being drawn from a greater number of states. . . . Although the Connecticut-born have migrated to all the states in the Union, their greatest concentration has been in the Middle Atlantic States and in Massachusetts."

Burnight, Robert G. *See* 364.

C

58. Catapusan, Benicio T., and Flora E. Diaz Catapusan

    1956 "Displaced Migrant Families in Rural Philippines," *Sociology and Social Research,* 40:186-89 (January-February).

    Rural immigrant families in the Philippines. Interview data. Displaced migrant families and their adjustment problems resulting from migration. Interpretive statement.

    The grievances of the migrants seemed to center on the poor location of the farm lands, nonavailability of irrigation water all year round, and the failure of the hacienderos to comply with contracts. The severing of social ties and bonds in one area and their reestablishment in another area are of great import in changing migrant behavior. The shift is generally followed by frequent maladjustments in the newly adopted community until the situation stabilizes itself after a period of exploration, testing, and assimilation of the way in the new environment.

Catapusan, Flora E. Diaz. *See* 58.

Cho, Chang-Soo. *See* 72.

Christiansen, John R. *See* 63.

59. Cleland, Courtney B.

    1956 "North Dakota Population Changes," North Dakota Agricultural Experiment Station Bimonthly Bulletin 19, pp. 63-65.

    People of North Dakota. Data derived from U.S. census reports. "What happens to people born in North Dakota? How many stay, and how many leave? And how many people settle there who were born elsewhere?"

    About 70 percent of North Dakota's 1950 population was born within the state. Minnesota, Washington, California, Montana, and Oregon received the bulk of North Dakota's out-migration. North Dakota received far more population born in Minnesota than from any other state. The migration pattern has changed little since 1950.

60. Clements, R. V.

    1955 "Trade Unions and Emigration, 1840-80," *Population Studies,* 9:167-80 (November).

    British trade unions and emigrants, 1840-1880.
    "Despite criticism, the assumption still lingers that between 1850 and 1880 trade unions, particularly those of the Junta group, subscribed to middle-class views on economics and on the function of trade unions. It

has been sustained by a mistaken idea of the motivation and importance of trade union encouragement of emigration. . . . [T]he complex motives behind their [trade union leaders] interest in emigration derived less from orthodox economics than from the never abandoned quest to strengthen trade union bargaining power. Traditional methods, irreconcilable with orthodox economics, were not given up, and emigration encouragement was usually intended to reinforce them. Emigration encouragement sprang from varied circumstances—migration into large towns, technological change, excessive burdens on union funds, strikes, lockouts, despair of the future, or the desire to add to the list of benefits. All sections of unionism exhibited some interest at some time, and probably the Junta showed least."

61. Coalson, George Otis

    1956 "The Development of the Migratory Farm Labor System in Texas: 1900-1954," unpublished doctoral dissertation, University of Oklahoma, 108 pp.

    A study of the importance of migrant workers to the agriculture of Texas and some of the problems associated with migrant labor.

    The mechanization of preharvest cotton operations and the development of the fruit and vegetable industries in South Texas resulted in a demand for seasonal labor. In response to this demand, Mexican immigrants entered the country and settled in South Texas, forming a reservoir of cheap labor. By 1900 certain patterns of migration of these workers were established. During the winter months, they were employed in South Texas, usually in the fruit and vegetable fields. In the summer they followed the cotton harvest across the state. After the cotton harvest they returned to their homes in South Texas to begin the cycle anew.

62. Coe, Paul E.

    1955 "Nonwhite Population Increases in Metropolitan Areas," *Journal of the American Statistical Association,* 50:283-308 (June).

    Nonwhites in metropolitan areas. Most data derived from U.S. censuses. Analysis devoted primarily to nonwhite population changes in standard metropolitan areas from 1940 to 1950.
    (1) The nonwhite population in the entire nation had begun to increase at a faster rate than the white. (2) The nonwhite population was being distributed generally. (3) Nonwhites living in SMA's increased over twice as fast as did the white population from 1940 to 1950. (4) In-migration accounted for an estimated almost two-thirds of the nonwhite population increase in SMA's and in their central cities, for almost half of their increase in the SMA suburbs. (5) In their movement to SMA's nonwhites have gravitated very sharply to the central parts of the cities. (6) Regional nonwhite increases were numerically largest in the North Central SMA's and relatively largest in the SMA's of the West. (7) There were great concentrations of nonwhites in a few SMA's (half of all nonwhites in the 168 SMA's and one-fourth of all nonwhites in the nation live in 10 SMA's). (8) Nonwhites did not increase equally in all SMA's: in 9 they decreased in number; in 31 they

doubled; and in 3 they tripled. White population doubled in only one SMA. (9) Nonwhites were not present to the same degree in all SMA's. (10) The reasons for the nonwhite population surge to SMA's cannot be quantified, but include such considerations as better employment opportunities, the search for greater freedom from segregation, and the appeal of urban life.

63. Coleman, A. Lee, Albert C. Pryor, Jr., and John R. Christiansen

    1956 *The Negro Population of Kentucky at Mid-Century,* Kentucky Agricultural Experiment Station Bulletin 643, 43 pp.

A study of the Negro population in Kentucky, using 1950 census data and related information.

Relatively high out-migration was a major factor in accounting for the decreasing population of Negroes in Kentucky's total population. A definite migration pattern could be seen. Kentucky-born Negroes went primarily to the four states directly north (Ohio, Indiana, Illinois, and Michigan), and the majority of the in-migrant Negroes came from the four states directly south of Kentucky (Tennessee, Alabama, Georgia, and Mississippi). Kentucky appeared to be a "way point," in that it receives Negroes from the areas of dense Negro population to the south and sends its own native Negroes on to the states further north.

64. Coller, Richard Walter

    1959 "Geographic Mobility of Selected Rural Minnesota Male High School Graduates," unpublished doctoral dissertation, University of Minnesota, 262 pp.

Male graduates for the years 1948, 1950, 1952, 1954, and 1956 from five Minnesota rural high schools (three in northeastern Minnesota, a low-farming income area; two in southwestern area, a high-farming income area). Information from 581 young adults. An attempt to test the validity of a social explanation of migration which viewed migratory patterns as adaptations to social pressures for success.

"All the findings relate to three aspects of geographic mobility—range, destination, and frequency of migration. Northeastern migrants tended toward either short- or long-distance moves, whereas the southwesterners clustered at intermediate locations. Variables most significantly associated with range were occupational aspiration, military experience, and career advancement. Early residence and reasons for migrating showed the least association. Destinations of Northeastern migrants were most often large or small communities. ...." Migrants from the southwest went to medium-sized centers.

65. Cowgill, Donald O.

    1961 "Value Assumptions in Recent Research on Migration," *Sociological Quarterly,* 2:281-92(October).

Study based on the author's review of some 35 articles and monographs on migration listed in *Sociological Abstracts* in recent years. Effect of value judgements on migration research.

Earlier sociological writings on migration and mobility tended to stress the disorganizing aspects. This was true of the research relating to immigration from abroad and it tended also to be true of the ecological studies of the 1920s and 1930s. This negative value orientation has tended to disappear in recent years, being replaced by more neutral attitudes or even positive ones in some cases.

66. Crane, Robert I.

    1955 "Urbanism in India," *American Journal of Sociology,* 60:463-70 (March).

More than one-third of the residents of major cities were studied, using data from Davis' existing study, to understand the role migration was playing in urbanization of India.

Despite recent rapid migration to urban centers, India remains predominantly rural. Migrants are never quite assimilated to city life. They float back to their families in rural areas after they have worked in the city for a time.

67. Cumpston, I. M.

    1956 "A Survey of Indian Immigration to British Tropical Colonies to 1910," *Population Studies,* 10:158-65 (November).

People of Indian origin in British Tropical Colonies with a view to understanding the advantages and abuses of the indenture system.

After the abolition of slavery in British colonies in 1834, many thousands of laborers left India under indenture for employment in colonial plantations. At the end of their indenture, many Indians decided to settle in their new homes, especially in British Guiana, Trinidad, Mauritius, and Fiji. The paper discusses the districts of origin in India, the conditions of service under the indenture system, and its advantages and abuses. It also discusses the opportunities open to the Indian laborer at the end of his indenture, and the facilities which the government or the planters provided for his settlement on the land. Those who did not settle on the land turned to the professions or trades, often with success. The paper describes the attitude of the "communities of reception" to the Indian during and after indenture, and his adjustment to a multiracial society.

68. Cunningham, Earl Harold

    1962 "Religious Concerns of Southern Appalachian Migrants in a North Central City," unpublished doctoral dissertation, Boston University Graduate School, 451 pp.

An exploratory study of 33 Southern Appalachian adult migrants in Cleveland, Ohio, centered around eight hypotheses. These hypotheses were concerned with migrants' disappointment in the city, the less strict ethics of the migrants, the correspondence of their attitudes to those of religious sects, passivity of the migrants to economic and psychological distress, their loneliness in the city, and the weakening of the migrants' religious life.

Analysis of the data showed that the migrants were not disappointed in the city, that ethically more strict migrants came from lower social status groups, and that they actively and constructively dealt with their economic and psychological stress situations. These migrants were not lonely in the city, but had friends and relatives who helped them to get settled. There was some weakening in the migrants' religious life, but those who prayed more frequently appeared to be less distressed and passive to their conditions. Implications of these conclusions are presented and suggestions for further research given.

D

69. Dambaugh, L. N.

1958 "Role of Migratory Agricultural Labor in South Florida" [abstract], *Association of American Geographers Annals*, 48:258 (September).

A study of migrant agricultural laborers in South Florida. Emphasis on employment, health, and housing problems connected with the movement of these seasonal workers.

In spite of the rapid adoption of technology, an increase in farm operations has increased the demand for labor. Southern Negroes, Texas-Mexicans, Puerto Ricans, and a few whites and Bahamians are recruited by the Department of Labor, Bureau of Employment Security. When crops, weather and market demand are normal, there is full employment for the migrants from November through April.

70. Danley, Robert A.

1959 *Population Estimates for Kentucky Counties and Economic Areas, July 1, 1958*, Kentucky Agricultural Experiment Station Progress Report 79, 17 pp.

Analysis of Kentucky's population growth based on census reports, utilizing the migration-and-natural-increase method, developed by the Population and Housing Division of the U.S. Bureau of Census. Tables and maps.

Kentucky's net population gain was due to the natural increase exceeding out-migration. Two trends continued, namely population losses due to migration throughout most of the state and marked gains in industrialized urban areas.

71. Davis, Billie

1956 "And Here is Your Desk . . . ," *Journal of the National Education Association*, 45:337-38 (September).

A case study of a child of migrant parents, emphasizing the part played by the public school system in the U.S.

The essence of this article is that the free public school had provided for the child a desk, a symbol of its chance to participate in the world of real people.

72. DeFleur, Melvin, and Chang-Soo Cho

1957 "Assimilation of Japanese-Born Women in an American City," *Social Problems*, 4:244-56 (January).

A study of 80 Issei women—40 Buddhists, and 40 Christians—residing in Seattle, Washington. An attempt to test the following hypotheses: (1) "Religious affiliation and participation are significant factors in assimilation." (2) "Cultural assimilation will be in part a function of the following premigration factors: rural-urban origin, educational attainment, occupation in the mother country and age at entry." (3) "Cultural assimilation will be in part a function of the following postmigration factors: number of children, personal occupation, years of stay in the U.S., and present age." An index of assimilation, comprising six general areas of behavior, is used.

The first hypothesis was supported; the second was only partially supported; and the third was not supported. The methodological aspects of the investigation were felt to be more important than the actual findings in that the assimilation index yielded results which indicate that its further refinement would be fruitful.

73. DeGroot, Dudley Edward

1957 "The Assimilation of Postwar Immigrants in Atlanta, Georgia," unpublished doctoral dissertation, Ohio State University, 117 pp.

Post-World War II immigrants to U.S. Samples of immigrants who had settled in Columbus, Ohio, and in Atlanta, Georgia. One hundred twenty-five postwar immigrants in the metropolitan area of Atlanta, Georgia, were intensively interviewed. "A major focus of the study was upon the relationship between motives for immigration and degree of assimilation." An eight-item index of assimilation.

"Age, marital status, religion, motivation for migration, presence of children in the family, and a number of adverse comments about the U.S. were significantly related to the degree of assimilation. . . . Those immigrants who because it was physically impossible for them to maintain themselves in their original environment were placed in a 'survival' category. Immigrants whose motivation was primarily a desire to improve their social status or economic position were placed in· a 'socio-economic' category. Finally, those immigrants who migrated because of problems of ideological or political compatability in their native lands were placed in a 'political' category. Configurational analysis revealed 8 clusterings of the variables which were significantly related to assimilation. Four assimilation 'types' were apparent in these 8 clusterings." (1) Low in assimilation—old married or previously married Jewish "survivals" without children. (2) The most highly assimilated type—young "socio-economics," married and without children, who were either Protestant or Greek Orthodox. (3) Medium assimilation—young Jewish "survivals," married and with children. (4) Medium assimilation—old "politicals," married and without children. "While intragroup differences in the rate of assimilation did appear, it was clear that postwar immigrants in Atlanta, Georgia, as a total group were assimilating quite rapidly."

74. Denton, Alfred Maxey

1960 "Some Factors in the Migration of Construction Workers," unpublished doctoral dissertation, University of North Carolina, 148 pp.

White migrant families around Atomic Energy Commission's Savannah River Plant in South Carolina, 1952-1953. A study of 821 families.

The migrant families were slightly smaller than the average for all white families in the U.S. and tended to be young with husband and wife under 35 years old, with about 75 percent of the children under 10 years of age. "The data indicated there was little or no relationship between size of family and distance migrated, but distance was related to other variables. (1) The longer the distance migrated the more likely a family was to have made several previous moves. (2) The longer the distance migrated the higher the family income tended to be. (3) The longer the distance migrated the more likely a wage earner was to have sought job information from formal sources and he was more likely to have contracted for a job before moving. It was found that many 'job information networks' exist among the workers who move frequently. . . . Such movement may enable them to achieve some of the same 'marks' of middle-class status that more sedentary families in the white-collar occupations achieve."

Diégues, M., Jr. *See* 229.

75. Dietrich, T. Stanton

1960 "Nature and Directions of Suburbanization in the South," *Social Forces*, 39:181-86 (December).

Hypothesis: "The South has experienced a remarkable redistribution of its population primarily due to changes in agricultural production; that the large number of agricultural out-migrants who have remained in the region have not been attracted to the larger industrial cities, but to the many smaller towns and cities and non-farm areas scattered about the region; and that industry has tended to move to rural territory rather than rely upon drawing labor to urban-located plants."
Hypothesis was upheld. There is need for a vigorous community research program to test these assumptions concerning the forms and processes of suburbanization in the new urban South.

76. Dobriner, William Mann

1956 "The Impact of Metropolitan Decentralization on a Village Social Structure: A Study in Suburbanization and Social Change," unpublished doctoral dissertation, Columbia University, 257 pp.

Residents of a Long Island village. Information through 275 (random sample) questionnaires and 60 interviews of community leaders to do an "empirical case analysis focused on the impact of the newcomer suburbanites on the 'oldtimer' social structure on a Long Island village."
"(1) The newcomers were intensely involved with individuals, groups and events outside of the local village in the metropolitan area. In contrast, the villagers were much more dependent on the local village. (2) Due largely to their cosmopolitan orientations and metropolitan attachments, the suburbanites do not perceive the village as a community whose ultimate destiny is intimately linked to theirs. In spite of the local ori-

entations of the oldtimers there has been a substantial decline in the perception of the village as a unit of solidarity. (3) The delineating characteristic of the suburbanite world seems to be the residence location of the family. Many of the changes being effected in the village are directly traceable to the concentration of functions centered on the family."

78. Doerflinger, Jon Arno

1962 "Patterns of Internal Migration Related to Institutional and Age-Sex Structure of the U.S.," unpublished doctoral dissertation, University of Wisconsin, 167 pp.

Migrants in the U.S. An attempt to understand the patterns of internal migration related to institutional and age-sex structure of U.S.
Most frequently involved in migration were the family, housing, and occupation. "Family structure was shown to have evolved from a more inclusive kin group which may have inhibited migration to the present form of nuclear family which may facilitate migration. Housing was shown to have developed to a stage where our present accommodations are tailored closely to the size of family at a given family cycle stage. Thus it was concluded that some migration could be accounted for by a desire for more space as the family increased." The occupational structure revealed the following trends which might influence migration: (a) separation of place of work and place of residence; (b) working for others versus self-employment; (c) larger more impersonal work aggregates; (d) greater division of labor; (e) rationalization of work; (f) reduction in time devoted to work; (g) increased occupational participation by women; (h) shifting regional patterns of occupational distribution; and (i) greater occupational mobility. It was concluded that the general effect of these trends was toward greater mobility.

78. Doerflinger, Jon A., and Douglas G. Marshall

1960 *The Story of Price County, Wisconsin: Population Research in a Rural Development County*, Wisconsin Agricultural Experiment Station Research Bulletin 220, 32 pp.

People of Price County, Wisconsin. The data sources were: census materials; historical data; a survey of a 20 percent sample of the open-country population done in 1956; and a population enumeration conducted in 1958. The study was an attempt to discover the causes and consequences of population change in an area of high out-migration, and to provide factual information to facilitate the Rural Development Program.
The population has a high proportion of older people and a low one of working-age persons when compared to the state as a whole. Migration from Price County has been age-sex selective. Young people leave the county and the older persons remain giving a high dependence ratio in the population. Lower population density also raises costs of services. With more adequate planning at county level in cooperation with many state, federal, and educational agencies a better balance of the use of resources to population is being achieved.

79. Ducoff, Louis J.

1955 "Trends and Characteristics of Farm Population in Low-Income Farming Areas," *Journal of Farm Economics*, 37:1399-1407 (December).

Low-income farmers in nine generalized areas in the U.S.: (1) Appalachian Mountains and Border areas; (2) Southern Piedmont and Coastal Plains; (3) Southeastern Hilly; (4) Mississippi Delta; (5) Sandy Coastal Plains of Arkansas, Louisiana, and Texas; (6) Ozark-Ouachita Mountains and Border; (7) Northern Lake States; (8) Northwestern New Mexico; and (9) Cascade and Rocky Mountain areas. Data derived mostly from reports of the Agricultural Marketing Service. Some of the demographic and other relevant characteristics of this population group were studied.

During 1940-1950 "an estimated one-half of the expansion in the nonagricultural labor force was supplied by migration from the farm population and over half of this was from the low-income farming areas. The most distinctive characteristic of the farm population in these areas is the high proportion of children and youths and the low proportion of adults in the productive ages. . . . This emphasizes the importance of focusing programs on greater investment in the children and youth of these areas."

80. Duncan, Otis Dudley, and Stanley Lieberson

1959 "Ethnic Segregation and Assimilation," *American Journal of Sociology*, 64:364-74 (January).

Seventy-five community areas of Chicago in 1930 and 1950. Census and special compilations of unpublished census data. Hypotheses: (1) The degree of residential segregation of a group of foreign stock at any given time is inversely related to appropriate indicators of its socioeconomic status and degree of assimilation and directly related to indicators of its "social distance" from the population of native stock. (2) Ethnic segregation patterns are relatively stable over time, but change in direction is to be anticipated on the basis of the positive correlation between assimilation and length of time that the immigrant group has been established in the United States. Index of dissimilarity between residential distributions, index of centralization, index of assimilation, index of socioeconomic status, and social distance scale used.

"Changes in residential patterns in Chicago between 1930 and 1950 were in the direction expected on the basis of a positive relationship between assimilation and length of residence; but such changes did not disrupt a pattern of differential segregation and spatial separation of ethnic colonies, this pattern exhibited remarkable stability over the twenty-year period."

81. Duncan, Otis Durant

1956 "The Theory and Consequences of Mobility of Farm Population," in *Population Theory and Policy*, ed. Joseph J. Spengler and Otis Dudley Duncan (Glencoe, Ill., The Free Press), pp. 417-34.

A study that tries to integrate a large number of empirical studies and statistical information from official government bureaus on migration with a fourfold purpose: the causes of human migration; the direct effects of migration on farm population; size and specific groups involved in this migration; and consequences of migration.

The conditions for migration are classified under the following five causes: economic and technological, social, personal, natural, and miscellaneous. Types of movements based on distance moved and the volume of these movements are discussed. Migration is age and sex selective. Unmarried persons are more mobile than married ones, partly because of the greater expense of moving families than single individuals. Cities seem to attract the extremes of population in physical traits, social ranking, and intelligence. The essay points out some of the positive and negative consequences of migration.

82. Durgin, O. B.

1957 *Population of New Hampshire: Effects of Migration on the Small New Hampshire Town*, New Hampshire Agricultural Experiment Station Bulletin 437, 30 pp

Twenty towns in New Hampshire. Basic data mostly derived from reports of Bureau of Census. Hypotheses: "(1) During the time interval of 1930-50 the measured characteristics of population for two samples of towns, one sample of towns increasing and the other decreasing during this period, will become more alike. (2) By 1950 there will be an apparent contrast in the general economic structure of the towns gaining and those losing population. (3) By 1950 only minor differences will exist between the towns gaining and those losing population for economic factors analyzed. Such minor differences as do exist will be in favor of the increasing towns."

"(1) Population characteristics have become more alike during the period 1930-50. (2) Census residence categories are of relatively little value in the analysis of the small northern New England town. (3) There are some differences in agricultural adjustments between farms in towns losing population and those in towns gaining populations. . . . (4) There appears to be some general difference in the economic orientation of the decreasing and increasing towns. . . . (5) In small towns in areas of long and stable settlement, differences in economic orientation and adjustment do not create difference in population characteristics."

Durgin, O. B. *See* 40 and 41.

83. Dyer, W. G., and Marylin Affleck

1958 "Labor Mobility and Industrialization in a Utah County," *Social Forces*, 36:214-17 (March).

Past and present employees of a major steel plant six miles northwest of Provo, Utah. Study included one out of every 40 terminated employee personnel folders and one out of every 15 active employees (350 schedules). "Hypothesis 1: The number of people employed by the steel plant previously residing in a given area is inversely proportional to the distance of that area from the work plant. Hypothesis 2: The age of the migrants at the time of employment is inversely related to the distance of the residence before migration to the work plant. Hypothesis 3: Labor turnover is a function of migratory tendencies, age, and education. Hypothesis 4: The residence of immigrant workers is a function of closeness and accessibility to the work plant, and available community services."

It was found in this study that the majority of industrial workers came from the local labor market within the county. Following this, workers migrated into the county from contiguous counties in the state. There was no direct inverse correlation between age and distance of migration. The younger workers had a higher termination record than older workers. Terminated workers had less education on the average than those who continued their employment.

84. Dynes, Russell R.

1956 "Rurality, Migration and Sectarianism," *Rural Sociology*, 21:25-28 (March).

Adults in Columbus, Ohio. A sample of 360 cases (53 percent returns) from the city directory of Columbus. Answers were sought to the following questions: (1) Do individuals reared in rural areas hold sectarian attitudes and beliefs after they move to a metropolitan area? (2) Is the sectarian a recent arrival to the city and therefore susceptible to "cultural shock"? (3) Does the sectarian change occupation and residence more often than others? Twenty-four item Likert-type scale measuring sectarianism and denominationalism.

"The general proposition that sectarianism functions as a cushion for the rural migrant in his adaptation to a hostile urban environment seems to have little validity. . . . While sectarianism may have functioned at one time as an accommodative device for rural migrants, the narrowing differentials between rural and urban areas may have modified this. . . . Urbanization, mass communication, and modern transportation have minimized the differences. . . . The sect cushions the 'culture shock' of the rural migrant *if* he is from a lower socioeconomic level. . . . The significance of sectarianism lies in its association with lower socioeconomic status."

E

85. Eames, E.

1954 "Some Aspects of Urban Migration from a Village in North Central India," *Eastern Anthropology*, 8:13-26 (September-November).

Migrants from Madhopur, a village in the southeastern part of the state of Uttar Pradesh. A study of 91 families with regard to aspects of urban migration.

1) More than 50 percent of the people from Madhopur now living in urban centers range in age from 20-29; a large majority are married and have children but do not take their families to the city with them. 2) Most of those who go to cities travel a long distance and give as their reasons a desire to obtain better wages, ease of finding employment, or just having relatives and friends to help them make initial adjustment to city life. 3) Sixty percent of those now working in cities have been there less than five years, 13 percent more than 10, and five percent more than 15 years. 4) On the whole, it seems that those who migrated to the city have adjusted, though only 13 families of the 91 represented had moved to the cities.

5) The greatest number of migrants return to the village once a year for holidays, family illness, marriage, or a family visit, although a substantial number never return. 6) Migration has caused little change in the village social structure.

86. Eckerson, Helen F.

1958 "United States and Canada: Magnets for Immigration," *Annals of the American Academy of Political and Social Science*, 316:34-42 (March).

U.S. and Canadian immigrants. Data derived from *Demographic Yearbook*, 1952 and 1954, and *Year Book of Labour Statistics*, 1956. The study is a descriptive comparison of immigration to the U.S. and to Canada, 1946-1957.

The United States remains the largest immigrant-receiving country in the world. Under the national-origins-quota system and emergency legislation, 2.6 million immigrants were admitted in 1946-1957: roughly one fourth displaced persons and refugees, one fourth Western Hemisphere immigration, one fourth families of citizens, and one fourth quota other than displaced persons. Admission of 1.5 million immigrants in 1946-1956 made Canada the second largest immigrant-receiving country. Included are immigrants from Commonwealth countries, displaced persons and Netherlands farm families, relatives of Canadian residents, and immigrants selected for occupational placement.

87. Edwards, E. P.

1960 "Children of Migratory Agricultural Workers in the Public Elementary Schools of the United States: Needs and Proposals in the Area of Curriculum," *Harvard Educational Review*, 30:12-52 (Winter).

Children of migratory agricultural workers in the U.S. The problems involved in educating migrant children and some of the attempts to meet these problems are outlined in some detail.

Migrant children show educational retardation because of, among other things, mobility, limited family income, and a feeling of rejection when they go to school. Among the problems which schools face in regard to migrant children are a lack of previous school records on the children, a lack of trained personnel for dealing with the migrant child, the burdens placed on the school with the influx of a large group of children for a few months of the year, and a lack of community responsiveness in helping with the migrant problem. The author suggests that the curriculum planned for migrant children must concern itself with three basic areas: fitting them for citizenship, helping them to partake in the culture of their nation and their time, and giving them what they need to make the fullest growth of which they as individuals are capable.

88. Eicher, Joanne Bubolz

1959 "Social Factors and Social Psychological Explanations of Non-Migration," unpublished doctoral dissertation, Michigan State University, 148 pp.

One hundred and sixty-eight (25 percent sample) of nonmigrant family heads, Ontonagon County, in the Upper Peninsula of Michigan. A study of the "relationship of two social factors, ethnic background and age, with explanations for non-migration." Three components were used to explain the decision-making process: satisfactions, aspirations, and social costs. Three general hypotheses were formulated for each variable, associating each of the two factors with the three components, giving a total of six general hypotheses.

"Statistical results support only one hypothesis, namely, older age is highly associated with aspirations obtainable within the community. . . . Seven out of 11 objective indices for community satisfaction supported association with older age. . . . The overwhelming majority of non-migrants of all age and ethnicity groups seem extremely satisfied with the community; for few seriously intend to leave."

89. Elkan, W.

1959 "Migrant Labor in Africa: An Economist's Approach, with a Discussion," *American Economic Review* (Papers and Proceedings), 49:188-202 (May).

African migrant laborers. The author examines the causes of the persistence of temporary or short-term labor migration in Africa.

"It is in most parts of Africa the common practice to seek only temporary employment in mines or towns or on plantations and sooner or later to return to homes on peasant farms in the countryside." Since hardly anywhere in Africa can a man obtain compensation for vacating his land and, on the other hand, cannot normally maintain his right to it unless he or his family are in actual occupation, he has no inducement to vacate it and he is therefore bound to regard employment as in some sense temporary.

90. Elkholy, Abdo A.

1960 "Religion and Assimilation in Two Muslin Communities in America," unpublished doctoral dissertation, Princeton University, 361 pp.

Two Arab-Muslin communities in the U.S.: one in Toledo, Ohio, and the other in Detroit, Michigan. "It is the thesis of this study that assimilation of an immigrant group is not necessarily hindered by adherence to an original religion differing from the religion prevailing in the adopted culture."

"The statistics showed the invalidity of assuming an antithesis between assimilation and original religiosity; Toledo community was found to be more assimilated than the Detroit community; yet it also proved to be more religious. . . . The different occupational patterns of Toledo and Detroit Muslims were found to be related to the difference in the two communities' assimilation and religiosity. . . . Besides delaying the process of assimilation, the residential concentration of the Detroit community has perpetuated the traditional concepts of family and social relations, as well as of religion and of the sectarian conflict between Sunnis and Shiahs. . . . The Toledo community, through cooperation between its two sects, has managed to build a common religious front to fortify its faith and preserve its religious identi-

ty. . . . [whereas] the sectarian dispute in Detroit, which is related to residential concentration and a low degree of assimilation, has prevented the promotion of religion in the community." Practical and theoretical implications of the findings are spelled out.

F

91. First, J. M.

1961 "Educationally Deprived," *Michigan Educational Journal*, 39:194-99 (October).

Migrant agricultural families in U.S. The problems resulting from migrancy are discussed, and the question of how to help the migrant children receive education is examined.

The seasonal farm labor force, totaling about a half million, represents the lowest economic and social plateau of American society. Because the migrant families seldom establish residency in a state, they live beyond the reach of most public welfare programs. Family illiteracy, poverty, mobility, and frustration are among the reasons why a great many migratory children are retarded in their schooling. Summer schools for migrant children have proved valuable, but financing such schools remains a major problem.

92. Fite, Gilbert C.

1959 "Flight from the Farm," *Nebraska History*, 40:159-76 (September).

A study of the farm people in Kansas and Nebraska in the late nineteenth century, utilizing data from U.S. census reports, with a view to understanding the reasons for their migration from farms in that period.

Author suggests the following reasons for the migration from farms in Kansas and Nebraska in the late nineteenth century: economic privation, debt, poverty, disappointment in the West, increased population, increased use of machinery, dislike of hard work by women, lack of convenience, low social prestige, and lack of intellectual stimulation and challenge.

93. Folger, John K.

1958 "Models in Migration," in *Selected Studies of Migration Since World War II*, Proceedings of the 34th Annual Conference of the Milbank Memorial Fund, New York, 1957, Part III, pp. 155-64.

A methodologically oriented paper, which discusses a new model and some of the limitations of existing models. Directions for developments in model building are suggested.

The mathematical relationships developed to date to explain or describe migration have demonstrated clearly that population movements are clearly patterned and can be described fairly well by introducing only one or two variables. Two best known models are: Zipf's P_1P_2/D hypothesis and Stouffer's hypothesis about opportunities and intervening opportunities. In spite of its limitations, the opportunities and intervening opportunities concept provides a useful approach to analysis of migration, and with a multivariate approach to the definition of opportunities, it provides a basis for considerable additional research. A study of social and psychological factors affecting migration based on interviews which obtained migration histories, reasons for moving, and general attitudes toward migration might be more useful in focusing other migration analyses, and illuminating some of their conceptual problems than any other type of study.

94. Ford, Thomas R.

1958 *Population Estimates for Kentucky Counties and Economic Areas, July 1, 1957*, Kentucky Agricultural Experiment Station Progress Report 66, 20 pp.

Population estimates for Kentucky counties and economic areas, July 1, 1957, using the migration-and-natural-increase method.

"The two most significant features of population change in Kentucky since 1950 have been the relatively slow rate of population growth for the state as a whole and the relatively rapid growth of larger urban areas while most rural sections of the state were losing population. . . . It is estimated that from 1950 to mid-1957 Kentucky lost nearly a third of a million residents in its exchange of migrants with other states, while additional losses were incurred through the induction of Kentuckians into the armed forces. The observed net loss through migration is not a new phenomenon for Kentucky, but rather continues a trend of the past half-century. . . . The relatively slow growth of Kentucky's total population indicates that most of the migrants are moving to other states."

95. Form, William H. and Julius Rivera

1958 "The Place of Returning Migrants in a Stratification System," *Rural Sociology*, 23:286-97. (September).

An examination of the place that returning Mexican migrants from the U.S. occupy in the stratification system of a border community, utilizing data gathered from 130 adult male workers in Sonoyta, Sonora, New Mexico.

Local residents perceived a three-strata system, making special distinctions within the lower economic category. The application of an index of status characteristics revealed certain ambiquities and inconsistencies in the stratification system which were not made evident by the use of subjective observation devices. "Returning migrants tended to be found in the lower middle ranges of the status, class, and power orders of the community."

96. Forman, Robert Edgar

1959 "The Ideology of Mobility: Some Attitudinal Aspects of Migration," unpublished doctoral dissertation, University of Minnesota, 285 pp.

A study of 1770 Minnesota high school students. "This study represents an attempt to consider mobility within the field of general sociology." Community Satisfaction Scale (CSS) and Mobility Justification Approval scores (MJA) were used.

"When considering conditions which might keep them in the community or make them move, respondents' answers appeared to be determined not by the conditions themselves, but by their mobility attitudes and community satisfaction."

97. Francis, H. T.

1962 "Travelers and Floaters: Educating Britain's Sub-Culture," *Times Educational Supplement*, 2457:1287 (June 22).

An interpretive statement, using the author's impressions as source materials. Emphasis of the statement is on problems of educating the children of migrant parents.

The children of the migrants come to school for about five or six months out of the year. The "parents did not wish to continue the travellers' life, but had no other alternative open to them. To plan for progress in education and in social services and to omit from the planning the fact of these forgotten thousands, is to ignore part of the facts of the problem of progress."

Freedman, Deborah. *See* 98.

98. Freedman, Ronald, and Deborah Freedman

1956 "Farm-Reared Elements in the Nonfarm Population," *Rural Sociology*, 21:50-61 (March).

The data for this study were gathered from an area sampling of 1,887 adults, 21 years of age or over, of a cross-section of the U.S. in order to answer the following questions: "(1) Are farm migrants concentrated in distinctive social and economic positions in the urban society? (2) Do farm-reared elements of our urban population have low rates of social participation?"

"The farm-reared are concentrated in low-status positions, as measured by education, income, occupation, or self-perception of class. . . . The relationship between social participation rates and farm background varies with the type of activity considered. The farm-reared are less active politically and have less confidence in political action. The farm-reared element is found to have a lower rate of activity in voluntary groups and higher rates of church attendance."

99. Freeman, Howard E., Ozzie G. Simmons, and Bernard J. Bergen

1960 "Residential Mobility Inclinations Among Families of Mental Patients," *Social Forces*, 38:320-24 (May).

Families of mental patients in Boston. Two-hundred and nine case of former mental patients. Interview data. Study emphases: (1) to see if residential mobility patterns are different for families of mental patients than for typical urban dwellers; (2) to see if families of mental patients are inclined to move for reasons associated with their illness. Scale of dissatisfaction of having a mental patient in the household.

The following tentative conclusions were drawn: (1) Most families of former mental patients desire to move for the same reasons as other families. (2) Mobility among families of former patients may, more often than not, also be adaptive. (3) Findings do not deny possible relationships between mental illness and residential mobility. Investigation of the relationship between residential mobility and mental illness first requires an accounting of the extent to which the mobility of such families represents adaptation to changes in their housing needs.

100. Freeman, Thomas W.

1959 "Rural Migration in Ireland," in *Rural Migration*, Papers presented at the 1st Congress of the European Society for Rural Sociology, Brussels-Louvain, September, 1958 (Bonn, privately published), pp. 64-68.

A descriptive essay.

"One notable effect of the reduction of the rural population by two-thirds since 1845 has been the enlargement of farms; but there are still thousands of very small farms, though their number is decreasing annually. . . . Only to a small extent has the recent industrial program of the Irish Republic provided work for rural migrants. . . . As long as employment is plentiful in Great Britain, emigration from rural Ireland is likely to remain heavy."

101. Fugitt, Glenn V.

1959 "Part-Time Farming and the Push-Pull Hypothesis," *American Journal of Sociology*, 64:375-79 (January).

Entire population of farmers in Wisconsin studied, using the 1950 censuses of agriculture and population. It is the object of this paper to test the push-pull hypothesis, using a number of ecological areas as the basic units.

The hypothesis that the proportion of farm operators engaged in part-time farming is directly related to off-farm opportunities and inversely related to opportunities in agriculture by counties for Wisconsin has been supported in the analysis of preceding data for all farmers considered together and for commercial farmers separately. For non-commercial farmers, on the other hand, the results do not explicitly agree with the hypothesis. Explanation for this seeming disagreement is suggested.

G

102. Galloway, Robert E.

1956 *Part-Time Farming in Eastern Kentucky (A Study of Economic Area 8)*, Kentucky Agricultural Experiment Station Bulletin 646, 28 pp.

Part-time farm families in Eastern Kentucky, based on the data collected from 333 rural families in Economic Area 8.

One or more members had migrated away from more than a third of the families. More males than females migrated and the migrants had a higher educational level than those who remained. They either left the state or remained within the home counties.

103. Geschwind, R. D., and V. W. Ruttan

1961 *Job Mobility and Migration in a Low Income Rural Community*, Indiana Agricultural Experiment Research Bulletin 730, 23 pp.

A study of male workers heading households between 31 and 65 years of age, in Brookston (White County) and Shoals (Martin County), Indiana, based on information gathered from 106 households. The study was intended to ascertain the factors influencing job mobility and migration in the low income rural community of Shoals in southern Indiana, using the high income rural community of Brookston in northern Indiana for comparison.

"A comparison of the job-mobile and the non-mobile individuals showed no difference in age, level of income and education. Mobile individuals did, however, tend to occupy a relatively low social position. Individuals who changed occupations had more thorough knowledge of available job opportunities than was characteristic of the non-mobile persons. . . . In both Brookston and Shoals, movement from farming to local non-farm employment resulted in a decline in social status. . . . In both Brookston and Shoals movement out of agriculture occurred primarily among farmers in the group with lowest gross sales of farm products. More of the former farmers in the Brookston community were tenants than owners. In the Shoals community there were as many former owners as tenants among former farmers."

104. Giffin, Roscoe

1962 "Appalachian Newcomers in Cincinnati," in *The Southern Appalachian Region: A Survey*, ed. Thomas R. Ford (Lexington, University of Kentucky Press), pp. 79-84.

Migrant families with at least one child in a grade below high school in Cincinnati. The research was based on data from 211 households (1141 persons). The study "was designed to determine by empirical means whether or not Southern Appalachian newcomers participate in the organizations of Cincinnati more or less frequently than do their neighbors of comparable social class."

People from the Southern Appalachian region did not differ significantly in their social participation from those coming from other regions; however, adults from the Southern Appalachians did participate much less often in voluntary organizations such as lodges, unions, neighborhood clubs, and community center activities. Generally people of lower social status, to which group most Southern Appalachian newcomers belong, were found to be less well-adjusted to urban life than those of higher social status. "The present host of unresolved problems of the city, particularly in those areas where newcomers of lower status cluster, actually multiply and complicate the all-too-numerous inadequacies for urban living of the Southern Appalachian newcomer."

105. Gillion, K. L.

1956 "The Sources of Indian Emigration to Fiji," *Population Studies*, 10:139-57 (November).

Report on a study of people of Indian origin in Fiji, based mainly on the Emigration Proceedings of the Governments of India, Bengal, and Madras.

"Most Indian emigrants to Fiji went as indentured labourers from 1879 to 1916. . . . Emigration under the indenture system was stimulated by labour recruiters, was highly commercialised and attended by many abuses in recruitment. . . . There was little family emigration. . . . Most emigrants were paupers when recruited. . . . Emigrants were a fair cross-section of Indian village life with a larger proportion of high caste people than might have been expected given the preference for agriculturists."

106. Godwin, Joseph Randall

1960 "Subregional Migration, 1935-40: An Analysis of the Structure of Migrant Characteristics Across Metropolitan and Non-Metropolitan Migration Streams," unpublished doctoral dissertation, University of Illinois, 160 pp.

A study of Illinois migrants around the following hypotheses: "(1) An analysis of the characteristics of migrants across metropolitan and nonmetropolitan subregional migration streams would reveal a structuring of migrant characteristics in terms of common factors, and (2) that these common factors are similarly patterned across all migration streams."

"Although the basic classification and tabulation of census data restricted a meaningful interpretation of factors, the findings suggest the major question of whether migration phenomena are a function of the age structure of population aggregates or whether the incidence of migration is a function simply of decisions of persons who do migrate. . . . The conceptual framework of metropolitan and nonmetropolitan migration streams provides a basic analytical model within which probability theory may be employed as a means of describing the expectancies of migration phenomena"

107. Goldsmith, Harold Frank

1962 "The Meaning of Migration: A Study of the Migration Expectations of High School Students," unpublished doctoral dissertation, Michigan State University, 322 pp.

High school students in Ontonagon County, Michigan, were studied to provide a "model for explaining the initial stage of voluntary migration."

"The desire to migrate can be accounted for chiefly by the relative attractiveness of social situations." Both community satisfaction and the degree to which expectations can be met outside primary community "were found to affect independently the students' desire to migrate." Evidence supported the conclusion that obligations in migrants' community of origin played a critical and perhaps the most important role in determining consideration of migration. To the extent that students' considering migration had facilities for migrating, it was predicted that they would expect to migrate." Some modifications necessary to improve the predictive efficiency and explanatory value of the model are suggested.

108. Goldstein, Sidney

1955 "Migration and Occupational Mobility in Norristown, Pennsylvania," American Sociological Review, 20:402-408 (August).

A 10 percent random sample of all male residents of Norristown, who were listed in the city directories from 1910 to 1950 were studied, using birth certificates, death certificates, and city directories of Norristown. The purpose of the study was to determine what relationship, if any, exists between occupational mobility and the migration patterns.

The study suggested that, the more Norristown was able to meet the changing needs for its labor force by attracting persons from outside, the less need there would be for occupaional mobility by those gainfully employed in the local economic structure.

109. Graham, F. P.

1958 "People Who Are Poor," American Federationist, 65:13-14 (June).

An interpretive essay discussing the plight of the agricultural migrants and small farmers.

As contrasted with the industrial workers, the agricultural workers "are still without long-overdue equal rights and privileges in organization, collective bargaining and participation in the determination of fair conditions of life and labor. . . . In a world of organized power, the farm laborers and the migratory workers need union organization and the support of the labor movement."

Gregory, C. L. See 250 and 251.

Grigg, Charles M. See 366.

110. Grimshaw, Allen D.

1958 "Relationships Between Agricultural and Economic Indices and Rural Migration," Rural Sociology, 23:397-400 (December).

Migrants from Wisconsin and Missouri, 1940-1950. The purpose of this research was to consider differences and similarities in the findings in two reports: A. D. Grimshaw's Internal Migration in Missouri, 1940 to 1950 and Margaret J. Hagood and Emmit F. Sharp's Rural-Urban Migration in Wisconsin, 1940-50.

Certain conclusions were tentatively drawn: "(1) Considerable caution should continue to be exercized in generalizing findings in one state regarding effects of agricultural and economic factors on net rural migration. (2) While there are consistent tendencies for relationships to appear between selected indices and net migration, these relationships are small and cannot be given as important a causal role as has been sometimes attributed to them. . . . (3) . . . mechanization as reflected in percent change in number of tractors and changes in Farm Operator Living Index are most influential among factors studied in determining patterns of net migration in rural areas."

111. Gulbrandsen, Odd

1959 "The Structural Transformation in Swedish Agriculture and Migration 1750-1970," in Rural Migration, Papers presented at the 1st Congress of the European Society for Rural Sociology, Brussels-Louvain, September, 1958 (Bonn, privately published), pp. 131-43.

Farmers in Sweden. Information based partly on an investigation by the Industrial Research Institute and partly on subsequent material obtained by the Royal Central Bureau of Statistics and the Agricultural Research Institute. Structural problems facing Swedish agriculture, and the questions of migration connected therewith are discussed.

"From 1750 to 1880 the number of farmers in Sweden rose from about 225,000 to roughly 385,000. This meant a splitting up of agriculture land in more holdings, forced by an excess of births in farm population, which could not be relieved by migration to other occupations or by emigration. The better income possibilities caused by the emigrations after 1850 and by the industrial revolution some decades later, made a growing number of people to leave the agricultural profession." Since 1935, migration from agriculture and auxiliary occupations has accelerated very heavily and it is estimated that since the 1950s the employees in agriculture have declined at a rate of 7.5 percent per year. "This migration has been pulled by the better incomes in other occupations and pushed by the substitutionary forces of mechanization, called forth by new machines and lower machine prices in relation to agricultural wages. . . . As a consequence about two thirds of the farmers have no permanent employees (neither family workers nor hired labour), the rest having as an average 1½ employees."

112. Gulliver, P. H.

1960 "Incentives in Labor Migration," *Human Organization*, 19:159-63 (Fall).

African workers in general, and those in Tanganyika and Rhodesia in particular. This article considers the hypothesis that "there are two general types of labor migration in which the motivations of African workers and the effects on them and their families and communities are significantly different. The two types may be termed 'low-wage, rural employment' and 'higher-wage, industrial employment' respectively."

"In the low-wage, rural employment there is relatively little change brought about in the lives and expectations of the people involved . . . ; there is, therefore, only a relatively slight incentive to continued and prolonged wage-labor and this is usually restricted to younger men. In higher-wage, industrial employment there is considerable and marked change in the lives and expectations of the men, their families and kin; there is the desire, felt with a strong sense of necessity and even of urgency, not merely to maintain new, higher standards but also to follow the idea that there are even higher standards within reach. There is change and the desire for further change with all dependent on continued wage-labor. . . . It is emphasized that . . . [t]he men leave home to obtain money, material wealth; they do not leave it if a reasonable standard is obtainable by labor and enterprise at home."

113. Gupta, Ajit Das

1959 "Types and Measures of Internal Migration," *International Population Conference Proceedings* (Vienna: International Union for the Scientific Study of Population), pp. 619-24.

A theoretical discussion of types and measures of internal migration.

Three types of migration are discussed: "(1) voluntary or (2) obligatory movement of the head or the independent individual; and (3) sequential movement of dependents. . . . A high degree of interdependency occurs between certain types, forms and motivations of migration. The various pushes and pulls, particularly social or political, could exercise opposite influence on different population groups. The reason of migration could thus be sometimes equivocal and resultant of diverse pulls. Various measures of migration are needed for different purposes and call for different approaches. Generation migration and cumulated lifetime migration since birth of the individual which go back longitudinally into the distant past, are of historical and sociological interest; but do not portray current conditions. Net migration over short intervals, specially if available as a series, is good enough for most practical purposes. But measures of flow migration are necessary to understand current processes fully. Surveys for measurement of migration can conveniently collect information on commuting (and transit): as also on motivations. While the time interval is divisible, the space dimension is not; and this is the problem of migration statistics. It is suggested that the area of the spatial segment is not so important as internal homogeneity, and that a plausible device is to split the country into homogeneous segments by characteristics like economic opportunities and living conditions, in a manner analogous to stratification in sampling." Illustration is given from Indian National Sample Survey, and the functional relationship between flow and net migration discussed theoretically.

114. Gupta, Savita

1961 "Net Migration in Michigan, 1950-60: An Analysis of Population Change in Relation to the Demographic, Socioeconomic, and Occupational Variables," unpublished doctoral dissertation, Michigan State University, 159 pp.

A study of Michigan migrants, 1950-1960, based on census data. "The first task of this thesis was to establish the validity of using net migration, the central variable, as a measure of population change in terms of redistribution of the population." The second one was "to study the nature of the changes which characterize the social organization when net migration takes place, and to study also the influence of population characteristics on net migration as a process."

"The results of the thesis indicate that net migration is as valid a measure for studying population change as other measures, such as total increase in population. The patterns of net migration are also closely related to recent past growth, and respond closely to the socio-economic changes in Michigan in terms of location of the industries, transport and communications, and raw materials. . . . [T]he findings show that when net migration increases, the sex ratio, population density, educational level, median family income, and percent employed in manufacture also increase; on the other hand, when net migration increases, the dependency ratio, the percent employed in agriculture, and the percent 65 years and over in age, decline."

H

115. Hadwiger, Don F.

1960-61 "Political Effects of Farm Population Changes," *Farm Policy Forum*, 13(2):20-28.

A study of changes in farm labor force with special emphasis on agriculture's strategy of rural bipartisanship.

In the legislatures, both state and national, farmers have had a disproportionate influence. The president, however, has responded more to urban influences. Recent changes in the labor force have meant a decline of rural influence in Congress.

116. Hagerstrand, Torsten

1959a "A Century of Migration To and From a Rural Parish in Sweden," in *Rural Migration*, Papers presented to the 1st Congress of the European Society for Rural Sociology, Brussels-Louvain, September, 1958 (Bonn, privately published), pp. 144-51.

A study of migrants to and from the parish of Asby in south Sweden, 1840 to 1945, using data from Swedish population registers to discover any existing patterns of migration.

"The net loss was constantly only a fraction of the total circulation. . . . Most people moved several times. The movements within Sweden followed a spatial pattern which remained amazingly constant during the century. Short-distance migration dominated. . . . The stability of the 'migration field' (especially its permanent deviations from the inverse distance rule) seems to indicate that the migrant tended to choose a destination according to information about vacancies obtained through a well established network of social contacts."

117. Hagerstrand, Torsten

1959b "Rural Demography," in *Rural Migration*, Papers presented to the 1st Congress of the European Society for Rural Sociology, Brussels-Louvain, September, 1958 (Bonn, privately published), pp. 37-41.

A study of the redistribution of population, causes and consequences, and the mechanism of interior migration. Swedish census and related information were used. The chief aim of the study was to discover the extent to which the redistribution of population and the mechanism of interior migration were not identical.

"Interior migration in the sense of changes of residences may . . . take place, and takes place extensively, without any immediate change of the population distribution at all. . . . One should not be misled to think that the movements behind the redistribution of population form a simple pattern. . . . We have reason to believe that the patterns are different in different economic, cultural and institutional environments. The net loss (or net gain) of an area is usually only a small part of the total circulation. . . . "

118. Haller, A. O.

1960 "The Occupational Achievement Process of Farm-Reared Youth in Urban Industrial Society," *Rural Sociology*, 25:321-33 (September).

A study based on information from 109 (70 percent of the total age group) 17-year old farm boys in school in Lenawee County, Michigan, spring, 1957. "The objective of the paper is to explore differences among farm boys who do and do not plan to farm . . . so as to formulate a tentative explanation for the low levels of nonfarm occupational aspiration of farm-reared

people." Among the various measures used were: Occupational Aspiration Scale; 16 P-F Test; MSU Work Belief Check-List; and Test of G-Culture Free.

"The data suggests three kinds of things which may result in planning not to farm: (1) The development of an unusually well-controlled, independent, and inquisitive personality, probably as a consequence of early training; (2) being the son of parents who are more oriented toward the nonfarm world than is usual; (3) perceiving farming as being an unattainable occupation." The early vocational self conception of farm boys tends to be that of a farmer. "[T]he occupational importance of higher education is more apparent to those who are least identified with farming. [I]t is hypothesized that the one who plans not to farm is, by virtue of his occupational self-conception, more highly motivated to seek out information which will enable him to be a success in the nonfarm occupational world."

119. Hamilton, C. Horace

1955 "How Many of Our Farm Families Are Leaving the Farm?" *Research and Farming*, 14:12-13 (Summer-Autumn).

A study of trends of migration from farms in North Carolina, using U.S. census data.

During 1940-1950 nearly 33 percent of the persons living on North Carolina farms moved away from the farms. The migration rate was the same for both sexes, and for whites and nonwhites. The highest migration rates for the males was in the 20-24 age group, and for the females in the 17-20 age group. In general migration to rural-nonfarm areas was twice as heavy as to cities. Negroes tended to leave North Carolina at a much higher rate than the whites, bypassing her cities. About 50 percent of the net migration from farms can be accounted for by population pressure. The rest of the rural-urban migration needs to be explained by the differential between economic opportunities in the city and the country.

120. Hamilton, C. Horace

1956 "Population Pressure and Other Factors Affecting Net Rural-Urban Migration," in *Demographic Analysis: Selected Readings*, ed. Joseph S. Spengler and Otis Dudley Duncan (Glencoe, Ill., The Free Press), pp. 419-24.

Describes and evaluates the application of several statistical techniques to a study of certain factors affecting net migration from farms.

Topics discussed are: "Methods of Estimating Net migration"; "Independent Variables"; "Statistical Procedure"; and "Results of the Analysis."

121. Hamilton, C. Horace

1958a "Educational Selectivity of Rural-Urban Migration: Preliminary Results of a North Carolina Study," in *Selected Studies of Migration Since World War II*, Proceedings of the 34th Annual Conference of the Milbank Memorial Fund, New York, pp. 110-22.

A study of North Carolina migrants, using residual survival rate data taken from U.S. census reports sample survey analysis. Six hundred and eleven households in Stokes and Montgomery counties were included in the study.

"The residual-survival rate analysis, applied to the rural-farm population 20-34 of age in 1940, tends to show that net migration takes its heaviest toll from the extremes of the educational distribution and its lightest toll from the middle. However, . . . as age increases, the selectivity of net migration shifts from the higher to the lower educational levels. . . . The field surveys show . . . rates of net migration *from* rural areas increase with education, and no tendency to select from the extremes is found, as was the case with the Census analysis. The difference in the results obtained by the two approaches tends to confirm the hypothesis that the pattern of educational selectivity by migration changes with age. . . ."

122. Hamilton, C. Horace

1958b "Whither Our Youth?" *Research and Farming*, 16:9 (Spring).

Persons in two all-rural North Carolina counties (Montgomery and Stokes), between the ages of 15 and 39 who had resided with their parents at some time since January 1, 1947. The data were derived from a sample survey of 638 cases. The question explored was, "Will your child stay on the farm?"

In the 20-24 years age group, education and migration, especially to cities, were related positively. "Migration from farms and from the state [is] less in older groups. . . . Race difference becomes progressively greater as education increases. . . . Losses are 5 to 10% greater for males than females in each color group having more than a fifth grade education." Nearly 50 percent left home permanently at some time during the ten-year interval. "There is a high relationship between the residence of parents and the destination of their children. Also, there is a strong association between distance and residential class of destination."

123. Hamilton, C. Horace

1959 "Educational Selectivity of Net Migration of the South," *Social Forces*, 38:33-42 (October).

Persons over 15 years of age in U.S., in southern region listed in *U.S. Census of Population, 1940-1950*. A study of educational selectivity of migration to and from the southern region of the U.S.

(1) Migration from South during 1940-1950 was selective of both the educationally inferior and superior elements of the parent population. However, the selective effect was not a marked one. The highest loss was in the no-education category. (2) "Net migration of adult nonwhite population from the South, 1940-50, was selective of the well-educated population only; whereas net migration of adult white population was largely selective of the poorly educated and only moderately selective of the well educated." (3) "Selective patterns of net migration from the South and from farms change with age: from selection at the extremes among young adults to selection of the poorly educated among middle aged and old aged adults." (4) "Net migration has substantially lowered the educational level of the urban and rural-nonfarm areas to which migrants have gone both in and out of the South."

124. Hamilton, C. Horace

1961 "Some Problems of Method in Internal Migration Research," *Population Index*, 27:297-307. (October).

A brief analysis of some of the problems of research method in migration studies.

The author concludes "that the present generation of experienced demographers, doing migration research, should continue to sharpen their tools, improve their research designs, and invent and develop new techniques of analysis."

125. Hamilton, C. Horace, and Herbert Aurbach

1958 *What's Happening to North Carolina Farms and Farmers*, North Carolina Agricultural Experiment Station Bulletin 407, 47 pp.

North Carolina farms and farmers studied, using data derived from 1954 Census of Agriculture. A general description of what is happening to North Carolina farms and farmers, including their heavy out-migration.

"Two factors are responsible for the heavy migration from farms: (1) Population pressure caused by higher birth rates in the country than in the city, and (2) relatively greater economic opportunity in the city than on farms. . . . Negroes migrate from farms at about the same rate as do the whites . . . but . . . when non-whites migrate from the farm they are much more likely than whites to leave the state."

Hart, John F. *See 196.*

126. Hathaway, D. E.

1960 "Migration from Agriculture: The Historical Record and Its Meaning," *American Economic Review: Papers and Proceedings*, 50:379-91, 413-18. (May).

A study of migrants from agriculture in U.S. using census materials, which "examines the impact of the recent out-migration from agriculture to see whether this prescription is enough, or whether some serious secondary symptoms should be treated at the same time."

Migration had left unsolved many pressing problems it had created. These include urban-rural income inequalities and strain on social structure of the communities.

Hawley, Amos H. *See 383.*

127. Heberle, R.

1955 "Types of Migration," *Southwestern Social Science Quarterly*, 36:65-70 (June).

A theoretical discussion of concepts which could form a basis for a general theory of human migration.

"Migration can be classified in many ways." The more advanced the economic structure of a society, the greater the importance of intrinsic and social, instead of extraneous and natural, factors in determining volume and direction of migration. It is important to keep semivoluntary migration (transfer of employees, wives and dependents of heads of households, etc.) in mind, especially when dealing with selective effects of migration. "A typology of migration should also take into consideration the qualitative differences in the social order of the areas between which migrants move. . . . As a rule, voluntary migrants move from areas of lower to areas of higher technological achievement. . . . Selectivity of migration is also a factor. Age at migration, education level, and the premigration class-position of migrants must be taken into account." Involuntary, voluntary, and semivoluntary migration are discussed.

128. Heberle, R.

1956 "Note on Riesman's *The Lonely Crowd,*" *American Journal of Sociology*, 62:34-36 (July).

A theoretically suggestive note which tries to relate three types of "directedness" to phases in the growth of population.

The statement criticizes Riesman's theory and suggests that "other directedness" be linked to migratory mobility rather than to "incipient population decline." It further suggests a hypothesis which reverses Riesman's postulates, i.e., "the possibility that changes in values and attitudes may influence the pattern of population growth."

129. Hill, L. D.

1962 "Characteristics of the Farmers Leaving Agriculture in an Iowa County," *Journal of Farm Economics*, 44:419-26 (May).

Migrants in a county in a general farming area in north central Iowa, with 82.5 percent of its total land area under cultivation and 60 percent of its 1,700 farms classified as in income Class III or above in the 1959 Census of Agriculture. The data pertain to 19 families who had left the farm to take urban employment. Factors influencing migration from farm to nonfarm occupations are studied.

"Many people in agriculture are looking for an alternative. They feel that the returns from agriculture are insufficient considering the effort, investment, and risk involved. . . . There appear to be fewer owner-operators leaving agriculture than tenant-operators. . . . The unemployment problem of the economy has been forced upon agriculture."

Hillery, George A., Jr. *See* 48.

Hirzel, Robert K. *See* 269.

130. Hitt, Homer L.

1956 "Population Movements in the Southern United States," *The Scientific Monthly*, 82:241-46. (May).

A study of the people of 12 states: Alabama, Arkansas, Florida, Georgia, Kentucky, Louisiana, Mississippi, North Carolina, Oklahoma, South Carolina, Tennessee, and Virginia. Most data derived from U.S. censuses of population. An attempt is made to add details regarding such aspects of the recent population movements as the sources and destinations of migrants, the approximate magnitude of the population transfer, and some conception of the population redistribution that has taken place.

"Data provide a composite picture of . . . the urbanization of the South. This process . . . has been generally similar to that which occurred earlier in the Northeast and Far West. Rural areas of the South have furnished migrants . . . and have been progressively depopulated while doing so. Urban centers and urban fringe areas have grown rapidly, and the people of the South are increasingly becoming concentrated in the larger cities and metropolitan areas. Moreover, interurban migrations are even more frequent than the more highly publicized rural-urban movements."

131. Hitt, Homer L.

1957 "Migration Between the South and Other Regions, 1949-1950," *Social Forces*, 36:9-16 (October).

Migrants from the South, 1949-1950, aged one year and over. Basic data from a Special Report of the 1950 Census of Population, "Population Mobility-States and State Economic Areas." "Attention was focused exclusively upon the exchange of population between the South and the other regions of the country during a limited period of time, 1949-50."

"These data indicate that the census South joined the West as a net importer of population from other sections of the nation between 1949 and 1950. Corresponding figures for the 11 states of the Southeast reveal that the region so defined also registered a net interregional migration gain. If valid, these data are significant because either they mark the end of a demographic era or they single out a unique year in the interregional migration experience of the South."

132. Hodgell, Murlin Ray

1960 "Low-Income Rural Families in an Urbanizing Society," unpublished doctoral dissertation, Cornell University, 446 pp.

A study of low-income rural families with emphasis on four segments: "the low-income subsistence farmer; the stranded farmer who has been forced off the farm in the consolidation process and who may be found at every economic level; the migratory worker; and the rural non-farm worker."

"The root-causes of the plight of such people are investigated and the interrelationships between these elements of rural society and between their problems and the larger problems of agricultural and urban development are discussed. . . . Special attention is given to such urban problems as the rapid growth of slums, housing for minority groups, functional illiteracy, suburban sprawl, employment and industrialization, all of which have been greatly complicated by the farm-to-city migration. Rural industrialization for small cities and rural communities is suggested as one key to solving many of the seemingly diverse problems which plague both rural and urban areas. . . . "The study deals extensively with techniques of rural redevelopment and industrialization.

133. Hohn, Elfriede

1955 "Sociometric Studies on the Adjustment Process of Displaced Persons," *International Social Science Bulletin*, 7(1):22-29.

Refugee children in southwestern Germany were studied in order to understand the influence of social situation on personality. Sociograms were repeated at intervals of several months, reflecting changes in the group ranking. Scholarly performance measured, handwriting and drawings evaluated, and projective techniques (TAT., Tree Test, Rohrschach test or Zulliger's Z-test, story completion test) were applied.

"The results may be summarized as follows: There are certain social situations which are so highly important for the individual that the general effects are the same for everybody, notwithstanding characteristic personality traits. The adjustment process the refugee newcomer had to undergo when he entered the established group of resident children provided a typical illustration of this statement. Social situations of this kind modify the personality in a very clear way. The final outcome of the adjustment process, however, is determined by individual personality traits."

134. Hotz, Marie Brase

1955 "A Study of Cohort Migration in the U.S.: 1870-1950," unpublished doctoral dissertation, Washington University, 127 pp.

This thesis is a study of migration of cohorts of the native white population in the U.S. between 1870 and 1950. The following hypotheses were investigated: (1) the present distribution of the aged population in the U.S. differs from the distribution of the younger population. (2) Younger persons in the nation's population migrate more than the older members of the population. (3) The number of migrations undertaken by a given cohort are in part dependent upon the time at which they were born. The more recently born are more likely to migrate. (4) Age alone cannot account for migration currents in the U.S.

It was concluded that the cohorts method provided an adequate measure for migration. Hypotheses (1), (2) and (4) were supported by the data, but hypothesis (3) was not validated by the available evidence.

135. Howard, H.

1958 "Toll Road Tommy," *Michigan Education Journal*, 35:224-25 (February).

A migrant child's story of his school experiences.
A migrant child, discouraged and depressed about his schooling because he had attended five schools in one year, adjusted well in the sixth school because of the attention he received from his teacher. When moving time came again, he was excited rather than depressed because his teacher had shown him that moving could be an adventure.

136. Howard, R. B.

1956 "Better Health for Colorado's Migrant Children," *Children*, 3:43-48 (March).

Agricultural migrant workers in Colorado studied in two projects: one at Fort Lupton Camp in Weld County and the other at Palisade Camp in Mesa County. A discussion of how teamwork between the State and local communities is striving for better health for Colorado's migrant children.

To improve health conditions for migrants a program for improving the quality and availability of health services to mothers and children of migrant agricultural workers who came into Colorado was set up in two counties in Colorado. It was concluded that a successful "local program must be so oriented that it can eventually become part of the health services available to all residents of the community throughout the year."

137. Huie, J. M.

1962 "Migration of Rural Residents," *Alabama Agricultural Experiment Station Highlights of Agricultural Research*, 9:14 (Summer).

Migrants in four counties of Alabama (Clark, Monroe, Montgomery, Tallapoosa) in 1961. A discussion of the degree of out-migration and the characteristics of out-migrants.

Although many factors contributed to the rural population loss in the counties, by far the most important was out-migration. The migrants were almost equally divided between the sexes, and were predominantly unmarried and more educated than the nonmigrants. "Out-migration of the better trained people represents one of the basic problems that low-income counties and states must overcome to increase income levels of the area."

138. Hutchinson, Bertram

1957 "Some Evidence Related to Matrimonial Selection and Immigrant Assimilation in Brazil," *Population Studies*, 11:149-56 (November).

Men and women residents of the city São Paulo who at the time of interview were aged 20 years or more. Study based on a sample of 2500. The study emphases were matrimonial selection, immigrant selection, and social mobility in Brazil.

"Intermarriage occurs most frequently between Brazilian and those of Mediterranean origin, least so with Japanese. It is concluded that common cultural characteristics facilitate intermarriage. . . . Matrimonial selection and linquistic assimilation appear to be equally useful measures of immigrant absorption. . . . The rate of intermarriage between foreign-born and persons of *any* nationality other than their own is roughly constant, except in the case of the Japanese among whom exogamy is infrequent. . . . [I]ntermarriage tends to occur among immigrants who are rising in the social scale. This conclusion is consistent with recent sociological studies in São Paulo which show that intermarriage with a Brazilian may be a symbol of rejection of the primary immigrant group by the economically successful."

139. Hutchinson, Bertram

1958 "Structural and Exchange Mobility in the Assimilation of Immigrants to Brazil," *Population Studies*, 12:111-20 (November).

A study of 1056 males who were 20 years or more and a permanent resident in the city of São Paulo in August, 1956. The analysis sought "to show how far an immigrant population, as it becomes assimilated, ceases to differ from the host population in the rate of vertical social mobility it displays."

"The proportion rising in social status greatly exceeds those who fall—a phenomenon made possible by changes in the socio-economic structure of the city. A distinction must thus be made between exchange mobility and structural mobility, and a possible means of calculating the latter is suggested. . . . [A]nalysis shows the immigrants and their children profited more than pure Brazilians by the opportunities offered by structural change. . . . [T]he process of immigrant assimilation is marked by an initially high rate of social mobility which decreases in subsequent generations as their dispersion through the status scale gradually approximates the dispersion of the native population."

140. Hutchinson, Bertram

1961 "Fertility, Social Mobility and Urban Migration in Brazil," *Population Studies*, 14:182-89(March).

A study of 5250 men and women in eight cities in southern Brazil (Rio de Janeiro, São Paulo, Belo Horizonte, Curitiba, Londrina, Americana, Volta Redonda, and Juiz de fora) in 1959-1960. The study focus was to understand the process and social consequences of urban growth in southern Brazil.

"The results generally corroborate those of J. Berent for England and Wales—that is, that fertility is inversely related to class status, and that for a given class, the lower the class of origin, the higher the fertility. There was no confirmation, however, of J. Goldbert's findings in Detroit that the inverse relationship between class and fertility is due to the presence in urban populations of the rural-born, and suggestions are put forward which may explain this result in Brazil."

Huyck, Earl I. *See* 167.

I

141. Ianni, Francis A. J.

1957 "Residential and Occupational Mobility as Indices of the Acculturation of an Ethnic Group," *Social Forces*, 36:65-72 (October).

The Italian-American colony in Norristown, Pennsylvania, from 1900 to 1950. City directories, informants, and file of marriage license applications provided the sources for the data. The hypothesis tested was that there existed a positive relationship between acculturation and social mobility.

There was a general trend of increasing vertical mobility and the diffusion of the ethnics throughout the occupational hierarchy as acculturation proceeded in the 50-year period. The movement of immigrants into the higher status occupations was in those areas of business where lack of formal training was not a hardship and where ethnicity may be an advantage. Residential mobility out of the colony existed, but was slow.

142. Icken, Helen Margaret

1962 "From Shanty Town to Public Housing: A Comparison of Family Structure in Two Urban Neighborhoods in Puerto Rico," unpublished doctoral dissertation, Columbia University, 321 pp.

Two urban neighborhoods in Puerto Rico were studied, using a sample of 474 individuals in 200 households. The study "attempts to analyze the process of adaptation of rural migrants to the new socio-economic conditions of the urban milieu. It concentrates on a comparison of basic patterns of family and community life in two urban neighborhoods, one—a 'shanty town,' a product of crescive growth, the other—a public housing project, a result of planned development."

"It was found that families in the shanty town and in public housing conform closely to what has been termed a 'matrifocal' form of family structure. That is, strong ties between a woman, her children and her female relatives contrast with the marginal position of the male in the household and in the kin group. . . . Public housing, while it aims at strengthening the conjugal tie in lower-class households, seems to weaken further the man's status in the family and in the neighborhood, and hence reinforces the trend toward matrifocality already inherent in the family structure of the shanty town. . . . Urbanization, insofar as it fosters the growth of a homogeneous landless, wage-earning, storebuying, corporately employed proletarian class, sets the stage for the development of the matrifocal family, not only in Puerto Rico but in other complex societies." Shanty town has not felt the full effects of urbanization. The primary orientation of these families "is *inward* to the local community. Shanty town families are bound together in a highly connected network which shields them from the impersonal outside world and makes it possible for them to preserve the characteristics of a folk society within the non-folk society of the city. For the majority of project residents, on the other hand, the local community has little meaning in their lives. They are oriented *outward* to a more dispersed association of friends and relatives, spread over the entire metropolitan area. The strong attachment to the local community has begun to be replaced by a class reference group, the interests of which are often seen to conflict with those of other groups in the society."

143. Iga, Mamoru

1957 "The Japanese Social Structure and the Source of Mental Strains of Japanese Immigrants in in the U.S.," *Social Forces*, 35:271-78 (March).

Japanese immigrants to U.S. in Davis County, Utah. A study of possible sources of mental strains and conflicts of Japanese immigrants which develop from the character of the Japanese social structure.

The "first generation" Japanese or Japanese immigrants to the United States maintain quite strongly the traditional Japanese values as evident in the fact that in many cases they engage in farming (directly correlated with conservatism), acquire little formal education (limiting cultural contact), retain non-Christian practices (retarding assimilation), migrate without family or relatives (reducing social contacts). Thus it may be concluded that the Japanese immigrants retain Japanese culture to a considerable extent. Consequently they undergo the mental strains due to conditions inherent in the structure of the Japanese society, not to mention those resulting from new environments, cultural contact, and difficult relations with their American-educated children.

144. Ikle, Fred C.

1955 "Comment on Theodore R. Anderson's 'Inter-metropolitan Migration: A Comparison of The Hypotheses of Zipf And Stouffer' (and Reply to Ikle by Theodore R. Anderson)," *American Sociological Review*, 20:713-14 (December).

Ikle criticizes Anderson's research design; Anderson thinks the criticism theoretically sound.

Ikle's major points are: (a) that it is unsatisfactory to select arbitrarily and to test parameter points when the parameter space is quantitative, a better procedure being to select a parameter value which maximizes or minimizes something (presumably the accuracy of reproduction or the errors of reproduction); and (b) that the method he suggests is a satisfactory method of making such maximizing estimations. Anderson agrees with the first point, but rejects the method Ikle suggests because it gives unequal weights to small and large streams.

145. Ipsen, Gunther

1959 "Rural Depopulation," in *Rural Migration*, Papers presented to the 1st Congress of The European Society for Rural Sociology, Brussels-Louvain, September, 1958 (Bonn, privately published), pp. 46-47.

An inquiry into the factors responsible for large scale migration of rural workers to towns and some of the possible consequences of this movement.

"Since the 1880's, mass migration from the country to towns has been observed in Germany, and deplored. . . . [T]he reasons for migration were not to be sought in the prevailing rural conditions, but in the process of industrial agglomeration, this being a result of the choice of sites for factories and the technical concentration of industrial work. . . . [T]he loss of agricultural manpower, . . . if continued for a long time, . . . must lead to a depletion of all working reserves in the countryside. . . . Larger farms . . . may . . . have to employ families of agricultural workers."

146. Isaac, Julius

1959a "Cultural and Economic Problems of Jewish Migration in the Post-War Period," *Jewish Journal of Sociology*, 1:234-41 (December).

A study of the Jewish migrants after World War II. It suggests reasons why resettling of Jewish migrants following the Second World War became a less difficult task than it might have been under conditions different from existing ones.

The decimation of the Jewry in Central and Eastern Europe and the restrictions on migration of the Jews imposed by the countries under Soviet rule considerably reduced the Jewish migration potential at a time when emigration became a dire necessity for many. Thus the ingathering of exiles into Israel reduced the total number of Jews to be resettled in non-Jewish countries and provided a home for those who would not have been eligible for admission to any other country. The immigration into Israel involved, besides the Jews in Europe, communities in Asia and Africa, which had

never participated in the great migratory movements beginning in the 1880s and which had ethnic and cultural characteristics significantly different from those of European Jewry.

147. Isaac, Julius

1959b "Israel—A New Melting Pot?" in *The Cultural Integration of Immigrants*, ed. W. D. Borrie and others (Paris: UNESCO), pp. 234-66.

A study of immigrants into Israel, with emphasis on the extent of their economic absorption. The data used in the study are largely drawn from the *Government Year Book*.

"Estimates [on] the number of immigrants admitted since May, 1948 which the State of Israel has successfully absorbed, are therefore meaningless, unless the degree of integration to which the estimate refers can be clearly defined. Not much enlightenment can be expected from the construction of complex composite indices."

148. Isbell, Eleanor Collins

1956 "Internal Migration in Sweden and Intervening Opportunities", in *Demographic Analysis: Selected Readings*, ed. Joseph J. Spengler and Otis Dudley Duncan (Glencoe, Ill., The Free Press), pp. 406-18.

An attempt to test Stouffer's theory of intervening opportunities as a generalized expression of the relationship between migration and distance.

The results of this study emphasized the need for testing Stouffer's theory with more homogeneous data than were available, if a conclusive demonstration was to be had. Increasing the similarity of opportunities and of the group of migrants under consideration repeatedly strengthened the evidence supporting the theory, but that evidence was still inconclusive. It was suggested that more convincing tests of theory would depend upon refinement of definitions of opportunities.

149. Israel, Joachim

1955 "Personality Change in a Socially Disturbed Rural Community," *International Social Science Bulletin*, 7(1):15-22.

A study of 200 inhabitants of Forestville, a small rural community in northern Sweden, aimed at testing the hypothesis that there developed a discrepancy between the roles and values of the people and the social conditions prevailing in Forestville when the population declined by about 30 percent, mostly because of migration, causing schools and stores to close, most existing organizations to dissolve, and the population to split up into belligerent cliques preventing all cooperative action.

Assuming "that values are central concepts in the definition of personality, we can say that in spite of the important changes in the social structure of the community, the value-structure of the personalities of the Forestvillers seemed to have remained little changed. . . . We would also point to another factor: the old roles of the Forestvillers were clearly defined, i.e. an eventual discrepancy between the prescribed roles and the subjective roles would be small because the unambiguous prescribed roles would restrict perceptual distortion. In a state of transition, new prescribed roles are assumed to be vague and ambiguous, in part because the norm-senders themselves are exposed to new conditions, and further because it may not always be evident who is acting as a norm-sender. That may easily lead to a discrepancy between prescribed and subjective roles. Such a discrepancy may not only create insecurity but . . . under certain conditions it may be punitive, especially if the gap between prescribed and subjective roles becomes too wide. Therefore, not only clinging to old inappropriate roles, but also behaving in accordance with the requirements of new roles, not adequately known, may result in a state of insecurity. In addition the process of acquiring new roles seems to be influenced by the size of the discrepancy between old and new roles. The greater this discrepancy the more will new roles be perceived as threatening, and therefore the tendency to stick to old values may increase."

J

150. Jaffe, A. J.

1962 "Notes on the Population Theory of Eugene M. Kulischer," *Milbank Memorial Fund Quarterly*, 40:187-206 (April).

An interpretation of the writings of Eugene Kulischer in the area of population theory.

In Kulischer's opinion "a theory which would account for changes in the size of the population within a specified geographic area, and for changes in the characteristics of the population (whatever factors might be subsumed under the term 'characteristics'), would be but part of a larger theory of social change." According to him the following items are all intimately interrelated: population, technology, the economic structure, natural resources, the political structure, political developments (including war), and man's psychology and personality. Eight of Kulischer's major propositions that interrelate these factors are listed.

151. Jehlik, Paul J.

1955 "Patterns of Net Migration and Changes in Crude Birth Rates in the North Central States, 1940-50," *Rural Sociology*, 20:282-88 (September-December).

A study of migrants of 13 north central states, 1940-1950, using 173 state economic areas. Basic sources of data were the U.S. census reports of population for 1940 and 1950, and publications from agricultural experiment stations in the 13 states. "The focus of this paper is on an analysis of the significant patterns of net migration and of changes in crude birth rates and of their relationship in 13 north central states during the decade 1940-1950."

"Analysis of the data clearly shows the concentration of population through net in-migration in the rural parts of metropolitan areas, and especially in the older and larger metropolitan areas. The 64 state economic areas of net in-migration had gains of 19, 36, and 14 percent in total, rural, and urban population respectively. The 109 areas of net out-migration maintained a stationary total population, lost five percent in rural population and gained 10 percent in urban population."

152. Jehlik, Paul J., and Ray E. Wakeley

1955 *Population Change and Net Migration in the North Central States, 1940-1950*, Iowa Agricultural Experiment Station Research Bulletin 430, 351 pp.

A study of the 13 north central states, using data from censuses and from unpublished data supplied by the National Office of Vital Statistics. The study was focused on the population changes and their components for the period 1940-1950.

Although the North Central States have had a history of continuous population growth, net out-migration lowered the natural increase during 1940-1950 decade. The urban population increased 13 percent, whereas rural population increased only 7 percent during the period. The North Central Region's population will continue to grow, but its proportionate share of the national population will decline in the future.

153. Johnson, Elmer H.

1955 "Methodological Note on Measuring Selection in Differential Migration," *Social Forces*, 33: 289 (March).

Male migrants aged 25-34 during 1935-1940 period were studied, using data from census reports. Two methods of measuring differences between several populations in the force of selection in differential migration are examined.

"If the relationship between the specific net migration rates and a given demographic characteristic can be described as linear, the force of selection for the total range of this characteristic can be expressed by a single statistic. . . . Inspection of the education-specific rates for the four regions led to the conclusion that linearity may be assumed if only the five highest educational groups (7 or more years of schooling) are considered."

154. Jones, F. E.

1956 "Sociological Perspective on Immigrant Adjustment," *Social Forces*, 35:39-47 (October).

A theoretical discussion. The question is raised whether or not immigrant adjustment could be a legitimate sociological problem.

The point is raised that migrants need to be studied with respect to their interaction patterns. Suggestions made for the study of migrants included the following: (1) to analyze what happens to immigrants or between immigrants and natives in terms of the broader concept of socialization rather than adjustment; (2) to subject the problem of socialization to functional analysis. These suggestions lead at least to two approaches to the problem: (1) "To study what occurs between socializer and socializee as interaction structured in a system of roles. This socialization role system can then be regarded as a social system and the interaction analyzed in terms of the functional requirements of the system. (2) To study the significance of new members to a social system with emphasis on the relation of the system's functional requirements to its methods of dealing with new members."

155. Jordan, Terry G.

1962 "Aspects of German Colonization in Southern Brazil," *The Southwestern Social Science Quarterly*, 42:346-53 (March) pp. 346-53.

A study of one million inhabitants of German descent living in three southernmost Brazilian states. "This paper attempts (1) to explain why Germans migrated to Brazil, (2) to review the problems involved in adapting to the new physical and cultural environment and (3) to describe the procedure of woodland settlement employed by the colonists."

"This brief study shows that (1) it was German colonists who first opened the forests of southern Brazil to agricultural settlement; (2) this was accomplished in a climate which is decidedly warmer than that of northern Europe; and (3) once the early isolation of the settlements was overcome, the German way of life was influenced by and in turn had an influence upon the Luso-Brazilean culture. The process of assimilation, when completed will have produced a way of life and a landscape which will be neither German nor Portuguese, but distinctively southern Brazil."

156. Jutikkala, Eino

1959 "Geographical Distribution of Emigration in Finland," in *International Population Conference Proceedings* (Vienna, International Union for the Scientific Study of Population), pp. 640-47.

Emigrants from Finland were studied utilizing *Finland's Official Statistics* and emigration statistics.

"Overseas emigration from Finland grew into a mass movement in the 1880's. Disregarding the new emigration movement of the last few years, it ended around the year 1930. It was so concentrated in a limited area, Southern Ostrobothnia, that this province which was inhabited in 1890 by only a good eighth of Finland's total population sent to America nearly a half of the emigrants. The 'push' theory can be at the most no more than a partial explanation for the very different emigration rate in Southern Ostrobothnia compared with the other provinces of Finland. There were many economic, social, political and cultural special features in the district which had a bearing on the lively emigration."

157. Jyrkila, Faina

1959 "Effects of Migration on the Adjustment of Finnish Rural Youth," in *Rural Migration*, Papers presented to the 1st Congress of the European Society for Rural Sociology, Brussels-Louvain, September, 1958 (Bonn, privately published), pp. 173-76.

Finnish young people were studied, and data was obtained from 1,578 young people, aged 10-29. The paper is concerned with the interrelation of migration and social adjustment among Finnish youth. Hypothesis: "Migrants in cities with city backgrounds are better adjusted than migrants in cities with rural backgrounds."

"The data shows that rural youth migrants in cities participate less in formal organizations . . . than city migrants and natives. When small and large cities are studied separately . . . the social participation decreases among rural migrants only in large cities. In smaller cities the rural migrant's membership in formal organizations even increases compared to city natives. Also visiting shows higher frequency among rural migrants in small cities compared to large cities. And the general social apathy . . . is greatest among rural migrants in large cities. Migration between two rural environments does not cause change in membership of formal organizations, neither in visiting nor in social apathy. Our data shows that when the two environments are markedly dissimilar difficulties in adjustment might appear."

K

158. Kalbach, Warren Edwin

1960 "Residential Mobility and Its Implications for Family and School Adjustment in an Urban Community," unpublished doctoral dissertation, University of Washington, 233 pp.

A 10 percent sample of senior high school students, Seattle, Washington, was studied. "The central problem of this thesis is the . . . differential residential mobility of a school population and its relationship to school and family adjustment." Longitudinal design.

"The strongest evidence of the disorganizing effects of mobility is found in moderate negative relationship between frequency of movement and (1) school participation for the white-collar migrants and the blue-collar intra-city movers, and (2) satisfaction with school for the lower status families within each of the white and blue-collar groups. Where intra-city movement appears to be a reflection of an increase in social status, as it does in the case of the white-collar intra-city movers, frequency of movement is positively but moderately related to (1) favorable attitudes toward education, (2) school participation, (3) number of strong friendships. . . . The analysis suggests the desirability of controlling for recency of mobility in studies of relationships between mobility and attitudes and behavior."

159. Kallay, F. P.

1955 "Repopulation of Sardinia," unpublished doctoral dissertation, University of Michigan, 127 pp.

"The purpose of this study is to analyze the major causes of underpopulation in Sardinia and to indicate ways by which the present . . . economic conditions can be improved. . . ." It is a "detailed analysis of physical, agronomical and cultural factors governing the use of Sardinia's land."

The detailed analysis reveals that reclamation of pasture land for the production of grains and citrus fruits, and intensified emphasis on mineral extraction could very well support twice the present population at a higher standard of living.

160. Kanel, Don

1954-55 "Nebraska Births Exceed Deaths: Migration Cuts Population Gain," *Nebraska Agricultural Experiment Station Quarterly*, 3:6-8 (Winter).

A study of Nebraska's population during the past 35 years, based on census and related information.

Nebraska's farm population has been altered by heavy out-migration in four categories: (1) young people taking nonfarm employment; (2) older people retiring from their farms; (3) the children of the migrating families; and (4) established farm operators changing to other employment.

161. Kant, Edgar

1962 "Classification and Problems of Migrations," in *Readings in Cultural Geography*, ed. Philip L. Wagner and Marvin W. Mikesell (Chicago, University of Chicago Press), pp. 342-54.

A theoretical essay, partly integrating statements on migration typology by such men as Arbos, Heberle, and T. Lynn Smith. It opens up problems and prospects in migration research for cultural geographers, particularly for those with interest in cartographic analysis.

Discusses briefly various theories of human migration from prehistoric times to the present. Arbos' dichotomous division of pastoral types, and Lynn Smith's classification of international and internal movements are especially mentioned. Heberle's analysis based on "ideal" types and Torsten Hagerstrand's classification using country, city, and "urbanlike agglomerations" are suggested as further alternative typologies available to the analyst. The author has proposed his own typology based on a dichotomy of "intralocal (intraregional) migration" and "interlocal (interregional) migration."

162. Kasahara, Yoshiko

1958 "The Influx and Exodus of Migrants Among the 47 Prefectures in Japan, 1920-1935," unpublished doctoral dissertation, University of Michigan, 185 pp.

Migrants in 47 prefectures in Japan were studied, using census information. The aim was to reconstruct the historic trends in migration over the fifteen years from 1920 to 1935.

Results indicate that "the patterns of population change due to migration varied widely by age, by sex, and by locality as well as over time." The large-scale population movement toward urban centers accelerated its pace as Japan's industrial economy matured. More men tended to migrate than women. The most mobile population over years studied was at ages 10-24, with maximum migration among 15-19 age group. Occupational migration among peasant boys and girls was impressive, but for the group aged 25 and older net migration decreased sharply. "Variations observed in the volume and direction of migration by age and sex as well as over space and time, when taken as a whole, support the proposition that migration is in general a reflection of the 'push' relationships between the sending and the receiving areas."

163. Kaufman, Harold F., and George L. Wilber

1959 "Social Changes and Their Implications for Southern Agriculture," *Sociology and Rural Life Series 11* (State College, Mississippi, Agricultural Experiment Station) 19 pp.

A descriptive study of Southern agriculture in the U.S. The changing pattern of farming and the char-

acteristics and behavior of farmers, the rapidly changing rural community, and the great influence of the growing urban society on rural life are examined.

"A study in Mississippi of migration for the year immediately preceding the taking of the 1950 census showed that college graduates, persons of higher income, and professional and white collar workers were more likely to migrate and move longer distances than others. . . . Perhaps no social changes occurring in the South and the nation as a whole are more significant than those described by the term urbanization. Urban growth has resulted not only in massing of populations but also in the concentration of power and authority."

164. Kempinski, T.

1961 "Rural Migration," *Rural Sociology*, 26:70-73 (March).

This is the substance of a report made by the author to the European Society for Rural Sociologists, September, 1958, Louvain, Belgium. Economic causes, political reasons, problems, social and psychological effects, advantages, and regulation of migration are discussed.

Rural exodus is caused mainly by the fall in farm labor requirements ("push") and by the attractions of urban life ("pull"). Where good town-jobs are scarce, rural people emigrate abroad. Problems of rural refugees from former Eastern German territories and from Eastern Germany are mentioned. There are social and psychological difficulties both in farm-to-town and farm-to-farm migration, but there are also economic advantages for the countryside and for the nation. Various proposals for state regulation and aid for rural migration and for encouraging rural people to remain in the countryside are summarized. The trend toward commuting creates problems of urban over-spill which interests both rural sociologists and town-planners.

165. Ketch, Clarence Willard

1961 "A Situational Analysis of the Effects of Drouth as a Disaster on the Mobility of a Selected Rural-Farm Population," unpublished doctoral dissertation, Louisiana State University, 295 pp.

All residents of each of three selected census precincts in Mills County, Texas, and all migrants who were within a 60-mile radius of the study area and who had migrated there between 1950 and 1958 were studied. Data were collected from 879 persons, and supplementary data from U.S. census reports were used. The effort was to understand the role of drouth in the lives of farm operators and their household members and to determine the nature and extent of changes made to cope with drouth.

"Drouth is not associated with migration to the extent commonly assumed. However, dry-land farmers move more frequently in times of drouth than do ranchers. Persons moving because of drouth do not find migration a satisfactory adjustment." The same general characteristics of age, sex, and education, are found as in migrants generally. Reactions to drouth are manifested in changes in farming practices, off-farm work, use made of farm agencies, use of programs such as Soil Bank Programs and the Federal Drouth Relief Program. "The over-all conclusion of the study is that empirical research is needed to establish whether or not drouth represents a unique and crisis experience to the residents of a particular area."

166. Kirk, Dudley

1958 "Major Migrations Since World War II," in *Selected Studies of Migration Since World War II*, Proceedings of the 34th Annual Conference of the Milbank Memorial Fund, New York, 1957, Part III, pp. 11-28.

Major migratory movements of international migrants since 1946 Conference of the Milbank Memorial Fund on postwar problems of migration are discussed.

"The first postwar decade has witnessed the successful liquidation of the huge legacy of displaced persons and refugees directly caused by World War II. In Europe political and military influences were dominant but the lasting movements were also usually in the direction of economic pressures. . . . Overseas migration from Europe has been resumed. . . . Almost all European emigration went to overseas areas already occupied by Europeans, and within these to the cities rather than the country side. . . . Overseas migration within Asia . . . has come to a standstill owing to restrictions on migration imposed by the Asian countries of immigration, most of which have gained independence since the war. Political and ethnic frontiers are replacing geography as the chief barriers to international migration. . . . It is doubtful if there is any country in the world where there has not been some rural-urban migration and growth of urbanization since World War II. . . . The most important migrations today are the internal and largely unrecorded migrations from rural to urban areas and within metropolitan areas."

167. Kirk, Dudley, and Earl Huyck

1956 "Overseas Migration from Europe Since World War II," in *Demographic Analysis: Selected Readings,* ed. Joseph J. Spengler and Otis Dudley Duncan (Glencoe, Ill., The Free Press), pp. 297-306.

This paper discusses various aspects of postwar overseas voluntary "free" migrations from Europe since World War II.

The topics discussed are: (1) how large it was, (2) where did it come from, (3) where did it go, (4) how did it go, (5) who went, (6) significance of postwar immigration, and (7) future prospects. Comparisons of the postwar movements with the great overseas migrations of the past are made.

168. Kiser, Clyde V.

1956 "Cultural Pluralism," in *Demographic Analysis: Selected Readings,* ed. Joseph J. Spengler and Otis Dudley Duncan (Glencoe, Ill., The Free Press), pp. 307-20.

The theme of the essay is the manner in which various historical antecedents have combined to produce the present population of the United States.

The following topics are discussed: "Colonial Origins of Ethnic Diversity," "Composition of Our Population in 1790," "Subsequent Increases in Diversity," "Mother Tongue" (definitions and interpretations, intermarriage among foreign-white stock, "Some National Origin" marriages), and "The Melting Pot Versus Cultural Pluralism" (assimilation a slow process).

169. Kleiner, Robert J., and Seymour Parker

1959 "Migration and Mental Illness: A New Look," *American Sociological Review,* 24:687-90 (October).

An analysis of 2013 first-admission Negro mental patients to Pennsylvania state psychiatric hospitals. The study "reexamines question of first admission rates to mental hospitals of interstate migrant and nonmigrant Negroes in Pennsylvania."

"The data clearly indicate that the southern Negro migrant population is under-represented and that both the northern migrants and natives are over-represented in the statistics on first admissions. . . . [The] data tend to support those investigations that cast doubt on the psychopathogenic qualities of the interstate migration experience *itself* as an important factor in mental disorders."

170. Knowlton, Clark S.

1955 "Spatial and Social Mobility of the Syrians and Lebanese in the City of São Paulo, Brazil," unpublished doctoral dissertation, Vanderbilt University, 350 pp.

A study of Syrians and Lebanese in São Paulo, Brazil. The study attempts "to discover why they migrated to Brazil, to analyze their demographic characteristics, to to trace their spatial and social mobility, and to study changes in their major social institutions produced by immigration and residence in São Paulo."

"The great majority of immigrants were single, poorly educated young males. In comparison with other immigrant groups, few women or children migrated. . . . Most of the immigrants came from rural villages and were Christians, mostly of the Maronite and Greek Orthodox denominations. Although many migrated to escape an inferior socio-religious position, the majority left the old country as temporary emigrants in order to make enough money to better their socio-economic position in their native villages. They went to Brazil either because they could not enter the U.S., or because they believed Brazil offered the best economic opportunities, or else to join friends and relatives. . . . They prefer urban to rural areas. . . . In Brazil they began as peddlers, moved into retailing and then into wholesaling, and many began to manufacture textiles and similar products. . . . In the course of this movement they have modified many of the institutions and associations brought with them from Syria and Lebanon and have developed new ones. The major finding of this study is that the sequence of spacial and social mobility of the Syrio-Lebanese in the city of São Paulo closely resembles those of immigrant groups in cities of the U.S."

171. Kohlmeyer, F. W.

1956 "Northern Pine Lumber Men: A Study in Origins and Migrations," *Journal of Economic History,* 16:529-38 (December).

One hundred and thirty-one northern pine lumber men, identified with the Lake States' lumber industry, studied in order to understand the factors of their origin, migration, training and experience, character and outlook, and the pattern of their rise as business leaders.

So many of these men are of approximately equal rank that instead of a handful of men dominating an industry, one finds a profusion of partnerships and coalitions of partnerships amid a general environment of intense competition. Their nationality fell within a narrow range, no fewer than 106 being of English-speaking stock. The parents of over half the leading lumbermen were farmers. The formal education of 78 percent of the future leaders was limited to the common schools. The varied experience gained during their formative years in farming, lumbering, teaching, and numerous other occupations undoubtedly contributed to their future business success. The transitory nature of the lumber industry in any given area impelled frequent migrations.

172. Kosa, John

1957 "A Century of Hungarian Emigration, 1850-1950," *American Slovac and East European Review*, 16:;01-14 (December).

A survey of Hungarian emigration for the period 1850-1950, utilizing census information. The study inquires into the reasons for this emigration.

"This survey of Hungarian emigration over a century clearly shows certain cycles, the volume of emigration increasing and diminishing in different periods. The peaks and troughs of the cycles cannot be tied to population increase of the country. They are connected rather with such factors as the general social problems and with political events which affected a large part of the population. Social problems and political circumstances are factors which must be considered important in appraising emigration from many European countries."

173. Kötter, Herbert

1962 "Economic and Social Implications of Rural Industrialization," *International Labour Review*, 86(1):1-14.

A comparative study of Kreis "County," Germany, and Groningen, Overijssel, and Braband Parishes in the Netherlands. The data were derived from census materials. The study was aimed at understanding social and economic implications of rural industrialization.

The survey endorsed the initial assumption that industrialization has favorable effects in small-farm areas in the following areas: (1) utilization of surplus manpower made available by technical progress in agriculture; (2) intensification of local division of labor; (3) establishment of contacts with outside world, thereby increasing migration to offset initial population increase, and extending zones of intermarriage; and (4) improvement of community services. "For most backward rural areas industrialization is probably the most powerful instrument available to a regional policy which aims at a thorough and lasting improvement in the economic and social structure."

174. Krueger, Nancy Moore

1955 "Assimilation and Adjustment of Postwar Immigrants in Franklin County, Ohio," unpublished doctoral dissertation, Ohio State University, 138 pp.

One hundred and twenty-five post-World War II immigrants in Franklin County, Ohio, were studied to understand the rapidity and the degree of assimilation and adjustment achieved by them.

"On the average, the older the immigrant, the poorer his English. The longer the immigrant has lived in the U.S., the better adjusted and assimilated he is. Youth also appears to be related to assimilation and adjustment. The Latvians were exceptions. . . . The larger the family unit, the lower the assimilation index. The similarity of the occupation in the U.S. to the occupation held in the native land appears neither to enhance nor to retard assimilation, but occupational similarity did appear to be related to the individual's adjustment indices. On the whole, the immigrants and repatriates had adjusted to their new environment and were self-supporting."

175. Ktsanes, Thomas, and Leonard Reissman

1959-60 "Suburbia—New Homes for Old Values," *Social Problems*, 7:187-95 (Winter).

The paper argues "that Suburbia is no different in its social forms than the city to which it sociologically belongs."

The argument is phrased around three themes generally found in literature on the subject: (1) suburbs are homogeneous, and undesirably so; (2) suburbia is overwhelmingly a middle class environment; and (3) suburbs nurture and encourage social conformity. Arguments against these three themes are presented. "What Suburbia means . . . is a question that can be answered by viewing it more as a continuation of the older values that still exist rather than a new phenomenon that has somehow taken the worst of all features of American life. . . . Perhaps the fact that Americans are moving in such numbers from the unplanned city to the poorly planned suburb is symbolic that really nothing much has changed except the time and the place."

176. Kurtz, Richard Allen

1959 "Resident Adjustment Patterns in the Rural-Urban Fringe," unpublished doctoral dissertation, Michigan State University, 265 pp.

A random sample of residents (representing farmers, part-time farmers, and non-farmers) of the fringe area surrounding Lansing, Michigan were studied. In this study of the rural-urban fringe, scalogram analysis of integration and typologies based on direction, content, and depth of identification were used.

Distributions and typologies "suggest that the conclusions of investigators who described the fringe area as an 'institutional desert' cannot be accepted. Over 40 percent of the respondents exhibit high participation patterns and more than 90 percent may be classified as positively identified with the area. . . . It was ascertained that long-time residence, relative stability, rural and non-Lansing background, and commitment to the area are all associated with a high degree of within-area participation. . . . It was found that definitions of the area, as either rural or urban, are affected by adjustment. Respondents who exhibit high degrees of integration, whose identifications with the area are based on friendship patterns and familiarity with it, and who had no prior choice for living in the area, define their place of residence as rural, rather than urban." The data suggest that "patterns of integration and identification do exist in the fringe, and that these are influenced by the residential experiences of residents and by commitment to the area."

177. Kuznets, Simon, and Dorothy S. Thomas

1958 "Internal Migration and Economic Growth," in *Selected Studies of Migration Since World War II*, Proceedings of the 34th Annual Conference of the Milbank Memorial Fund, New York, 1957, Part III, pp. 196-211.

This paper presents some general propositions on the relation between economic growth and internal migration. The data were primarily derived from census reports.

In the first part, Kuznets defines economic growth and outlines three relevant modern characteristics of this process: (1) A rise in per capita income and in population numbers; (2) high rates of growth of population, of economic product per capita, and of total economic product; (3) high rates of growth in per capita national income, associated with rapid shifts in the industrial and related aspects of the productive structure of the economy. He then states the functions of internal migration in relation to the process of economic growth, and suggests further hypotheses and questions. In the second part, Thomas summarizes the nature of the framework and methodology of the University of Pennsylvania's study of "Population Redistribution and Economic Growth." Essentially the study begins with the conception that economic growth and population redistribution are linked by a continuous chain of interdependent variables. It then proceeds to prepare and evaluate estimates of a number of these variables to provide a firm basis for empirical analyses of interrelations, over time and among spatial units. The four major sections of the study are concerned with population redistribution, levels of income, labor force, and production.

L

178. Larcheveque, R. L. J.

1959 "Results of the Rural Migration Policy in France from 1949 to 1955," *Industry and Labor*, 15: 340-43 (April).

This is a report from the French Ministry of Agriculture on their experiences in planning for 3700 migrant farm families.

In 1949 subsidies were paid by the French Ministry of Agriculture to farmers who could not settle in overcrowded areas and who agreed to settle in other parts of France. This policy had resulted in setting free land in the zones of origin and in bringing cultivated areas in line with family needs.

Larson, Olaf F. *See* 297.

179. Larson, Olaf F., and Emmit F. Sharp

1960 *Migratory Farm Workers in the Atlantic Coast Stream I: Changes in New York, 1953 and 1957*, Cornell University Agricultural Experiment Station Bulletin 948, 62 pp.

Migratory farm workers, New York. The study is based on information gathered from two samples, one in 1953 and the other in 1957. The study was aimed at understanding such things as changes in composition, employment, migration practices, and other related aspects of migratory farm workers.

The majority of the seasonal workers employed in farm and food-processing plants in New York in 1957 were southern Negroes. The analysis suggests the importance of (a) economic motivation, (b) the roles of state employment services, crew leaders, and informal contacts in recruiting the labor force, and (c) kinship and friendship ties in large, northern, urban centers, and (d) aspirations for nonfarm work as factors that contribute to dropping out of the migrant labor stream. Some useful recommendations are made to improve worker productivity.

180. Lasker, Gabriel W.

1960 "Migration, Isolation and Ongoing Human Evolution," *Human Biology*, 32:80-88 (February).

The effects of migration and isolation on ongoing human evolution are discussed from a genetic point of view of adaptation to environment.

It is indicated that isolation through random genetic drift, though conditions for it are now rare, may be responsible for some of the local racial differences in man. Interbreeding and migration in the genetically effective sense is the reason for the universal presence in man of his distinctive adaptive evolutionary advances.

Lee, Anne S. *See* 184.

181. Lee, Everett S.

1955 "Negro Intelligence and Selective Migration: A Philadelphia Test of the Klineberg Hypothesis," in *Demographic Analysis: Selected Readings*, ed. Joseph J. Spengler and Otis Dudley Duncan (Glencoe, Ill., The Free Press), pp. 432-37.

This study is an attempt to test Klineberg's hypothesis that there is a significant improvement in the intelligence test scores of southern-born Negro children as the length of residence in Philadelphia increases.

"There is a significant and continuous upward trend in the intelligence test ratings of southern-born Negro children as their length of residence in Philadelphia increases."

182 Lee, Everett S.

1957 "Migration Estimates," in *Population Redistribution and Economic Growth: U.S., 1870-1950. Volume I: Methodological Considerations and Reference Tables*, Everett S. Lee and others

(Philadelphia, American Philosophical Society), pp. 9-361.

An extensive study of U.S. migrants, utilizing data derived mostly from U.S. census reports. The study objectives were: (1) descriptions of procedures developed to convert masses of disparate and defective data from censuses and other administrative collections into sets of analysis-directed estimates; (2) evaluation of the validity and reliability of these estimates; and (3) the estimates themselves.

The study contains estimates of net migration derived by the forward census survival method by age, sex, color or race, and nativity of whites for each state and each intercensal period from 1870 to 1950. There are special sections on: (1) spatial and temporal units; (2) estimating net migration from census age distributions; (3) estimating migration from state-of-birth data; (4) comparison of estimates of net migration by census survival and state-of-birth methods; and (5) rural-urban series (1870, 1880, 1890, 1900, 1910, 1920, 1930 and 1940, 1950).

183. Lee, Everett S.

1958 "Migration and Mental Disease: New York State 1949-1951," in *Selected Studies of Migration Since World War II*, Proceedings of the 34th Annual Conference of the Milbank Memorial Fund, New York, 1957, Part III, 141-50.

A study of persons admitted for the first time for mental disease in New York State during the three-year period centering around the census of April 1, 1950. It is an investigation of 56,000 persons in order to understand the relationship between migration and mental disease.

"Rates of first admission to hospitals for mental disease in N.Y. State for the 3-yr. period, 1949-51, are higher for migrants than for nonmigrants when age, sex, and color are controlled. Furthermore, the differential in favor of nonmigrants holds for most of the specific psychoses as well as for all psychoses combined. . . . There are, however, differences between whites and nonwhites. . . . [T]he nonwhite group with the lowest rates of first admission is the foreign born." Qualifications attached to the conclusion are: "First admissions are not ideal indicators of the incidence of mental disease. . . . The same factors that impel migration may also result in mental disease, or the early stages of mental disease may be accompanied by migration . . . there is a possibility that higher rates of mental disease among migrants to N. Y. State simply reflect higher rates in the states or country of origin than in N.Y. State, and therefore, are unrelated to migration, *per se*."

184. Lee, Everett S., and Anne S. Lee

1960 "Internal Migration Statistics for the U.S.," *Journal of American Statistical Association*, 55: 664-97 (December).

A discussion of the uses and limitations of the internal migration statistics for the U.S. The data were derived from Bureau of Census and Department of Agriculture reports.

"[T]here is no one body of materials which gives a reasonably complete picture of migration within the U.S. Much, however, can be pieced out from the essentially complementary series which exist. These are: the state-of-birth data of the decennial censuses . . . ; the five-year migration data of the 1940 census and the one-year migration data from the 1950 census; the Current Population Survey . . . ; and the Department of Agriculture estimates of migration to and from farms. . . . In addition, the age-sex-nativity data of the decennial censuses can be used in connection with birth and death registrations or with survival ratios to obtain migration estimates. . . . The data are such that generalizations about trends and gross movements can be made with confidence, and it is only in regard to small and relatively unimportant shifts that doubt exists."

185. Lee, Rose H.

1957 "Chinese Immigration and Population Changes Since 1940," *Sociology and Social Research*, 41:195-202 (January-February).

Chinese population in the United States is studied, using census data. The paper deals with (1) "new immigration policies affecting persons of Chinese ancestry and (2) changes in the demographic characteristics of this group."

"The Chinese population shifted from a stationary to a lusty growing group after 1946. Earlier predictions as to its composition and demographic characteristics were rendered invalid by the repeal and modification of immigration laws and our policy of 'promoting family unity.' . . . After a century of residence and adaptation, the socioeconomic characteristics of the Chinese were becoming more akin to those of other ethnic groups."

186. Lee, Y. L.

1962 "The Population of British Borneo," *Population Studies*, 15:226-43 (March).

Families in British Borneo were studied in order to understand the pattern of migration which has influenced population growth and economic factors. The data were derived from census information.

"In general, the outstanding feature of the population distribution is the coastal concentration of the immigrant peoples. . . . [The] wide difference in economic status between the immigrant (especially the Chinese) and the aboriginal tribes . . . [points up the] important demographic fact . . . that in no other country of southeast Asia is there such a large portion of the indigenous people still living in primitive and backward conditions in the wilds of the country. . . . [I]t will take a long time before the division between ethnic and economic groupings will disappear."

187. Leslie, Gerald R., and Arthur H. Richardson

1961 "Life-Cycle, Career Pattern, and the Decision to Move," *American Sociological Review*, 26: 894-902 (December).

Two hundred and one (50 percent probability sample) households in Vinton Homes area, Lafayette, Indiana, were interviewed. Explanation was sought through two contrasting approaches, life-cycle and career pattern. Rossi's Mobility Potential Index and five items reflecting the influences of the career pattern were included in the interview schedule.

"Survey data supporting the utility of the career pattern approach are presented and inconsistencies among existing studies are interpreted as reflecting differences in the populations studied. A paradigm based upon 'life-cycle stage' and 'vertical mobility potential' is used to develop a model for further research. The decision to move is seen as a function of these two variables, with complaints about the present dwelling appearing as an intervening variable."

188. Leven, Charles L.

1959 "Population, Migration, and Regional Economic Development," *Current Economic Comment*, 21:31-42 (November).

A discussion of the relationships among population, migration, and regional economic development.

Some of the forces behind migration—such as the declining farm population, the declining demand for trade and service facilities of rural small towns, improved personal transportation and suburbanization—and also some of the problems of population receiving areas (cost to manufacturing and cost of expanding services) and population-sending areas (loss of business by retail merchants, narrowing of local tax base and per capita costs of maintaining local government outlays) are discussed.

189. Lieberson, S.

1961 "The Impact of Residential Segregation on Ethnic Assimilation," *Social Forces*, 40:52-57 (October).

A study of ten ethnic groups in ten U.S. cities (Boston, Buffalo, Chicago, Cincinnati, Cleveland, Columbus, Philadelphia, Pittsburgh, St. Louis, and Syracuse) using census data. It examines the impact of ethnic residential patterns on other aspects of their assimilation. Indices of dissimilarity between the actual occupational distribution of selected groups of second generation males and the occupational distribution expected on the basis of intergenerational mobility patterns are employed.

"The magnitude of an immigrant group's residential isolation from the native white population in a city influences other dimensions of the group's assimilation. Highly segregated groups are less apt to become citizens or speak English. . . . In addition, the degree of intermarriage is influenced by an immigrant group's residential segregation. . . . Finally, applying intergenerational mobility tables to the occupational patterns of second generation groups in five metropolises for which such data were available, it was found that highly segregated first generation groups were more apt to have second generation members deviate from the general pattern of intergenerational occupational choice. . . . Examination of the spatial distributions of human populations or social institutions is not merely a convenient tool or indicator for research purposes . . . but is, additionally, a potentially significant factor in interpreting and predicting differences in social behavior."

Lieberson, Stanley. *See* 80.

190. Lijfering, J. H. W.

1959 "Selective Aspects of Rural Migration in the Netherlands," in *Rural Migration*, Papers presented to the 1st Congress of the European Society for Rural Sociology, Brussels-Louvain, September, 1958 (Bonn, privately printed), pp. 95-105.

Ex-elementary pupils of 262 country schools in the Netherlands were studied, using information gathered from 1,934 of them. The following hypotheses were tested: "(1) Intelligence score increases with migration to a more urbanized residence. (2) Intelligence score increases with migration over a longer distance. (3) Intelligence score increases with level of education. (4) Intelligence score increases with the degree of social status of the occupation."

In general, all the four hypotheses were supported by the data. The evidence showed that rural boys of above-average intelligence were selected by the educational system and trained for occupations in urban areas.

191. Lipset, Seymour Martin

1955 "Social Mobility and Urbanization," *Rural Sociology*, 20:220-28 (September-December).

A study of the principal wage earners in 935 households in Oakland, California. The relationship between geographical and occupational mobility was tested.

"The findings indicate that the larger a person's community of orientation (the community in which he spent his teens), the more likely he has been upward mobile. This suggests a continuing pattern of social mobility in which migrants to metropolitan centers from rural areas or small urban communities take over the lower-status positions, while native urbanites move up on the occupational structure. Hypotheses are suggested to explain why large cities are more likely to be characterized by high rates of social mobility than other communities, and why natives of metropolitan centers are more prone to be upward-mobile than those originating in other parts of the country."

192. Litwak, Eugene

1960 "Geographic Mobility and Extended Family Cohesion," *American Sociological Review*, 25: 385-94 (June).

A study of 920 white married women, living in Buffalo, New York (mostly young, middle-class, and native-born). The following hypothesis was tested: extended family relations can be maintained in an industrial, bureaucratized society despite differential rates of geographical mobility.

The data substantiated the hypothesis. They also revealed that (1) those geographically separated from their families retained their extended family orientation; (2) close family identification did not make migration for occupational reasons less likely, and (3) those who were upwardly mobile occupationally were likely to move away and still receive family support. The findings also showed that (1) institutional pressures forced the extended family to legitimize geographical mobility; (2) technological improvements in communication systems have minimized the socially disruptive forces of geographical distance; and (3) that an extended family can provide important aid to the nuclear families without interfering with the occupational system.

193. Liu, William Thomas

1958 "A Study of the Social Integration of Catholic Migrants in a Southern Community," unpublished doctoral dissertation, Florida State University, 163 pp.

A study of Roman Catholics in a small urban parish in the upper part of Florida, 1957-1958. Information was gathered from 98 couples. The hypotheses tested were: "(1) The length of residence in the host community was directly related to the general integration pattern of the individual; (2) the degree of Catholicity was inversely related to the general integration of the couples; (3) the degree of Catholicity was inversely related to the degree of southern identification; and (4) the socioeconomic characteristics of the individual tended to modify the pattern of general integration." Four scales represented a composite area of "religio-social" attitude. One scale measured the degree of southern identification. In addition, the Chapin Social Participation Scale and the Wallin Women's Neighborliness Scale were used. The degree of the individual's Catholicity was measured by the modified criteria of Fichter's typologies.

The following inferences were drawn: (1) Church doctrine and birth control attitudes were related to Catholicity; (2) church doctrine, birth control, and race issues scales were influenced by the mobility pattern of the individuals; (3) religious education had no influence on the religio-social attitude; (4) older persons were more conservative toward race issues; (5) favorable Catholic attitude toward birth control issues on the part of the wife was influenced by the occupational and income prestige of the husband; (6) longer length of residence was found to be responsible for the more conservative attitude toward race issues; (7) the extent of participation in formal groups was influenced not only by socioeconomic status of migrants, but also by degree of Catholicity; (8) degree of southern identification was found to be influenced by the length of residence, family income, and age; (9) more conservative attitudes toward race and labor issues were found to be identified with the higher scores on the Southern Identification Scale.

194. Liu, William Thomas

1959 "Marginal Catholics in the South—A Revision of Concepts," American Journal of Sociology, 65:383-90 (January).

A study of 196 (98 couples) married, white, migrant Roman Catholics in an urban community of northern Florida. "The present study deals with the patterns of migration and adjustment of the Roman Catholic population of one southern community as an empirical test of the validity of the concept of the marginal man." Six scales were used: (1) the Church Doctrine Scale, (2) Labor Attitude Scale, (3) Birth-Control Attitude Scale, (4) Race Attitude Scale, (5) Social Participation Scale, and (6) Southern Identification Scale.

"It was found that manifestation of attitudinal inconsistency seemed to have been distinctive of the 'high' Catholicity group rather than of the 'low.' Class values seem significant in determining both the verbal attitudes and the overt social participation in such cases. The concept of 'marginal Catholic,' therefore, cannot be measured by using only a single continuum."

195. Livingston, J. W.

1960 "Migrant Workers and Trade Unions," American Federationist, 67:8-9 (February).

This article deals with the plight of the domestic migrant workers, and the obstacles that are encountered in attempts to organize trade unions for these workers.

Until the migrant worker organizes for collective bargaining, he will be forced to accept the wages and other conditions, set by his employer. The author has pointed out some of the problems involved in organizing the migrant workers.

196. Luebke, B. H., and John F. Hart

1958 "Migration from a Southern Appalachian Community," Land Economics, 34:44-53 (February).

Present and former residents of the Chestnut Hill area (eastern edge of the Great Valley of East Tennessee) with migration experience. Information was gathered from 177 of them. An attempt was made to understand the mechanics of migration from the hills and the problems of peoples' adjustment to their new environments.

The people of Chestnut Hill were adjusting the local economy to that of the nation, by responding to the national labor market through migration. The traditional mountain yeomen culture made it difficult for the migrants to adjust to urban life.

M

197. McCleary, George Frederick

1955 "Dispersal by Mass Migration," in Peopling the British Commonwealth, ed. George Frederick McCleary (London, Faber and Faber), pp. 146-63.

This paper is a discussion of the pros and cons of the proposal to redistribute the population of the British Commonwealth through migration to the Dominions.

198. McDonagh, E. C.

1955 "Attitudes Toward Ethnic Farm Workers in Coachella Valley," Sociology and Social Research, 40:10-18 (September).

Residents of Coachella Valley in California were studied, using two samples: 125 high school students and 100 ranchers. It was an attempt to learn the attitudes of the respondents toward American Filipinos, American Mexicans, American Negroes, Mexican nationals, and Mexican wetbacks. An ethnic test adapted from the work of Buchanan and Cantril was used.

The conclusions are that (1) both students and ranchers apply a wide range of stereotypes to ethnic groups employed as farm labor; (2) students appear to be more ethnocentric than ranchers; and (3) the great social distance between the ranchers and domestic migratory labor may account for the steady demand that a large pool of Mexican nationals be maintained as a dependable source of labor.

199. McDonald, Stephen L.

1955 "Farm Out Migration as an Integrative Adjustment to Economic Growth," *Social Forces*, 34:119-28 (December).

A study of farm families in the U.S. The aim was to restate a broad theoretical approach to agricultural problems in their historical setting.

A special burden of adjustment to national economic growth rests upon farm people, with depressing effects upon their average incomes. With every genuine "integrative adjustment" the problem of further adjustments will be reduced, as the size of farm population declines, and the spatio-cultural barrier dwindles.

200. McDonald, Stephen L.

1961 "On the South's Recent Economic Development," *Southern Economic Journal*, 28:30-40 (July).

A study of population shifts and industrialization in the southern U.S., with some emphasis on migration and its relationship to increase in per capita personal income.

The South's recent progress toward income parity is the result of two processes: the growth of aggregate earning power in the region and the relative reduction of the number of persons dependent upon that aggregate earning power through out-migration.

201. MacGaffey, Wyatt

1961 "The History of Negro Migrants in the Northern Sudan," *Southern Journal of Anthropology*, 17:178-97 (Summer).

A study of the peoples of Northern Sudan in order to test the hypothesis that many ethnographic features of the area are the result of an immigration of Negroes speaking Eastern Sudanic (Nilotic) languages from the south in the third century A.D.

The findings show that the Northern Sudanese share an association with the Eastern Sudanic (Nilotic) language group and with traditional histories of migration from a Nile valley homeland. Other recurrent features include symbiotic clanship and the office of king-maker, secondary shrines associated with local groups and subordinate chiefships within the tribe, and a history of conquest and the assimilation of alien groups linked to the royal clan through women. These findings appear to support the hypothesis.

McKnight, Robert K. *See* 22.

202. McNamara, Robert L.

1955 "Population Change Poses Problems in Supplying Adequate Health Service," *Journal of Osteopathy*, 62:9-14 (April).

A study of people of Missouri using data mostly derived from Census reports in order to assess changes in population, reasons for the changes, and some of their implications, particularly in the area of health maintenance.

It was concluded that migration is not to be regretted. "[M]igration is an important means of adjusting population to economic resources and opportunities . . . keep[ing] the man-land relationship in proper balance. . . . On the other hand, migration and the aging of our population have brought us serious social problems." Health, work with retirement, and housing are perhaps the major needs of aging citizens.

203. McQueen, Albert James

1959 "A Study of Anomie Among Lower Class Negro Migrants," unpublished doctoral dissertation, University of Michigan, 215 pp.

Seventy-five male Negro migrants, aged 20 to 50, to urban Ypsilanti, Michigan, during 1940-1957. The study focused on adjustment of Negro migrants to an urban community, assumed that alienation, apprehension, and purposelessness would be high among migrants who experienced trouble in the areas of family and occupation.

The most alienated and apprehensive persons were generally unsettled and dissatisfied with their situation in the community. These were 20-30 years old, veterans, late arrivals, non-voters, non-church-goers, and persons knowing little about the community. "Higher income respondents tended to be the least alienated, apprehensive, and purposeless as did those persons who thought their jobs were worthwhile and important. Service workers were less apprehensive than unionized laborers about job security, but were more alienated."

204. Maddox, James G.

1960a "Tar Heel Farmers Pay When Youth Leave Farms," *Research and Farming*, 18:11 (Spring).

Youths aged 10 to 20 who left North Carolina farms from 1950-1960. The study was aimed at finding out the cost of young people leaving the farm, using census data.

"North Carolina's farm families are bearing the cost of one of the adjustments now taking place in our agricultural economy . . . the cost of the young people leaving the farm. [T]he incomes which the youth will earn and spend will benefit the urban areas. . . . There are at least two ways in which this uneven distribution of gains and losses could be lessened. One way would be through financial aid to education. Another would be to expand industry into areas nearer the supply of rural labor."

205. Maddox, James G.

1960b "Private and Social Costs of the Movement of People Out of Agriculture," *American Economic Review: Papers and Proceedings*, 50: 392-402, 413-18 (May).

A study of the problems involved in people leaving agriculture in the U.S. since 1940, particularly for the farm people. "The aim of this paper is to identify some of the costs of off-farm migration and to draw a few conclusions about their relevance to policy formulation."

Despite high costs associated with it "off-farm migration is almost certain to continue at relatively high levels unless there is an unforeseeably large and continuing increase in the demand for farm products or, conversely, a prolonged and serious decline in the employment in the nonfarm sector of the economy." Rural communities which experience either a rapid decline in total population or a sustained outflow of a large proportion of the maturing young people are the types of areas in which public action is most necessary to ameliorate the inequities arising from the shift of people out of agriculture.

206. Maitland, Sheridan T.

1956 *The Hired Farm Working Force of 1954*, Agricultural Marketing Service 103 (U.S. Department of Agriculture), 26 pp.

The hired farm-working force of 1954 was studied, using data from a national sample of approximately 25,000 households obtained by the Bureau of the Census. The topics examined included migratory farm workers, their employment and earnings, and some characteristics of their children.

"Migrants worked fewer days, earned more per day and averaged slightly higher annual farm wage income than nonmigrant farm workers in 1954. Age differences between migratory and nonmigratory farm workers were less in 1954 than in 1952 and earlier years. The ratio of female to male migratory workers was about the same as for nonmigrants. . . . [Over] 150,000 children under the age of 18 traveled with migratory farm workers during 1954. About the same number of children remained at the migratory worker's home base with some member of the household or in other households."

207. Manis, Jerome G.

1959 "Agricultural Migration and Population Prediction," *Rural Sociology*, 24:29-34 (March).

Migrants into Van Buren County, Michigan, in the summer of 1957, based on 417 interviews. General characteristics of migrant workers were sought.

These migrants were primarily agricultural workers before migration. June was the month of most intensive migration. Over 50 percent came dirctly from their home state. One in six stopped in other states before working in Michigan. Attitudes regarding the desire to stay or leave were about equally divided. It was found that the migrant is not a wanderer or a hobo type, but rather half are work seekers, the others are settlers.

208. Marhoefer, Gilbert Lionel

1960 "Background and Economic Aspects of Immigration to the U.S. and the World Refugee Problem," unpublished doctoral dissertation, University of Pittsburgh, 273 pp.

Immigrants and refugees in U.S. Background and economic aspects of immigration to the U.S. with special emphasis on the world refugee problem were studied using census information.

"The history of the U.S. demonstrates experience with voluntary, involuntary, and refugee immigration. Three periods are discernible: (1) The Colonial period of 1882, characterized by the need for immigrants as a part of the policy of economic growth and development; (2) 1882 to World War II, marked by a growing fear of immigrants as an economic threat; and (3) the decade of the 1950's in which immigration has been linked to foreign economic policy." This new concept was reflected in the emergency Refugee Relief Act. "The operation of the refugee program has supplied important information as to the possible future consequences of similar legislation and immigration policy. For the U.S. the value of these refugees to its economy far outweighed their cost of acquisition. . . . Much of the potential benefit was dissipated, however, because of the lack of a complete program to handle the problem of the refugee."

209. Maris, Ic. A.

1959 "The Efflux of Labour from Agriculture in Europe," in *Rural Migration*, Papers presented to the 1st Congress of the European Society for Rural Sociology, Brussels-Louvain, September, 1958 (Bonn: privately published), pp. 48-57.

A discussion of the conditions under which a balance between the level of welfare in agriculture and rural depopulation can be maintained, with especial reference to the problems confronting the youth.

Europeans "are faced with the question of how this highly desirable efflux of younger people from farming can be fostered and directed into the right channels." Its lack of past direction was to the disadvantage of both town and country. [T]he most appropriate way would be to provide the rural population with advice and information about the choice of schools and occupations, . . . [together with the] redistribution of industry over regional centres and . . . the modernization of the countryside's equipment. [S]tructural changes in agriculture need not . . . lead to the depopulation of rural areas."

210. Markoff, S.

1957 "Sweatshops Under Blue Skies," *American Federationist*, 64:18-19 (October).

The substandard living and working conditions of the migrant farm workers are discussed. Some of the special problems of the children of migrants are emphasized.

Despite past efforts, migrants "remain virtually unorganized and consequently are easy prey for exploitation." Child labor, due to parental poverty, is commonplace among migrants. "Migrancy, even if many of its bad features were controlled, would serve to prevent a normal home life for parents and children. Because of that reason it would be desirable to develop public policies which would reduce migrancy to the minimum necessary for our national needs. This can be done through an expansion of employment opportunities at fair wages in the migrants' home areas, or in the areas to which they migrate, and through more effective utilization of the manpower available to a community."

211. Marshall, Douglas G.

1959a "*Wisconsin's Population: Changes and Prospects*. Wisconsin Agricultural Experiment Station Research Bulletin 194 Rev., 49 pp.

A general analysis of the changes in population in Wisconsin from 1900-1955 using census data.

"Migration is a selective factor. The young unmarried people who have completed their high school education tend to be moving from the farm into the small town and city, and particularly into the city. Young married people are moving into the suburbs. In addition, the older people, those retiring from agriculture, are moving, but tend to move into the small town. This expansion of the city and its suburbs and the small town population probably will continue. The impact of migration will also be felt generally on the age and sex distribution. There will tend to be more males than females in the farm population; more females in the towns and cities."

212. Marshall, Douglas G.

1959b *Population Characteristics, Resources, and Prospects in the North Central Region,* Wisconsin Agricultural Experiment Station Research Bulletin 209, 80 pp.

North Central Region of U.S. (East North Central and West North Central states as defined by the Bureau of the Census, plus Kentucky). Most data derived from U.S. census reports. A descriptive report on population changes, including those resulting from migration.

Migration's "relative importance in determining demographic changes often outweighs the vital processes of fertility and mortality, especially in modern times. The streams of migration in the North Central Region might be characterized in five groups: (a) movement from farms of families, (b) movement of youth from farms, (c) movement of hired farm workers and their families, (d) movement of persons and families from small towns and cities to large urban centers, and (e) movement to rural areas of urban employed persons."

Marshall, Douglas G. *See* 78.

213. Martin, Joe A.

1958 *Off-Farm Migration: Some of Its Characteristics and Effects Upon Weakley City, Tennessee,* Tennessee Agricultural Experiment Station Bulletin 290, 43 pp. Based on the author's doctoral dissertation. (*See* 214).

214. Martin, Joe Allen

1955 "The Impact of Industrialization upon Agriculture: A Study of Off-Farm Migration and Agricultural Development in Weakley County, Tennessee," unpublished doctoral dissertation, University of Minnesota, 149 pp.

One hundred eighty-one farm operators in Weakley County, Tennessee, were interviewed in 1951. "The objectives of this study are: (1) to reveal some of the social and economic characteristics of off-farm migration, and (2) to reveal some of the effects of a reduction in labor supply upon resource use on farms in Tennessee and the Southeast generally."

"The following characteristics of off-farm migration were revealed in the study: (1) migration is highly selective of the younger age groups in the population; (2) people in the tenure status of hired labor and share-cropper are moving off-farm faster than other tenure groups; (3) prior to World War II the better educated tended to be selected for movement out; in the period from 1946 to 1951 the level of education was not a significant factor in migration; (4) information regarding nonfarm employment in distant cities is provided to farm people almost exclusively by members of the family or friends from the community who had moved to the distant cities; (5) a significantly larger proportion of the migrants in the young age group (17-28 years) were married than of the nonmigrant population; (6) a negative correlation was found between acres of crop and pasture land per unit of labor and off-farm migration; and (7) as employment of labor on farms increased, off-farm movement declined."

215. Martinson, Floyd M.

1955 "Personal Adjustment and Rural-Urban Migration," *Rural Sociology,* 20:102-10 (June).

Graduates in the classes of 1945 through 1949 of five Minnesota high schools, all essentially rural. Information from 1289 cases. The following hypothesis was tested: "There are aspects of personal adjustment which are related to, and perhaps causative of, migration from rural communities." Bell Adjustment Inventory, Kuder Preference Record, and California Test of Personality were used.

"In general, then, it would appear that the migrants were less well adjusted to family and community and better adjusted to the life of the high school, a symbol of what the world outside the local rural community has to offer—academic, scientific, and literary pursuits."

216. Masters, Kenneth Whaley

1955 "Population Redistribution in the U.S., 1840-1860," unpublished doctoral dissertation, University of Pennsylvania, 165 pp.

The main sources of data utilized were the federal censuses of 1840, 1850, and 1860. The purpose of the study was: "To describe population distribution among states and regions in the U.S. by decade for the 1840-1860 period; to analyze the roles of fertility, natural increase, net internal migration, and immigration in population redistribution; and to study the relationships between the component factors of population redistribution and measures of economic growth."

"Three measures of economic development were employed: estimated per capita income in 1840; percentage of population urban in 1840, 1850, and 1860; and percentage of gainfully employed workers in non-agricultural pursuits in 1840, 1850, and 1860. The relationship between these measures and net intercensal migration were analyzed and suggestions made for further study."

217. Maxwell, G. N.

1955 "Opening New Doors for Children of Migrants Through a Girl Scout Program," *Social Service Review,* 29:148-52 (June).

This study is a discussion of the purposes, difficulties, and learnings of two projects—in Colorado and in the San Joaquin Valley of California—set up by the National Girl Scout Organization concerned with the organization of scout programs for migrant girls.

In this effort the Girl Scouts have learned several things: that teamwork with other organizations is essential; that care must be taken in recruiting volunteers; that prejudice waned when tempered by direct personal contact; and that Girl Scout troops could be organized among girls coming from widely scattered farms as well as among those living close together.

218. Mayer, P.

1962 "Migrancy and the Study of Africans in Towns," *American Anthropologist*, 64:576-92 (June, Part I).

Migrants in East London, Cape Province, between 1955 and 1959. The study investigated two things: (1) the individual migrant's personal relationships so as to determine the balance of town and out-of-town ties and the possibility of change in these ties and (2) investigation of patterns of behavior, values, and attitudes with special reference to aspiration and desire for change.

Two types of behavior were found. In one type all of the migrant's most important personal ties were contained within the town. In the opposite type, ties with nontownsmen remained paramount. In East London a migrant's propensity to change culturally was related to the fate of his extra-town ties. These mechanisms of (a) home-visiting, and (b) organization of relations between "amakhaya" while in town serve to keep the extra-town ties in force. No East Londoners had urbanization thrust upon them. Some of the migrants began to change; but others voluntarily incapsulated themselves in something as nearly as possible like the tribal relations from which their migration could have liberated them.

219. Metzler, William H., and Frederic O. Sargent

1960 *Incomes of Migratory Agricultural Workers*. Texas Agricultural Experiment Station Bulletin 950, 12 pp.

Migratory farm workers in San Antonio, Crystal City, Eagle Pass, Laredo, Weslaco, and Robstown, Texas, 1956-1957. Four hundred and forty-six households (1334 workers) were studied to find answers to questions concerning incomes of migratory workers located in south Texas during the winter of 1956-1957.

The "workers showed considerable skill in timing and planning their itinerary. . . . One-third worked in only one area away from the home base. . . . Average earnings per family varied closely with the size of the family work force and averaged $2,208. . . . Less than one-fourth of this was earned at the home base; hence, migratory labor was a major source of their income." Approximately half of the workers were household heads or their wives. "Working wives were only a little more than half as numerous as working husbands. . . . One-fifth of the workers were school children. . . . One-third of the school youth who worked were under 14 years of age. . . . Several major trends are working toward an improved situation for migratory workers. They are (1) permanent movement of migratory workers to other states and reduction of labor surpluses at the home base during the winter; (2) development of annual

workers' plans which correlate movement of workers with local labor needs during the season; (3) development of better means of school-attendance administration so as to reduce the loss in educational advantages; and (4) more careful regulation of transportation, housing and sanitation so as to bring the living and working conditions of these people more in line with acceptable minimum standards."

220. Metzler, W. H., and Frederic O. Sargent

1962 "Problems of Children, Youth and Education among Mid-Continent Migrants," *Southwestern Social Science Quarterly*, 43:29-38 (June).

Migrant workers in six cities in southern Texas, 1957. A sample of 446 households (1334 migrant workers) provided the data. Problems of children, youth, and education among midcontinent workers are dealt with in this paper.

"The very direct conflict between the economic and the educational needs of these families calls for considerate rather than arbitrary action. . . . The rate at which migratory agricultural workers find better and steadier employment depends to a large extent upon their ability to speak English and upon their educational background. . . . Since a dependable seasonal work force is vital to the agriculture of the midcontinent area, long-range policies are needed that will build up such a force without creating heavy social costs. The present system of seasonal labor is based on a migrant family supporting its children through child labor and the sacrifice of their educational opportunities. . . . A comprehensive program to reduce the movement of large families and to check on the timing of those who must migrate would be socially advantageous."

Miller, Vincent A. *See* 289.

221. Moss, J. Joel

1956 "Newcomer Family Acceptance: Rejection of the Community and the Process of Assimilation," *Rural Sociology*, 21:302-306 (September-December).

Newcomer families living in Barnwell and Williston, South Carolina, 1953. A study of 162 families (20 percent random sample) to test the following hypotheses: "(1) Families that expect the community to be open and receptive to them will more fully accept it than families that expect it to be closed and defensive, (2) Close-knit families will more fully accept the community than will families that are less close-knit, and (3) Families that are given many receptive experiences by the community will more fully accept it than will families that have fewer receptive experiences." The following scales and scores were used: Jansen's Family Solidarity Scale, family's expectations score, and a scale developed by Vreeland and Glick to measure attitudes of students toward their home and college community was used.

"The evidence from the study is that family organization, family reception by a community, expectations of permanence, social participation, and the family's position in the assimilation process are related to the attitude a family takes toward the community."

222. Moss, J. Joel

1957 *West Virginia and Her Population*, West Virginia Agricultural Experiment Station Bulletin 403, 51 pp.

A general demographic survey of the people of West Virginia using data derived from U.S. census reports. Special attention is given to changes occurring in population characteristics over the 1940-1950 decade.

The population is growing older. The number of females in the state population is increasing. Out-migration is attracting males who are in their most productive years. "This means that greater occupational attraction for males must be made by the State or else its activities may need to be more oriented to the contribution of women and older people." Population pressure and low median income are reasons for the loss of males.

223. Mumey, G. A.

1959 "Parity Ratio and Agricultural Out-Migration," *Southern Economic Journal*, 26:63-65 (July).

This paper is a discussion of the extent to which the principle of parity ratio might influence out-migration of farm population.

"An absence of negative correlation between farm prices and farm out-migration has been shown, and an attempt has been made to reconcile, deductively, this conclusion with the existing body of economic theory. The study suggests that farm income maintenance does not impede the movement of labor into non-agricultural jobs, and that the pricing system, alone, will not solve the farm problem."

224. Munzer, Jean Howard

1961 "A Study of the Relationships Between Mobility and Academic Achievement of Third-Grade and Sixth-Grade Children," unpublished doctoral dissertation, University of Michigan, 210 pp.

Third- and sixth-grade children of the Wayne Community School District, Wayne, Michigan, were studied, using two samples: 781 third-grade children and 765 sixth-grade children. "The purpose of this study was to examine the relationship between the mobility of elementary school children in an urban school district and their academic achievement." Academic achievement was measured by Iowa Tests of Basic Skills. Within the limitations of the study, very little relationship was found between mobility and mean academic achievement of third- and sixth-grade students in Wayne, Michigan, in 1959. This remained true within intelligence and sex groups.

N

225. Nagi, Saad Zaghloul

1958 "Migration and Communicative Integration in a Rural Fringe Population," unpublished doctoral dissertation, Ohio State University, 109 pp.

Residents of the rural fringe of Columbus, Ohio, were studied, using information from 303 cases (25 percent sample). "The purpose of this study is to determine the degree of communicative integration among old residents and among in-migrants, as well as between the two segments, in the population of the rural fringe of Columbus, Ohio." An index of communicative integration devised on the basis of both formal and informal social participation scores was used.

"Old residents showed a significantly higher degree of integration in their communities of residence than the migrants. The migrants' integration scores in communities other than those of residence are significantly higher. Both the old residents and the migrants showed a significant tendency to choose new friends from within their respective groups." Among the migrants, the following showed positive association with integration: femaleness, farming, educational and occupational attainment, number of children, length of residence, and stability. The degree of their integration in the previous communities of residence showed a negative relationship. "Old residents in the rural fringe communities are more local bound in their social relationships than migrants."

226. Nam, Charles Benjamin

1959 "Nationality Groups and Social Stratification: A Study of the Socioeconomic Status and Mobility of Selected European Nationality Groups in America," unpublished doctoral dissertation, University of North Carolina, 232 pp.

Five male groups from "old" immigration countries and five male groups from "new" immigration countries were studied, using data mostly derived from census reports. Answers were sought for the effect of certain variables on nationality groups in their social mobility. These variables were language facility, generational length of stay in the country, education, and geographical location.

Nationality groups have shared significantly in the status mobility afforded by the open-class system in the United States. Educational attainment is most important explanation for this mobility. As these groups increasingly become assimilated, association of their members with ethnic origins diminishes.

227. Nash, E. F.

1959 "Rural Migration; The Economic Background," in *Rural Migration*, Papers presented to the 1st Congress of the European Society for Rural Sociology, Brussels-Louvain, September, 1958 (Bonn, privately published), pp. 445-53.

An essay that supports the basic economic explanation of migration, namely that rural people migrate to urban areas in order to seek better income sources. Basic economic cause of the exodus from agriculture is disequilibrium between demand and supply, leading to relative fall in profit and income-levels in agriculture and setting up a tendency to labor transfer from agriculture. Some of the factors influencing demand and supply of agricultural products are: elasticity of demand for food; effects on supply of resource distribution between agriculture and other industries and of relative rates of growth in productivity; and persistence of relative agricultural oversupply. Resistance of agriculture to economic change prolongs the relative oversupply of agricultural products. Most measures of government support to agriculture have a similar effect.

228. Nasrat, Mohamed Mohiey Eldin

1958 "Conceptual Variable Analysis of Rural Migration in Iowa," unpublished doctoral dissertation, Iowa State University, 104 pp.

Using available data on migration of people in Iowa and related factors, the following hypotesis was tested: "Cohesion varies indirectly with deprivation." Three indices of deprivation were developed: (1) coefficient of variation, (2) coefficient of deprivation, and (3) coefficient of relative rewards.

Analysis indicated that the relationship between cohesion and the three indices of deprivation was in the expected direction. The relationships between the variables have been examined in more detail for groups of Iowa counties, classified according to the size of the largest incorporated center that exists in each county, by the simple and multiple regression techniques.

Nasrat, Mohamed Mohiey Eldin. *See* 356.

229. Neiva, A. H., and M. Diégues, Jr.

1959 "The Cultural Assimilation of Immigrants in Brazil," in *The Cultural Integration of Immigrants*, by W. D. Borrie and others (Paris, UNESCO), pp. 181-233.

A study of immigrants to Brazil. The aim was to discover some of the major factors facilitating the cultural assimilation of immigrants to Brazil.

"Thus the process of adjusting the foreign to the basically Portuguese Brazilian cultures operates by mutual interaction with reciprocal modifications in a process of transculturation—a term which seems to us happier than acculturation to indicate the process taking place in Brazil. . . . The trend in Brazil is for immigration operations to be followed up by planned group settlements, so that the foreign group is located in a milieu where the conditions meet its needs and aspirations. And with the growth of a genuinely urban industrial system, the requisite avenues to satisfactory adjustment are likewise provided even for that part of the immigrant intake which seeks the towns. The place of cultural assimilation of immigrants in the Brazilian scene is, then, closely bound up as a process with the aims of immigration, and the immigrant is not brought in to be abandoned to his fate nor to be stripped of the cultural values to which he holds." The National Institute of Immigration and Settlement has played an important part in this process.

230. Nelson, Philip Jacob

1957 "A Study in the Geographic Mobility of Labor," unpublished doctoral dissertation, Columbia University, 336 pp.

Migrants between states, 1935-1940 and 1949-1950. Census data used. Answers were sought for the following questions: "What variables are most effective in explaining the distribution of migration? What behavior patterns produce these statistical relationships?"

"For the earlier period the following variables proved to have a statistically significant relationship to the logarithm of migration rates: distance, two measures of industrial similarity, the percent of the native population born outside their state of residence as an origin variable, destination income, and destination unemployment. These variables explain 81% of the variance in the logarithm of migration rates. We contend that these statistical results can best be explained by the distribution of labor market information."

231. Newman, Jeremiah

1959 "The Viability of the Village in Relation to Size," in *Rural Migration*, Papers presented to the 1st Congress of the European Society for Rural Sociology, Brussels-Louvain, September, 1958 (Bonn, privately published), pp. 77-79.

People of the county of Limerick, Ireland. The basic question for inquiry was: How large should a village be in order to be viable under the conditions of rural-urban migration?

"[T]he depopulation of the smaller villages and more rural parishes is much more serious than appears from general rural statistics for the county as a whole. . . . [T]he real extent of rural depopulation in Ireland can only be gauged . . . [by] surveys at the district and the parish levels. . . . [I]f the village of the future is to be viable, it must be of a sufficient size [at least 1000 population] to offer a satisfactory social [and economic] life."

232. Nishiura, Eleanor Noble

1959 "Internal Migration in Indiana," unpublished doctoral dissertation, Purdue University, 293 pp.

Migrants in Indiana. Census reports were used as the source of the data. "Instead of simply listing the characteristics of migrants or the characteristics of areas of origin or destination, [this study] has attempted to draw together within one theoretical framework these traditional kinds of findings."

"Our analysis showed that the three sets of data which refer to two different periods of time showed consistency among each other and did not contradict the theory which was being tested. These findings showed that census data can be extremely useful at one stage in the testing of a theory and in this particular instance, with a minimum of costs they convince us that Sara Smith's theoretical framework 'makes sense' in terms of empirical data."

Nishiura, Eleanor Noble. *See* 24.

233. Nixon, J. W.

1959 "Occupations of Immigrants into the Principal Countries of Immigration in 1950-1954," *International Population Conference Proceedings* (Vienna, International Union for the Scientific Study of Population), pp. 619-24.

A study of immigrants into principal countries of immigration during 1950-1954. The data were taken mostly from United Nations' *Economic Characteristics of International Migrants: Statistics for Selected Coun-*

tries 1918-1954. The study focus was needed uniformity in classifying migrants by economic activity.

"About three quarters of all international immigration is directed to about 8 countries, and a summary of the data for these countries throws much light on world immigration. . . . Owing to the differences in the classifications by economic activities, it is difficult to draw many definite conclusions but for the four largest countries of immigration (U.S.A., Canada, Australia and Israel) a similarity in classification enables some idea to be obtained of the proportions in the principal categories such as farm workers, manual workers, non-manual workers, liberal professions and personal service. . . . Compared with previous periods, the period 1950-54 shows a decline in the proportion of semiskilled and unskilled and an increase in the professional and non-manual groups. A greater uniformity in the system of classification of migrants by economic activity is much to be desired."

234. Norman, A. M. Z.

1956 "Migration to Southeast Texas: People and Words," *Southwest Science Quarterly,* 37:149-58 (September).

A study based on intensive interviewing of three age groups of informants in Jefferson County, Texas. Each group consisted of four males and females: one group less than 39 years old; another, 40-49 years old; and the third group with members in the 70 years and older category. Besides these interview data, U.S. census reports were used. The study focus was to determine the relationship between migration of people and that of words.

With a few exceptions, it may be said that the Southern dialect words which penetrated into southeast Texas were those which earlier got across the mountains into the South Midland. Furthermore, it seems likely that all of the words from the southern coast are limited to the east Texas area. The dialect vocabulary of the southeast Texas area is made up of about five parts Southern terms, two parts Midland expressions, and one part Northern words.

O

235. Olson, Philip Gilbert

1959 "Socio-Economic Factors Affecting Labor Mobility in an Indiana Rural Community," unpublished doctoral dissertation, Purdue University, 143 pp.

One hundred thirty-two heads of households of a central Indiana rural farming community. "The fundamental objective of this study is to lay out a conceptual framework of labor mobility and migration, and to test its adequacy from empirical data collected in a rural farming community in central Indiana."

The differences between the three mobility types (job mobile, migrant, and job mobile-migrant) "with regard to age, education, income, social status, and occupation led to the conclusions that the *migrant* was primarily motivated by desire for social betterment, the *job mobile* for economic betterment, and the *job mobile-migrant* by both desires." The largest

proportion of involuntary job mobility occurred among the job mobile population, and largest proportion of voluntary, among the job mobile-migrant population.

236. Olson, Philip Gilbert

1960 *Job Mobility and Migration in a High Income Rural Community,* Purdue University Agricultural Experiment Station Research Bulletin 708, 23 pp.

Based on the author's doctoral dissertation. (*See* 235).

237. Omari, Thompson Peter

1956 "Factors Associated with Urban Adjustment of Rural Southern Migrants," *Social Forces,* 35:47-53 (October).

Two hundred Negro migrants in Beloit, Wisconsin. They were male, 18 years and over, and had had at least one year's residence in the community. The study emphasis was to determine the factors that contribute to the adjustment of Negro migrants.

It was concluded that: (1) Relatives contribute significantly to the adjustment of the migrant; (2) in determining the nature of the adjustment of the migrant to his new community, attention should be paid to both premigration as well as postmigration factors; (3) the length of time the migrant has lived in his new community is the most important factor in the process of his adjustment.

O'Neal, P. *See* 268.

238. Osborne, Richard H.

1956 "Scottish Migration Statistics: A Note," *Scottish Geographic Magazine,* 72:153-59 (December).

People of Scotland. Most of the data were taken from annual reports of the Registrar-General for Scotland. It is largely a descriptive study of migration in and out of Scotland during 1861-1951.

During the 90-year period only three counties had a net gain through migration; the country as a whole continually lost through migration. The destinations of most emigrants were England, the Commonwealth, and the United States.

Owens, G. P. *See* 291.

P

Parker, Seymour. *See* 169.

Parrish, Barnard D. *See* 324.

239. Patton, J. W.

1960 "Letters from North Carolina Emigrants in the Old Northwest, 1830-1834," *Mississippi Valley Historical Review,* 47:263-77 (September).

This paper is a collection of letters written by North Carolinia migrants to new territories and states in the 1830s to friends and relatives remaining in North Carolina.

Indiana and Illinois were especial beneficiaries of this migration. In 1850 there were 33,175 natives of North Carolina living in Indiana and 13,851 in Illinois. The migrants often compared conditions in North Carolina unfavorably with those which they found on the fertile prairies of the West.

240. Payne, Raymond

1956 "Occupational and Migration Expectations," *Rural Sociology*, 21:117-25 (June).

All eighth and twelfth grade boys in Georgia County schools who were in school the day the schedule was administered. Four hundred thirteen cases in all. Answers were sought for the following questions: How, when, and in what situations does the adolescent as a member of the community learn about occupational, educational, and migration alternatives? How does he come to perceive one or another of these as having greater relative value or applicability for him and his emerging life situation?

"[I]n general, informal interpersonal situations contributed most to the formation of such expectations, and . . . the educational expectation was typically formed first, followed by the occupational choice, with the decision concerning future place of residence being dependent upon the first two. The absence of direct influence of formal occupational counseling was noted. The boys were found to be aware of the prestige value of occupations, and they were predominantly choosing above their parents; also, they were choosing occupations which were more urbanlike than their parents', and were usually expecting to leave their present communities to live and work as adults."

241. Pedersen, Harald A.

1956 *Migration from Mississippi*, Mississippi Agricultural Experiment Station Information Sheet 536 (reprinted from *Mississippi Farm Research* 19: 6) (May).

A study of migrants from Mississippi using data partly from U.S. census reports, vital statistics reports, and partly from a study of 111 high school graduates. The study emphasizes some of the consequences of out-migration for Mississippi.

The process of rearing children through their years of dependency only to lose them when they become producers is an economic drain on the state. Opportunities which will attract and hold a cross-section of each generation are badly needed in Mississippi. In a study of high school graduates in a small Mississippi county seat town it was concluded that the community can only expect to reap the benefit from the investment in education for one-fourth of its high school graduates.

242. Pedersen, Harald A., and Lelia H. Thomas

1957 *Estimated Population Trends in Mississippi, 1950-56*. Mississippi Agricultural Experiment Station Bulletin 550, 17 pp.

A general study of population changes in Mississippi, with emphasis on the importance of migration in the adjustment of the people to available resources, using U.S. census data.

Six of the counties which showed increases in population had large urban concentration. The critical factor affecting the population situation in Mississippi was that, despite the sizable increases in urban centers, Mississippi remained predominantly a rural state.

243. Petersen, William

1958 "A General Typology of Migration," *American Sociological Review*, 23:256-66 (June).

Migrants and migration in general are considered in an attempt to bring together into one typology some of the more significant analyses of both internal and international migration.

A typology is developed in this paper and is summarized in a table form. The principal purpose of the typology was to offer, by an ordering of conceptual types, a basis for the possible development of theory. The author urges that the most general statement that one can make concerning migration should be in the form of a typology, rather than a law. (*See* 244)

244. Petersen, William

1961a "The General Determinants of Migration," in *Population* (New York, Macmillan), pp. 592-621.

A theoretical discussion aimed at differentiating types of migration.

The typology developed is based on observations on migratory selection (age, sex, family status, occupation, and psychical factors) and the relation between migration and population growth. When the push-pull polarity has been refined by distinguishing innovating from conservative migration and by including in the analysis the migrants' level of aspiration, it can form the basis of a typology. Five broad classes of migration are defined: (1) *primitive migration* including the two subtypes, wandering and ranging; (2) *impelled migration;* (3) *forced migration;* (4) *free migration;* and (5) *mass migration.*

245. Petersen, William

1961b "Internal Migration," in *Population* (New York, Macmillan), pp. 153-78.

A theoretical discussion, based on current work in internal migration and aimed at alerting researchers and others about problems in interpreting the findings of various studies in the U.S.A.

The U.S. Census Bureau's definition of migration takes into account basically a measure of distance and the significance of distance to the move. In order to differentiate significant migration by any other criterion, one must delineate the culture areas within the U.S. It is not possible to define these precisely, for regional subcultures, to the degree that they exist at all within the all-pervasive national culture, blend into one another gradually. The four regions used by the Bureau of the Census, and to a smaller degree the divisions within them, probably represent the most homogeneous groups of whole states that could be selected.

Peterson, John M. *See* 52.

246. Petrini, Frank

1959 "The Demographic Development of the Agricultural Population", in *Rural Migration*, Papers presented to the 1st Congress of the European Society for Rural Sociology, Brussels-Louvain, September, 1958 (Bonn, privately published), pp. 4-5-408.

Swedish agricultural population was studied in order to understand the factors involved in the demographic development of the agricultural population. The aim was to predict the size of one of the primary branches, namely agriculture.

The definition of a permanent farm as stated by the Royal Board of Agriculture is critically reviewed. The author has suggested additional economic and social factors that need to be taken into consideration if one is to understand the full meaning of the demographic conditions existing on the farms, including migration. Among these factors are distance to the market, the quality of the buildings used, the possibility of getting off-farm work, attractiveness of the village, sense of belongingness to the village, and the value orientation concerning rational behavior and cultural change.

247. Phillips, Coy T.

1956 "Population Distribution and Trends in North Carolina," *The Journal of Geography*, 55:182-94 (April).

North Carolina's entire population and its distribution, using data derived mostly from U.S. census reports.

General trends are discussed, which take into account changes brought about by migration.

248. Pierson, G. W.

1962 "M-Factor in American History," *American Quarterly*, 14:275-89 (Summer).

An essay on what the author calls the M-factor (movement, migration, mobility) in American history.

"What made and kept [the U.S.] different was not just the wildness of the North American continent, nor its vast and empty spaces, nor even its wealth of resources. . . . It was , first of all, the M-factor: the factor of movement, migration, mobility." The author contends that the M-factor has been: "(1) the great Eliminator; (2) the persistent Distorter; (3) and arch-Conservator; (4) an almost irresistible Disintegrator or Atomizer; (5) a heart Stimulant or Energizer; and (6) the prime source of Optimism in the American atmosphere, a never-failing ozone of hope. Also, (7) the Secularizer and Externalizer of our beliefs, and (8) the Equalizer and Democratizer of social classes."

249. Pihlblad, C. T., and Dagfinn Aas

1960 "Residential and Occupational Mobility in an Area of Rapid Industrialization in Norway," *American Sociological Review*, 25:369-75 (June).

Norwegian youth and young adults in the Rana region (west coast of Norway, a few miles below the Arctic Circle) 1930-1953. The data were gathered from 1197 youths between the ages of 17 and 37 from ten rural school districts. The purpose of the study was to measure the volume of residential and occupational mobility, and to analyze some of the factors affecting mobility among youth.

The study has demonstrated a method whereby changes in the volume of migration, age at the time of migration, origin and destination, and occupations of migrants may be related to socioeconomic changes taking place in an area undergoing rapid transformation.

250. Pihlblad, C. T., and C. L. Gregory

1957a "Occupation and Patterns of Migration," *Social Forces*, 36:56-64 (October).

A study of 1553 male and 1862 female high school graduates in 116 Missouri small communities, ten years earlier than the study. The following hypothesis was tested: migration is selective of occupation.

"[T]he general conclusion [was drawn] that emigration from the small towns of Missouri has been selective of the professions, students—most of whom are probably embarking on professional careers—and skilled workers. . . . Since . . . a higher order of ability and talent is necessary for entrance into the professions and related white collar occupations than . . . for common labor and farming, the process of occupational selection is largely responsible for the tendency of those with higher intelligence . . . to migrate more frequently, to move longer distances, to be attracted more by the larger than the smaller cities, and to move toward certain regions of the country rather than toward others."

251. Pihlblad, C. T., and C. L. Gregory

1957b "Occupational Mobility in Small Communities in Missouri," *Rural Sociology*, 22:40-49 (March).

Missouri youth who completed their high school in 116 small communities 1939-1941 and whose whereabouts in 1952 were known. The data were gathered from 1504 males and 1495 females. An attempt was made to answer questions about the extent of influence of parental occupations on students' occupational choices.

Study justifies "the conclusions that the open-class system is still the predominant pattern when it comes to the selection of occupations. . . . The most significant shift was away from farming and agricultural pursuits toward the professions, clerical work, and business pursuits. A distinct tendency for subjects to gravitate toward the same occupational level as that of their fathers appeared. . . . Nearly all persons occupied in farming were sons of farmers. Women showed a distinct tendency to marry into occupations at the same level as that of their fathers. Upward mobility, from lower status toward higher status occupations, was more marked than the reverse."

252. Pipping, Knut

1959 "A Community Self-Survey of Rural Depopulation," in *Rural Migration*, Papers presented to the 1st Congress of the European Society for Rural Sociology, Brussels-Louvain, September, 1958 (Bonn: Privately published), pp. 177-79.

Migrants and possible migrants, aged 15-30 years, from Aland Islands to Sweden. The study was based on a probability sample of the total population. Rural depopulation of Aland Islands, including a detailed description of the structure of the moving youth population, was studied. An interim report.

The report dealt with the study design and with any findings.

253. Ploch, L. A.

1957 "Grass is Always Greener," *Maine Agricultural Experiment Station Farm Research*, 5:3-6 (July).

A study of the people of Maine, using data derived from a regional population project. It outlines the major movements of people to and from the state.

Since 1870 "there were more persons who were born in Maine living in other states than there were persons living in Maine who were born in other states. . . . In general, the bulk of the persons migrating into Maine from other states have come from . . . nearby states . . . . In recent years there has been a trend for both in-migrants and out-migrants to travel shorter distances than formerly. An exception is California which continues to be an attractive destination for Maine migrants. A pronounced factor in this shift has been the growing importance of Connecticut as both a source and destination of persons migrating to and from Maine."

254. Pocock, D. C. D.

1960a "Migration of Scottish Labour to Corby New Town," *Scottish Geographical Magazine*, 76: 169-71 (December).

A study of the origin of the Scottish labor force among the steel workers in Corby, a Northamptonshire town which greatly expanded with the coming of Stewarts and Lloyds steel industry.

Corby, with the arrival of the iron and steel works, has grown from a village of 1500 to a new town of 34,000, where some 10,000 are presently employed in steel-making. "Almost the whole labour force has been imported; at first by special transfer, later by wide recruitment campaigns. Most of the initial transfer was from the firm's established plants in Lanarkshire. This, together with the subsequent success of Scottish recruitment drives, has resulted in over half of the present workers being of Scottish origin compared with less than a third from within England." Concerning the pattern of Scottish migration, the period from 1933 to 1944 under the system of direct labor transfer was one of restricted geographical origin, compared with the more widespread postwar pattern which is the result of a general advertising campaign for the whole of Scotland in conjunction with the Ministry of Labour.

255. Pocock, D. C. D.

1960b "Some Features of the Population of Corby New Town," *Sociological Review*, 8:209-21 (December).

Six thousand employees of Stewarts and Lloyds. Census reports and other related information used.
(1) During the prewar and postwar periods immigra-
tion has made a more significant contribution than natural increase to the total population growth. (2) Two-thirds of the total migration to Corby are of non-English origin, with an especially high number from Scotland. (3) The pattern reveals a more restricted distribution during the early period than since the end of the war. (4) The immigration of English workers forms only 30 percent of the total. One-third of the workers has been drawn from the villages and towns within a ten-mile radius. (5) The highly unbalanced employment structure has militated against the growth of a large group of people in the professions. (6) Assimilation has proceeded effectively. (7) Contact is maintained with friends and relations elsewhere in the British Isles and Europe. "After almost 30 years of expansion Corby is still a town with several unusual features, prominent among which is the diversity of its population."

256. Prescott, J. R. V.

1959 "Migrant Labor in the Central African Federation," *Geographical Review*, 49:424-27 (July).

The federal pattern of the labor movements of the Central African Federation (Southern and Northern Rhodesia, and Nyasaland) are examined and the findings compared with the conclusions of two earlier studies.
"The rising volume of labor migration demonstrates the increasing importance of this element in the boom economy of the Central African Federation and provides a strong economic argument in favor of continued federation. Changes in the alien occupation pattern, particularly in Southern Rhodesia, suggest hitherto undetected qualities of versatility and adaptability in the mobile labor force. Finally, the small proportion of migrant labor drawn from territories other than the Federation and Mozambique serves to underline the the economic affinity between these two territories, which is already apparent in communications."

257. Price, Charles A.

1959 "Immigration and Group Settlement," in *The Cultural Integration of Immigrants*, W. D. Borrie and others (Paris, UNESCO), pp. 267-87.

European settlers in Australia, Canada, and the U.S. The study is focused on the relationship between immigration and group settlement (group settlement defined as "something which covers the greater part of members' lives, encourages within itself numerous social, cultural, and primary group relationships and which frequently acts as members' agent for contact with outside persons and organizations").

The origin and growth of group settlements; village, district, regional, and national group settlements; and the consolidation, transformation, and breakdown of group settlements are explained and discussed.

258. Price, Charles A., and Jerry Zubrzycki

1962a "The Use of Inter-Marriage Statistics as an Index of Assimilation," *Population Studies*, 16:58-69 (July).

A study of members of immigrant groups and families who have intermarried, using marriage statistics of intermarriage among immigrant groups. It is also a review of the problems involved in using marriage statistics as a means of assessing the speed with which immigrant, racial, or ethnico-religious groups shed their ethnic identity.

"This paper . . . concludes that though inter-marriage is a reasonable measure of assimilation, the ratios in common use greatly overstate or distort the extent of inter-marriage. The paper then puts forward two much more reliable ratios—one measuring the tendency to inter-marry on the part of those having some opportunity to inter-marry, and the other measuring the actual extent of inter-marriage in the ethnic group as a whole—and suggests that the best assessment comes from using these two in conjunction. Though these ratios are readily obtainable from field and documentary surveys they cannot be derived from official published statistics; the paper therefore puts forward another ratio which is obtainable from official statistics but is more reliable than the ratio in common use."

259. Price, Charles A., and Jerzy Zubrzycki

1962b "Immigrant Marriage Patterns in Australia," *Population Studies*, 16:123-33 (November).

A study of the immigrant population of Australia, 1947-1960, in order to understand the marriage patterns, using marriage statistics of immigrant groups.

"In general it appears that three-quarters of British male immigrants, and two-thirds of females, have married into the older Australian stock; that about one-half of Dutch and Maltese male immigrants (though considerably fewer females) have intermarried but that solid family migration has more than counterbalanced the tendency to disrupt ethnic group solidarity; that eastern European males have been intermarrying with British-Australians and other immigrants, largely because of inability to obtain brides from Iron Curtain countries; that Greeks and Italians, both male and female, have intermarried very little and this, plus large-scale family migration, has greatly strengthened ethnic-group solidarity. With second generation southern Europeans intermarriage has increased amongst males but not amongst females, largely because of the competition for brides caused by a surplus of immigrant bachelors."

260. Price, Daniel O.

1955 "Examination of Two Sources of Error in the Estimation of Net Internal Migration," *Journal of American Statistical Association*, 50:689-700 (September).

A study aimed at examining the errors arising from the use of a single set of survival rates in all 48 states and errors from underenumeration of the population, using U.S. census data.

"It is estimated that about 1/3 of the estimates of net migration are in error by 25% or more due to the effects of underenumeration. . . . We can be fairly certain that the methods most frequently used to estimate net migration give us estimates that are likely to include an appreciable percentage error. For this reason caution must be exercised in interpreting such figures and small relative differences between states and decades should not be taken too seriously."

261. Price, Daniel O.

1959 "A Mathematical Model for Migration Suitable for Simulation on an Electronic Computer," in *International Population Conference Proceedings*, (Vienna, International Union for the Scientific Study of Populaton), pp. 665-73.

The present paper reports progress on the development of a model of internal migration that can eventually simulate internal migration for a country on an electronic computer.

On the assumption that electronic computers are not being efficiently utilized in social science, the author is suggesting that we must learn to simulate social behavior with electronic computers. The first problem is to assign an individual a probability of migrating across a state boundary during a one-year period on the basis of certain selected characteristics of the individual. The paper shows how this can be done, using such characteristics as color, age, sex, marital status, employment status, and how other variables will be added.

Pryor, Albert C., Jr. *See* 63.

Purington, M. S. *See* 41.

R

262. Ramsey, C. E., and W. A. Anderson

1958 *Migration of the New York State Population*, Cornell Agricultural Experiment Station Bulletin 929, 22 pp.

A study of migrants of New York state, based on U.S. censuses, 1870-1940.

A detailed description of the size of migration into and out of New York state is given. There was no relationship between sex and the amount of migration in the urban, rural-nonfarm, or rural-farm populations. Movement from nonfarm to farm residence involved more distances, on the average, than other types of migration. Migrants were younger, and more educated than the nonmigrants in all economic areas. The labor force participation rate was higher for persons who moved than for nonmovers. Professional and technical workers moved to and from economic areas more than skilled workers, but the latter moved more within nonmetropolitan areas. There was some tendency for migrants to have lower median incomes than nonmigrants.

263. Ramsey, C. E., and W. A. Anderson

1959 *Some Problems in the Regional Study of Migration*, Cornell Department of Rural Sociology Bulletin 53, 46 pp.

The people of the northeastern U.S. were studied. The study raised three questions: (1) Is the extent of loss or gain through net migration of single counties sufficient to warrant study separate from that of total population growth? (2) Can net migration be analyzed or predicted on a regional basis? (3) What factors for predicting migration are most fruitful for further analysis?

The study reached affirmative conclusions on the first two questions. The ecological, occupational, and status patterns appear most fruitful for further analysis.

264. Raup, Philip M.

1960-61 "Impact of Population Decline on Rural Communities," *Farm Policy Forum*, 13(2):28-36.

An essay dealing with the relationship between out-migration of farm population and availability of local services in small, rural communities. Secondary data sources used.

"Explanation for small town decline is not necessarily to be found in immutable trends toward fewer and bigger farms and toward business in marketing and retailing functions. A part of the explanation lies in the absence, at the small town level, of services that we recognize at the farm level under the names of supervised credit and agricultural research and extension. . . . Because of migration, some of these communities are surplus to our needs for the services that they have traditionally performed. The extent to which they are 'surplus' will not be accurately appraised until we have explored more thoroughly the steps that could be taken to render them economically viable."

Reissman, Leonard. *See* 175.

265. Richardson, Alan

1957a "The Assimilation of British Immigrants in Australia," *Human Relations*, 10:157-66 (May).

Three groups of 17 each of British immigrants in Australia who had resided there for 11 weeks, for 7 months, and for 12 months respectively, were studied. A control group of 25 native-born Australians was compared to these groups in factors relating to British immigrants' assimilation in Australia, such as satisfaction with life in Australia, identification with Australia, and acculturation to some aspects of the Australian culture. A degree of assimilation scale was employed.

There was no evidence to support the view sometimes held, that when a person goes to another country having the same language and the same primary institutions as the one he left behind, the assimilation process is usually complete in most essentials within the first few months after his arrival. However, certain factors such as age, sex, length of residence, and occupational status are related to the degree of assimilation.

266. Richardson, Alan

1957b "Some Psycho-Social Characteristics of Satisfied and Dissatisfied British Immigrant Skilled Manual Workers in Western Australia," *Human Relations*, 10:235-48 (August).

Thirty-four male, white, married skilled manual workers of British birth who had been living in western Australia between May, 1952, and May, 1953. Out of these, the ten most satisfied and the ten most dissatisfied workers were studied. Perceived Difference Index was used to measure the difference in certain beliefs between British immigrants and native Australians.

Satisfied immigrants tended more often to be found in the building industry. They were fundamentally more "conservative" and significantly more often visited the homes of Australian friends. Their image of Australians was more positive. They believed, significantly more than the dissatisfied ones, that there was equal opportunity for all in Australia. Further, they significantly less often believed that their views and those of other British immigrants differed from Australian views. Also, they showed a greater positive predisposition to change than the dissatisfied immigrants.

267. Richardson, Alan

1959 "Some Psychosocial Aspects of British Emigration to Australia," *British Journal of Sociology*, 10:327-37 (December).

British skilled, manual workers intending to emigrate to Australia under the Assisted Passage Scheme. Eighty intending migrants compared with a carefully matched group of eighty nonmigrants. Five different psychological aspects were investigated. Fifteen personal attitudes were investigated using a modified version of the Sachs Sentence Completion Test.

The typical skilled manual worker emigrating to Australia did not find life in Britain impossible economically or otherwise. He had moved around more and probably had a wider circle of acquaintances than the nonmigrant. Of special importance was the fact that he more often knew of someone who had already emigrated to Australia and corresponded with him. From his contact with people in Australia and other sources, he came to view Australia as relatively more attractive than Britain. He was more likely to come from a family having three or more children, and this might have made it easier to emigrate in terms of economic and social responsibility of parents. His anticipation of his future life in Australia was mixed with some apprehension. Anxiety was inherent in the decision to emigrate, and was likely to result in some perceptual and cognitive distortions which, through preserving a highly favorable image of Australia, functioned to protect him from excessive awareness of this anxiety.

Richardson, Arthur H. *See* 187.

Rivera, Julius. *See* 95.

268. Robins, L. C., and P. O'Neal

1958 "Mortality, Mobility, and Crime: Problem Children Thirty Years Later," *American Sociological Review*, 23:162-71 (April).

Of the 524 persons seen as children at the St. Louis Municipal Psychiatric Clinic between 1924 and 1929, those expatients were studied who thirty years later met the following criteria: age under 18 years at first clinic contact; Caucasian race; IQ not less than 80 (Stanford-Binet); referral because of problem behavior. A control group of 100, randomly selected from the records of the St. Louis Public Schools to match the patient group with respect to sex, race, year of birth, and matching home neighborhoods, was used.

Findings suggest that these disturbed children grew into adults who not only were highly mobile, but contributed a disproportionate share to serious social problems such as violent death by homicide, suicide, and other types of crime. The disproportionate contribution to mental hospital population, to divorce rate, and to breeding of a second generation of disturbed offspring may occur in a relatively circumscribed segment of the population, characterized by a lifelong failure to conform to the social mores. However, many earlier patients are well adjusted as adults.

269. Rohrer, Wayne C., and Robert K. Hirzel

1959 *Population Change in Urbanization in the Northeast,* Maryland Agricultural Experiment Station Miscellaneous Publication 358, 45 pp.

A study of migrants in the Northeast U.S., using published censuses and census analyses. The report deals with the movement of population into, out of, or within the Northeast, and with urbanization and suburbanization that accompanied population change.

"Population growth and change in the Northeast have been closely related to urban-industrial expansion. The region's metropolitan counties account for the bulk of its population and exert an influence beyond their borders to nonmetropolitan places inside and outside the region. . . . The development of suburban areas has come about. . . . Farming, too, has been affected by urban-industrial expansion. Farmers close to the city have more than likely taken on off-farm work while they managed present acreages more intensively than have farmers more removed from metropolitan areas. Rural areas near the cities are the scene of land use competition. . . . Community development efforts in rural areas probably will result in even further urbanization of the population."

270. Romualdi, S.

1955 "Cooperation is Paying Dividends: U.S. and Mexico," *American Federationist* 62:25-27 (November).

American and Mexican laborers. This article deals with the results of the cooperative efforts of the labor movements of the United States and Mexico, particularly with respect to eliminating the problem of migrant labor from Mexico to the U.S.

"The outstanding success of this cooperation . . . has been the almost complete elimination of the 'wetback' problem. . . . " The Joint U.S.-Mexico Trade Union Committee is committed to working toward the elimination of the differentials in wages and working conditions that exist between the two countries.

271. Rooney, J. F.

1961 "Effects of Imported Mexican Farm Labor in a California County," *American Journal of Economics and Sociology,* 20:513-21 (October).

This is a study of the effects of imported Mexican contract labor upon the economy and social structure of one of the leading agricultural counties in the state of California.

"These workers constitute an official part of the farm economy and standardize the wage scale at the rate paid to imported aliens. . . . The resulting low wage forces reliable agricultural workers to seek employment in industry, resulting in further labor shortages and in the importing of more Mexican nationals at the established wage rate. The continuing inflation in the American economy results in an ever-increasing inequity between farms and industries with respect to wages, conditions of work and social protections, so that more workers are motivated to leave agriculture. This causes the native farm force to be composed, to a continually greater extent, of those workers incapable of qualifying for industrial employment. Thus the domestic farm force consists to an increasing extent of alcoholics and vagabonds. The greater difficulty in employing reliable men prompts many farmers to use labor contractors to hire and to manage work crews. These contractors take a percentage of the worker's earnings and transport men daily from skid row . . . the farm labor policy is producing one of the largest and most severe skid rows on the West Coast. . . . "

272. Rose, A. J.

1958 "The Geographical Pattern of European Immigration in Australia," *Geographical Review,* 48: 512-27 (October).

Immigrants of continental Europe and Maltese origin in Australia. Study based on "County of Birth" data in the Australian census of 1954. The study focus was distribution patterns in Australia of immigrants of continental European and Maltese origin, with reference to whom the description "New Australians" is reserved.

The trend between 1947 and 1954 in the distribution of immigrants was toward concentration in the economically stronger southeast. Immigrants show a distinct tendency to settle differentially in certain kinds of environment, of which four are distinguished: state capitals, industrial cities, rural-urban centers, and rural areas. Besides being responsible for more than two-fifths of the population increase in Australia since the war, the net immigration has altered the internal demographic structure by its contribution to the working-age group, particularly on the male side and in primary and secondary industry.

273. Rose, Arnold M.

1958 "Distance of Migration and Socio-Economic Status of Migrants," *American Sociological Review,* 23:420-23 (August).

In-migrants to the Minneapolis area. All 1221 of those who moved to the Minneapolis area from March 15 to July 1, 1955, and who were customers of the Northern States Power Company, were included in the study. All data were furnished by the Northern States Power Company or taken from census data on tracts and suburbs in the Minneapolis area. The following hypothesis was tested: Higher status persons, seeking the better jobs or opportunities, must move a greater distance to find them, on the average, than do persons seeking less desirable opportunities.

"These data indicate that the 'upper class' neighborhoods are being disproportionately filled with persons who have migrated a long distance, while the opposite is true for the 'poorer class' neighborhoods. The exception is for the poorest class of neighborhoods, but most of these contain disproportionate numbers of Negro residents who are being augmented significantly by migrants coming all the way from the South."

274. Rose, Arnold M., and Leon Warshay

1957 "The Adjustment of Migrants to Cities," *Social Forces*, 36:72-76 (October).

Migrants to Minneapolis (and adjoining areas serviced by the Minneapolis Electric Company) who came from outside a 40-mile radius of the city between March 1, 1955, and May 31, 1955. The data were gathered from 217 migrants. The following hypotheses were tested: "(1) Migrants who move from one urban area to another are likely to act more 'efficiently' in solving their adjustment problems than do migrants from rural areas. . . . (2) Migrants with already existing primary group contacts in the new community are more likely to remain isolated from the rest of the community and/or to remain isolated longer, than migrants without such contacts. . . . (3) Migrants without already existing primary group contacts in the new community are more likely to feel disheartened and/or pessimistic about their life accomplishments and life chances than are those with such contacts. . . . (4) Migrants without already existing primary group contacts in the new community are more likely to feel distrust in, or lack sympathy for, other people."

The hypotheses can be regarded as "confirmed, in general. . . . [R]ural-urban background differences of the migrants were less important than the presence in the new community of relatives and friends. . . . The theory used here has been found useful in predicting and accounting for the observed empirical relationships."

275. Rosenthal, Erich

1960 "Acculturation Without Assimilation? The Jewish Community of Chicago, Illinois," *American Journal of Sociology*, 66:275-85 (November).

Jewish population in Chicago was studied by participant observation, census data, and newspaper analysis. The aim of the study was to delineate the movement of Jewish communal life since the late twenties and to determine to what extent cultural, social, and psychological forces had made an impact upon the community.

Migration within the city of Chicago by Jews is a result of the housing market and a desire for voluntary segregation.

276. Ross, H. Laurence

1962 "Reasons for Moves to and From a Central City Area," *Social Forces*, 40:261-63 (March).

Two hundred and fifty residents of a central area in Boston were studied in order to find out the reasons for moves to and from a central city area. Respondents were divided into local movers, centralizers, and distance migrants.

"The reasons for moves to this central city area differ considerably according to the length of the move. Local movers cite features of the house and changes in family status to the relative exclusion of other reasons. . . . On the other hand, among distance migrants in particular, and also among centralizers to a marked extent, the convenience features of the location are predominant. . . . Furthermore, it is noteworthy that none of the groups places a great deal of emphasis on

class reasons, suggested by Whitnay and Grigg. . . . The results suggest that distance and direction of move may be useful as classificatory principles in the further analysis of residential mobility."

277. Roy, P.

1961 "Factors Related to Leaving Farming," *Journal of Farm Economics*, 43:666-74 (August).

Data were gathered from 260 (10 percent sample) of farm households in Stevens County, Washington. Four hypotheses were tested: "(1) There is an inverse relationship between success in farming and aspiration to leave farming, (2) the level of aspiration would be inversely related to age and mobility, (3) the level of aspiration would be directly related to socio-economic status as measured by education, level of living, or family income, and (4) parental and sibling, past and present non-farm occupational associations would tend to be related to the aspiration to leave farming."

Level of aspiration was not related to any of the five measures used for performance on the farm. Inverse associations were found between level of aspiration and age, and level of aspiration and years in farming. Education, family income, and level of living were not related to level of aspiration. No association was found between level of aspiration and the number of nonfarm jobs the operator had worked in, nor the number of additional skills he had from which he felt he could make a living. Results indicate that the aspiration to leave farming for people in chronically low-income counties does not fit the expected economic and sociological patterns. The general hypothesis that nonfarm association would be related to a high aspiration to leave farming was rejected.

278. Rozman, David, and Ruth Sherboure

1959 *Migration in Massachusetts on a State and Local Basis*, Massachusetts Agricultural Experiment Station Bulletin 512, 28 pp.

Migrants in Massachusetts, 1945-1955. Basic data from the 1945 and 1955 state censuses, state vital statistics, and the 1955 U.S. Census of Agriculture. Changes in population caused by migration in Massachusetts during the decade ending in 1955 are analyzed.

"All of the central cities in the state's nine metropolitan areas experienced declines, but the districts outside the central cities in all except one metropolitan area had increases. Only towns classified as urban sustained losses through migratory movements. . . . Selected characteristics of nonmobile persons and migrants in the western, central, and eastern areas of Massachusetts during 1949-50 are presented, utilizing special tabulations of data from the U.S. Census of 1950. Compared with the nonmobile, persons who migrated were younger, had higher education level, and were to a greater extent professional and technical workers."

279. Rubin, Ernest

1958 "Immigration to the U.S. under our Current Laws and Policies 1946-1957," in *Selected Studies of Migration Since World War II*, Proceedings of the 34th Annual Conference of the Milbank Memorial Fund, New York, 1957, Part III, pp. 95-103.

The purpose of this paper was to review briefly the principal legislative developments with regard to immigration since 1946 and to suggest certain revisions of current immigration laws and policies.

"During and since World War II, the immigration laws and policies have tended to a form of labor recruitment for unskilled and skilled persons. . . . Secondly, there is the general inadequacy of the present national origins quota concept, especially so in times of emergency." The basis for permanent admission should not be solely occupational criteria. "A rational immigration policy may accomplish the objectives of the present recruitment provisions more effectively and at the same time more ethically." Suggestions are made for such a rational immigration policy.

280. Rubin, M.

1958 "Localism and Related Values among Negroes in a Southern Rural Community," *Social Forces*, 36:263-67 (March).

A study of 114 Negro heads of households in Houston and surrounding countryside of west Chickasaw County, Mississippi, 1956. The aim of the study was to understand the attitudes of those who had not migrated toward their local situation, as well as toward migration in general. Five indices were used: (1) Locality Satisfaction, (2) Locality Orientation, (3) Institutional Conservatism, (4) Projection of Local Opportunities, and (5) Success Themes.

The findings revealed a folk society influx. Migration was draining off young persons who sought work and the products that high wages in urban industry would buy. The older generation that once preferred country living to city living, had changed their point of view in favor of northern industrial cities. The study confirmed that migration was directed specifically to industrial cities where close relatives already lived and worked.

281. Rubin, Morton

1960 "Migration Patterns of Negroes from a Rural Northeastern Mississippi Community", *Social Forces*, 39:59-66 (October).

A study of Negroes from Houston, Mississippi, and its surrounding countryside in western Chickasaw County, Mississippi. The data were gathered from 114 heads of households. The study was focused on migration patterns of Negroes from rural northeastern Mississippi.

The study revealed a heavy out-migration that had been accelerated since World War II. Migration destinations had changed over the years. Rural Negro out-migration was directed to communities where better economic opportunities were available, but not including southern cities. Farm owners had had the least personal experience in migration and urban living, yet they had provided a proportionately large number of kin migrants.

282. Ruttan, V. W.

1955 "Industrial Progress and Rural Stagnation in the New South," *Social Forces*, 34:114-18 (December).

A general discussion of the economical conditions in the southern U.S., emphasizing the relationships between farm employment, farm income, migration, and industrialization. Existing information utilized.

"The experience of the 1939-49 decade indicates rather clearly that the extensive declines in farm employment that did occur have not had an adverse effect on the farm output of the region. . . . Low farm incomes are agriculture. . . . Those areas of the Southeast in which farm people have made the greatest economic gains have generally been located in close proximity to developing urban centers. . . . The level of welfare achieved by rural farm people, both in the Southeast and the nation, bears a direct and positive relationship to the extent of urban-industrial development in the same general areas." Most of the existing agricultural education and conservation programs must be continued, and vocational training of farm youth must emphasize skills that will be useful outside agriculture.

283. Ruttan, V. W.

1959 "Farm and Nonfarm Employment Opportunities for Low Income Farm Families," *Phylon Quarterly*, 20:248-55 (Fall).

An essay on the future of agricultural labor opportunities. The author makes predictions on future migration trends.

"(1) Employment opportunities in Southeastern agriculture will be extremely limited during the next decade for those individuals who are unwilling to accept extremely low levels of incomes. (2) Expanding urban employment within the region will offer substantial non-farm opportunities to migrants from Southeastern farms. But white migrants will have a comparative advantage as far as higher paying industrial jobs in the Southeast are concerned. (3) Assuming continued expansion of the national economy, employment opportunities for southern migrants to the Northeast and Midwest will continue to expand."

Ruttan, V. W. *See* 103.

S

Sargent, Frederic O. *See* 219 and 220.

284. Sariola, Sakari

1960 "A Colonization Experiment in Bolivia," *Rural Sociology*, 25:76-90 (March).

Bolivian peasants from ten villages in the Cochabamba Valley. Data were gathered from 33 prospective colonizers (experimental group) and 41 valley peasants (control group). It is a study of the impact of the initial motives of Cochabamba Valley peasants to move and the impact of the peasant's colonizing experiences upon the success of a colony.

The findings could be summarized as follows: "(1) The colonizers experienced a drastic change in environment and were confronted with experiences which were new and unanticipated. . . . (2) The colonizers' value-attitudes were not sufficiently compatible with the long-term planning and deferred need-gratification implied by colonization. . . . (3) The social distance be-

tween the Indian and Mestizo Colonizers and the officials of European extraction in charge of the colony
resulted in inhibitions on the part of the former from
coming forward to describe their problems or ask for
guidance. ... (4) Sex-graded differences in value-attitudes ... made it difficult to inititate a migratory
movement which whole families would join. ... (5)
The colony structure itself determined that some colonizers gained status and others remained in low-status
positions. ... (6) Social relationships between the colony
and its neighboring villages might later on gain in
importance in determining the success of the colony.
Ethnic differences and prejudices between the colonizers
and the native population were already evident on both
sides, impeding assimilation and intergroup marriages.
... (7) There was insufficient co-ordination between
national agencies providing the services needed in the
colonization effort, and the individual agencies failed
to attend to the colony's needs."

285. Saville, John

1959 "Rural Migration in England and Wales," in
Rural Migration, Papers presented to 1st Congress of the European Society for Rural Sociology, September, Brussels-Louvain, 1958 (Bonn,
privately published), pp. 58-63.

An essay on the general characteristics and the main
sequences of rural-urban migration in England and Wales.
Existing information was utilized.

"In the last half century the traditional 19th pattern
of internal migration has continued, though in greatly
diminishing volumes because of the shrinkage of the
rural sector; and a new more powerful pattern has
emerged of movement from one urban area to another.
... The major factor involved in the rural exodus
has been the steady decline of work and employment
in the rural community and the parallel centralisation
of employment opportunities in the towns. ... The main
consequences of the rural exodus have been (i) the ab-
solute population decline in rural areas ... , (ii) the
devitalisation of much of rural social life, (iii) an un-
balance of age and sex structure in the rural areas
compared with the national population."

286. Savitz, Leonard David

1960a "Delinquency and Migration," unpublished
doctoral dissertation, University of Pennsylvania, 178 pp.

A study of the boys attending Philadelphia public
school system in 1957 who resided in one of the four
highest delinquency areas in the city, and who were
born between 1939 and 1945. The present study reports
primarily on the 890 Negroes in the population. The
objective of the study was to examine whether a causative link between migration and delinquency existed.

"The Philadelphia-born population engaged in delinquency to a greater extent than did a migrant cohort
of the same age exposed to a similar 'risk' of delinquency. ... They committed their first delinquency at
an earlier average age and had longer delinquency careers. Finally, if one measures the 'delinquency potential' of any neighborhood by the probability of an
individual acquiring a delinquency record if he resides

in the area for the full 11 years of delinquency exposure (from ages 7 through 18), ... 63% of the Philadelphia-born and 50% of the migrants who were in
Philadelphia by the time they were 7 ultimately became delinquent."

287. Savitz, Leonard David

1960b "Delinquency and Migration," Philadelphia
Commission on Human Relations, 19 pp.

Based on the author's dissertation. (*See* 286)

288. Schaller, L. E.

1961 "Vocational Migration—From Agriculture to
Public Service," *Public Management,* 43:53-58
(March).

The main thesis of the essay is that local government has overtaken agriculture as a source of full-time
employment for the citizens of the U.S., in spite of
the general historical orientation of the society to be
proagriculture and antigovernment. Measures of this
change, gaps in the existing statistics, and implications
of this shift from agriculture to governmental services
are discussed.

Under the last item, the author discusses implications for political process, for personnel, for college
training, for research, for investment, for federal ex-
penditures, and for federal-urban relations.

289. Schmid, Calvin F., Vincent A. Miller, and Baha Abu-
laban

1959 "Impact of Recent Negro Migration on Seattle
Schools," *International Population Conference
Proceedings* (Vienna, International Union for
the Scientific Study of Population), pp. 674-84.

All principals and an average of two teachers from each
of the schools in the central area of Seattle, Washington
were interviewed. The study was aimed at assessing
the impact of Negro migration on Seattle schools.

"It was not until after the outbreak of World War II
that the Negro population of Seattle showed any considerable growth. ... In view of the heavy influx of
Negroes to the city of Seattle in recent years ... [and
their] [pronounced segregation], ... the locus of most of
the problems is to be found in the central area. ... The
most frequently mentioned problems were related to
discipline and behavior, and to the unconcern of a large
proportion of the pupils for school work."

290. Schmitt, Robert C.

1957 "Areal Mobility and Mental Health on Oahu,"
Sociology and Social Research, 42:115-18 (November-December).

A study of the Honolulu Standard Metropolitan Area,
using U.S. census data. The relationship between mental
disorders and areal mobility was investigated.

"The correlations found between mobility and mental
health seem quite low. Areas with populations of high
long-term mobility or low short-term mobility tended
to have high mental hospital admissions rates, but
neither relationship was free from numerous exceptions.

The two measures of mobility in combination left as much as five-sixths of the variation in hospitalization rates unexplained."

291. Schnittker, J. A., and G. P. Owens

1959 *Farm-to-City Migration: Perspective and Problems*, Kansas Agricultural Experiment Station, Agricultural Economics Reports 84, 32 pp.

A study of farmers (non-professional, non-supervisory male workers) who had moved to industrial jobs. Interviews were taken from 46 respondents who had been employed for fewer than five years and who listed farm operation among their last three previous jobs. "The small study reported here was undertaken with the deliberate intention of reviewing many of the changes occurring in the relationship of the farm sector of the economy to the nonfarm sector."

One half of the excess labor supply on the farms in Kansas was employed off the farm in 1954. A small group of men who had moved from farms to industrial jobs in the past five years showed considerable adaptability to new jobs, and had improved their incomes, but they still preferred farm life. Managers of employment offices and of manufacturing firms in Kansas indicated ready acceptance and, in some instances, a small preference for workers with farm backgrounds for certain types of jobs.

292. Schnore, Leo Francis, Jr.

1955 "Patterns of Decentralization: A Study of Differential Growth in the Metropolitan Areas of the U.S., 1900-1950," unpublished doctoral dissertation, University of Michigan, 438 pp.

Standard metropolitan areas of U.S. One hundred and sixty-eight SMA's identified by the Census Bureau in 1950 were projected backward to 1900. "This study attempts to identify some structural characteristics of communities associated with population decentralization within metropolitan areas."

"Within metropolitan areas, it was found that higher growth rates shifted from the central city to the ring, from urban to rural ring areas, and from incorporated to unincorporated rural ring areas. But decentralization occurred in two distinct stages. At first, urban places in the ring grew faster than the central city, while both parts of the rural ring grew more slowly than the center. Later, overall decentralization was accelerated by rural-ring growth in excess of urban-ring growth while urban places in the ring continued to grow faster than the central city. . . . Both the timing and the extent of decentralization were found to be related to population *size*. . . . Decentralization was also found to be related to the *density* of population within the central city, *geographic features* of the central city site, and average family *income* in the metropolitan area although the control of size and regional location reduced the originally observed associations. . . . [D]ifferences between the central city and the ring in *rent level* and in the *proportion of professionals* in the employed labor force showed clear associations with past centrifugal growth that remained in all their details within size classes and regional groupings."

293. Schnore, Leo Francis, Jr.

1958 "Components of Population Change in Large Metropolitan Suburbs," *American Sociological Review*, 23:570-73 (October).

Residents of suburbs of New York, Chicago, Los Angeles, Philadelphia, and Detroit. U.S. census reports used as the data source. It was hypothesized that "areas exhibiting broad functional similarities tend to experience analogous patterns of population change."

"The *overall* pattern revealed in the combined data for all five areas are in clear accord with the substantive hypotheses that gave rise to the study. More detailed analysis within individual metropolitan areas, however, revealed significant exceptions to these overall patterns. . . . In areas growing rapidly by immigration (for example, Los Angeles) patterns of suburban growth were substantially different from those observed in areas experiencing relatively limited inmigration (for example, the older metropolitan areas of the east coast). . . . The research design employed here now appears to have been particularly deficient in failing systematically to explore the implications of overall growth for the growth of such constituent parts as suburbs. . . . [T]he metropolitan area is an integrated functional entity, no part of which may be understood without reference to the whole."

294. Schorr, A. L.

1956 "Mobile Family Living," *Social Casework*, 37: 175-180 (April).

One hundred twenty-two mobile families receiving casework service through the United Community Defense Services were studied to determine the special needs, special problems, and special adjustments of mobile families.

"In twenty-two months of casework service in an 'atomic area,' cohesiveness and resilience were observed among mobile families. . . . Three hypotheses are presented as partial explanation of this strength: (1) that mobile families feel a strong sense of group unity; (2) that families able to move and still to continue to be healthy and well adjusted have learned to 'settle in' in each place they live; and (3) that escape or independence is an adequate device in meeting the needs of some families."

295. Scruggs, O. M.

1961 "The United States, Mexico, and the Wetbacks, 1942-47," *Pacific Historical Review*, 30:149-64 (May).

This article is a factual account of the events and problems confronting the United States in its relations with Mexico which stemmed from the influx of "wetbacks" in 1942-1947.

"The workers came principally because American farm wages, low as they were, were two and three times higher than wages in underdeveloped Mexico." In 1942 the U.S. and Mexico passed an agreement to establish a program "based on contracts providing for the temporary employment in the United States of *braceros*, contract Mexican laborers, and guaranteeing them a minimum wage and satisfactory living and working conditions." The program was not successful, for its requirements fostered rather than discouraged illegal entry.

296. Senior, Clarence

1955 "Puerto Rico: Migration to the Mainland," *Monthly Labor Review*, 78:1354-58 (December).

Puerto Rican migrants to the U.S.A. were studied in order to understand the relationship of this migration to the American labor market, differences between farm labor migrants and city migrants, dispersion of the migrants, and the Commonwealth of Puerto Rico's migration program.

Migration from Puerto Rico is extremely sensitive to business conditions. "Two streams of migration flow from the island; they differ significantly in origin, destination, and length of stay. One flows out in the spring and back in the fall; the other flows out and remains permanently. One is fairly highly organized; the other spontaneous. The first consists of farm-workers; the second of city people." Though the Commonwealth neither encourages nor discourages migration, it attempts to aid those who decide to move.

297. Sharp, Emmit F., and Olaf F. Larson

1960 *Migratory Farm Workers in the Atlantic Coast Stream. II. Education of New York Workers and their Children, 1953 and 1957*, Cornell University Agricultural Experiment Station Bulletin 949, 20 pp.

The focus of the present study is "(1) To provide information regarding educational progress and attainment of migrant children within those age groups in which education is normally still in progress, and (2) to provide information on the educational attainments of the adult migrants and the factors relating to or influencing this attainment." (See the sample description in item 179.)

"[T]he general pattern of school attendance and achievement is much like that of American society as a whole, except at a lower level. . . . The problem of providing adequate schooling for migrant children is clearly an inter-community and inter-state problem. . . . The summer schools for migrant children conducted in two localities in New York on an experimental basis in 1956 and 1957 offer one approach to [solving this problem]. The limited formal education of many adult migrants, especially the older ones, suggests the difficulty encountered by employers and agencies who work with migrants in using written media of communication. Heavy reliance must be placed on face-to-face communication and on the use of key individuals in migrant crews and camps."

Sharp, Emmit F. *See* 179.

298. Sharp, Harry P.

1955 "Migration and Voting Behavior in a Metropolitan Community," *Public Opinion Quarterly*, 19:206-209 (Summer).

A sample of adults in Detroit, Michigan. The aim of the study was to discover differences in the pattern of voting, if any, between migrants and non-migrants. "Voting appears to indicate a level of involvement in and adjustment to the community which is much more closely associated with length of residence in the new area than with the place and type of previous residence," socioeconomic status, and demographic characteristics.

299. Sharp, Paul F.

1955 "Three Frontiers: Some Comparative Studies of Canadian, American and Australian Settlement," *Pacific Historical Review*, 24:369-77 (November).

Settlers in America, Canada, and Australia. The purpose of the study was to suggest some of the usefulness of comparative studies of settlement of regions outside the U.S. and to examine several such comparisons in Australian and Canadian history.

"At least three conditions seem essential for close and profitable comparative analysis. Settlement must occur during the same historical period. The cultural heritage of the pioneers must possess basic similarities and a corresponding technology. Finally, the physical environment must possess a general likeness."

Sherburne, Ruth. *See* 278.

300. Shryock, Henry S., Jr.

1956a "Population Redistribution Within Metropolitan Areas: Evaluation of Research," *Social Forces*, 35:154-59 (December).

This paper is a brief evaluation of some of the research on redistribution of population within metropolitan areas that has been carried out by social scientists working in universities. It deals primarily with research using census data for the United States.

There is no rigid dichotomy of producers and consumers in this field. Although the Census Bureau has usually waited for outside expressions of urgent need for a new or modified statistical area, it has occasionally been the innovator in an areal concept. There must be a greater measure of cooperation between the Census Bureau and research workers in universities, foundations, and other agencies in order to improve the quality of the data through better operational definitions. Brief comments are made on the research frame, concepts used, specific tools developed, completeness of analysis of the redistribution process, and some of the misuses or misinterpretations of the census data.

301. Shryock, Henry S., Jr.

1956b "Redistribution of Population: 1940 to 1950," in *Demographic Analysis: Selected Readings*, ed. Joseph J. Spengler and Otis Dudley Duncan (Glencoe, Ill., The Free Press), pp. 386-405.

A consideration of the not so spectacular, but significant, movement of people within the U.S. during the 1940-1950 decade. Publications of the Bureau of Census utilized as data sources.

Topics discussed are: "Inequalities of Population Change"; "The Roles of Natural Increase and Migration"; "Gross Migration"; "Differentials in Population Redistribution"; and "The 1950 Program of Migration Statistics."

302. Shryock, Henry S., Jr.

1959 "The Efficiency of Internal Migration in the United States," *International Population Conference Proceedings* (Vienna, International Union for the Scientific Study of Population), pp. 685-94.

The efficiency of internal migration, defined as "The percentage that net migration for an area forms of the sum of its in-migration and out-migration," in the U.S. is discussed on the basis of information derived from the census.

"Several ways of summarizing the efficiency of internal migration over a set of areas are considered. On the basis of these measures, it appears that internal migration within the United States has been less efficient in the postwar period than during World War II or during the late 1930's (a period of economic depression). This decrease may represent part of a longtime trend. . . . [T]he efficiency of migration may be . . . considerably higher for most subgroups than for the population as a whole." The efficiency of internal migration varies with race, education, and occupation; the relationship to age is complex, and to sex, lacking.

303. Shuval, Judith T.

1959 "The Role of Ideology as a Predisposing Frame of Reference for Immigrants," *Human Relations*, 12:51-63 (February).

Two thousand immigrants in temporary transit camps during their first year in Israel, 1949-1950. Male respondents only. Three hypotheses were tested: (1) With a given exposure, Zionist immigrants will absorb more information about Israel, about its customs and way of life, than non-Zionist immigrants. (2) Immigrants with a Zionist frame of reference will make constructive use of information acquired in helping themselves to formulate decisive plans concerning their future. (3) For non-Zionist immigrants, such information will not be functional and will induce increased ambiguity rather than decisiveness of plans. Guttman-type scales were constructed for three variables: Zionism, information about Israel, and plans for settlement.

Within the limits of the data, all three hypotheses were supported.

304. Siegel, A. I.

1957 "The Social Adjustments of Puerto Ricans in Philadelphia," *Journal of Social Psychology*, 46:99-110 (August).

A study of Puerto Rican residents of Philadelphia on the basis of the information obtained from 102 interviews from Puerto Ricans and 102 interviews from native American neighbors. The study emphases were: (1) the number and rate of increase of Puerto Rican population; (2) its major demographic features such as age, health, ratio of males to females, marital status, nativity, and mobility; (3) social adjustments these migrants were making. Bogardus Social Distance Scale was used.

The migrant population was weak in English and was aware of it. They were more like their Protestant neighbors than like the Roman Catholics in the emphasis on religion in daily life. They looked upon the Philadelphia milieu as being somewhat unfriendly. The migrants' commonest way of communication among themselves was conversation. They had some knowledge of the laws and were apprehensive of the police. Their main problems were primarily economic, followed by problems in the area of housing and health facilities. Their vocational aspiration was high as indexed by their desire for steady employment and white collar and professional jobs for their children.

Simmons, Ozzie G. *See* 99.

305. Sizer, Leonard M.

1957 *Population Changes in West Virginia, 1900-1950*, West Virginia Agricultural Experiment Station Bulletin 401, 8 pp.

A study of distribution of the people of West Virginia. The data were derived from the U.S. census reports.

The factors which may be used to explain West Virginia's population decline are: (1) a continuing decline in the number of persons engaged in agriculture; (2) the decline in the number of persons employed in mining; (3) the continuing suburban developments which cross country and state boundaries; and (4) the beginning of or continuing industrial developments.

306. Skinner, G. William

1959 "Overseas Chinese in Southeast Asia," *Annals of the American Academy of Political and Social Science*, 321:136-47 (January).

A descriptive account of overseas Chinese issues in five major Southeast Asian countries (Thailand, Philippines, South Vietnam, Indonesia, Malaya) as follows: (1) the economic role of overseas Chinese who dominate or control major segments of the nonagricultural economy throughout Southeast Asia; (2) the education of the local-born Chinese children; (3) determination of citizenship and problems of dual nationality arising from China's citizenship claims over all persons of Chinese descent; and (4) the political integration of overseas Chinese into the new national states of Southeast Asia.

Approximately 10 million overseas Chinese reside in Southeast Asia where they have economic power and political significance out of all proportion to their numbers. The Southeast Asian governments are determined to loosen the Chinese grip on their national economies, to achieve an unequivocal clarification of citizenship status of resident Chinese, to end foreign political activity among, and to proceed with educational and political integration of their citizens of Chinese descent.

307. Skrabanek, Robert L.

1955 *Characteristics and Changes in the Texas Farm Population*, Texas Agricultural Experiment Station Bulletin 825, 15 pp.

Texas farm population. Most data derived from U.S. census reports. The bulletin concerns itself mainly with farm population trends and an explanation of why these trends occurred.

"Farm population trends in Texas generally have been in the same direction as in the nation and the West South Central division. . . ." Before 1937, the speed of decline was less rapid and after 1945, more rapid than the nation's. "Age differentials are largely the result of variations in the rates of migration into or out of the different classes of residential areas, with youth being the most important group. In Texas, 70% of the youngsters living on farms in 1940 between the ages of 10 to 15 were no longer farm residents in 1950."

308. Skrabanek, Robert L.

1956 *Agriculture's Human Resources in Cherokee County,* Texas Agricultural Experiment Station Progress Report 1888, 6 pp.

This report outlines some of the significant features of agriculture's human resources in Cherokee County, Texas. It is part of an overall study to determine the adjustments needed for improving the economic conditions among farm people in east Texas.

Cherokee County's farm population is characterized by declining numbers, especially of youth, low education, large percentage of Negroes, and increasing, but still low levels of living.

309. Skrabanek, Robert L., and Gladys K. Bowles

1957 *Migration of the Texas Farm Population,* Texas Agricultural Experiment Station Bulletin 847, 8 pp.

Texas farm population. Data from U.S. census reports and reports of the Agricultural Marketing Service. The study focuses on migration as it affects the farm population of Texas.

A decided drop in the number of people leaving farms has occurred since 1954. Between 1940 and 1950 the net loss through migration was greater than for the two previous decades combined. In this period, rates of net out-migration were higher among youth, nonwhites, females, and residents of certain economic areas.

310. Smith, Eldon D.

1956 "Non-Farm Employment Information for Rural People," *Journal of Farm Economics,* 38:813-27 (August).

A study of 157 migrants in Indianapolis. The investigation was aimed at discovering possibilities of creating better opportunities for rural people to obtain a higher level of living through farm and nonfarm work. The following hypothesis was tested: "Information is a limitational factor in migration."

The following conclusions were drawn: When considerable distances are involved in rural-urban migration, special problems are created that are not ordinarily dealt with by conventional employment media. Evidence indicated that lack of specific information about pay and social requirements resulted in doubts and fears that may contribute to immobility. Information supplied to areas with large numbers of underemployed Negroes is likely to result in substantially more migration than if supplied to either Northern agriculture areas, or areas of predominantly white population in the South.

311. Smith, Louis P. F.

1959 "Studies in a Declining Population," in *Rural Migration,* Papers presented to the 1st Congress

of the European Society for Rural Sociology, September, Brussels-Louvain, (Bonn, privately published), pp. 69-76.

A study of Irish migrants. Census data used. The emphasis of the study was the effects of migration and extreme rural population decline in Ireland.

Some important effects of Ireland's declining rural population are: "A reduction in the number of farms leading to fragmentation of holdings and lateness of succession. Lateness and uncertainty of succession leading to marriage at a late age and a migration of women. Disparity in age between man and wife which, combined with normal higher age expectancy of women, gives a higher proportion of farms held by widows. This means untrained, conservative management and an average age of succession to control by the son of 45 years. ... In the high emigration area there is a psychological state of inertia caused by the easy escape of those who are discontented. This may be seen for example in the small membership of the National Farmers' Association where average ages of farmers are high. There is a resource drain in the cost of rearing, educating and dowering those who have left farming. This 'investment' is as great as that applied to modernizing agriculture. There is also an unusually high dependency burden due to investment of the past in roads, schools and other facilities which are now redundant and expensive to maintain."

312. Smith, Raymond T.

1959 "Some Social Characteristics of Indian Immigrants to British Guiana," *Population Studies,* 13:34-39 (July).

Indian immigrants to British Guiana. Information was extracted from the archives of the Immigration Agent General's Office—embarkation records pertaining to 9393 indentured immigrants arriving in the colony between 1865 and 1917. The purpose of this paper was to supplement the existing accounts of Indian emigration.

"[T]he sample study material presented here reflects the origins of the whole Indian population of British Guiana. The characteristics of the immigrants to British Guiana correspond closely to those of the immigrants to Fiji. ... This correspondence ... is of particular interest for the comparative study of their present-day culture and social structure, since it provides a firm base line to which divergent developments can be referred. ... [T]here has been a great deal of change in the beliefs and practices of the Hindus. Caste has come to be of minor significance and its vast original complexity has disappeared in favour of a set of simple concepts focussing on the high ritual status of Brahmins."

313. Smith, T. Lynn

1959 "Migration from One Latin American Country to Another," *International Population Conference Proceedings* (Vienna, International Union for the Scientific Study of Populations), pp. 695-702.

A study of migrants in 20 Latin American countries. The data were derived from censuses and vital statistics reports sought out in the countries. The focus of the study was migrations of population from one Latin American country to another.

"[T]he principal migratory currents between the various countries ... are as follows: (1) A large migration of Haitians to the easternmost portions of Cuba; (2) a heavy flow of persons born and reared in El Salvador across the border and well across the Republic of Honduras; (3) the push of Nicaraguans into the low-lying areas along both coasts in Costa Rica; (4) a constant flow of population northward from Ecuador into Colombia and a recent flood of refugees from Colombia into the Pacific coastal plain in Ecuador; (5) a large migration of people from the mostly rural sections of the Andean highlands in southern Peru to LaPaz, the capital of neighboring Bolivia; (6) a strong out-migration of agricultural workers from southern Bolivia to the sugar cane and other plantations in northern Argentina; (7) a heavy and long-sustained migration of people from Paraguay to Buenos Aires, the metropolis of the southern portion of South America; and (8) the movement in large numbers of Paraguayans to southwestern Brazil."

314. Solien, N. L.

1961 "Family Organization in Five Types of Migratory Wage Labor," *American Anthropologist*, 63:1264-80 (December).

An exploratory attempt to classify various types of migratory wage labor and to suggest some of the probable effects of each type of migration on family organization. The nature of the period of absence from the home village is the basis for classification. The categories discussed are: (1) seasonal migration; (2) temporary, nonseasonal migration; (3) recurrent migration; (4) continuous migration; and (5) permanent removal.

There are several essentially different patterns of behavior which are usually lumped together in discussions of migracy and the family. The main conclusion was that migrancy would be reflected in the social organization in different ways depending upon the nature of the sociocultural system affected, as well as upon the type of migrancy itself. Some types of migrant labor appeared to have little effect on the family, regardless of what the traditional family form might have been. Other types of migrancy seemed to be more compatible with some forms of family and household organization than with others.

315. Solomon, Darwin Dale

1957 "Value Factors in Migration: Rural Residence Values Associated with Rural to Urban Migration," unpublished doctoral dissertation, Cornell University, 281 pp.

Open-country (56) and urban (56) residents of Broome County, N. Y. The theoretical proposition was that situational factors being equal, measurable value concepts which people have regarding the relative desirability of particular aspects of the rural versus urban enviroments (residence values) are important factors in the selectivity of migration. The specific hypothesis tested was that, other things being equal, the married sons and daughters of native-born, open-country residents of Broome County, N.Y., who were living in the open country at least four years previous to 18 years of age and are now between 19 and 50 years of age, will differ in their evaluation of specific aspects of rural versus urban conditions of living by rural and urban residence. Anderson's Values of Rural Living Scale and a Values Ranking Scale after Woodruff and Reeder were used.

It was concluded that the evidence supported the major hypothesis, even though the *ex post facto* design made acceptance somewhat tentative.

316. Sovain, N. V.

1959 "Potential Out-Migrants and Removable Surplus Population in Three Districts of Orissa (India)," *International Population Conference Proceedings* (Vienna, International Union for the Scientific Study of Population), pp. 703-709.

Potential out-migrants in rural households in three districts of Orissa, India: 10,091 households in Sambalpur, 23,090 households in Cuttack, and 10,493 households in the Puri sample. It is a study of earners in families who were willing to migrate out of the village for a part (temporarily) or whole of the year (permanently) without affecting the household occupation in which they were engaged, or current production.

Of the households only one percent reported potential seasonal out-migrants but about nine percent reported potential permanent out-migrants. The proportion of households reporting potential *permanent* out-migrants was relatively large in households with little or no land engaged in agricultural labor. The data qualify to a certain extent the theory of rapid urbanization.

317. Spengler, Joseph J.

1956 "Some Economic Aspects of Immigration into the U.S.," in *Demographic Analysis: Selected Readings*, ed. Joseph J. Spengler and Otis Dudley Ducan (Glencoe, Ill., The Free Press), pp. 277-96.

This paper deals with the economic aspects of American immigration—among them, the capacity of the American economy to absorb immigrants and the probable response of the American economy to variations in the size of immigration.

The first four parts are analysis. In Part V, conclusions for policy based upon the preceding historical and analytical sections are indicated, including the permissible size of immigration without upsetting the economic conditions seriously.

318. Spengler, Joseph J.

1958a "The Commonwealth Demographic Dimensions: Implications," in *Commonwealth Perspectives*, by Nicholas Mansergh and others (Durham, N.C., Duke University Press), pp. 86-124.

The present essay presents a demographic picture of the British Commonwealth, points out some implications of this picture, and indicates whether the demographic forces presently operative in the Commonwealth are essentially centrifugal or centripetal, assuming that demographic ties and associated economic interdependence reinforce various sources of subjective solidarity.

There are not enough Englishmen to migrate to the Commonwealth countries, thereby forming nuclei of pro-Commonwealth sentiment. Such "sentiments must rest on other grounds. Among these grounds is the capacity of the Commonwealth, and above all, the United Kingdom, to supply capital, technical assistance, and opportunities for profitable trade. Insofar as the United Kingdom is concerned, however, this capacity is not likely to be great enough or to grow rapidly enough. . . . It is quite possible, therefore, that the participation of India, [Ceylon], and Pakistan in the Commonwealth will diminish . . . . Malaya is more likely, on economic and politico-military grounds, to continue its adherence. For South Africa, [and the Federation of Rhodesia and Nyasaland] there is no practical alternative to adherence . . . . A similar, but less overpowering, argument might be made for the continued adherence of Ghana and Nigeria; but [they do not accept it yet]. . . . [T]he Caribbean Federation . . . must either participate in the Commonwealth or pass under American protection."

319. Spengler, Joseph J.

1958b "The Economic Effects of Migration," in *Selected Studies of Migration Since World War II*, Proceedings of the 34th Annual Conference of the Milbank Memorial Fund, New York, 1957, Part III pp. 172-92.

An essay in international migration and economic theory of migration. The nature of particular effects of migration are identified, isolated, and assessed.

In discussing migration as part of the longer-run economic growth process, the following observations are made: "Even if migration is set in motion by essentially non-economic changes, it produces economic effects and thus makes the extent and the course of economic growth, if not the actual sequency of economic events, different than they otherwise would have been. Migration is thus related (to phrase it loosely) 'causally' and 'effectually' to a number of the elements that enter into the process of economic growth, its course is subject to fluctuation even as is that of economic growth, particularly when, as in the 19th century, migration is subject to few constraints or stimuli of governmental origin. For, except in periods when men seek to escape persecution for their religious or political beliefs, migration is primarily a form of behaviour designed to improve the economic and/or the social situation of the migrant and his family."

320. Spiegelglas, Stephan

1961 "Role of Industrial Development as a Factor Influencing Migration to and From Wisconsin Counties, 1940-50," *Journal of Farm Economics*, 43:128-37 (February).

A study of the migration pattern in the state of Wisconsin. The data were derived from publications of the *U.S. Census of Population*. The following hypothesis was tested: "Migration changes in the 71 Wisconsin counties were essentially contingent upon changes in industrial employment in those counties."

The hypothesis was supported by the analysis of the data.

321. Stanislawski, D.

1957 "Migration and Environment," *Association of American Geographers Annals*, 47:179 (June).

A study of migration in Iberia. The purpose of the study was to understand the effects of migration upon Iberian life.

None of the early migrations of various groups failed to make its impact upon Iberian life.

322. Stanton, W. J.

1955 "Purpose and Source of Seasonal Migration to Alaska," *Economic Geography*, 31:138-48 (April).

The paper reports on a questionnaire survey of 44 percent of all southbound passengers who departed from Alaska between June 1 and September 30, 1952. The paper discusses some of the economic and geographical patterns of migration to Alaska that emerged from the study.

During this period 38.9 percent went to Alaska for vacation only; 28.6 percent for business only; 11 percent for business-vacation; 9.4 percent to visit family; 8.3 percent for military; 3.1 percent government; and .7 percent other. Significant correlation existed between (1) the number of visitors a region sent to Alaska and (2) the combination of (a) the population total of the region and (b) the distance it is from Alaska.

323. Stewart, Charles T., Jr.

1960 "Migration as a Function of Population and Distance," *American Sociological Review*, 25: 347-56 (June).

"[T]he allometric growth hypothesis is checked against both migration models and historical data. This hypothesis regards the growth rate of (urban) population as an increasing function of its rank in the system of cities."

"Limited empirical data do not support the hypothesis that migration is proportional to the population of the city of destination, nor that it is inversely proportional to the distance of migration . . . But the historical development of city-size distributions does not support the hypothesis of allometric growth except during a major structural shift from agriculture to industry . . . and possibly from subsistence to commercial agriculture. . . . A study of the historical development of many city hierarchies is needed both as a rough measure of migration rate differential by size of city and of growth-rate differentials of cities by size or by rank."

324. Straus, Murray A., and Barnard D. Parrish

1956 *The Columbia Basin Settler: A Study of Social and Economic Resources in New Land Settlement*, Washington Agricultural Experiment Station Bulletin 566, 51 pp.

A study of a sample of 210 farmers in the Columbia Basin Project in the state of Washington in 1954. "This report is the first of a series which will analyze different aspects of the settlement of the Columbia Basin Project. In this report, data on the social and economic resources which farmers in the Basin have had available to undertake the task of transforming desert land into farms and homes are presented. . . ."

"The settlement of Columbia Basin Project through 1954 has taken place under relatively favorable economic and technological conditions. . . . [The settlers] have made considerable financial progress, as indicated by the income figures and growth in net worth. . . . The restrictions on settlement opportunities growing out of the relatively large sums required to develop a Columbia Basin farm, the development of a pattern of multiple unit operations, and the widespread occurrence of absentee ownership and rental arrangement run contrary to the philosophy on which the Project was based. Overall, however, the findings of this study point to the conclusion that the expenditure of public funds for this and similar projects is providing many families with the opportunity to achieve some of the social and economic values which the American people have traditionally considered important."

325. Stub, Halger R.

1962 "The Occupational Characteristics of Migrants to Duluth: A Retest of Rose's Hypothesis," *American Sociological Review*, 27:87-90 (February).

Seven hundred thirty-five persons—heads of each family moving into Duluth and visited by the "Welcome Wagon" in Duluth in 1958—were studied. The hypothesis retested was as follows: Higher status persons, seeking the better jobs or opportunities, must move a greater distance to find them, on the average, than do persons seeking less desirable opportunities.

The data supports Rose's findings that professionals and managers migrate longer distances than do lower status migrants. Also, the higher status migrants are more likely to come from eastern urban centers while middle and lower status groups come from rural areas, small cities, and towns lying west of the Mississippi.

Stueber, R. K. *See* 341.

326. Sutton, E.

1957 "The World of the Migrant Child," *Educational Leadership*, 14:221-28 (January).

Children of agricultural migrants in the United States. This article describes the life of migratory children and relates their situation to the challenges presented to the schools to meet their special needs.

"The two outstanding facts of the migrant child's school experience are retardation and frustration, even though there are some exceptions. . . . The majority of migratory children most need experiences which will help them develop a sense of personal belief in themselves, a realization of their worth as individuals." Additional facilities and curriculum adaptations are the two main demands made on the schools by the migrant children.

327. Sutton, E.

1961 "When the Migrant Child Comes to School," *NEA Journal*, 50:32-34 (October).

Children of migratory agricultural workers in the U.S. This article deals with the problems that migrant children face in regard to their education, and the author makes suggestions as to how teaching may be made beneficial to the migrant children.

"Irregular schooling, periodic uprooting and readjustments, lack of cultural background—these and many other factors make the migrant child feel frustrated and inadequate in the schoolroom." Effective learning cannot take place until rapport with teacher and classmates and a sense of belonging have been established. Contacts the teacher has with the child's parents are also important. The teacher can help the migrant child to profit from past travel experiences. He should also prepare the child for educational experiences along the way as his family moves again. When the migrant child leaves a school, the recognition given him by his teacher and classmates often encourages him to re-enter another school in a new location.

328. Swanson, Lloyd Phillip

1961 "An Investigation of the Relationship Between Selected Characteristics of Junior High School Children and the Number of Schools Attended," unpublished doctoral dissertation, Purdue University, 188 pp.

Junior high school children in the sixth, seventh, and eighth grades in a midwest town near a large Air Force Base. The data were derived from a sample of 578 students. "The purpose of this study was to investigate the relationship between the number of different school systems attended, and the following mental and personality traits: (1) intelligence, (2) achievement, (3) personal adjustment, (4) participation in extra-curricular activities, (5) attitude towards minority groups and other social issues, (6) habits of citizenship, and (7) academic grades." Pintner Achievement Test of General Ability, the Metropolitan Achievement Tests, the S. R. A. Junior Inventory, and five attitude scales measuring attitudes towards Negroes, Jews, integration, labor unions, and the United Nations were employed.

"It was found that the different mobility groups had no significantly different scores in performance on standardized intelligence tests, standardized achievement tests, personal adjustment, participation in extra-curricular activities, attitudes toward minority groups and other social issues, habits of citizenship."

T

329. Taeuber, Conrad

1959 "Economic and Social Implications of Internal Migration in the United States," *Journal of Farm Economics*, 41:1141-54 (December).

This is largely a study of the effects of off-farm migration on such economic and social aspects as occupational mobility, social mobility, industrial growth, and suburbanization.

"The decrease in the number of farms and of farm population has created significant problems of organization for agencies that are accustomed to functioning on a county basis. . . . As a result of the continued intermingling of rural and urban people, the distinctions involved in the dichotomy, rural and urban, are becoming increasingly blurred. . . . The fact that Americans exercise their freedom to move has been an important factor in developing national homogeneity. . . . There will continue to be a need for high levels of mobility in the population if the economy is to function at the levels of which it is capable. Rural-urban migrations will contribute, but they may well become less and less significant in the total pattern of internal migration."

330. Taeuber, Irene B.

1958 "Continuities in Internal Migration in Japan," in *Selected Studies of Migration Since World War II*, Proceedings of the 34th Annual Conference of the Milbank Memorial Fund, New York, 1957, Part III, pp. 39-74.

A study of Japanese migrants, based on data derived from Japanese census reports. The focus of the study was the following hypothesis: "If migration is a function of the location of people in relation to the location of industries and cities, any given area should lose migrants to areas more industrial than itself and gain migrants from areas more agricultural than itself. Distance and geographic location should be modifying factors rather than determinants of migration."

"Analysis of gross population changes, of the net life-time migrations shown in place-of-birth statistics, of current movements that involve change of residence, and of the movements between place of work and place of residence alike verified the fundamental hypothesis. . . . As the industrialization of the total economy and the urbanization of the regional populations proceeded, migration became increasingly an interchange between industrial areas as well as a direct movement from the rural areas to the metropolitan centers. And as transportation and communication developed, labor mobility within the cities and residential developments outside the cities created patterns of daily movement comparable to those in the metropolitan areas of other industrial countries."

331. Taeuber, Karl E.

1961 "Duration-of-Residence Analysis of Internal Migration in the U.S.," *Milbank Memorial Fund Quarterly*, 39:116-31 (January).

This paper discusses the migration information provided by a question on duration of residence and presents the first national migration data derived from this approach. Most of the data was from Current Population Reports.

"The most distinctive feature of duration data, however, is the glimpse they give into migration as part of the life history of persons. An individual's changes of residence are not independent of previous changes of residence; neither are the migrations of a given year independent of the changing residential patterns of the nation. A single question on duration in current residence can provide but a small proportion of the data needed to proceed very far with the longitudinal analysis of migration. A second question, on place of previous residence, is necessary to permit duration analysis of specific migration streams. More questions are necessary to provide more complete longitudinal data. Analysis of the basic duration data continually suggests the need for such additional information. Duration-of-residence analysis is but a preliminary step in the systematic study of migration within the context of the life cycle of the individual and the population redistributions of the nation."

332. Taft, Ronald

1957 "A Psychological Model for the Study of Social Assimilation," *Human Relations*, 10:141-56 (May).

A theoretical paper, aimed at analyzing the stages of assimilation and at considering the extent of their covariation and some possible sequences in which they may occur.

This model represents only a first tentative step, but it may suffice to provide a common set of concepts required for studies of assimilation, to be mutually comparing and reinforcing.

333. Taft, Ronald

1961 "The Assimilation of Dutch Male Immigrants in a Western Australian Community: A Replication of Richardson's Study of British Immigrants," *Human Relations*, 14:265-82 (August).

A study of Dutch immigrants (1949-1955) in Australia. Forty males in a suburban town of 2500 in western Australia were studied in an attempt to relate assimilation in the host society to satisfaction with life in and identification with the host society. Guttman-type scale of satisfaction was developed.

This replication of Richardson's study supported the earlier investigator's hypotheses. The background variables showing a positive relationship with degree of assimilation were dissatisfaction with the country of origin (Holland), satisfaction with job prospects in Australia, and never being unemployed since arrival. Good knowledge of English, small town background in Holland, and a high self-rating on ability to adapt also contributed to better assimilation.

334. Tarver, James D.

1957a *Population Change and Migration in Oklahoma, 1940-50*, Oklahoma A&M Agricultural Experiment Station Bulletin B 485, 39 pp.

A study of the people of Oklahoma, 1940-1950, using data derived mainly from census reports.

This study showed that the growth in "the suburban areas accounted for virtually all of the migration increase in the Oklahoma population. . . . On the other hand, the population in each of the 11 nonmetropolitan economic areas declined because of out-migration. Recent Oklahoma population estimates indicate a continuation of the 1940-50 trends, except in a few counties."

335. Tarver, James D.

1957b "Bureau of the Census Data on the Selectivity of Migration from Farms," *Rural Sociology*, 22:162-63 (June).

The author studied off-farm migrants, using U.S. census data. The objectives of the study were to show the paucity of published census data on certain characteristics of migrants, especially those migrating from farms, and to suggest a new classification of migrants that should make possible further analysis to fill this gap in research knowledge.

"In order to maximize the usefulness of published census data in migration research, there is a need for the following additional types of classification: (1) By type of residence at both origin and destination. (2) By the four types of migration according to the unit of migration. . . . (3) By characteristics of family head and size of family at the date of migration."

336. Tarver, James D.

1961 "Predicting Migration," *Social Forces*, 39:207-14 (March).

A study of the 1940-1950 intra-censal net migration rates of whites, nonwhites, and the total population of the U.S. The major hypothesis tested was that demographic, economic, and social variables are interdependent in explaining spatial mobility.

Although migration is not the effect of a single element, the economic factor is more important than any other in explaining white migration rates. The three sets of variables together explain 87 percent of nonwhite migration. The economic variable, however, is not so important as the other two in explaining the non-white migration.

337. Taves, Marvin J.

1959 "Mobility Among High School Graduates," in *Sociology of Rural Life* (Minnesota Agricultural Experiment Station), 32 pp.

Male graduates from six high schools in northeastern and southwestern Minnesota. Interviews were taken from a sample of 739 respondents. The purpose was to determine vocational and geographic mobility patterns of high school graduates for selected years of the last decade.

"Fewer than half of all the graduates still lived, at the time of the survey, in the community in which they had attended high school. . . . Father's occupation most often reported by all graduates was farming. . . . Men in both [high and low income] groups received information about jobs currently held from similar sources. . . . 'Money' was mentioned most frequently as the influence that caused the graduates to accept their jobs. . . . Other reasons mentioned frequently were opportunity for experience, good working conditions and employee relations, security, nearness to home, chance for advancement, and only job available."

338. Taves, Marvin J.

1961 "Population Loss Affects Everyone," *Minnesota Farm and Home Science*, 19:12, 21 (Fall).

A descriptive statement, attempting to answer the following questions: Does migration affect a community? Is migration bad or good? What are the costs of migration?

A community becomes increasingly a less desirable place to live when out-migration prevents it from growing and from providing adequate professional and other services. Current studies show that this tends to generate a circular pattern. A serious investigation considering the well-being of the local community, the state, and the nation will be needed to guide any decision to encourage or to discourage redistribution of populations.

339. Thomas, Brinley

1956 "International Movements of Capital and Labour Since 1945," *International Labour Review*, 74:225-38 (September).

A study based mostly on a survey of intercontinental migration in the postwar period prepared for the World Population Conference (1954) by the Population Division of the United Nations. The author has examined the volume and the pattern of international capital and migratory movements since the Second World War and the consequences of the changes which have taken place in recent years.

"The outlook for intercontinental migration, particularly from Europe, will be affected by the following factors. First, the time is approaching when the age group 15-25 will begin to reflect the sharp rise in the birth rate in the years immediately following the war, the strength of the traditional emigration age groups will be relatively high. Secondly, since Western economies are now passing through major construction booms simultaneously, there may be a general recession involving a higher rate of unemployment than has been known since the war. . . . Thirdly, there may be changes in policy in sending and receiving countries. . . . Moreover, there may be a rapid advance towards closer integration in Europe, entailing a greater degree of intra-European mobility of labour. . . . Once countries realize that they profit best when there is a reasonably flexible two-way traffic . . . interesting possibilities will open up. The fund of expertise and operational experience now existing in the Intergovernmental Committee for European Migration could be the basis for an advance towards more effective international action to develop the international mobility of labour."

340. Thomas, Brinley

1959 "International Migration," in *The Study of Population*, by Philip M. Hauser and Otis Dudley Duncan (Chicago, University of Chicago Press), pp. 510-43.

An essay on various phases of international migration, since the beginning of the nineteenth century.

The author discusses the following phases of international migration: data, methods, summary of existing knowledge, and next steps in research.

341. Thomas, D. R. and R. K. Stueber

1959 "No Desk for Carmen," *Teachers College Record*, 61:143-50 (December).

The persistent difficulties of educating migrant children in the U.S. are examined, using children of Mexican ancestry for purposes of illustration.

There are five points to remember in trying to solve the problems of educating migrant children: their cultural isolation, their unstable existence, the general public's lack of concern for them, a lack of continuity in the efforts to help them, and a lack of structural coordination among the several states which must deal with them. These problems are not insurmountable.

342. Thomas, Dorothy Swaine

1956 "Selective Internal Migration: Some Implications for Mental Hygiene," in *Demographic Analysis: Selected Readings,* ed. Joseph J. Spengler and Otis Dudley Duncan (Glencoe, Ill., The Free Press), pp.425-31.

A brief resume of the present empirical foundation of knowledge regarding selective internal migration (physical fitness, intelligence levels, mental fitness, and familial adjustment).

The evidence, though not clear-cut, suggests that migrants, particularly cityward migrants from rural areas, are somewhat better physical risks than nonmigrants; of average or slightly better than average intelligence; disproportionately young adults and adolescents; often disproportionately females; and more successful than their nonmigrant brothers and sisters in establishing marital ties. From the standpoint of mental hygiene, these findings suggest that migrants, by and large, will represent more favorable than unfavorable risks. However, problems of selective migration have not yet been sufficiently worked up on the empirical side to give us definite answers in regard to the extent and nature of the selection or shifting of population classes in the process of migration, of their effects in modifying the environments of both sending and receiving areas through the withdrawal or introduction of diverse cultural and personal elements.

343. Thomas, Dorothy Swaine

1958 "Age and Economic Differentials in Interstate Migration," *Population Index,* 24:313-25 (October).

Interstate migrants were studied, using data derived from U.S. census reports, unpublished summaries of the University of Pennsylvania data, and Current Population Surveys. The study emphasized age differentials by sex and economic differentials in interstate migration.

Examination of the age-specific rates showed the following: (1) wide fluctuations by decades for both sexes; (2) generally higher rates for males than for females; and (3) a consistent age-differential pattern for each sex within each decade, with rates rising to pronounced peaks at ages 25-29 and thereafter declining fairly regularly, to minima at the oldest ages. "The net gains of interstate migrants were highly concentrated in a very narrow age range for both sexes. . . . Differences in the *levels* of net migration in periods of high and low economic activity have been demonstrated. It should, therefore, follow that the age and sex classes most likely to respond to variations in economic activity, that is, young people, and especially young males, seeking economic betterment, would show a correspondingly greater *intensity* of migration during high than during low activity periods. In general this is true."

Thomas, Dorothy Swaine. *See* 177.

Thomas, Lelia H. *See* 242.

344. Thomas, Sister Mary Eloise

1960 "A Study of the Causes and Consequences of the Economic Status of Migratory Farm Workers in Illinois, Indiana, Michigan, and Wiscon-

sin, 1940-1958," unpublished doctoral dissertation, University of Notre Dame, 456 pp.

Migratory farm workers in Illinois, Indiana, Michigan, and Wisconsin, 1940-1958. The study was undertaken (1) to demonstrate the seriousness and persistence of the low economic status of the migratory farm worker in the above states; (2) to examine some causes and consequences of this economic status and to account in part for the persistence of this aspect of the migratory problem in the four states; and (3) to examine some of the means proposed to improve the economic status of the migrant.

The study showed that the bargaining position of the migrant was weak compared to that of his employer. This inferior position existed despite the importance of the services of the migrant to the agricultural economy and was largely responsible for low wage rates and income. His largely unprotected civil status and his lack of established residence militated against his securing such items as education and health services through public channels.

345. Thomlinson, Ralph

1960 "A Mathematical Model for Migration: A Methodological Study to Improve the Quantitative Analysis of Migration Data by Controlling for Certain Spatial Demographic Variables," unpublished doctoral dissertation, Columbia University, 119 pp.

This is a methodological study attempting to improve the quantitative analysis of migration data by controlling for certain important spatial variables.

Construction of the model involved a number of series of equidistant concentric circles used to approximate a double-integral formula for the probability of migration between any two areas. After an exploratory pretest taking New England as the universe, states as areas, and Bogue's state economic areas as sub-areas, this model was applied to migration between regions of the U.S., using 1935-1940 census data. The results provided overwhelming support for the usefulness of the model. A fuller validation of the model should wait additional research, including an application to international migration.

346. Thomlinson, Ralph

1962 "The Determination of a Base Population for Computing Migration Rates," *Milbank Memorial Fund Quarterly,* 40:356-66 (July).

A discussion of the determination of a base population for computing migration rates, using seven base populations. Four criteria were used for establishing the adequacy of a base population for computing migration rates: (1) the base population must correspond exactly to the population exposed to the event in question; (2) the data must be customarily available; (3) the data must be accurate, or the magnitude and direction of error must be known; and (4) the computation of the base must not be too cumbersome.

Among seven bases analyzed, no one population base was entirely suitable. The final choice in many parts of the world appeared to be a compromise. The criteria for this compromise base are spelled out.

347. Thompson, A. N.

1956 "The Mexican Immigrant Worker in Southwestern Agriculture," *American Journal of Economics and Sociology*, 16:73-81 (October).

This study is primarily concerned with the problems associated with the exploitation of the Mexican agricultural worker in the southwestern region of the United States.

It would be good for all concerned, including the Mexican workers, the U.S. farmers, and the two countries in general, if these migrant workers would organize themselves into unions.

348. Thompson, John L.

1956 "A Case Study of Interregional Labor Migration," *Association of American Geographers Annals*, 46:277-78 (June). (Paper presented at the 52nd Annual Meeting of the Association of American Geographers, Montreal, Canada, April 1-5, 1956.)

This is a case study of interregional labor migration of Eastern Kentuckians to southwestern Ohio. The paper is based partly on facts gathered from industrial administrators and partly on existing documents.

While Kentuckians were not as numerous as Ohio-born employees, their influence as a source of cheap labor for expansion and attraction of industry was disproportional to their numbers. Remoteness and a low standard of living in Kentucky had created clannish attitudes which were evident in migration. The newly arrived Kentucky-born migrants had created industrial problems, e.g., absenteeism, and social problems in their community.

349. Tomasek, Robert Dennis

1958 "The Political and Economic Implications of Mexican Labor in the U.S. Under the Non Quota System, Contract Labor Program, and Wetback Movement," unpublished doctoral dissertation, University of Michigan, 318 pp.

There were three purposes to this study: (1) to compare the methods by which Mexican labor has entered the U.S.; (2) to examine how political decisions are made on the subject of Mexican labor in the U.S., and (3) to determine the extent of Mexican labor in the U.S.

Four general conclusions were drawn from the study. (1) The contract labor program had been a better method for Mexicans to enter the U.S. than the unregulated migration under the non quota system or the "wetback" method. (2) Mexico had had more bargaining power on the question of Mexican labor in the U.S. than was generally known. (3) Pressure groups in the U.S. had had great influence in determining policy on Mexican labor in the U.S., while in Mexico the president and official party leaders had monopolized the decision making on the subject. (4) Mexican labor in the U.S. has led to foreign policy complications.

350. Tower, J. A.

1955 "Negro Exodus from the South," *Association of American Geographers Annals*, 45:301-302 (September). (Abstracts of papers presented at meeting of the Association of American Geographers, Montreal, Canada, April 1-5, 1955.)

Migration of Negroes from the South, especially from Alabama. Census data used, with corrections of the census data to allow for birth and deaths in the intercensus years.

The available evidence indicated greater migratoriness for the Negro than for the white, at least in the South. The increased dispersion of the Negro to other parts of the country was making him increasingly a national problem.

V

351. Valibouja, Joseph

1958 "Postwar Population Movements in Europe," *Association of American Geographers Annals*, 48:458-72 (December).

This is a review of recent and significant studies of the migration problems of postwar population movements in Europe.

The review consisted of the following studies: (1) general studies—research and analysis concentrated on the apparently disordered migrations in order to establish their causes and clarify their chronology, numerical composition, and qualitative characteristics; (2) the case of Germany—studies recognizing the unique problem of postwar migration in regards to Germany; (3) other regional studies —Austria, Finland, Sweden, United Kingdom, France, North Africa, Algeria, Belgium, Netherlands, Italy, Spain, Portugal, Greece, and Turkey.

352. Vance, Rupert B.

1958 "Prerequisites to Immigration: Elements of National Policy," in *Selected Studies of Migration Since World War II*, Proceedings of the 34th Annual Conference of the Milbank Memorial Fund, New York, 1957, Part III, pp. 75-88.

This study's purpose is to point out certain requirements that must be met if immigration is to be economically and socially sound.

Favorable to immigration are the following conditions in the host country: (1) the native population is insufficient for full economic development or defense; (2) there is a seasonal or continuing labor shortage; (3) there is a specialized need for certain skills and technology; and (4) there are the twin phenomena of an aging population and a declining rate of natural increase. The following conditions and qualities of the migrant facilitate his migration and adjustment: (1) lack of feeling of exclusion; (2) active participation in community life; (3) immigration as a family unit; (4) free, individual immigration rather than group removals and transfers; (5) similarities of characteristics between the recipient population and immigrants. "Little has been accomplished toward lessening the pressure toward migration throughout the world. The supply is greater than the demand. . . . The problem of the refugee, the once unwanted stateless masses in the world, has come nearer solution than most could have hoped."

353. Van Valen, M. B.

1956 "Approach to Mobile Dependent Families," *Social Casework*, 37:180-86 (April).

A study of six mobile dependent families who applied to the Family Service Association in Piketon, Ohio. The characteristics of the mobile dependent family are described, tentative diagnoses are made, and treatment suggestions are given.

The six mobile dependent families applying for financial aid presented striking similarities. The family ties were strong. They had no awareness of the reasons behind their impulsive mobility. They expected their needs to be met by others, if not in one place, then in another. All six families fell into the same pattern. Various psychoanalytic characteristics of the men and women involved are described.

354. Varley, Andrew

1962 "Migration Studies," *Population Research and Administrative Planning*, Mississippi State University, Division of Sociology and Rural Life, Conference Series No. 10, pp. 62-64.

A review of migration research studies in progress. Also planned migration research projects are discussed.

"The research being carried on in the field of migration can be classified loosely as describing migration that is taking place, as interpreting migration in a cause and effect type of analysis, and as research primarily concerned with data problems." Analysis, interpretation, and projection are becoming increasingly important in the field of migration research.

355. Veidemanis, Juris

1961 "Social Change: Major Value-Systems of Latvians at Home, as Refugees, and as Immigrants," unpublished doctoral dissertation, University of Wisconsin, 2 vols., 769 pp.

The study compared the major social values in Latvian society during (1) the period of independence (1918-1940), (2) refugee life in Western Germany and Austria (1945-1950), and (3) life in resettlement in the U. S.-specifically in Milwaukee, Wisconsin (1949-1950). The question was: What patterns of change in kinds of values can be discerned over these three phases? In the Milwaukee phase of the study, data were obtained through three questionnaire studies reaching two-thirds of all Latvian households in Milwaukee. Becker's method of constructive typology and his sacred-secular conceptual framework were utilized in the research and analysis. Culture case studies were made.

The following hypothesis was derived from a comparison of the nomothetic types and from their contexts: *If* (1) a nationality group whose major value systems accord closest to the prescriptive-sacred type lives in exile, and (2) the majority of its members have acted in more than children's roles in this nationality's subsystems for at least as many years as in solely children's roles, *then* there is high probability that changes, if any, in this group's major value systems will not be sufficient for reclassifying them under a different sacred or secular primary subtype. On the nomothetic level, the study revealed no changes in the kinds of values maintained during the refugee and resettlement phases.

W

Wakeley, Ray E. *See* 152.

356. Wakeley, Ray E., and Mohiey Eldin Nasrat

1961 "Sociological Analysis of Population Migration," *Rural Sociology*, 26:15-23 (March).

A study of 99 Iowa counties, using census data. The study had two main purposes: (1) To illustrate the application of the conceptual variable analysis in the study of population migration, and (2) to explain and attempt to predict net migration by use of a theory of human relationships. The following hypothesis was tested: net migration is (1) directly related to the coefficient of variation, (2) inversely to the coefficient of deprivation, and (3) inversely to the coefficient of comparative rewards. Contrived indices for coefficients of variation, deprivation, and comparative reward were developed.

A logical explanation for migration was attempted, but when tested empirically it did not predict. Statistically significant relationships were found between the measures of cohesion and two of the three measures of deprivation. The relationships between the measurement variables were sufficient to give support to the empirical hypotheses. These results support the conceptualized framework, but do not prove it. They indicated ways in which these concepts might be used in setting up a research or an action program involving migration into or from a social system.

357. Walz, Orry C.

1960 "Migration of Ranch County Youth," *Southwestern Social Science Quarterly*, 41(supp.):283-89 (March).

All individuals in Ranch County who enrolled in the ninth grade in the fall of 1954, and those who joined this class in the Ranch County schools after the fall of 1954. Seventy-five males and 75 females were included in this study. Comparison between some of the characteristics of the migrants and a group of nonmigrants was the emphasis of the study.

The girls had left the county in greater numbers and at earlier ages than the boys and created an unfavorable sex ratio. Comparing the migrant girls as a group with the nonmigrant girls, a larger percentage of the migrants came from nonfarm homes, a larger percentage were married, a much larger percentage came from homes of working mothers, a much larger percentage held clerical or sales positions, and a much higher percentage made "above average" grades in school. Among the boys, a larger percentage of the migrants came from nonfarm homes, a much higher percentage were married, a much higher percentage came from broken homes and from homes of working mothers, a much higher percentage worked as operatives and clerks, while all of the boys with "above average" grades either migrated or attended college.

358. Walz, R. B.

1958 "Migration into Arkansas 1834-1880," unpublished doctoral dissertation, University of Texas, 601 pp.

Migrants to Arkansas, 1834-1880. Data from U.S. censuses. The aim of the study was to show whence and at what rate families migrated into Arkansas and its various physiographic and political subdivisions, 1834-1880.

Most Arkansas immigrants until 1880 were farm families. Negro and white immigration alike almost ceased during the Civil War and reached a pre-1880 high in 1878-1880. Most families migrated short distances. Nearly two-thirds of the estimated white immigrants and even more of the Negroes came from adjacent states. Approximately one-third of the whites and one-fifth of the Negroes had made one or more detectable interstate moves prior to the move into Arkansas.

359. Ward, William

    1961 "Continuities and Discontinuities in Denominational Loyalty: A Lehigh Valley Study of Residential Movement," unpublished doctoral dissertation, University of Pennsylvania, 428 pp.

A systematic study of 168 households, Bethlehem, Pennsylvania. The data were collected and analyzed around the central hypothesis, "The denominational loyalty of mobile residents is a product of three interrelated sets of factors: (1) the integrative strength of the denomination which was influential in the formative years; (2) the impact of unique experiences during the life history (crises, mixed marriages, etc.); and (3) the effect of changes in family situation which accompany change from one stage to another of the life cycle of the family."

The clearest denominational loyalty was shown by the Roman Catholics, individuals reared in denominations most akin to Roman Catholicism, and persons who were not involved in mixed marriages. "(2) Those most likely to *cross denominational lines* were: individuals with non-liturgical Protestant background, Protestants who married other Protestants of a different specific denomination, individuals who experienced a clear break in membership continuity during their life histories, and persons who had a late start in their relationships with organized religion. (3) Those most likely to remain *technically loyal* to their denominations, but prone toward 'dormancy' or 'marginality' in church relationships were: Respondents who did not resolve religious differences after a mixed marriage, and persons whose motives for current congregational membership were strongly influenced by family ties and local traditions. (4) The nature of Protestant congregational life fosters more *change* in the *intensity of participation*, after a residential move, among Protestants than among Roman Catholics. (5) Among the *life cycle changes* which influence membership and participation are marriage, and the approach of one's children toward the age of full congregational membership. However, life cycle changes are followed by more fluctuation in Protestant than in Roman Catholic participation. (6) Among the respondents, *upward occupational mobility* had at least two effects: it promoted *membership* and it improved the chances for *leadership* within a congregation."

Warshay, Leon. *See* 274.

360. Watson, Walter Bingham

    1959 "Metropolitan Migration in the U.S. 1949-1950," unpublished doctoral dissertation, University of Wisconsin, 118 pp.

Migrants between the 128 Standard Metropolitan Areas in U.S., 1949-1950. Most data were taken from 1950 census data on mobility. The purpose of the study was to understand the relative importance of factors related to metropolitan migration in the U.S. for the year 1949-1950.

Fifty-six of 128 SMA's had net migration losses during 1949-1950. Contrary to expectation, net and gross migration rates were *negatively* correlated with level of living measures. However, both rates correlated positively with measures of economic opportunity as distinct from level of living. Gross migration was high and net migration was positive for trade centers. These trends were reversed for manufacturing centers. However, both rates correlated positively with the expansion of manufacturing activity. Net and gross migration rates were related negatively to maturity of the SMA as measured by age, size, density, and suburbanization. Net migration rates were greatest in SMA's most isolated from other SMA's. With only three concepts it was possible to explain 81 percent of the variance of gross migration. Functional type of SMA, maturity of SMA, and regional location of SMA were each independently important in the explanation, but none alone was sufficient.

361. Weaver, Robert C.

    1959 "Non-White Population Movements and Urban Ghettos," *Phylon Quarterly*, 20:235-41 (Fall).

The study raised the following questions: Will the metropolitan areas of tomorrow in the U.S. have a core of low-income, colored families surrounded by middle- and upper-income whites in the suburbs? Does this mean Negro political domination in the larger urban communities? Will downtown business and cultural institutions wither away from lack of support?

The study shows that the racial occupational patterns, if ignored, are likely to threaten established businesses and cultural institutions in most of the larger and some of the smaller metropolitan areas in the U.S. This does not have to happen, and there are straws in the wind which suggest that it may not. The most encouraging sign is the tendency of those dedicated to the preservation of these great cities to approach the problem of residential segregation with a new realism, which might lead to constructive solutions.

362. Webber, Irving L.

    1956 "The Effect of Migration on the Number and Distribution of the Aged in Florida," *Journal of Gerontology*, 11:323-27 (July).

A study of migrants, 55 years and over in 1940, to Florida. The study was based on data derived from U.S. censuses. The purpose of the investigation was to measure, as accurately as possible, the volume and relative importance of movements into the state and its 67 counties during the decade ending in 1950.

A large proportion (96 percent) of the 66,500 aged

migrants to the state during 1940-1950 were white. The counties which gained the largest numbers of older white persons were found in the central and southeastern parts of the peninsula. With minor exceptions those counties which received the largest volume of migrants, absolutely and relatively, of either or both races had high rates of growth for the total population during the decade and were located on seacoasts.

363. Wertheim, W. F.

1959 "Sociological Aspects of Inter-Island Migration in Indonesia," *Population Studies*, 12:184-201 (March).

People of Java and the Outer Islands of Indonesia were studied in an attempt to test the assumption of Dr. Akbar, an Indonesian Moslem scholar, that family planning can be avoided by implementing transmigration, exploiting the virgin woods which still abound in this country, and by many other endeavors.

Organized resettlement in irrigated areas tended to reproduce the overpopulation pattern prevalent in Java. "Spontaneous" migration, without governmental planning and supervision, was still less satisfactory as it exposed the cleared soils to erosion, after a few harvests. The analysis showed that the concept of overpopulation should be made more precise. In relation to the modes of cultivation practiced among most of the peoples outside Java, many regions in the Outer Islands may be regarded as overpopulated, in spite of their low population densities. The absorptive capacity of the Outer Islands should not be measured in spatial terms only, but sociological and psychological factors also must be taken into account. Assimilation of the Javanese migrants with Sumatrans would seem unlikely, given the present system of rural resettlement. A solution of the overpopulation problem of Java, and of the resettlement problem, would call for efficient planning to bring about basic changes in the economic structure of the whole archipelago, including a program for industrial development.

364. Whetten, Nathan L., and Robert G. Burnight

1956 "Internal Migration in Mexico," *Rural Sociology*, 21:140-51 (June).

Internal migration of the people of Mexico was studied, using their birth data from the 1940-1950 Mexican censuses.

The rate of "net lifetime migration" in Mexico was only about half that in the U.S. in 1950. The Federal District, which includes Mexico City, experienced the greatest volume of net gain in migration, a gain which was experienced also by the tier of states along the northern border contiguous to the U.S. A fifth of the population increase experienced by eight Mexican states, including the Federal District, during 1940-1950 could be attributed to interstate migration. Large scale rural-to-urban migration was indirectly indicated in the analysis. Correlational analysis strongly suggested that interstate migration in Mexico, between 1940 and 1950, improved the distribution of population in relation to the distribution of economic opportunities.

365. Whitney, Vincent H.

1960 "Changes in the Rural-Nonfarm Population, 1930-50," *American Sociological Review*, 25:363-68 (June).

An analysis of the U.S. rural-nonfarm population, 1930-1950, using U.S. census data by county. The hypothesis tested was that the rural-nonfarm population was primarily concentrated in the immediate vicinity of urban places in the two decades 1930 to 1950, and that the greater part of all rural-nonfarm *growth* in this period took place in such areas of urban dominance.

The hypothesis was supported by county census data for 1930, 1940, and 1950. The data suggest that a substantial proportion of statistically rural-nonfarm people were sociologically urban and lend support to changes in "urban" and "rural" definitions already made or under consideration by the Bureau of the Census.

366. Whitney, Vincent H., and Charles M. Grigg

1958 "Patterns of Mobility Among a Group of Families of College Students," *American Sociological Review*, 23:643-52 (December).

Undergraduate liberal arts students in 11 colleges and universities in the eastern U.S., 1947-1952. Information was obtained from 501 respondents through a questionnaire. The main purpose of the study was to test use of questionnaire method for ex post facto longitudinal studies of migration.

The migration pattern studied pertained to a 20-year period, the lifetime of the student respondents. The families included in the study were in general white, Protestant, middle-income, and aged between 40 and 50 years. The findings suggested the hypothesis that when a family migrated to a community, the initial migration would be followed by a number of local moves. These local moves tended to be largely for social class reasons. The study concluded that the questionnaire method could be used for historical longitudinal studies of migration.

367. Wilber, George L.

1962 "Determinants of Migration Research and Their Consequences," *Population Research and Administrative Planning*, Mississippi State University, Division of Sociology and Rural Life, Conference Series No. 10, pp. 52-61.

Investigation aimed at answering the following questions: (1) What major factors determine the points of concentration in migration research? (2) What are the consequences for migration research of these determinants? (3) What aspects of migration research can benefit most from reorientation?

The need for a theory encompassing the major aspects of migration, including ecological and demographic, is emphasized. Sample surveys should supplement the current heavy reliance on secondary sources of information. The level of migration research needs to be elevated and research results published on at least two levels, one for the layman, the other for the scientist. A multidisciplinary approach to migration should complement a resurgence of cause-effect analysis.

Wilber, George L. *See* 54 and 163.

368. Willsie, Roger H.

1958 *Why Farmers Sold Out in Central Nebraska in 1956-57*, Nebraska Agricultural Experiment Station Bulletin SB 445, 15 pp.

A sample of 133 farmers who sold farms in central Nebraska during 1956-1957. The aim of the study is contained in the title of the paper.

Those who sold out were, in general, in poor financial position, and were in effect forced out by financial difficulties. There were some exceptions. Some of the sales were due to retirement, poor health, and poor leasing arrangements.

369. Willson, E. A.

1957 *Off-Farm Residence of Families of Farm and Ranch Operators,* Montana Agricultural Experiment Bulletin 530, 50 pp.

A study in off-farm residence. Fifty-two rural school districts were selected as unit areas for study: 33 wheat-farming areas, eight general farming, and 11 stock ranching. A total of 83 off-farm residents were interviewed. This report is concerned with the factors influencing the migration of farm families from farm to town residence while they continue to operate the farm.

Among the reasons given for change of residence to towns are school facilities for their children, health, weather, poor roads, or town comforts and conveniences. Other reasons include income, modern conveniences, social life, and medical facilities. There are some disadvantages felt as a result of migration, such as increased living costs, inability to keep livestock, difficulty in doing farm work and maintaining equipment, and break-up of family. Migration has had no effects on the size of farms.

370. Winberg, Isak P.

1959 "Net Migration and Rationalisation in Agriculture in the Thinly Populated Districts of Southern and Central Sweden," in *Rural Migration,* Papers presented to the 1st Congress of the European Society for Rural Sociology, Brussels-Louvain, September, 1958 (Bonn, privately published), pp. 152-59.

Net migration and rationalization in agriculture in the thinly-populated districts of southern and central Sweden are the concerns of this paper. Census reports and related publications were used as information sources.

Sweden's total population has more than doubled during 1850-1957. The development has been even and not too much influenced either by the emigration in the latter half of the nineteenth century or by birth control. Behind this seemingly uniform development big regional differences are concealed. There is an obvious relationship between the net migration and the industrial and commercial structure. Migration from thinly-populated areas was often forced by local unemployment resulting from the rationalization of agriculture and related trades.

371. Windham, Gerald O.

1960 "Socio-Economic Status and Formal Social Participation of Rural Migrant Families in Pitts-

burgh," unpublished doctoral dissertation, Pennsylvania State University, 158 pp.

The data were collected from 1470 families in Pittsburgh Metropolitan Area. Relationship between the migrant status of the families and their socio-economic status, and that between the migrant status of husbands and wives and their formal social participation were studied.

"Urban migrants were more numerous and nonmigrants less numerous in the higher status classes. When education was controlled there was no association between migrant status and housing status or socio-economic status. . . . [H]ousing status did tend to improve with length of residence in the community, but this factor was not related to socio-economic status. . . . Nonmigrants of both sexes reported more organization memberships and attending more meetings per month than the other migrant groups. This relationship persisted when education and stage in family life cycle were controlled. Urban migrant wives followed by rural migrants held the most power positions proportionally. . . . The data on selectivity of participation showed no consistent relationship between migrant status and the three qualitative measures of social participation."

372. Windham, Gerald O.

1961 "Urban Identification of Rural Migrants," *Mississippi Quarterly,* 14:78-89 (Spring).

One hundred and five rural migrant families in Pittsburgh, Pennsylvania. The study was to test the hypothesis that the degree to which rural migrants identified with urban society was related to their position in the social and economic structure of the community. An index of urban identification was constructed from seven attitude items related to psychological adjustment.

The rural migrants did not identify closely with urban society. However, there is a significant association between scores on the urban identification index and four independent variables, namely housing status, social participation, formal education, and length of residence in the community. The evidence, in general, supports the hypothesis.

Wink, Anna T. *See* 3.

373. Winsemium, J.

1960 "Urbanisation in the Western Part of the Netherland," *Tijdschrift voor Economische en Sociale Geografie,* 51:188-99 (July).

This is a study in urbanization and its consequences, resulting from a variety of factors impinging upon the western section of Holland.

Industrialization would result in econmic competition in the labor market in Holland. This would encourage admission of foreign workers, i.e., immigrants to "Randstad." Other effects of this urbanization might include demand for recreational facilities, and development of capital intensive horticulture around the vicinity of urbanized regions. The author predicts that the conditions in this chain of deconcentrated and integrated towns would not be any less satisfactory than the conditions prevailing in the metropolitan areas in foreign countries.

374. Withington, W. A.

   1956 "Suburban Migration: A Case Study of Winchester, Massachusetts, 1930 to 1950," *Association of American Geographers Annals*, 46:281 (June). (Paper presented at the 52nd Annual Meeting of Association of American Geographers, April, 1956, Montreal, Canada.)

Fifteen thousand residents of Winchester, Massachusetts (eight miles northeast of Boston) between 1930-1950 were investigated in order to understand the phenomenon of suburban migration.

Most suburban migrants move short distances. The number of long-distance migrants are increasingly important. Peripheral areas of suburbs where new dwelling construction is greatest are most active as areas of in- and out-migration. Central, older residential areas of suburbs have the greatest amount of intramigration. The number of migrants into, out of, or within a suburb in a 20-year period may equal its total population.

375. Wolf, Eleanor Paperno

   1959 "Changing Neighborhood: A Study of Racial Transition," unpublished doctoral dissertation, Wayne State University, 306 pp.

An area-probability sample of households of the 670 dwelling units in a Detroit middle-class neighborhood, 1955-1957, was selected. This dissertation was focused on the racial invasion-succession sequence in private housing in urban neighborhoods.

In general, certain socio-economic characteristics (especially income and type of employment) are better indicators of which households would move away than are respondents' attitudes toward Negroes. By the time two and one-half years had elapsed a large majority of the white residents had come to define the area as fated to become predominantly Negro-occupied in the near future (because mobility greatly increased) and hence unsuitable for prolonged residence. Most had developed a highly temporary orientation to their stay in the neighborhood, despite the fact that their level of racial prejudice tended on the whole either to remain stable, or to move toward less prejudice as some stereotyped conceptions of Negroes were corrected.

376. Wood, Helen C.

   1958 "Children Who Move with the Crops," *Journal of the National Education Association*, 47:170-72 (March).

Children of migrant workers in Fresno County, California. A description of the efforts taken by educators in Fresno County to assure a better education for migrant children.

By working together on the problem of educating the migrant children, the schools have been able to reinforce one another's efforts. Efforts made by the schools show definite results when the curriculum is realistically based on a direct study of children's needs.

377. Wood, N.

   1962 "Summer-School Help for Migrant Workers' Children," *Journal of the National Education Association*, 51:18-19 (May).

The summer school program for the children of Spanish-American migrant workers at Liberty School in Colorado is described.

The state reimbursed the district for all current operating expenses. Attendance stayed up remarkably well for the whole season. Language was a barrier but never an insurmountable one. Only a few of the migrant children were on a grade level for their age. Health habits were taught and the children were checked by a nurse and given preventive shots.

X-Y-Z

378. Yaukey, David William

   1956 "A Comparison of Distribution by Classes of Migrants Within the State of Washington, 1949-50," unpublished doctoral dissertation, University of Washington, 189 pp.

Migrants into the state economic areas of Washington between 1949 and 1950 were studied, using information on 35,518 cases obtained through U.S. census reports. Answers were sought for the following questions: (1) What classes of migrants differed most in their distributions among available locations? (2) What characteristics of the locations best explained the differences between distributions? (3) What classes of migrants were attracted by these characteristics?

Position in the life cycle, as defined by age and marital status, and sex were basic distinctions among migrants. The old, higher status married, colored, and single females chose urban locations. Young single males and those migrants with farm backgrounds chose rural locations.

379. Zachariah, Kunniparampil Curien

   1962 *"Historical Study of Internal Migration in the Indian Sub-Continent, 1901-1931,"* unpublished doctoral dissertation, University of Pennsylvania, 402 pp.

The object was to measure and describe the pattern of interstate migration by decades in the Indian subcontinent during 1901-1931.

The major contribution is the quantitative analysis of the pattern of interstate migration. It was generally believed that the population of India was comparatively immobile and strongly attached to its original villages. The estimates support this view. Rural-urban migration has proceeded at an accelerated rate in certain states. The trends suggest that there is a close association between the nature of population redistribution and the economic organization in the country and that the future pattern is likely to become similar to that observed in the developed countries.

380. Zimmer, Basil G.

   1955 "Participation of Migrants in Urban Structures," *American Sociological Review*, 20:218-24 (April).

A random sample of dwelling units in a midwestern community (pop. 20,000) in 1951 was used. Interviews were then obtained from the married, male occupants of those dwellings. Two hypotheses were tested: (1) Migrants differed from the natives in level of participation, but became more similar to the natives in their behavior the longer they lived in the community. (2) Urban migrants tended to enter the activities of the community more rapidly than farm migrants.

Both hypotheses were substantiated. The adjustment process took at least five years, however, and status affected its success.

381. Zimmer, Basil G.

1956 "Farm Background and Urban Participation," *American Journal of Sociology*, 61:470-75 (March).

A study of a random sample of married male occupants in a midwestern community. Two hypotheses were tested: (1) Migrants as a group will differ in level of participation from the natives, but migrants who come from a similar environment will be more like the natives than migrants who come from a dissimilar environment. (2) The level of participation will vary inversely with the experience of migrants in a dissimilar environment.

Migration itself does not limit participation. The community of origin is a more important determinant. Movement from city to city put less limitations upon becoming assimilated to city life than did movement from rural to urban areas. High status tended to transcend the limiting influence of farm background. Any increase in amount of farm experience was closely related to a decrease in level of participation in the urban community.

382. Zimmer, Basil G.

1962 "The Adjustment of Negroes in a Northern Industrial Community," *Social Problems*, 9:378-86 (Spring).

Negroes in the central city of a northern community of 200,000 population. A random sample of 648 household heads was selected for study. The purpose of this paper was to describe the socioeconomic status of Negroes in a northern industrial community.

Historically, Negroes involved in a mass movement from the rural South to urban areas have been faced with the handicaps of race and lack of formal education with which to cope with the strange environment in urban places. But future movements of Negroes will involve those reared and educated in an urban environment. Gains would be realized by the settling down of Negroes in urban centers. It would seem that the Negro in urban communities is entering a period of population stability where social and economic adjustments could be worked out for a stable population, whose growth would be largely through natural increase rather than a rapid expansion in numbers due to a constant influx of migrants from rural areas.

383. Zimmer, Basil G., and Amos H. Hawley

1959 "Suburbanization and Church Participation," *Social Forces*, 37:348-54 (May).

Seven hundred household heads in the Flint, Michigan, city-fringe area are included in this study. The study is concerned with the relationship between frequency of church attendance and place of residence in a metropolitan area. Differences in rates of attendance were hypothesized to be different because of the effects of population redistribution in the area.

There is a city-fringe difference in church attendance, but the data do not reveal why. Place of residence is closely related to church participation. Attendance is lower in the rapidly growing fringe area, showing the effect of intracity migration.

384. Zubrzycki, Jerzy

1958 "The Role of the Foreign-Language Press in Migrant Integration," *Population Studies*, 12:73-82 (July).

This paper considers one aspect of the cultural framework of the process of migration, namely, the role of the foreign language press in the integration of migrants.

A brief survey of the natural history and contents of the foreign-language papers in the U.S., Canada, and Australia makes clear their principal function in preparing immigrants for good citizenship in the countries of settlement. They are an educational agency without equal in giving the immigrant the essential information about the customs, traditions, and institutions of his adopted country.

385. Zubrzycki, Jerzy

1959 "Across the Frontiers of Europe," in *The Cultural Integration of Immigrants*, by W. D. Borrie and others, (Paris, UNESCO), pp. 159-80.

An examination of three types of movements of the people of Europe: "normal" migration; refugees fleeing from political persecution or, as in the case of displaced persons, seeking a country; and the seasonal and frontier movement.

The traditional function of migration within Europe had been to relieve population pressure in the countries of eastern and southern Europe while supplying much needed manpower in the countries of northwestern Europe which have been undergoing rapid industrialization. Some history of the migrations is given. Neither migrations of displaced persons nor migrations of seasonal workers contributed to a significant extent to the problems of integration in the receiving countries. Seasonal migration accounted for a high proportion of all intra-European movements. The main movements were from Italy to France and Switzerland, from Belgium to France, and from Ireland to the United Kingdom. A discussion of national policies, with special reference to measures designed to assimilate the migrants, is presented in the paper.

Zubrzycki, Jerzy. See 36, 258, and 259.

II. UNANNOTATED BOOKS AND REPORTS

Adloff, Richard. *See* 631

387. Ali, Hassan Mohammad

    1955 *Land Reclamation and Settlement in Iraq* (Baghdad, Baghdad Printing Press), 210 pp.

388. Anderson, Henry P.

    1961 *The Bracero Program in California, with Particular Reference to Health Status, Attitudes, and Practices* (Berkeley, School of Public Health, University of California), 328 pp.

Apthorpe, R. J. *See* 576.

389. Arrington, Leonard J.

    1958 *Great Basin Kingdom: An Economic History of the Latterday Saints 1830-1900*, (Cambridge, Harvard University Press, published in cooperation with the Committee on Research in Economic History), 534 pp.

390. Aziz, M. A.

    1955 *Japan's Colonialism and Indonesia* (The Hague, Martinus Nijhoff, published under the direction of the Netherlands Institute of International Affairs), 271 pp.

391. Banton, Michael

    1955 *The Coloured Quarter: Negro Immigrants in an English City* (London, Jonathan Cape), 254 pp.

392. Banton, Michael

    1960 *White and Coloured: The Behavior of British Peoples Towards Coloured Immigrants* (New Brunswick, N. J., Rutgers University Press), 223 pp.

Bates, Margaret. *See* 413.

393. Beijer, G., and others

    1961 *Characteristics of Overseas Migrants* (The Hague, Government Printing and Publishing Office), 319 pp.

394. Berle, Beatrice B.

    1958 *Eighty Puerto Rican Families in New York City: Health and Disease Studies in Context* (New York, Columbia University Press), 332 pp.

395. Bernolak, Imre, and others

    1955 *Immigrants in Canada* (Montreal, Canadian Association for Adult Education), 63 pp.

396. Beyer, Glenn H., and J. Hugh Rose

    1957 *Farm Housing* (New York, John Wiley, published for the Social Science Research Council in cooperation with the U.S. Department of Commerce, Bureau of the Census), 194 pp.

397. Bhatta, J. N.

    1957 *Regarding Internal Migration in Indonesia (with Special Reference to S. Sumatra)* (Djakarta, Institute of Geography), 76 pp.

398. Billington, Ray A.

    1956 *The Far Western Frontier, 1830-1860* (New York, Harper), 324 pp.

399. Bjork, Kenneth O.

    1958 *West of the Great Divide: Norwegian Migration to the Pacific Coast, 1847-1893* (Northfield, Minn., Norwegian-American Historical Association), 671 pp.

400. Bladen, V. W. (ed,)

    1962 *Canadian Population and Northern Colonization*, Royal Society of Canada, Studia Varia 7 (Toronto, University of Toronto Press), 158 pp.

401. Blanco, Cicely

    1962 *The Determinants of Regional Factor Mobility* (The Hague, Pasmans), 143 pp.

402. Bleakley, J. W.

    1961 *The Aborigines of Australia: Their History, Their Habits, Their Assimilation* (Brisbane, Jacaranda Press), 366 pp.

403. Blishen, Bernard R., and others (eds.)

    1961 *Canadian Society: Sociological Perspectives* (Toronto: Macmillan), 622 pp.

404. Bogue, Donald J.

    1957 *Components of Population Change, 1940-1950: Estimates of New Migration and Natural Increase for Each Standard Metropolitan Area and State Economic Area* (Oxford, Ohio, Scripps Foundation), 145 pp.

405. Bogue, Donald J.

    1959 *The Population of the U.S.* (Glencoe, Ill., The Free Press), 873 pp.

406. Bogue, Donald J., H. S. Shryock, and S. A. Hoermann

    1957 *Subregional Migration in the United States, 1935-40, Volume I, Streams of Migrations Flows*

Between Environments (Oxford, Ohio, Scripps Foundation), 333 pp.

407. Borrie, W. D., and others

1959 *The Cultural Integration of Immigrants: A Survey Based upon the Papers and Proceedings of the UNESCO Conference Held in Havana, April, 1956,* Population and Culture Series 4 (Paris, UNESCO), 297 pp.

Brackel, P. O. M. *See* 660.

Brainerd, Carol P. *See* 530.

408. Brepohl, W., and others

1955 *Adjustment of Refugees to Their New Environment, R. E. M. P. Bulletin,* Vol. 3, Supp. 3, 32 pp.

409. Brooks, Melvin S.

1960 *The Social Problems of Migrant Farm Laborers; Effect of Migrant Farm Labor on Education of Children* (Carbondale, Ill. Southern Illinois University), 242 pp.

Bryant, Ellen S. *See* 666.

410. Bunting, Robert L., and Peter A. Prosper, Jr.

1960 *Labor Mobility Patterns in the Piedmont Industrial Crescent* (Chapel Hill, University of North Carolina), 70 pp.

411. Canada. Saskatchewan. Royal Commission on Agriculture and Rural Life

1956 *Movement of Farm People,* Report No. 7 (Regina, Royal Commission on Agriculture and Rural Life), 210 pp.

412. Catholic Institute for Social-Ecclesiastical Research

1955 *International Catholic Migration Congress, Organized by the International Catholic Migration Commission, Geneva, and the Central Catholic Emigration Foundation* (The Hague, Pax International), 442 pp.

413. Catholic University of America

1957 *The Migration of Peoples to Latin America,* Proceedings of the Conference on the Migration of Peoples to Latin America held under the auspices of the Institute of Ibero-American Studies of the Catholic University of America, April 27 and 28, 1956, ed. Margaret Bates (Washington, Catholic University of America Press), 113 pp.

414. Claude, Inis L.

1955 *National Minorities: An International Problem* (Cambridge, Harvard University Press), 248 pp.

415. Clausen, C. A. (ed.)

1961 *The Lady with the Pen: Elise Waerenskjokd in Texas* (Northfield, Minn. Norwegian-American Historical Association), 183 pp.

416. Collins, Sydney

1957 *Coloured Minorities in Britain* (London, Lutterworth Press), 258 pp.

Commager, Henry S. *See* 550.

417. Conference on Economic Progress

1955 *Full Prosperity for Agriculture; Goals for Farm Policy* (Washington, Conference on Economic Progress), 108 pp.

418. Conway, Alan

1961 *The Welsh in America: Letters from the Immigrants* (Minneapolis: University of Minnesota Press), 341 pp.

419. Corbett, David C.

1957 *Canada's Immigration Policy: A Critique* (Toronto, University of Toronto Press, published for the Canadian Institute of International Affairs), 216 pp.

420. Corsi, Edward

1956 *Paths to the New World: American Immigration—Yesterday, Today, and Tomorrow,* rev. ed. (New York, Anti-Defamation League of B'nai B'rith), 44 pp.

421. Coughlin, Richard J.

1960 *Double Identity: The Chinese in Modern Thailand* (Hong Kong, Hong Kong University Press); 222 pp.

422. Cowan, Helen I.

1961 *British Emigration to British North America: The First Hundred Years,* rev. and enlarged ed. (Toronto, University of Toronto Press), 321 pp.

423. Cronin, Vincent

1957 *The Last Migration* (New York. E. P. Dutton), 343 pp.

424. Crystal, David

1958 *The Displaced Person and the Social Agency: A Study of the Casework Process in Its Relation to Immigrant Adjustment* (Rochester, N. Y., United Hias Service), 182 pp.

425. Cunningham, Clark E.

1958 *The Postwar Migration of the Toba-Bataks to East Sumatra* (New Haven, Yale University), 189 pp.

426. Current, Tom, and Marke Martinez Infante

1959 " *... And Migrant Problems Demand Attention:" Being the Final Report of the 1958-59 Migrant Farm Labor Studies in Oregon. In-*

cluding Material from the Preliminary Report of the Bureau of Labor (July 1959) Entitled "We Talked to the Migrants" (Salem, Bureau of Labor), 218 pp.

Cuthbert, Norman. *See* 513.

427. Davison, Robert B.

1962 *West Indian Migrants: The Social and Economic Facts of Migration from the British West Indies* (London, Oxford University Press), 96 pp.

428. Dewhurst, J. Frederic, and others

1961 *Europe's Needs and Resources: Trends and Prospects in Eighteen Countries* (New York, Twentieth Century Fund), 1198 pp.

429. Diskalkar, P. D.

1960 *Resurvey of a Deccan Village, Pimple Saudagar* (Bombay, The Indian Society of Agricultural Economics), 160 pp.

430. Divine, Robert A.

1957 *American Immigration Policy, 1924-1952* (New Haven, Yale University Press), 220 pp.

Doczy, A. Gedeon. *See* 625.

431. Dodd, Arthur H.

1957 *The Character of Early Welsh Emigration to the United States* (Cardiff, University of Wales Press), 40 pp.

432. Duffy, James

1959 *Portuguese Africa* (Cambridge, Harvard University Press), 389 pp.

Duncan, Beverly. *See* 433.

433. Duncan, Otis Dudley, and Beverly Duncan

1957 *The Negro Population of Chicago: A Study of Residential Succession* (Chicago, University of Chicago Press), 368 pp.

Duncan, Otis Dudley. *See* 485, 610, 611.

434. Dvinov, Boris L.

1955 *Politics of the Russian Emigration* (Santa Monica, The Rand Corporation), 433 pp. (processed).

435. Dvinov, Boris L.

1956 *Documents on the Russian Emigration: An Appendix to Rand Paper P-768* (Santa Monica, Calif., The Rand Corporation), 227 pp.

436. Dworkis, Martin B. (ed.)

1957 *The Impact of Puerto Rican Migration on Governmental Service in New York City* (New York, New York University Press), 74 pp.

437. Dynes, Russell Rowe

1956 *Consequences of Population Mobility for School and Community Change* (Columbus, Ohio State University), 132 pp.

Easterlin, Richard A. *See* 528 and 530.

438. Edwards, R. Dudley, and T. Desmond Williams (eds.)

1957 *The Great Famine: Studies in Irish History 1845-52* (Dublin, Brown and Nolan), 519 pp.

439. Eisenstadt, S. N.

1955 *The Absorption of Immigrants: A Comparative Study Based Mainly on the Jewish Community in Palestine and the State of Israel* (Glencoe, Ill., The Free Press), 275 pp.

440. Elkan, Walter

1960 *Migrants and Proletarians: Urban Labour in the Economic Development of Uganda* (London, Oxford University Press, published on behalf of the East African Institute of Social Research), 149 pp.

441. Ericksen, E. Gordon

1962 *The West Indies Population Problem: Dimensions for Action* (Lawrence, University of Kansas Publications), 194 pp.

442. Erickson, Charlotte

1957 *American Industry and the European Immigrant* (London, Oxford University Press), 269 pp.

443. Espina, Vincente

1956 *Immigration and Alien Registration Laws of the Philippines; A Complete Compilation of the Aforementioned Laws Together with the Latest Regulations, Decisions, and Opinions in Immigration, Alien Registration and Citizenship Cases* (Manila, Educational Book Store), 303 pp.

444. European Society for Rural Sociology

1959 *Rural Migration*, Papers presented to the 1st Congress of the European Society for Rural Sociology, Brussels-Louvain, September, 1958 (Bonn, privately published), 476 pp.

Fair, T. J. D. *See* 469.

445. Farmer, Bertram Hughes

1957 *Pioneer Peasant Colonization in Ceylon: A Study in Asian Agrarian Problems* (London, Oxford University Press, issued under the auspices of the Royal Institute of International Affairs), 388 pp.

446. Field, Henry (comp.)

1962 *"M" Project for F. D. R.: Studies on Migration*

and Settlement (Ann Arbor, University of Michigan Press), 421 pp.

Floyd, J. S., Jr. *See* 541.

447. Ford, Thomas R. (ed.)

1962 *The Southern Appalachian Region: A Survey* (Lexington, University of Kentucky Press), 308 pp.

448. Francis, E. K.

1955 *In Search of Utopia: The Mennonites in Manitoba* (Glencoe, Ill., The Free Press), 294 pp.

449. French, Allen

1955 *Charles I and the Puritan Upheaval: A Study of the Causes of the Great Migration* (London, Allen and Unwin), 436 pp.

450. Fretz, J. W.

1962 *Immigrant Group Settlements in Paraguay: A Study in the Sociology of Colonization* (North Newton, Kans., Bethel College), 194 pp.

451. Fujii, Yukio, and T. Lynn Smith

1959 *The Acculturation of the Japanese Immigrants in Brazil: A Case Study*, University of Florida School of Inter-American Studies, Latin American Monograph Series, No. 8, 56 pp.

452. Galarza, Ernesto

1956 *Strangers in Our Fields* (Washington, Joint United States—Mexico Trade Union Committee, United States Section), 80 pp.

453. Gartner, Lloyd P.

1960 *The Jewish Immigrant in England, 1870-1914* (Detroit, Wayne State University Press), 320 pp.

454. Geisert, Harold L.

1962 *Population Growth and International Migration* (Washington, George Washington University), 57 pp.

455. George Washington University

1956 *A Report on World Population Migrations as Related to the United States of America: An Exploratory Survey of Past Studies and Researches on World Population Migration, with the View to Evaluating Areas Already Covered and Outlining Areas which Warrant Development* (Washington, George Washington University), 450 pp.

456. Gil, Benjamin Z.

1957 *Settlement of New Immigrants in Israel, 1948-53* (Jerusalem, Falk Project for Economic Research in Israel), 239 pp.

457. Ginsburg, Norton, and others

1958 *Malaya* (Seattle, University of Washington Press, published for the American Ethnological Society), 533 pp.

458. Glass Ruth

1961 *London's New-Comers: The West Indian Migrants* (Cambridge, Harvard University Press), 278 pp.

459. Goblet, Y. M.

1955 *Political Geography and the World Map* (London, George Philip and Son), 292 pp.

460. Goldstein, Sidney

1958 *Patterns of Mobility, 1910-1950: The Norristown Study* (Philadelphia, University of Pennsylvania Press), 254 pp.

461. Goldstein, Sidney

1961 *The Norristown Study: An Experiment in Interdisciplinary Research Training* (Philadelphia, University of Pennsylvania Press), 366 pp.

Goldstein, Sidney. *See* 546.

462. Goldstein, Sidney, and Kurt B. Mayer

1961 *Metropolitanization and Population Change in Rhode Island* (Providence, Planning Division, State Planning Section, Rhode Island Development Council), 60 pp.

463. Gourou, Pierre

1955 *The Peasants of the Tonkin Delta: A Study of Human Geography*, trans. Richard R. Miller (New Haven, Human Relations Area Files), 2 vols., 889 pp.

464. Govorchin, Gerald G.

1961 *Americans from Yugoslovia: A Survey of Yugoslav Immigrants in the United States* (Gainesville, University of Florida Press), 352 pp.

465. Graham, I. C. C.

1956 *Colonists from Scotland: Emigration to North America, 1707-1783* (Ithaca, Cornell University Press, published for the American Historical Association), 213 pp.

466. Great Britain. Commonwealth Relations Office

1956 *Second Report of the Oversea Migration Board, August, 1956*, Cmd. 9835 (London, H. M. Stationery Office), 40 pp.

467. Great Britain. Commonwealth Relations Office

1957 *Third Report of the Oversea Migration Board, December, 1957*, Cmd. 336 (London, H. M. Stationery Office), 36 pp.

468. Great Britain. East African Royal Commission

1955 *1953-1955 Report*, Cmd. 9475 (London, H. M. Stationery Office), 42 pp.

469. Green, L. P., and T. J. D. Fair

1962 *Development in Africa: A Study in Regional Analysis with Special Reference to Southern Africa* (Johannesburg, Witwatersrand University Press), 203 pp.

470. Griffith, J. A. G., and others

1960 *Coloured Immigrants in Britain: An Investigation Carried Out by the Institute of Race Relations* (London, Oxford University Press), 225 pp.

Grigsby, William G. *See* 572.

471. Gulliver, P. H.

1955 *Labour Migration in a Rural Economy: A Study of the Ngoni and Ndendeuli of Southern Tanganyika*, East African Studies, No. 6 (Kampala, Uganda, East African Institute of Social Research), 48 pp.

472. Hack, H.

1959 *Dutch Group Settlement in Brazil*, trans. Elizabeth Haig, *R. E. M. P. Bulletin*, Vol. 7, Supp. 4, 68 pp.

Hägerstrand, Torsten. *See* 481.

473. Hailey, Lord

1957 *An African Survey Revised 1956: A Study of Problems Arising in Africa South of the Sahara* (London, Oxford University Press, issued under the auspices of the Royal Institute of International Affairs), 1676 pp.

474. Hall, Douglas

1959 *Free Jamaica, 1838-1865: An Economic History* (New Haven, Yale University Press), 290 pp.

475. Hambro, Edvard

1955 *The Problem of Chinese Refugees in Hong Kong*, report submitted to the U.N. Commissioner for Refugees (Leyden, A. W. Sijthoff), 214 pp.

476. Hancock, Richard H.

1959 *The Role of the Bracero in the Economic and Cultural Dynamics of Mexico: A Case Study of Chihuahua* (Stanford, Calif., Hispanic American Society), 146 pp.

477. Handlin, Oscar

1959a *Boston's Immigrants: A Study in Acculturation* (Cambridge, The Belknap Press of Harvard University Press), 382 pp.

478. Handlin, Oscar (ed.)

1959b *Immigration as a Factor in American History* (Englewood Cliffs, N. J., Prentice-Hall), 206 pp.

479. Handlin, Oscar

1959c *The New Comers: Negroes and Puerto Ricans in a Changing Metropolis* (Cambridge, Harvard University Press), 171 pp.

480. Handlin, Oscar, and others

1955 *The Positive Contribution by Immigrants* (Paris, UNESCO), 200 pp.

481. Hannerberg, David, Torsten Hägerstrand, and Bruno Odeving (eds.)

1957 *Migration in Sweden: A Symposium,* Lund Studies in Geography, Series B., Human Geography, No. 13 (Lund: The Royal University of Lund), 336 pp.

482. Hanson, E. P.

1955 *Transformation: The Story of Modern Puerto Rico* (New York, Simon and Schuster), 416 pp.

483. Hasluck, A.

1959 *Unwilling Emigrants: A Study of the Convict Period In Western Australia* (Melbourne, Oxford University Press), 165 pp.

484. Hauser, Philip M. (ed.)

1958 *Population and World Politics* (Glencoe, Ill., The Free Press), 298 pp.

485. Hauser, Philip M., and Otis Dudley Duncan (eds.)

1959 *The Study of Populations* (Chicago, University of Chicago Press), 864 pp.

486. Hawley, Amos Henry

1956 *The Changing Shape of Metropolitan America* (Glencoe, Ill., The Free Press), 177 pp.

487. Hempel, J. A.

1959 *Italians in Queensland; Some Aspects of the Postwar Settlement of Italian Immigrants* (Canberra; Department of Demography, Australian National University), 185 pp.

488. Higham, John

1955 *Strangers in the Land* (New Brunswick, N.J., Rutgers University Press), 431 pp.

Hoermann, S. A. *See* 406.

489. Hoglund, William A.

1960 *Finnish Immigrants in America 1880-1920* (Madison, University of Wisconsin Press), 213 pp.

490. Holborn, Louise W.

1956 *The International Refugee Organization: A Spe-*

cialized Agency of the United Nations: Its History and Work, 1946-52 (New York, Oxford University Press), 805 pp.

491. Hoover, Edgar M., Raymond Vernon, and others

    1959 *Anatomy of a Metropolis: The Changing Distribution of People and Jobs within the New York Metropolitan Region*, New York Metropolitan Region Study Series, No. 1 (Cambridge, Harvard University Press), 345 pp.

492. Horigan, Francis D.

    1962 *The Israeli Kibbutz: Psychiatric, Psychological, and Social Studies with Emphasis on Family Life and Family Structure: A Survey of Literature* (Bethesda, Md., U.S. National Institute of Health), 62 pp.

493. Hovne, Avner

    1961 *The Labor Force in Israel* (Jerusalem, Falk Project for Economic Research in Israel), 88 pp.

494. Hutchinson, Edward Prince

    1956 *Immigrants and Their Children, 1850-1950* (New York, John Wiley, published for the Social Science Research Council in cooperation with the U.S. Department of Commerce, Bureau of the Census), 391 pp.

Immigration Reform Group. *See* 577.

495. India. West Bengal. State Statistical Bureau.

    1956 *Rehabilitation of Refugees: A Statistical Survey, 1955* (Alipore, West Bengal Government Press), 96 pp.

496. Indonesia. Biro Perantjang Negara.

    1960 *Report on the Execution of the Five-Year Development Plan 1956-1960, Covering the Years 1956-1957 and 1958* (Djakarta, Biro Ekonomi dan Keuangan), 421 pp.

Indonesia. Ministry of Defense. *See* 397.

497. Institute for Mediterranean Affairs

    1958 *The Palestine Refugee Problem: A New Approach and a Plan for a Solution* (New York, Institute for Mediterranean Affairs), 133 pp.

498. Inter-African Labour Institute

    1962 *Migrant Labour in Africa South of the Sahara: Proceedings under Item II of the Agenda of the Sixth Inter-African Labour Conference, Abidjan, 1961, and Other Relevant Papers*, Scientific Council for Africa South of the Sahara Publication 79 (London, Commission for Technical Co-operation in Africa), 338 pp.

499. Intergovernmental Committee for European Migration

    1962 *Report for the Year 1 January/31 December 1961* (Geneva, Intergovernmental Committee for European Migration), 51 pp.

International African Institute. *See* 652.

500. International Catholic Migration Congress, 3rd, Assisi, 1957

    1957 *Third International Catholic Migration Congress*, ed. Information Centre of the International Catholic Migration Commission (Geneva, International Catholic Migration Commission), 342 pp.

501. International Catholic Migration Congress, 4th, Ottawa, 1960

    1960 *The Integration of Catholic Immigrants*, International Catholic Migration Congress (4th) Ottawa, 21-25 August (Ottawa, International Catholic Migration Commission), 533 pp.

International Catholic Migration Commission. *See* 614.

502. International Conference of Agricultural Economics

    1960 *Proceedings of the Tenth International Conference of Agricultural Economists*, Mysore, 1958 (London, Oxford University Press), 535 pp.

International Economic Association. *See* 651.

503. International Labour Office

    1955 *International Labour Conference, 38th Session, Geneva, 1955*, Report V(2), *Migrant Workers (Under-developed Countries)* (Geneva, International Labour Office), 85 pp.

504. International Labour Office

    1956 *Social Aspects of European Economic Co-Cooperation: Report by a Group of Experts* (Geneva, International Labour Office), 179 pp.

505. International Labour Office

    1959a *International Migration 1945-1957* Studies and Reports, New Series, No. 54 (Geneva, International Labour Office), 414 pp.

506. International Labour Office

    1959b *International Migration of Labour in the Construction Industry* (Geneva, International Labour Office), 122 pp.

507. International Labour Office

    1960 *Why Labour Leaves the Land: A Comparative Study of the Movement of Labour Out of Agriculture*, New Series, No. 59 (Geneva, International Labour Office), 229 pp.

508. International Labour Office

    1961a *Employment Objectives in Economic Development: Report of a Meeting of Experts*, Studies and Reports, New Series, 62 (Geneva, International Labour Office), 255 pp.

509. International Labour Office

1961b *Social Security for Migrants and Non-Nationals* (Geneva, International Labour Office), 61 pp.

510. International Labour Organization

1960 *First African Regional Conference, 1960*, Report I, Report of the Director-General (Geneva, International Labour Organization), 90 pp.

International Sociological Association. *See* 651.

511. Iowa State University Center for Agricultural and Economic Adjustment

1961 *Labor Mobility and Population in Agriculture* (Ames, Iowa State University Press), 231 pp.

512. Ireland. Commission on Emigration and Other Population Problems, 1948-1954.

1955 *Reports* (Dublin, Stationery Office), 418 pp.

513. Isles, K. S., and Norman Cuthbert

1957 *An Economic Survey of Northern Ireland* (Belfast, Ministry of Commerce), 646 pp.

514. Jackson, R. N.

1961 *Immigrant Labour and the Development of Malaya, 1789-1920* (Kuala Lumpur, Government Printer), 160 pp.

515. Jones, Maldwyn A.

1960 *American Immigration* (Chicago, University of Chicago Press), 359 pp.

516. Kaplan, Benjamin

1957 *The Eternal Stranger: A Study of Jewish Life in the Small Community* (New York, Bookman Associates), 198 pp.

517. Kaplan, Deborah

1959 *The Arab Refugees: An Abnormal Problem*, trans. Misha Louvish (Jerusalem, Rubin Mass), 230 pp.

518. Keep, George R.

1956 *The Irish Migration to Montreal, 1847-1867*, Canadian Studies Series, No. 19 (Rochester, University of Rochester Press), 131 pp.

519. Kephart, Calvin

1960 *Races of Mankind: Their Origin and Migration* (New York, Philosophical Library), 566 pp.

520. Klass, Morton

1961 *East Indians in Trinidad: A Study of Cultural Persistence* (New York, Columbia University Press), 265 pp.

521. Knoellinger, F. C. E.

1960 *Labor in Finland* (Cambridge, Harvard University Press), 300 pp.

522. Koehl, Robert L.

1957 *RKFDV: German Resettlement and Population Policy, 1939-1945: A History of the Reich Commission for the Strengthening of Germandom*, Harvard Historical Monographs, 31 (Cambridge, Harvard University Press), 263 pp.

523. Koos, Earl Lomon

1957 *They Follow the Sun* (Jacksonville, Bureau of Maternal and Child Health, Florida State Board of Health), 55 pp.

524. Koren, Elisabeth

1955 *The Diary of Elisabeth Koren: 1853-1855*, ed. David T. Nelson (Northfield, Minn. Norwegian-American Historical Association), 381 pp.

525. Kulldorff, Gunnar

1955 *Migration Probabilities*, Lund Studies in Geography, Series B., Human Georgraphy, No. 14, Royal University of Lund (Lund, C. W. K. Gleerup), 44 pp.

526. Kuper, Hilda

1960 *Indian People in Natal* (Natal, The University Press), 305 pp.

527. Kuper, Leo, and others

1958 *Durban: A Study in Racial Ecology* (London, Jonathan Cape), 254 pp.

528. Kuznets, Simon, Ann Ratner Miller, and Richard A. Easterlin

1960 *Population Redistribution and Economic Growth: U. S., 1870-1950, Volume II: Analyses of Economic Change* (Philadelphia, The American Philosophical Society), 289 pp.

529. Landis, Benson Y.

1961 *Protestant Experience with U. S. Immigration, 1910-1960: A Study Paper* (New York, World Church Service), 81 pp.

Lee, Everett S. *See* 542.

530. Lee, Everett S., and others

1957 *Population Redistribution and Economic Growth: U. S., 1870-1950, Volume I: Methodological Considerations and Reference Tables*, prepared under the direction of Simon Kuznets and Dorothy S. Thomas (Philadelphia, American Philosophical Society), 759 pp.

531. Lewis, E. D.

1959 *The Rhondda Valleys: A Study on Industrial Development from 1800 to the Present Day* (London, Phoenix House), 312 pp.

532. Lias, Godfrey

1956 *Kazak Exodus* (London, Evans), 230 pp.

533. Lichtenberg, Robert M.

    1960 *One-tenth of a Nation: National Forces in the Economic Growth of the New York Region*, New York Metropolitan Region Study, No. 7 (Cambridge, Harvard University Press), 326 pp.

534. Lipscomb, J. F.

    1955 *White Africans* (London, Faber and Faber), 172 pp.

535. Lorimer, Frank, and Mark Karp (eds.)

    1960 *Population in Africa* (Boston, Boston University Press), 88 pp.

536. Lucas, Henry S.

    1955 *Netherlands in America: Dutch Immigration to the United States, 1789-1950* (Ann Arbor, University of Michigan Press), 744 pp.

537. Lutz, Vera C.

    1962 *Italy: A Study in Economic Development* (London, Oxford University Press, under the auspices of the Royal Institute of International Affairs), 342 pp.

538. McCaskill, Murray (ed.)

    1962 *Land and Livelihood: Geographical Essays in Honour of George Jobberns* (Christchurch, New Zealand Geographical Society), 280 pp.

539. McCleary, George Frederick

    1955 *Peopling the British Commonwealth* (London, Faber and Faber), 174 pp.

540. McCulloch, Merran

    1956 *A Social Survey of the African Population of Livingstone*, The Rhodes-Livingstone Papers, No. 26 (Manchester, Manchester University Press, published on behalf of the Rhodes-Livingstone Institute), 86 pp.

541. Maclachlan, John M., and J. S. Floyd, Jr.

    1956 *This Changing South* (Gainesville, University of Florida Press), 154 pp.

542. Malzberg, Benjamin, and Everett S. Lee

    1956 *Migration and Mental Disease: A Study of First Admissions to Hospitals for Mental Disease, New York, 1939-1941* (New York, Social Science Research Council), 142 pp.

Manley, Douglas. *See* 598.

543. Marris, Peter

    1961 *Family and Social Change in an African City: A Study of Rehousing in Lagos* (London, Routledge and Kegan Paul), 180 pp.

Martinez Infante, Marke. *See* 426.

544. Mathewson, J. Edward

    1957 *The Establishment of an Urban Bantu Township* (Pretoria, J. L. Van Schaik, Ltd.), 143 pp.

545. Mayer, Adrian C.

    1961 *Peasants in the Pacific: A Study of Fiji Indian Rural Society* (Berkeley, University of California Press), 202 pp.

546. Mayer, Kurt B., and Sidney Goldstein

    1958 *Migration and Economic Development in Rhode Island* (Providence, R. I., Brown University Press), 63 pp.

547. Mayer, Phillip

    1961 *Townsmen or Tribesmen: Conservatism and the Process of Urbanization in a South African City* (Cape Town, Oxford University Press, published in behalf of the Rhodes University Institute of Social and Economic Research), 306 pp.

548. Metzler, William H., and Frederic O. Sargent

    1960 *Migratory Farm Workers in the Midcontinent Streams*, U.S. Agricultural Research Service, Research Report No. 41 (Washington, Government Printing Office), 61 pp.

549. Milbank Memorial Fund

    1958 *Selected Studies of Migration Since World War II*, Proceedings of the 34th Annual Conference of the Milbank Memorial Fund, at the N. Y. Academy of Medicine, October 30-31, 1957, Part III (New York, Milbank Memorial Fund), 244 pp.

Miller, Ann Ratner. *See* 528 and 530.

550. Minnesota, University of.

    1961 *Immigration and American History: Essays in Honor of Theodore C. Blegen*, ed. Henry S. Commager (London, Oxford University Press), 166 pp.

551. Mol, Johannes Jacob

    1961 *Churches and Immigrants (A Sociological Study of the Mutual Effect of Religion and Immigrant Adjustment)*, *R. E. M. P. Bulletin*, Vol. 9, Supp. 5, 86 pp.

552. Moser, Claus A., and Wolf Scott

    1961 *British Towns: A Statistical Study of Their Social and Economic Differences* (Edinburgh, Oliver and Boyd), 169 pp.

553. Mulder, William

    1957 *Homeward to Zion: The Mormn Migration from Scandinavia* (Minneapolis, University of Minnesota Press), 375 pp.

554. Murphy, H. B. M., and others

    1955 *Flight and Resettlement*, Population and Culture Series II (Paris, UNESCO), 228 pp.

555. Norwegian-American Historical Association

    1956 *Norwegian-American Studies and Records*, Vol. XIX, 217 pp.

Odeving, Bruno. *See* 481.

556. Padilla, Elena

    1958 *Up from Puerto Rico* (New York, Columbia University Press), 317 pp.

557. Paikert, G. C.

    1962 *The German Exodus: A Selective Study on the Post-World War II Expulsion of German Populations and Its Effects* (The Hague, Martinus Nijhoff, published for the Research Group for European Migration Problems), 97 pp.

558. Palmer, Mabel

    1957 *The History of the Indians in Natal*, Natal Regional Survey, Vol. 10 (Cape Town, Oxford University Press), 197 pp.

559. Patterson, Sheila

    1957 *The Last Trek: A Study of the Boer People and the Afrikaner Nation* (London, Routledge and Kegan Paul), 336 pp.

560. Pellegrini, Angelo

    1956 *Americans by Choice* (New York, Macmillan), 240 pp.

561. Petersen, William

    1955 *Planned Migration: The Social Determinants of the Dutch-Canadian Movement* (Berkeley, University of California Press), 273 pp.

562. Petersen, William

    1961 *Population* (New York, Macmillan), 652 pp.

Philippines, Republic of. *See* 443.

563. Philosophical Society of Sudan, and Department of Statistics, Republic of Sudan

    1958 *The Population of Sudan*, Report of the Sixth Annual Conference held in the University of Khartoum, 16-17 January, 1958 (Khartoum, Philosophical Society of Sudan), 110 pp.

564. Pinner, Walter

    1959 *How Many Arab Refugees? A Critical Study of UNRWA's Statistics and Reports* (London, Macgibbon and Kee), 65 pp.

565. Pisani, Lawrence Frank

    1957 *The Italian in America* (New York, Exposition Press), 293 pp.

566. Pollitt, Daniel H.

    1960 *The Migrant Farm Worker in America: Background Data on the Migrant Worker Situation in the U.S. Today* (Washington, U. S. Government Printing Office), 79 pp.

567. Powesland, P. G.

    1957 *Economic Policy and Labor: A Study in Uganda's Economic History* (Kampala, East African Institute of Social Research), 80 pp.

Prosper, Peter A., Jr. *See* 410.

568. Prothero, R. Mansell

    1959 *Migrant Labour from Sokota Province, Northern Nigeria* (Kaduna, Government Printer, Northern Region of Nigeria), 46 pp.

569. Proudfoot, Malcolm J.

    1956 *European Refugees, 1939-52: A Study in Forced Population Movement* (Evanston, Ill., Northwestern University Press), 542 pp.

570. Radspieler, Tony

    1955 *The Ethnic German Refugee in Austria, 1945 to 1954*, Studies in Social Life II (The Hague, Martinus Nijhoff), 197 pp.

571. Rand, Christopher

    1958 *The Puerto Ricans* (New York, Oxford University Press), 178 pp.

572. Rapkin, Chester, and William G. Grigsby

    1960 *The Demand for Housing in Racially Mixed Areas: A Study of the Nature of Neighborhood Change* (Berkeley, University of California Press), 177 pp.

573. Read, James M.

    1962 *The United Nations and Refugees: Changing Concepts*, International Conciliation, No. 537 (New York, Carnegie Endowment for International Peace), 60 pp.

574. Reader, D. H.

    1961 *The Black Man's Portion: History, Demography, and Living Conditions in the Native Locations of East London, Cape Province*, Xhosa in Town, 1 (Cape Town, Oxford University Press, published on behalf of the Institute of Social and Economic Research, Rhodes University), 180 pp.

575. Reubens, S. P.

    1960 *Migration and Development in the West Indies*, Studies in Federal Economics, 3, Institute of Social and Economic Research (Kingston, Jamaica, University College of the West Indies), 84 pp.

Rhodes-Livingstone Institute. *See* 668.

576. Rhodes-Livingstone Institute for Social Research, Eleventh Conference

    1958 *Present Interrelations in Central African Rural*

and Urban Life, being the Proceedings of the Eleventh Conference of the Rhodes-Livingstone Institute for Social Research Held at Lusaka, Northern Rhodesia, January 14th-17th, 1958, ed. R. J. Apthorpe (Lusaka, The Rhodes-Livingstone Institute), 176 pp.

577. Rivett, Kenneth (ed.)

1962 *Immigration: Control or Colour Bar? The Background to "White Australia" and a Proposal for Change,* 2nd edition, rev, and enlarged (Parkville, Melbourne University Press, for the Immigration Reform Group), 171 pp.

Robbins, Richard. *See* 624.

578. Roberts, George W.

1957 *The Population of Jamaica* (Cambridge, Eng., University Press, published for the Conservation Foundation), 356 pp.

579. Robertson, A. H.

1961 *The Council of Europe: Its Structure, Functions and Achievements;* 2nd ed. (London, Stevens, published under the auspices of the London Institute of World Affairs), 288 pp.

Rose, J. Hugh. *See* 396.

Roskamp, Karl W. *See* 620.

580. Rossi, Peter H.

1955 *Why Families Move: A Study in the Social Psychology of Urban Residential Mobility* (Glencoe, Ill., The Free Press), 220 pp.

581. Rowley, Charles D.

1958 *The Australians in German New Guinea, 1914-1921* (Melbourne, Melbourne University Press), 371 pp.

582. Rozenberg, M.

n.d. *The Measurement of the Economic Absorption of Israel's New Immigrant Sector from a National Point of View* (Jerusalem, The Hebrew University, The Eliezer Kaplan School of Economics and Social Sciences), 129 pp. (processed).

583. Ruck, S. K.

1960 *The West Indian Comes to England* (London, Routledge and Kegan Paul), 187 pp.

584. Saksena, R. N.

1961 *Refugees: A Study in Changing Attitudes* (London, Asia Publishing House), 119 pp.

585. Salera, Virgil

1960 *U. S. Immigration Policy and World Population Problems* (Washington American Enterprise Association), 37 pp.

586. Sampson, R.

1956 *They Came to Northern Rhodesia; being a Record of Persons Who Had Entered What is Now the Territory of Northern Rhodesia by 31st December 1902* (Lusaka, Government Printer), 49 pp.

Sargent, Frederic O. *See* 548.

587. Savan, David

1955 *Newcomers from Israel* (Toronto, Research Committee, Canadian Jewish Congress, Central Region), 43 pp.

588. Saville, J.

1957 *Rural Depopulation in England and Wales, 1851-1951* (London, Routledge and Kegan Paul), 253 pp.

589. Schauff, J. (comp.)

1956 *Immigrant Colonization in Brazil, as Seen by European Experts, With the Cooperation of 24 Experts in Rural Settlement* (Geneva, International Catholic Migration Commission), 36 pp.

590. Schechtman, Joseph B.

1962 *Postwar Population Transfers in Europe, 1945-1955* (Philadelphia, University of Pennsylvania Press), 417 pp.

591. Schnell, E. L. G.

1955 *For Men Must Work: An Account of German Immigration to the Cape with Special Reference to the German Military Settlers of 1857 and the German Migrants of 1858* (London, M. Miller), 300 pp.

592. Schrier, Arnold

1958 *Ireland and the American Emigration, 1850-1900* (Minneapolis, University of Minnesota Press), 210 pp.

593. Schwarz, Leo W.

1957 *Refugees in Germany Today* (New York, Twayne), 172 pp.

Scott, Wolf. *See* 552.

594. Sen, Probhat K.

1962 *Land and People of the Andamans* (Calcutta, Post-Graduate Book Mart), 197 pp.

595. Sen, S. N.

1960 *The City of Calcutta: A Sociological Economic Survey, 1954-55 to 1957-58* (Calcutta, Bookland Private Ltd.), 269 pp.

596. Sen, Satyabrata

n.d. *Report on the Sample Survey of Displaced Persons in the Urban Areas of Bombay State, July-September 1953,* The National Sample Survey

No. 9 (Calcutta, Eka Press, for the Cabinet Secretariat, Government of India), 98 pp.

597. Senior Clarence

1961 *Strangers Then Neighbors: From Pilgrims to Puerto Ricans* (New York, Freedom Books), 88 pp.

598. Senior, Clarence, and Douglas Manley

1955 *A Report on Jamaican Migration to Great Britain* (Kingston, Jamaica, Government Printer), 68 pp.

599. Shannon, James P.

1957 *Catholic Colonization of the Western Frontier,* Yale Publications in American Studies, Vol. 1 (New Haven, Yale University Press), 302 pp.

600. Shepperson, Wilbur S.

1957 *British Emigration to North America: Projects and Opinions in the Early Victorian Period* (Oxford, Blackwell), 302 pp.

601. Shotwell, Louisa Rossiter

1961 *The Harvesters: The Story of Migrant People* (Garden City, N. Y., Doubleday), 242 pp.

Shryock, H. S. *See* 406.

602. Sicron, Moshe

1957 *Immigration to Israel, 1948-1953,* Falk Project for Economic Research in Israel and Central Bureau of Statistics, Special Series, No. 60 (Jerusalem, The Falk Project for Economic Research in Israel), 138 pp.

603. Simpson, Richard L., and others

1960 *Occupational Choice and Mobility in the Urbanizing Piedmont of North Carolina* (Chapel Hill, Institute for Research in Social Science, University of North Carolina), 257 pp.

604. Sklare, Marshall (ed.)

1958 *The Jews: Social Patterns of an American Group* (Glencoe, Ill., The Free Press), 670 pp.

605. Slotkin, James Sydney

1960 *From Field to Factory: New Industrial Employees* (Glencoe, Ill., The Free Press, published for the Research Center in Economic Development and Cultural Change, University of Chicago), 156 pp.

Smith, T. Lynn. *See* 451.

606. Solomon, Barbara M.

1956 *Ancestors and Immigrants, A Changing New England Tradition* (Cambridge, Harvard University Press), 276 pp.

607. South Africa, Union of. Bureau of Census and Statistics.

1960-1961 *Official Yearbook of the Union and of Basu-* *toland. Bechuanaland Protectorate and Swaziland, No. 30-1960* (Pretoria, Government Printer), 713 pp.

608. Southall, Aidan W. (ed.)

1961 *Social Change in Modern Africa: Studies Presented and Discussed at the First International African Seminar, Makere College, Kampala, 1959* (London, Oxford University Press, published for the International African Institute), 337 pp.

609. Sovani, N. V., and others

1956 *Poona: A Re-Survey: The Changing Pattern of Employment and Earnings,* Publication No. 34 (Poona, Gokhale Institute of Politics and Economics), 558 pp.

610. Spengler, Joseph J., and Otis Dudley Duncan (eds.)

1956a *Demographic Analysis: Selected Readings* (Glencoe, Ill., The Free Press), 819 pp.

611. Spengler, Joseph J., and Otis Dudley Duncan (eds.)

1956b *Population Theory and Policy: Selected Readings* (Glencoe, Ill., The Free Press), 522 pp.

612. Spicer, Edward H.

1962 *Cycles of Conquest: The Impact of Spain, Mexico, and the United States on the Indians of the Southwest, 1533-1960* (Tucson, University of Arizona Press), 609 pp.

613. Srole, Leo, and others

1962 *Mental Health in the Metropolis: The Midtown Manhattan Study,* Vol. I (New York, McGraw-Hill), 428 pp.

614. Stark, Tadeusz

1957 *Family Migration,* Special Working Group Report, Third International Catholic Migration Congress, Assisi, September 22-28, 1957 (Geneva, International Catholic Migration Commission), 203 pp.

615. Staudenraus, P. J.

1961 *The African Colonization Movement, 1816-1865* (New York, Columbia University Press), 323 pp.

616. Steigenga, William

1955 *Industrialization—Emigration: The Consequences of the Demographic Development in the Netherlands* (The Hague, Martinus Nijhoff, published for the Research Group for European Migration Problems), 69 pp.

617. Stenning, Derrick J.

1959 *Savannah Nomads: A Study of the Wodaabe Pastoral Fulani of Western Bornu Province, Northern Region, Nigeria.* (London, Oxford University Press, published for the International African Institute), 266 pp.

618. Stoessinger, John G.

 1956 *The Refugee and the World Community* (Minneapolis, University of Minnesota Press), 239 pp.

619. Stolper, Wolfgang F.

 1956 *Population Movements and Labor Force in the SBZ.* (Cambridge, Center for International Studies, Massachusetts Institute of Technology), 73 pp. (processed).

620. Stolper, Wolfgang F., and Karl W. Roskamp

 1960 *The Structure of the East German Economy* (Cambridge: Harvard University Press, published for the Center for International Studies, Massachusetts Institute of Technology), 478 pp.

621. Sutton, Elizabeth

 1960 *Knowing and Teaching the Migrant Child* (Washington, Department of Rural Education, National Education Association), 147 pp.

622. Taeuber, Conrad, and Irene B. Taeuber

 1958 *The Changing Population of the United States* (New York, John Wiley), 357 pp.

623. Taeuber, Irene B.

 1958 *The Population of Japan* (Princeton, Princeton University Press, published under the editorial sponsorship of the Office of Population Research, Princeton University), 462 pp.

 Taeuber, Irene B. *See* 622.

624. Taft, Donald R., and Richard Robbins

 1955 *International Migrations* (New York, Ronald Press), 670 pp.

625. Taft, Ronald, and A. Gedeon Doczy

 1961 *The Assimilation of Intellectual Refugees in Western Australia; with Special Reference to Hungarians, R. E. M. P. Bulletin,* Vol. 9, No. 4 and Vol. 10, Nos. 1-2, 82 pp.

626. Textor, Robert B.

 1961 *From Peasant to Pedicab Driver: A Social Study of Northeastern Thai Farmers Who Periodically Migrated to Bangkok and Became Pedicab Drivers* (New Haven, Yale University), 83 pp.

627. Thieme, Frederick P.

 1959 *The Puerto Rican Population: A Study in Human Biology,* Anthropological Papers, Museum of Anthropology, No. 13 (Ann Arbor, University of Michigan), 219 pp. (processed).

628. Thomas, Brinley (ed.)

 1958 *Economics of International Migration,* Proceedings of a Conference Held by the International Economic Association (London, Macmillan), 502 pp.

629. Thomas, Brinley

 1961 *International Migration and Economic Development: A Trend Report and Bibliography* (New York, Columbia University Press, published for UNESCO), 85 pp.

630. Thompson, Raymond H. (ed.)

 1961 *Migrations: In New World Culture History* (Tucson, University of Arizona Press), 68 pp.

631. Thompson, Virginia, and Richard Adloff

 1955 *Minority Problems in Southeast Asia* (Stanford, Stanford University Press, published for the International Secretariat, Institute of Pacific Relations), 296 pp.

632. Thompson, Warren S.

 1955 *Growth and Changes in California's Population* (Los Angeles, The Haynes Foundation), 377 pp.

633. Thornbrough, Emma L.

 1957 *The Negro in Indiana: A Study of a Minority,* Indiana Historical Collections, Vol. 37 (Indianapolis, Indiana Historical Bureau), 412 pp.

634. Tracey, Stanley J. (ed.)

 1956 *A Report on World Population Migrations as Related to U.S.A.* (Washington, McGregor and Warner), 450 pp.

635. Treadgold, Donald W.

 1957 *The Great Siberian Migration: Government and Peasant in Resettlement from Emancipation to to the First World War* (Princeton, Princeton University Press), 278 pp.

636. Turner, Roy (ed.)

 1962 *India's Urban Future* (Berkeley, University of California Press), 470 pp.

637. Tyler, Poyntz (ed.)

 1956 *Immigration and the United States,* The Reference Shelf, Vol. 28, No. 1 (New York, H. W. Wilson), 202 pp.

638. Uchida, Naosaku

 1959 *The Overseas Chinese: A Bibliographical Essay Based on the Resources of the Hoover Institution,* Hoover Institution on War, Revolution, and Peace, Bibliographical Series, 7 (Stanford, Stanford University), 134 pp.

639. United Nations

 1955a *Proceedings of the World Population Conference, 1954, Volume II, August 31-September 10, Rome* (New York, United Nations), 1040 pp.

640. United Nations

 1955b *Study on Expulsion of Immigrants* (New York,

Department of Economic and Social Affairs, United Nations), 77 pp.

641. United Nations

1956a *Analytical Bibliography of International Migration Statistics, Selected Countries, 1925-1950* (New York, United Nations), 195 pp.

642. United Nations

1956b *Report of the United Nations High Commissioner for Refugees* (New York, United Nations), 70 pp.

643. United Nations

1957 *Preliminary Report on Possibilities for International Co-operation in the Study of Internal Migration,* Item 13, Population Commission, Ninth Session, New York, 25 February—8 March 1957 (New York, United Nations), 32 pp.

644. United Nations

1958a *Report of the United Nations High Commissioner for Refugees, 1957-58,* United Nations General Assembly, Official Records, 13th Session, Supplement No. 11 (New York, United Nations), 59 pp.

645. United Nations

1958b *Survey of the Non-settled Refugee Population in Various Countries,* Report Submitted to the United Nations High Commissioner for Refugees by Professor Dr. Ph. J. Idenburg (New York, Executive Committee, United Nations Refugee Fund), 111 pp. (processed).

646. United Nations

1959a *Economic Characteristics of International Migrants: Statistics for Selected Countries, 1918-1954* (New York, Department of Economic and Social Affairs, United Nations), 314 pp.

647. United Nations

1959b *Final Report for the Ford Foundation Program for Refugees, Primarily in Europe, Implemented by Voluntary Agencies and Administered through the United Nations High Commissioner for Refugees* (Geneva, High Commissioner for Refugees, United Nations), 127 pp. (See other similar reports by the UN High Commissioner for Refugees.)

648. United Nations

1960a *Report, 1959-60,* General Assembly, Official Records, 15th Session, Supplement 11 (New York, United Nations, Office of the High Commissioner for Refugees), 35 pp.

649. United Nations

1960b *Internal Migration: Use of Census Data to Measure Volume and Characteristics of Migrants, and Reasons for Moving,* United Nations Seminar on Evaluation and Utilization of Population Census Data in Asia and the Far East, 20 June—8 July 1960, Bombay, India (New York, United Nations), 27 pp.

650. United Nations

1961 *The Mysore Population Study: Report of a Field Study Carried Out in Selected Areas of Mysore State, India,* Population Studies No. 34. (New York, United Nations), 443 pp.

651. United Nations Educational, Scientific, and Cultural Organization (UNESCO)

1955 *The Positive Contribution by Migrants,* A symposium prepared for UNESCO by the International Sociological Association and the International Economic Association. (Paris, UNESCO), 199 pp.

652. UNESCO

1956 *Social Implications of Industrialization and Urbanization in Africa South of the Sahara,* Prepared under the auspices of UNESCO by the International African Institute, London, Tension and Technology Series (Paris, UNESCO), 744 pp.

653. UNESCO

1957 *Human and Animal Ecology: Reviews of Research, No. 8* (Paris, UNESCO), 244 pp.

654. UNESCO. Research Centre on the Social Implications of Industrialization in Southern Asia.

1956 *The Social Implications of Industrialization and Urbanization; Five Studies of Urban Populations of Recent Rural Origin in Cities of Southern Asia* (Calcutta, Research Centre on the Social Implications of Industrialization in Southern Asia, UNESCO), 268 pp.

UNESCO. *See* 407, 480, and 629.

655. U. S. Bureau of the Census

1960 *Historical Statistics of the U.S. Colonial Times to 1957* (Washington, Bureau of the Census), 789 pp.

656. Vakil, C. N.

1956 *Government and the Displaced Persons: A Study in Social Tensions* (Bombay, Vora and Company), 144 pp.

657. Vamathevon, S.

1961 *Internal Migration in Ceylon, 1946-53,* Monograph 13 (Colombo, Department of Census and Statistics), 72 pp.

658. Veiter, Theodor (ed.)

1962 *Expulsion, Refuge, Domicile: Scientific Results of the Eleventh Congress of the Research Societies for Refugee Questions AER/AWR in Saloniki and Athens* (Vienna, W. Braumuller), 230 pp.

659. Vernon, Raymond

    1960 *Metropolis, 1985: An Interpretation of the Findings of the New York Metropolitan Region Study* (Cambridge, Harvard University Press), 251 pp.

Vernon, Raymond. *See* 491.

660. Verwey-Jonker, H., and P. O. M. Brackel

    1957 *The Assimilation and Integration of Pre- and Postwar Refugees in the Netherlands* (The Hague, Martinus Nijhoff, published for the Research Group for European Migration Problems), 55 pp.

661. Virginia, University of. Bureau of Population and Economic Research.

    1956 *The Impact of Industry in a Southern Rural Community: Changes in Road Use, Travel Habits and Socio-economic Characteristics in Charlotte County, Virginia, Five Years after the Establishment of a New Manufacturing Plant* (Richmond, Bureau of Population and Economic Research, University of Virginia, prepared in cooperation with the Division of Traffic and Planning, Virginia Department of Highways and the U.S. Bureau of Public Roads), 244 pp.

662. Wade, Richard C.

    1959 *The Urban Frontier: The Rise of Western Cities, 1790-1830*, Harvard Historical Monographs, 41 (Cambridge, Harvard University Press), 362 pp.

663. Weinberg, Abraham A.

    1961 *Migration and Belonging: A Study of Mental Health and Personal Adjustment in Israel*, Studies in Social Life V (The Hague, Martinus Nijhoff), 402 pp.

664. Westoff, Charles F., and others

    1961 *Family Growth in Metropolitan America* (Princeton, Princeton University Press), 433 pp.

665. White, Gilbert Fowler

    1958 *Changes in Urban Occupance of Flood Plains in the U. S.* (Chicago, University of Chicago), 235 pp.

666. Wilber, George L., and Ellen S. Bryant

    1962 *Population Research and Administrative Planning*, Conference Series No. 10 (State College, Division of Social and Rural Life, Mississippi State University), 74 pp.

667. Wilgus, A. Curtis (ed.)

    1957 *The Caribbean: Contemporary International Relations* (Gainesville: University of Florida Press), 330 pp.

668. Williams, Stuart

    1962 *The Distribution of the African Population of Northern Rhodesia*, Rhodes-Livingstone Communication 24 (Lusaka, Rhodes-Livingstone Institute), 37 pp. (with separately bound pamphlet).

Williams, T. Desmond. *See* 438.

669. Willmott, Donald E.

    1960 *The Chinese of Semarang: A Changing Minority Community in Indonesia* (Ithaca, N. Y., Cornell University Press, published under the auspices of the Modern Indonesia Project, Southeast Asia Program, Cornell University), 374 pp.

670. Wiskemann, Elizabeth

    1956 *Germany's Eastern Neighbours: Problems Relating to the Oder-Neisse Line and the Czech Frontier Regions* (London, Oxford University Press, issued under the auspices of the Royal Institute of International Affairs, 310 pp.

671. Wood, Arthur E.

    1955 *Hamtramck Then and Now: A Study of a Polish-American Community* (New York, Bookman Associates), 254 pp.

672. Woods, Harry D., and Ostry Sylvia

    1962 *Labour Policy and Labour Economics in Canada* (Toronto, Macmillan), 534 pp.

673. World Council of Churches. Division of Inter-Church Aid and Service to Refugees.

    1961 *In a Strange Land: A Report of a World Conference on Problems of International Migration and the Responsibility of the Churches, held at Leysin, Switzerland, June 11-16, 1961* (Geneva, World Council of Churches), 95 pp.

674. World Federation for Mental Health

    1960 *Uprooting and Resettlement*, Papers of 11th Annual Meeting of the World Federation for Mental Health, Vienna, Austria, August, 1958 (London, World Federation for Mental Health), 150 pp.

675. Young, Gordon

    1962 *The Hill Tribes of Northern Thailand: A Socio-Ethnological Report*, 2d ed. (Bangkok, Siam Society), 92 pp.

676. Zachodnia Agencja Prasowa (Journalists' Cooperative)

    1961 *Population Movements Between the Oder and Bug Rivers, 1939-1950* (Poznan, Wydawnictwo Zachodnie), 108 pp.

677. Zellerbach Commission on the European Refugee Situation

    1959 *European Refugee Problems 1959* (New York, Zellerbach Commission on the European Refugee Situation), 96 pp.

678. Zierer, Clifford M. (ed.)

    1956 *California and the Southwest* (New York, John Wiley), 376 pp.

679. Zubrzycki, Jerzy

    1956 *Polish Immigrants in Britain: A Study in Adjustment,* Studies in Social Life III (The Hague, Martinus Nijhoff), 219 pp.

680. Zubrzycki, Jerzy

    1960a *Immigrants in Australia: A Demographic Survey Based upon the 1954 Census* (Melbourne, Melbourne University Press, published on behalf of the Australian National University), 118 pp.

681. Zubrzycki, Jerzy

    1960b *Immigrants in Australia: Statistical Supplement,* Social Science Monographs, No. 18 (Canberra, The Australian National University), 108 pp.

III. OTHER UNANNOTATED MATERIALS

*682. Aagesen, Aage

1955 "The Japanese Population in Brazil," *Kulturgeografi,* 7:1-8 (February).

683. Ackley, G., and L. Spaventa

1962 "Emigration and Industrialization in Southern Italy: A Comment," *Banco Nazionale del Lavoro Quarterly Review,* No. 61:196-204 (June).

*684. Acsádi, György

1956 "Internal Migration of Population in Hungary," *Statisztikai Szemle,* 34:451-62 (May).

*685. Acsádi, György

1960 "Some Problems of Migration and Regional Planning," *Demografia,* 3 (3-4):390-423.

*686. Acsádi, György

1961 "Main Features of Hungarian Vital Statistics in 1960," *Demografia,* 4 (2):259-68.

*687. Acsádi, György, and Egon Szabady

1956 "Demographic Trends of 1955 in Hungary," *Statisztikai Szemle,* 34:821-52 (October).

Adloff, Richard. *See* 1871.

688. Agapitidis, Sotitios

1961 "Emigration from Greece," *Migration,* 1:53-61 (January-March).

689. Agarwala, S. N.

1958 "A Method for Estimating Decade Internal Migration in Cities from Indian Census Data," *Indian Economic Review,* 4:59-76 (February).

690. Agricultural Policy Institute. North Carolina State College.

1961 *The Farmer and Migration in the United States,* papers presented at a research workshop, 91 pp.

691. Ahmad, Kazi S.

1955 "A Geographical Study of the Refugee Population and Some of Its Problems," *Pakistan Geographical Review,* 10 (2):1-18.

*692. Ajo, Reino

1962 "The Rovaniemi Basin as Shown by the Geographical Variations in the Annual Growth of Population, and the Time Variation in the Net Migrational Rate for the Basin in the Light of Economic Fluctuations and in Conditions of Unrestricted Migration, 1866-1939," *Terra,* 74 (1):8-22.

693. Alabama, University of. Business Research Council.

1958 *Flight from the Soil,* 57 pp.

694. Allen-Price, E. D.

1957 "Some Sociological and Statistical Effects of Depopulation of a Rural Area," *Public Health,* 71:25-35 (April).

695. Alstrom, Carl

1958 "First-Cousin Marriages in Sweden 1750-1844 and a Study of the Population Movement in Some Swedish Subpopulations from the Genetic-Statistical Viewpoint: A Preliminary Report," *Acta Genetica et Statistica Medica,* 8 (3/4):295-369.

696. American Council for Judaism. Research Department.

1957 *Worldwide Jewish Migration, 1951-1957* (New York, Research Department, American Council for Judaism), 17 pp. (processed).

697. American Economic Association

1960 "Papers and Proceedings of the 72nd Annual Meeting of the American Economic Association, Washington, D. C., December 28-30, 1959," *American Economic Review,* 50:1-745 (May).

698. American Farm Economic Association

1959 "Proceedings of the Annual Meeting of the American Farm Economic Association, August 23-26, 1959, Cornell University, Ithaca, New York," *Journal of Farm Economics,* 41: 885-1586 (December).

699. American Jewish Committee

1961 *American Jewish Yearbook 1961* (New York, American Jewish Committee), Vol. 62, 514 pp.

700. American Statistical Association

1955 "Summaries of Papers Delivered at the 114th Annual Meeting of the American Statistical Association in Montreal, September 10-13, 1954," *Journal of the American Statistical Association,* 50:566-99 (June).

*The original work is not in English, but it includes a summary in English.

701. American Statistical Association

1956 "Summaries of Papers Delivered at the 115th Annual Meeting of the American Statistical Association in New York City, December 27-29, 1955," *Journal of the American Statistical Association*, 51:501-27 (September).

702. American Statistical Association

1960 "Summaries of Papers Delivered at the 119th Annual Meeting of the American Statistical Association, Washington, D. C., December 27-30, 1959," *Journal of the American Statistical Association*, 55:350-74 (June).

703. American Statistical Association

n.d. *Proceedings of the Social Statistics Section, 1960*, papers presented at the 120th Annual Meeting of the American Statistical Association, Stanford University, August 23-26, 1960, under the sponsorship of the Social Statistics Section (Washington, American Statistical Association), 211 pp.

704. American Statistical Association

1961 "Summaries of Papers Delivered at the 120th Annual Meeting of the American Statistical Association, Stanford, California, August 23-26, 1960," *Journal of the American Statistical Association*, 56:388-410 (June).

705. American Statistical Association

1962a "Summaries of Papers Delivered at the 121st Annual Meeting of the American Statistical Association, New York City, December 27-30, 1961," *Journal of the American Statistical Association*, 57:481-501 (June).

706. American Statistical Association

1962b *Proceedings of the Social Statistics Section, 1962*, papers and discussions presented at the 122nd Annual Meeting of the American Statistical Association, Minneapolis, Minnesota, September 7-10, 1962, under the sponsorship of the Social Statistics Section (Washington, American Statistical Association), 299 pp.

707. Amiral, Ilídio do

1960 *Aspects of the White Peopling of Angola*, Estudos, Ensaios e Documentos, Vol. 74 (Lisbon, Junta de Investigaçõ̃es do Ultramar), 83 pp.

708. Andrews, Wade H., and Saad Z. Nagi

1956 *Migrant Agricultural Labor in Ohio*, Ohio Agricultural Experiment Station, Research Bulletin 780, 27 pp.

709. Andrus, J. Russell, and Azizali F. Mohammed

1958 *The Economy of Pakistan* (London, Oxford University Press), 517 pp.

710. Appleyard, R. T.

1955 "Displaced Persons in Western Australia: Their Industrial Location and Geographical Distribution: 1948-1954," *University Studies in History and Economics*, 2:62-100 (September).

711. Appleyard, R. T.

1956 "The Economic Absorption of Dutch and Italian Immigrants into Western Australia," Part I, *R. E. M. P. Bulletin*, 4:45-54 (July-September).

712. Armistead, A. H.

1956 "Learn about Migrants," *International Journal of Religious Education*, 33:16-17 (December).

713. Armor, Murray

1962 "Migrant Labour in Africa South of the Sahara: Migrant Labour in the Kalabo District of Barotseland (Northern Rhodesia)," *Bulletin of the Inter-African Labour Institute*, 9: 5-42 (February).

Arrington, L. J. *See* 1854.

714. Artic Institute of North America

1955 "Arctic Research: The Current Status of Research and Some Immediate Problems in the North American Arctic and Subarctic," ed. Diana Rowley, *Arctic*, 7:113-376 (December).

*715. Asole, Angela T.

1958 "Migratory Movements of Sicilians into Sardinia," *Bollettino della Societa Geografica Italiana*, Ser. 8, 11:353-60 (June-August).

716. Association of Jewish Refugees in Great Britain

1955 *Dispersion and Resettlement: The Story of the Jews from Central Europe*, ed. Werner Rosenstock (London, Association of Jewish Refugees in Great Britain), 61 pp.

717. Augelli, J. P.

1962 "Agricultural Colonisation in the Dominican Republic," *Economic Geography*, 38:15-27 (January).

718. Australia. Commonwealth Bureau of Census and Statistics. Western Australian Office.

1959 *Statistical Register of Western Australia, 1957-8, Statistical from 1829.* (Perth, Government Printer), 22 pp.

719. Australia. Commonwealth Immigration Advisory Council.

1960 *First Report on the Progress and Assimilation of Migrant Children in Australia* (Canberra, Australia Commonwealth Immigration Advisory Council), 43 pp.

720. Australian School of Pacific Administration.

1956 "Migrant Labor and Permanent Labor in Africa," *South Pacific*, 9 (3):343-46.

721. Avila, Fernando Bastos de, S. J.,

1961 "Immigration, Development and Industrial Expansion in Brazil," *Migration*, 1:21-31 (July-September).

722. Awad, Mohamed

1959 "Settlement of Nomadic and Semi-Nomadic Tribal Groups in the Middle East," *International Labour Review*, 79:25-56 (January).

723. Baker, Colin

1961 "A Note on Nguru Immigration to Nyasaland," *Nyasaland Journal*, 14:41-42 (January).

724. Banco Nacional de México, S. A.

1956 "Migratory Movements and the Mexican Labor Force," *Review of the Economic Situation*, 32:5-7 (August).

725. Banco Nacional de México, S. A.

1958 "The Population Problem in Mexico," *Review of the Economic Situation of Mexico*, 34: 3-5 (June).

726. Bandini, Mario

1962 "Present Situation of Italian Agriculture," *Review of Economic Conditions in Italy*, 16: 375-90 (September).

727. Banfield, Edward C.

1957 "The Politics of Metropolitan Area Organization," *Midwest Journal of Political Science*, 1:77-91 (May).

728. Bang, James S., and others

1961 *Population Change and Migration: 1950-1960*, Population Series 1 (Madison, College of Agriculture, University of Wisconsin), 44 pp.

729. Bank of Hawaii. Department of Business Research, and Hawaiian Electric Company.

1960 *Employment, Population, and Housing on Oahu, 1951-1970* (Honolulu, Department of Business Research, Bank of Hawaii), 107 pp.

730. Banton, Michael

1957 *West African City: A Study of Tribal Life in Freetown* (London, Oxford University Press, for the International African Institute), 228 pp.

731. Barber, William J.

1961 "Disguised Unemployment in Underdeveloped Economies," *Oxford Economic Papers*, New Series, 13:103-15 (February).

*732. Barberis, Carlo

1957 "The Southern Peasant Takes Over Land in the North," *Rivista di Economia Agraria*, 12:324-50 (September).

*733. Barberis, Carlo

1959 "Some Aspects of the Inland Migration Policy in Italy," *La Previdenza Sociale nell-Agricoltura*, 10:282-87 (July-October).

734. Barbour, K. M., and R. M. Prothero (eds.)

1961 *Essays on African Population* (London, Routledge and Kegan Paul), 336 pp.

735. Bastos de Avila, Fernando

1957 "The Future of Immigration to South America," *International Labour Review*, 76:30-46 (July).

736. Baum, Samuel, and J. W. Combs

1959 *The Labor Force of the Soviet Zone of Germany and the Soviet Sector of Berlin*, International Population Statistics Reports, Series P-90, No. 11 (Washington: Government Printing Office), 30 pp. (processed).

Bazzanella, Waldemiro. *See* 866.

737. Beach, E. F., and J. C. Weldon (eds.)

1962 *Canadian Political Science Association Conference on Statistics, 1960, at Queen's University, Kingston, Canada: Papers* (Toronto, University of Toronto Press), 314 pp.

738. Beaglehole, Ernest

1957 "The Maori in New Zealand: A Case Study in Socio-Economic Integration," *International Labour Review*, 76:103-23 (August).

739. Beal, George M., Ray E. Wakeley, and Amy Russell

1957 *Iowa's People—1965* (Ames, Cooperative Extension Service, Iowa State College, MA-582), 39 pp.

740. Beegle, J. A.

1959 *Social Components in the Decision to Migrate* (Stresa, Congress of International Sociological Association), 12 pp. (mimeographed).

741. Behrendt, Richard F.

1955 "General Prospects for Immigration and Settlement in Central America," *I. C. M. C. News*, 4:1-4 (April).

742. Beijer, G.

1955 "Concluding Remarks on the Practical Implications of the Relations between International and Internal Migration," *Proceedings of the World Population Conference 1954, Summary Report* (New York).

743. Beijer, G.

1958 "Applicants for Emigration in Western Germany, 1950-56," *R. E. M. P. Bulletin*, 6: 88-92 (July-December).

744. Beijer, G.

1959 "Demographic Consequences of the Flight of Intellectuals, Highly Skilled, Skilled, and Unskilled Workers from Eastern to Western Germany," *R. E. M. P. Bulletin*, 7:100-105 (October-December).

745. Beijer, G.

1960 "Some Recent Publications on Dutch Emigration," *R. E. M. P. Bulletin*, 8:92-100 (October-December).

746. Bell, Howard H.

1959 "The New Emigration Movement, 1849-1854: A Phase of Negro Nationalism," *Phylon*, 20: 132-42 (Summer).

747. Berghe, Pierre van den

1962 "Indians in Natal and Fiji: A 'Controlled Experiment' Culture Contact," *Civilisations*, 12 (1):75-87.

*748. Berk, L. J. M. van den

1957 "Migration Movement in Eastern Germany and Brown Coal Mining," *Tijdschrift voor Economische en Sociale Geografie*, 48:288-90 (December).

*749. Berk, L. J. M. van den

1958 "Population Trends in East Germany," *Tijdschrift voor Economische en Sociale Geografie*, 49:203-204 (August-September).

750. Berry, Charles H.

1956 *Occupational Migration from Agriculture, 1940-1950* (Chicago, Library, University of Chicago), 106 pp.

751. Bertier de Sauvigny, G. de

1957 "Population Movements and Political Changes in Nineteenth Century France," *Review of Politics*, 19:37-47 (January).

752. Bienenstok, Theodore

1955 *Migration Movements of Children in New York State* (Albany, Division of Research, State Education Department, University of the State of New York), 17 pp. (processed).

Bingham, Sally. *See* 1628 and 1629.

753. Bird, Ronald, and others

1958 *Resources and Levels of Income of Farm and Rural Nonfarm Households in Eastern Ozarks, Missouri*, Missouri Agricultural Experiment Station Research Bulletin 661, 71 pp.

754. Bjork, Robert M.

1955 "The Italian Immigration into France, 1870-1954," unpublished doctoral dissertation, Syracuse University, 361 pp.

755. Blackwood, Paul E.

1957 *Report of Two Conferences on Planning Education of Agricultural Migrants* (Washington, U. S. Office of Education).

756. Blodgett, Louise Quigg

1960 *The Community Meets the Migrant Worker: Current Program and Trends* (Washington, Bureau of Labor Standards, Department of Labor), 62 pp.

757. Blumberg, Leonard

1958 *Migration as a Program Area for Urban Social Work* (Philadelphia, Urban League of Philadelphia).

758. Bogue, Donald J.

1955 *Methods of Studying Internal Migration*, paper prepared for a regional seminar on population in Central and South America, held in Rio de Janeiro, Brazil, December, 1955, 96 pp. (processed).

759. Boïarskii, A. Ia

1958 "An Experiment in the Theory of a Census with Control Rounds," *Revue de l'Institut International de Statistique*, 26 (1-3):48-55.

*760. Bologna, Luigi M.

1961 "Some Considerations on the Settlement of Nomadic Populations on the Land in the Countries of North Africa," *Rivista di Agricoltura Subtropicale e Tropicale*, 55:147-55 (April-June).

*761. Bonãc, V.

1956 "Population According to Place of Birth . . ." *Statisticka Revija*, 6:43-51 (June).

762. Bonné, A.

1959 "Trends in Occupational Structure and Distribution of Income Among the Jewish Population of Israel," *Jewish Journal of Sociology*, 1:242-49 (December).

763. Böök, Jan A.

1958 "Some Aspects of Practical Applications of the Theory of Population Genetics to Man," *Bulletin de l'Institut International de Statistique*, 36 (3):277-83.

764. Borrie, W. D.

1955 "Economic and Demographic Aspects of Post-War Immigration to Australia," *R. E. M. P. Bulletin*, 3:1-8 (January).

765. Borrie, W. D., and Ruth M. Dedman

1958 "Population Increase and Decrease 1947-1954," commentary on map in *Atlas of Australian Resources* (Canberra, Department of National Development), 27 pp.

766. Borrie, W. D., and Ruth Rodgers

n.d. *Australian Population Projections, 1960-1975: A Study of Changing Population Structure* (Canberra, Australian National University, Department of Demography, Institute of Advanced Studies), 27 pp. (processed).

767. Borts, G. H., and J. L. Stein

1962 "Regional Growth and Maturity in the United States: A Study of Regional Structural Change," *Schweizerische Zeitschrift für Volkswirtschaft und Statistik*, 98:290-321 (September).

768. Bottum, J. Carroll

1956 "The Impact of Anticipated Trends and Shifts of Population upon American Agriculture," in *Proceedings of Agricultural Industries Conference, June 21st through 23rd, 1956* (Ithaca, Cornell University, Graduate School of Business of Public Administration in cooperation with N. Y. State College of Agriculture), 43-49.

*769. Bouman, F. J.

1957 "The Irish Population Problem," *Tijdschrift voor Economische en Sociale Geografie*, 48: 14-20 (January).

770. Bouscaren, Anthony T.

1962 "Latin America in International Migrations," *R. E. M. P. Bulletin*, 10:109-14 (December).

771. Boutell, Robert M.

1955 "Migration Problems at the Rio Congress," *I. C. M. C. News*, 4:1-3 (September-October).

Bouvier, Mme. P. F. *See* 1346.

772. Bowles, Gladys K.

1960 *Some Previews of Population Changes in Low-income Farming Area* (Washington, U. S. Agricultural Marketing Service), 4 pp. (processed).

773. Bowles, Gladys K.

1962 *Adjustment Processes Associated with Migration, with Special Reference to Population Redistribution in the Great Plains between 1950 and 1960* (Washington, Farm Population Branch, U.S. Department of Agriculture), 20 pp.

774. Boyd, W. D.

1955 "James Redpath and American Negro Colonization in Haiti, 1860-1862," *The Americas*, 12 (2):169-82.

775. Bracey, H. E.

1958 "A Note on Rural Depopulation and Social Provision," *Sociological Review*, 6:67-74 (July).

776. Bradway, J. S., and A. E. Evans

1958 "The Refugee Problem—An International Legal Tangle," *American Bar Association Journal*, 44:333-37 (April).

777. Braithwaite, Lloyd

1957 "Sociology and Demographic Research in the British Caribbean," *Social and Economic Studies*, 6:523-71 (December).

778. Breton, Raymond, and Maurice Pinard

1960 "Group Formation among Immigrants: Criteria and Processes," *Canadian Journal of Economics and Political Science*, 26:465-77 (August).

779. Brice, Edward Warner

1961 *Education of the Adult Migrant* (Washington, Office of Education, U.S. Department of Health, Education and Welfare).

780. Brice, W. C.

1955 "The Turkish Colonization of Anatolia," *John Rylands Library*, Bulletin 38, 18-44.

781. Bridger, G. A.

1962 "Planning Land Settlement Schemes, with Special Reference to East Africa," *Agricultural Economics Bulletin for Africa*, No. 1: 21-54 (September).

782. Brookfield, H. C.

1960 "Population Distribution and Labour Migration in New Guinea: A Preliminary Survey," *The Australian Geographer*, 7:233-42 (February).

783. Brookfield, H. C.

1961 "The Highland Peoples of New Guinea: A Study of Distribution and Localization," *Geographical Journal U. S.*, 127:436-48 (December).

Brouwn, A. E. *See* 1369 and 1370.

784. Brown, Hugh H.

1955 "A Technique for Estimating the Population of Counties," *Journal of the American Statistical Association*, 50:323-43 (June).

785. Brown, James S., and Ralph J. Ramsey (comps.)

1958 *The Changing Kentucky Population: A Summary of Population Data for Counties, Ken-*

tucky Agricultural Experiment Station Progress Report 67, 74 pp.

786. Brown, L. B.

1957 "English Migrants to New Zealand: A Note on Differential Intelligence," *Australian Journal of Psychology*, 9:120-22.

787. Brown, Phillips H.

1959 "Arkansas Population Makes Another Advance," *Arkansas Economist*, 1:6-10 (Spring).

788. Browning, Robert H.

1961 *On the Season: A Report of a Public Health Project Conducted among Negro Migrant Agricultural Workers in Palm Beach County, Florida*, Monograph No. 2. (Jacksonville, Florida State Board of Health), 65 pp.

789. Buckley, Louis F.

1958 "The Migrant Worker Today," *Review of Social Economy*, 16:36-43 (March).

Buettner-Janusch, John. *See* 2026.

*790. Bunle, M. H.

1961 "Urban Hypertrophy," *Bulletin de l' Institut International de Statistique*, 38 (2):521-28.

791. Bunting, Robert L.

1961 "A Test of the Theory of Geographic Mobility," *Industrial and Labor Relations Review*, 15:75-82 (October).

792. Bunting, Robert L., and others

1961 "Labor Mobility in Three Southern States," *Industrial and Labor Relations Review*, 14: 432-45 (April).

Burchinal, Lee G. *See* 824.

793. Burford, Roger L.

1962a "The Diverse Southeast: Population Growth, 1950-1960," *Atlanta Economic Review*, 12: 20-21 (January).

794. Burford, Roger L.

1962b "An Index of Distance as Related to Internal Migration," *Southern Economic Journal*, 29:77-81 (October).

795. Burgess, E. W., and others

1955 "The Construction of Scales for the Measurement of Migration after Retirement," *Sociometry*, 18 (4):360-67.

796. Burnight, Robert G.

1956 *Suburban Migration and the Cost of Education*, Connecticut Agricultural Experiment Station Progress Report No. 15, 10 pp.

Burrus, John N. *See* 1440.

*797. Busca, M.

1956 "The Rural Exodus," *Riso*, 5:3-4 (September).

798. Butler, E. B.

1959 "The Migration of School Children and Local Authority Population Estimates," *Journal of the Town Planning Institute*, 45:135-36 (May).

799. Butterfield, Roy L.

1957 "On the American Migrations," *New York History*, 38:368-86 (October).

800. California, Fresno County.

1955 *Teaching Children Who Move with the Crops*, Report and recommendations of the Fresno County Project: The Educational Program for Migrant Children (Fresno: Fresno County Superintendent of Schools).

801. California. Santa Clara County.

1958 *Education Today—Self-Sufficiency Tomorrow*, Report on the Education Project for Season Farm Families (mimeographed).

802. California. State Department of Industrial Relations. Division of Labor Statistics and Research.

1958 *Migrant Workers in California, 1957*, 15 pp.

*803. Camargo, José Francisco de

1957 *The Rural Exodus in Brazil; An Essay on Its Forms, Causes and Principal Economic Consequences*, Boletim No. 1. Economia Política e História das Doutrinas Econômicas, No. 1, (São Paulo, Universidade de São Paulo, Faculdade de Ciências Econômicas e Administrativas), 233 pp.

804. Campbell, H. Murray

1961 "Mexico's Immigration Law: An Explanation," *Mexican-American Review*, 29:29-33 (May).

805. Campbell, K. O.

1960 "Rural Population Movements in Relation to Economic Development," in *Proceedings of the Tenth International Conference of Agriculture Economists (Mysore, 1958)* (London, Oxford University Press), 319 pp.

806. Campbell, Mildred

1955 "English Emigration on the Eve of the American Revolution" *American Historical Review*, 61:1-20 (October).

807. Campbell, Mildred

1960 " 'Of People Either too Few or too Many ; The Conflict of Opinion on Population and Its Relation to Emigration," in *Conflict in*

Stuart England: Essays in Honour of Wallace Notestein, ed. William A. Aiken and Basil D. Henning (London, Jonathan Cape; New York, New York University Press).

808. Canada. Department of Citizenship and Immigration. Statistics Section.

1956 *Immigration to Canada by Ethnic Origin from Overseas and Total from the United States, by Intended Occupation, 1946-55*, 16 pp.

809. Canada. Department of Citizenship and Immigration. Statistics Section.

1962 *Immigration, 1961*, 28 pp.

810. Canada. Department of Labour. Economics and Research Bureau.

1961 *Migration of Professional Workers into and out of Canada, 1946-1960*, Bulletin 11, 48 pp.

811. Canada. Dominion Bureau of Statistics. Health and Welfare Division.

1956 *Canadian Vital Statistics Trends, 1921-1954*, Reference Paper No. 70 (Ottawa, Queen's Printer), 56 pp.

812. Canada. Dominion Bureau of Statistics.

1956 *The Canadian-born in the United States*, Reference Paper No. 71 (Ottawa, Queen's Printer), 36 pp. (processed).

813. Canada. Royal Commission on Canada's Economic Prospects.

1957 *Some Regional Aspects of Canada's Economic Development*, By R. D. Howland, 302 pp.

814. Canadian Jewish Congress Research Committee, Central Region

1956 *The Smaller Jewish Communities of Ontario. Their History and Population Characteristics Based on Self-Surveys of Ten Ontario Jewish Communities* (Toronto: Canadian Jewish Congress Research Committee, Central Region), 25 pp. (processed).

*815. Cappelletti, Fausto

1955 "The Experience of Colonization from Overseas in Pedrinhas, Brazil," *Rivista di Agricoltura Subtropicale e Tropicale*, 49:14-24 (January-March).

816. Carr-Saunders, A. M., and others

1958 *A Survey of Social Conditions in England and Wales as Illustrated by Statistics* (Oxford, Claredon Press), 302 pp.

817. Caselli, R. R.

1962 "Summer School for Migrant Youngsters," *California Teachers Association Journal*, 58: 34-37 (April).

818. Cassinis, Umberto

1956 "Intra-European Movements of Italian Workers," *I. E. M. C. Migration News*, 5 :1-6 (July-August).

819. Central African Statistical Office

1956 "Immigration into the Federation of Rhodesia and Nyasaland in 1955," *Monthly Digest of Statistics*, 3:iv-x (April).

820. Central Mortgage and Housing Corporation (Ottawa)

1956 *Housing and Urban Growth in Canada: A Brief from Central Mortgage and Housing Corporation to the Royal Commission on Canada's Economic Prospects*, 35 pp.

821. Ceylon. Department of Labour.

1960 "Migration Statistics," *Labour Gazette*, 11: 145-150 (April).

822. Ceylon. National Planning Council.

1959 *Population Projections for Ceylon, 1956-1981*, By S. Selvaratnam (Colombo, Planning Secretariat), 57 pp.

*823. Chablani, S. P.

1957 "The Rehabilitation of Refugees in the Federal Republic of Germany," *Weltwirtschaftliches Archiv*, 79 (2):281-304.

824. Chancellor, Loren E., and Lee G. Burchinal

1962 "Relations among Inter-Religious Marriages, Migratory Marriages and Civil Weddings in Iowa," *Eugenics Quarterly*, 9:75-83 (June).

825. Chang-Rodríquez, Eugenio

1958 "Chinese Labor Migration into Latin America in the Nineteenth Century," *Revista de Historia de América*, 46:375-397 (December).

826. Chao Ku-chun

1957 "Agricultural Laborers in India," *Far Eastern Survey*, 26:24-31 (February).

827. Charanis, Peter

1961 "The Transfer of Population as a Policy in the Byzantine Empire," *Comparative Studies in Society and History*, 3:140-154 (January).

828. Chauhan, D. S.

1957 "Rural Migration and Regional Balance," *Agra University Journal of Research*, 5:1-11 (January), and 5:169-184 (July).

829. Chauhan, D. S.

1958 "Social Costs of Migration," *Journal of Social Sciences*, 1:29-51 (July).

*830. Chevallier, Raymond

1960 "Centuriation and Roman Colonization in the

Eighth Augustan Region (Emilia-Romagna),"
L'Universo, 40:1077-1104 (November-December).

*831. China (National Government). Directorate-General of Budgets, Accounts and Statistics.

1957 *Statistical Abstract of the Republic of China, 1956,* 594 pp.

832. Chiu, Tze Nang

1961 "Agricultural Resettlement in the Sai Kung Peninsula," *Journal of the Geographical, Geological and Archaelogical Society,* University of Hong Kong, Jubilee Issue, 1960-61.

833. Choh-Ming Li

1959 *Economic Development of Communist China, An Appraisal of the First Five Years of Industrialization* (Berkeley and Los Angeles: University of California Press), 284 pp.

834. Christensen, David E.

1956 *Rural Occupance in Transition, Sumter and Lee Counties, Georgia,* Department of Georgraphy Research Paper No. 43 (Chicago, University of Chicago), 162 pp. (processed).

835. Christian, David E.

1955 "Resistance to International Worker Mobility. A Barrier to European Unity," *Industrial and Labor Relations Review,* 8:379-391 (April).

836. Cisneros Cisneros, Cesar

1959 "Indian Migrations from the Andean Zone of Ecuador to the Lowlands," *América Indígena,* 19:225-231 (July).

Clark, Philip J. *See* 1823.

837. Clarke, John I.

1957 "Emigration from Southern Tunisia," *Geography,* 42:96-104 (April).

838. Clarke, John I.

1960 "Rural and Urban Sex-Ratios in England and Wales," *Tijdschrift voor Economische en Sociale Geografie,* 51:29-38 (February).

839. Cleland, Courtney B.

1957 *Changes in Rural Population on the Plains,* North Dakota Institute for Regional Studies Social Science Report 3, 13 pp.

840. Cleland, Courtney B., and others

1962 *Great Plains Sociology: A Symposium,* North Dakota Institute for Regional Studies Social Science Report No. 7. 24 pp. (processed).

841. Cochrane, Donald

1955 "Australian Post-War Immigration," *Banca Nazionale del Lavoro Quarterly Review,* 8: 49-55 (March).

842. Coe, Paul F.

1959 "The Nonwhite Population Surge to Our Cities," *Land Economics,* 35:195-210 (August).

843. Coene, R. de

1956 "Agricultural Settlement Schemes in the Belgian Congo," *Tropical Agriculture,* 33:1-12 (January).

844. Colorado. Department of Education.

1957 *General Summary: Migration Education Projects, 1957,* (Denver: Division of Instructional Services), mimeographed.

845. Colorado. Department of Education.

1959 *Migration Education Research Project.*
(or 1960)

846. Colorado. Legislative Council. Committee on Migratory Labor.

1960 *Migratory Labor in Colorado: A Progress Report to the Colorado General Assembly,* Research Publication 43, 37 pp.

Combs, J. W. *See* 736.

847. Comhaire, Jean

1962 "Leopoldville, Lagos, and Port-au-Prince: Some Points of Comparison," in *Nigerian Institute of Social and Economic Research, Conference Proceedings, December, 1960,* Ibadan, University College), pp. 73-83.

Comitas, Lambros *See* 1500.

848. Commission for Technical Co-operation in Africa South of the Sahara

1959 "The Housing of Workers in Urban Living Conditions in Africa" (three articles based on documentation prepared for the second session of the CCTA Inter-African Conference on Housing and Urbanization, Nairobi, January, 1959), *Bulletin of the Inter-African Labour Institute,* 6:62-71 (March); 6:58-83 (May); and 6:92-115 (July).

849. Committee for the Demography of the Jews in the Netherlands

1961 "Dutch Jewry: A Demographic Analysis," Part I, *Jewish Journal of Sociology,* 3:195-242 (December).

850. Conference of Non Governmental Organizations Interested in Migration

1957 *Re-migration. A Report Presented to the Conference of Non Governmental Organizations Interested in Migration by the International Catholic Migration Commission at the Request of the Liaison Committee of the Con-*

ference. (Geneva: Sixth International Conference of Non Governmental Organizations Interested in Migration, August 5-9, 1957, MC. NGO/6/3), 24 pp. (processed).

851. Conference on the Refugee Problem Today and Tomorrow, Geneva, 1957

    1957 *The Refugee Problem Today and Tomorrow,* Conference Report, 64 pp.

852. Conklin, Howard E., and Irving R. Starbird

    1958 *Low Incomes in Rural New York State: An Analysis of Causes and Lines of Remedial Action* (New York City, Interdepartmental Committee on Low Incomes), 37 pp. (processed).

853. Connecticut, University of. College of Agriculture. Agricultural Extension Service

    1955 *Population Estimates, Natural Increase and Net Migration, Connecticut Towns, 1950 to 1955,* Connecticut Population Reports No. 1, Progress Report 11, 10 pp.

*854. Constância, J. de Medeiros

    1962 "The Human Framework of the Island of Sao Miguel," *Boletim do Centro de Estudos Geograficos,* 3 (19):7-20.

855. Cook, Robert C.

    1957a "The American Melting Pot: 1850-1950," *Population Bulletin,* 13:113-130 (November).

856.   1957b "World Migration, 1946-1955," *Population Bulletin,* 13:77-95 (August).

857. Cooppan, S.

    1962 "Indian Population: A Small but Significant Minority," *Economic Opinion,* No. 9:37-42 (February).

858. Copeland, George

    1958 "Migratory Americans," *Industrial Bulletin,* 37:13-17 (May).

859. Copland, Douglas

    1960 *The Adventure of Growth. Essays on the Australian Economy and Its International Setting* (Melbourne, F. W. Cheshire), 148 pp.

860. Corbett, David C.

    1958a "Immigrants and Canada's Economic Expansion," *International Labour Review,* 77:19-37 (January).

861.   1958b "Immigration and Foreign Policy in Australia and Canada," *International Journal,* 13:110-123 (Spring).

862. Corden, W. M.

    1955 "The Economic Limits to Population Increase," *Economic Research,* 31:242-260 (November).

863. Corner, F. H.

    1955 "The Arab Refugees: A New Zealand View," *Jewish Frontier,* pp. 13-15 (December).

864. Cornevin, R.

    1956 "A Successful Transfer of Labour. Cabrais Colonisation in the Trustee Territory of French Togoland," *Bulletin of the Inter-African Labour Institute,* 3:8-15 (March).

865. Costa Pinto, L. A.

    1959 "Economic Development in Brazil: Its Sociological Implications," *International Social Science Journal,* 11 (4):589-597.

866. Costa Pinto, L. A., and Waldemiro Bazzanella

    1958 "Economic Development, Social Change, and Population Problems in Brazil," *The Annals of the American Academy of Political and Social Science,* 316:121-126 (March).

867. Coughlin, R. J.

    1955 "The Chinese in Bangkok: A Commercial-Oriented Minority," *American Sociological Review,* 20:311-316 (June).

868. Council of Europe

    1956 *Progress Report of the Council of Europe, Special Representative for National Refugees and Overpopulation to the Consultative Assembly,* 45 pp.

869. Council of Europe

    1957 *Second Progress Report of the Special Representative of the Council of Europe for National Refugees and Overpopulation,* Document 694 (Strasbourg, Consultative Assembly of the Council of Europe) 14 pp.

870. Council of Europe

    1961 *European Co-operation in 1960: Report of the Secretary-General, 1961,* 262 pp.

871. Council of Europe

    1962 *Resettlement Fund for National Refugees and Overpopulation in Europe* (Paris, Report of the Governor, 1961), 44 pp.

872. Cousens, S. H.

    1960 "The Regional Pattern of Emigration during the Great Irish Famine, 1846-51," in *Institute of British Geographers, Transactions and Papers, 1960,* pp. 119-134.

873. Cousens, S. H.

    1961 "Emigration and Demographic Change in Ireland, 1851-1961," *Economic History Review,* 2nd series, 14:275-288 (December).

874. Cowie, W. J. G., and A. K. Giles

1957 "An Inquiry into Reasons for 'the Drift from the Land,'" *Selected Papers on Agricultural Economics*, 5:71-113 (December).

875. Crist, Raymond E., and Ernesto Guhl

1957 "Pioneer Settlement in Eastern Colombia," in *Annual Report, 1956* (Washington, Smithsonian Institution) pp. 391-414.

876. Culen, Constanine

1958 "Slovak Emigration," *Slovakia*, 8:49-55 (June).

877. Cumberland, Charles C.

1960 "The United States-Mexican Border: A Selective Guide to Literature of the Region," Supplement to *Rural Sociology*, 25:235 pp. (June).

878. Cumper, G. E.

1956 "Population Movements in Jamaica, 1830-1950," *Social and Economic Studies*, 5:261-280 (September).

879. Cumper, G. E.

1957 "Working Class Emigration from Barbados to the United Kingdom, October, 1955," *Social and Economic Studies*, 6:76-83 (March).

880. Cumper, G. E.

1959 "Employment in Barbados," *Social and Economic Studies*, 8:105-146 (June).

881. Cyprus. Statistics and Research Department. Ministry of Finance.

1961 *Vital and Migration Statistics 1960*, 98 pp. (processed).

882. Cyprus. Statistics and Research Department. Ministry of Finance.

1962 *Vital and Migration Statistics, 1961*, 100 pp. (processed).

*883. Darrouy, H.

1955 "The Migration of North Africans into France," *La Nouvelle Revue Francaise d'Outre-Mer*, pp. 154-162 (April).

884. Davie, Maurice R.

1961 *The Papers of Maurice R. Davie*, ed. Ruby J. R. Kennedy (New Haven, Yale University Press), 311 pp.

Davis, Elizabeth Gould *See* 1936.

885. Davis, Kingsley

1960 "Colonial Expansion and Urban Diffusion in the Americas," *International Journal of Comparative Sociology*, 9:43-66 (March).

886. Davis, S. G.

1955a "Chinese Emigration through Hong Kong," *Ekonomi dan Keuangan Indonesia*, 8 (1): 25-39.

887. Davis, S. G.

1955b "Chinese Emigration through the Ages," *Far Eastern Economic Review*, 18:714-16 (June 9).

888. Davison, R. B.

1957 "Labour Migration in Tropical Africa," *Indian Journal of Economics*, 37:365-377 (April).

889. Dayal, P.

1959 "Population Growth and Rural-Urban Migration in India," *National Geographical Journal of India*, 5:179-85 (December).

Dedman, Ruth M. *See* 765.

890. DeJong, Gordon F.

1961 *The Population of Kentucky: Changes in the Number of Inhabitants, 1950-60*, Kentucky Agricultural Experiment Station Bulletin 675, 26 pp.

891. Denmark. Statistiske Department

1955 *Vital Statistics, 1953*, 94 pp.

Desclercs, R. *See* 1348.

*892. Deshamps, Hubert

1961 "Internal Migration in Madagascar," *Bulletin of the Inter-African Labour Institute*, 8: 26-49 (August).

893. Devernois, Guy

1958 "The Franco-African Community," *Civilisations*, 8 (4):585-610.

894. Dey, Mukul K.

1962 "The Indian Population in Trinidad and Tobago," *International Journal of Comparative Sociology*, 3:245-253 (December).

895. Dickinson, G. C.

*1958 "The Nature of Rural Population Movement-An Analysis of Seven Yorkshire Parishes Based on Electoral Returns from 1931-1954," *Yorkshire Bulletin of Economic and Social Research*, 10:95-108 (November).

896. Dimech, Victor G.

1961 "Some Problems of Maltese Emigration," *Migration News*, 10:11-14 (March-April).

Doerflinger, Jon. *See* 1396.

897. Dominedo, H. E., Francesco M.

1961 "How Migration Affects the Country of Emigration," *Migration*, 1:37-50 (October-December).

898. Donnison, D. V.

1961 "The Movement of Households in England," *Journal of the Royal Statistical Society*, Series A, 124 (1):60-80.

Dornbusch, Sanford M. *See* 1770.

899. Dovring, Folke

1961 "The Opportunity to Multiply: Demographic Aspects of Modern Colonialism," *Journal of Economic History*, 21:599-612 (December).

900. Dowsett, C. P.

1962 "Agriculture and Economic Development: Mexico," *Australian Quarterly*, 34:62-68 (March).

901. Dreyer, Heinrich M.

1961 "Immigration of Foreign Workers into the Federal Republic of Germany," *International Labour Review*, 84:1-25 (July-August).

902. Duffy, James

1961 "Portugal in Africa," *Foreign Affairs*, 39: 481-493 (April).

903. Duke University School of Law

1956 "Immigration," *Law and Contemporary Problems*, 21 (2): 212-426 (A series of articles).

Duncan, Beverly. *See* 905.

904. Duncan, J. S.

1962 "The Land for the People: Land Settlement and Rural Population Movements, 1886-1906," in *Land and Livelihood: Geographical Essays in Honour of George Jobberns*, ed. Murray McCaskill (Christchurch, New Zealand Geographical Society), pp. 170-190.

905. Duncan, Otis D., and Beverly Duncan (compilers)

1956 *Chicago's Negro Population: Characteristics and Trends: A Report by the University of Chicago, Chicago Community Inventory, to the Office of the Housing and Redevelopment Coordinator and the Chicago Plan Commission* (Chicago, University of Chicago, Chicago Community Inventory), 109 pp.

906. *East Africa and Rhodesia*

1956a "Land Settlement in Southern Rhodesia," *East Africa and Rhodesia*, 32:1420 (1652).

907. *East Africa and Rhodesia*

1956b "Uganda Labour Department's Report," *East Africa and Rhodesia*, 32:1842 (1663).

908. East African High Commission. Statistical Department.

1957 *Statistical Abstract, 1957* (Dar es Salaam, Government Printer), 56 pp.

909. East African Statistical Department. Kenya.

1956 *Report on Migration, 1949 to 1953*, 13 pp.

910. Easterlin, R. A.

1961 "The American Baby Boom in Historical Perspective," *American Economic Review*, 60: 869-911 (December).

911. Eberhard, Wolfram

1959 "Mobility in South Chinese Families," *Sinologica*, 6 (1):16-24.

912. Econometric Society

1960a "Report of Washington, D. C., Meeting (The American Winter Meeting) of the Econometric Society, December 1959, in Conjunction with the American Economic Association, the American Farm Economics Association, the American Statistical Association, and the Regional Science Association," *Econometrica*, 28:670-708 (July).

913. Econometric Society

1960b "Report of Amsterdam Meeting (21st European Meeting) of the Econometric Society, September 10 to 12, 1959," *Econometrica*, 28:647-669 (July).

914. *Economic Development and Cultural Change*

1961 "Essays in the Quantitative Study of Economic Growth, Presented to Simon Kuznets on the Occasion of His Sixtieth Birthday," *Economic Development and Cultural Change*, 9:225-560 (April).

915. *Economic Weekly* (Bombay)

1961 "Migration from East Pakistan (1951-1961)," *Economic Weekly*, 13:609, 611, 612 (April 15).

916. *Economist*

1957 "Hungarian Exodus," *The Economist*, 183: 379-380 (May 4).

917. *Economist*

1958a "Exploding Cities" (A series of 11 one- or two-page articles), *The Economist*, Vols. 186-189, Nos. 5967, 5979, 5974, 5977, 5981, 5984, 5989, 5993, 5998, 6003, and 6008 (January 4-October 18).

918. *Economist*

1958b "Refugees and Others. A Look at Refugees in Central Europe Shows That Migration Policies, As Well As the Refugee Machinery, Need Overhaul," *The Economist*, 189:1057-1059 (December 20).

919. Edgel, Ralph L.

1958 "New Mexico Population. Its Size and Its Changing Distribution," *New Mexico Business*, 11:2-13 (October).

Eisenhower, Dwight. *See* 1960.

920. Eisenstadt, S. N.

1956 "Sociological Aspects of the Economic Adaptation of Oriental Immigrants in Israel: A Case Study in the Problem of Modernization," *Economic Development and Cultural Change*, 4:269-278 (April).

921. Eisner, Gisela

1961 *Jamaica, 1830-1930: A Study in Economic Growth* (Manchester, Manchester University Press), 399 pp.

922. *Ekonomi dan Keuangan Indonesia*

1956 *The Population of Indonesia* (Djakarta, Reprint from *Ekonomi dan Keuangan Indonesia*), 27 pp.

Elkan, Walter. *See* 1345.

923. Enequist, Gerd M.

1959 *Geographical Changes of Rural Settlement in North-Western Sweden Since 1523* (Uppsala: Lundequistska Bodhandeln, Uppsala Universitets Arsskrift), 43 pp.

924. Enequist, Gerd, and Gunnar Noring, eds.

1960 "Advance and Retreat of Rural Settlement," papers of the Siljan Symposium at the XIXth International Geographical Congress, *Geografiska Annaler*, 42 (4):207-346.

Epstein, Fritz T. *See* 1975.

Evans, A. E. *See* 776.

925. Eversley, D. E. C., and D. M. R. Keate

1958 *The Overspill Problem in the West Midlands*, Studies in the Problems of Housing and Industrial Location No. 1, (N. p.: The Midlands New Towns Society), 57 pp.

926. Fairbairn, Ian

1961 "Samoan Migration to New Zealand: The General Background and Some Economic Implications for Samoa," *Journal of the Polynesian Society*, 70:18-30 (March).

927. Fall, Betty C.

1958 *Report on the Ottawa County Summer School for Migrant Children* (Curtice, Ohio) (mimeographed).

928. *Far Eastern Economic Review*

1955a "Problems of Population and Migration in Singapore," *Far Eastern Economic Review*, 19:468-469 (October 13).

929. *Far Eastern Economic Review*
1955b "Japan's Population Problem and Emigra-

tion," *Far Eastern Economic Review*, 19:520-521 (October 27).

930. *Far Eastern Economic Review*

1958 "Japanese Emigration in the Postwar Period," *Far Eastern Economic Review*, 24:365 (March 20).

931. Fennell, Rosemary

1961 "Economic Problems of Western Ireland," *Studies*, 50:385-402 (Winter).

*932. Fenyö, Imréné

1959 "The Organization of the Hungarian External Migration Statistics and Preliminary Data," *Demográfia*, 2 (1):130-134.

*933. Fenyö, Imréné, and Endre Sardi

1960 "Foreign Tourist Traffic and the Hotel Situation in 1958-1959," *Demográfia*, 3 (2):242-54.

934. Figueroa, John

1958 "British West Indian Immigration to Great Britain," *Caribbean Quarterly*, 5:116-130 (February).

935. Findeisen, Hans

1958 "The Colonization of Kazakhstan," *East Turkic Review*, No. 1:16-25.

936. Fischlowitz, Estanislau

1959 "Manpower Problems in Brazil," *International Labor Review*, 79:398-417 (April).

937. Fischlowitz, Estanislau

1960 "Manpower Problems and Prospects in Latin America," *Monthly Labor Review*, 83:900-916 (September).

938. Fisk, E. K.

1961 "The Mobility of Rural Labour and the Settlement of New Land in Underdeveloped Countries," *Journal of Farm Economics*, 43:761-778 (November).

939. Flapan, S.

1959 "One More Step is Needed," *New Outlook*, 2:9-13 (January).

940. Florida. Bureau of Maternal and Child Health.

1959 *Migrant Project; A Report of the Observations and Activities of a Public Health Team Working Directly with Agricultural Migrant Laborers in Palm Beach County, Florida* (Jacksonville, Bureau of Maternal and Child Health, Florida State Board of Health, and Palm Beach County Health Department).

941. Florida. Legislative Council and Legislative Reference Bureau.

1961 *Migrant Farm Labor in Florida: A Summary of Recent Studies*, 63 pp.

Florida. State Board of Health. *See* 788.

942. Ford, J. R., and C. M. Stewart

1960 "An Estimate of the Future Population of England and Wales," *Eugenics Review*, 52: 151-159 (October).

943. France. Ambassade de France. Service de Presse et d' Information.

1962 "Migration of Algerian Moslem Workers to France: Balance Sheet," *French Affairs*, No. 137, 4 pp. (processed).

*944. France. Institut National d' Etudes Demographiques.

1955 *Algerians in France. A Demographic and Social Study*, Travaux et Documents, Cahier No. 24 (Paris), 180 pp.

945. Francis, Roy G., ed.

1961 "A Symposium on Values in Demographic Research," *Sociological Quarterly*, 2:259-297 (October).

946. Fraser, J. M.

1955 "The Character of Cities: V. Singapore, A Problem in Population," *Town and Country Planning*, 23:505-509 (November).

947. Freedman, Maurice

1960 "Immigrants and Associations: Chinese in Nineteenth-century Singapore," *Comparative Studies in Society and History*, 3:25-48 (October).

948. Freedman, Ronald, and Doris P. Slesinger

1961 "Fertility Differentials for the Indigenous Nonfarm Population of the United States," *Population Studies*, 15:161-173 (November).

*949. Fussing, Hans H.

1957 *Urban Population, 1600-1660; Distribution of Occupations, Migration, Incomes* (Aarhus, Universitetsforlaget), 125 pp.

*950. Fyfe, Christopher

1962 *A History of Sierra Leone* (London, Oxford University Press), 733 pp.

*951. Gabriel, Juno R.

1960 *Patterns of Nuptiality and Fertility in Israel, with Special References to Differences Between Origin Groups and Their Assimilation* (Jerusalem: Department of Statistics, The Eliezer Kaplan School of Economics and Social Sciences, The Hebrew University), No. 275, 13 pp.

952. Gadgil, D. R.

1959 "Integration of Land Settlement Policies into the Economic and Social Development of Countries," *Monthly Bulletin of Agricultural Economics and Statistics*, 8:1-7 (October).

953. Gaffney, M. M.

1958 "Urban Expansion—Will It Ever Stop?" in *Yearbook of Agriculture* (Washington, U. S. Department of Agriculture), pp. 503-522.

954. Gaitskill, Arthur

1955 "The Gezira Scheme," *Journal of the Royal Society of Arts*, 104:67-86 (December 9).

Galloway, Robert E. *See* 1755.

955. Garcia, Trevino Rodrigo

1956 "The Wetback: A Mexican View of a Mexican Problem," *Central America and Mexico*, 4:3-6 (October).

956. Gartner, Lloyd P.

1960 "Notes on the Statistics of Jewish Immigration to England 1870-1914," *Jewish Social Studies*, 22:97-102 (April).

*957. Gayat, G.

1955 "Immigration of Asians into Madagascar," *Civilisations*, 1:54-64.

958. Gayler, J. L., and others

1957 *A Sketch-map Economic History of Britain* (London, George G. Harrap), 214 pp.

959. Geach, Gwen

1960 *State Migratory Labor Committees, Their Organization and Programs* (Washington: Bureau of Labor Standards, Department of Labor), 75 pp.

960. Geographical Association, The

1957 "Urbanization Among the South African White Population," *Geography*, 42:63-64 (January).

Gerland, Martin E. *See* 1508.

961. Germany. Federal Republic. Embassy to the U.S.

1958 *German Refugees and Conditions in the Soviet Zone of Germany: A Government Declaration Delivered by Federal Minister for All-German Affairs Ernst Lemmer at the Opening Session of the German Bundestag in Berlin on October 1, 1958* (Washington, German Embassy), 19 pp.

962. Germany. Federal Republic. Ministry for Expellees, Refugees and War Victims.

1958 "The German Losses by Expulsion. Final Results of the Population Balance Sheet 1939-50," by Werner Nellner, *Wirtschaft und Statistik*, 10:600-604 (November).

Gernes, Arthur C. *See* 1698.

*963. Geschwind, Henrik

1957 "Internal Migration 1951-1955. A Special Investigation based on the Population Sample Register," *Statistik Tidskrift*, 6:607-614 (November).

*964. Geschwind, Henrik

1958 "Mean Stay of Immigrants in Sweden. A Scheme for Researches Based on the Population Samples Register," *Statistik Tidskrift*, 7:134-136 (March).

965. Ghana. Office of the Government Statistician.

1958 *Migration Statistics 1953-1957*, Statistical Reports, Series VI, No. 1, 85 pp. (processed).

966. Ghana. Office of the Government Statistician.

1959 *Migration Statistics, 1958*, Statistical Reports, Series VI, No. 2, 25 pp.

967. Gibbs, Jack P., ed.

1961 *Urban Research Methods* (Princeton, Van Nostrand) 625 pp.

968. Gil, B.

1955 "The Selectivity of the North African Aliyah," *Alliance Review*, pp. 25-28 (February).

969. Gil, B.

n.d. "Planned Spatial Distribution of Population in Israel and Some of Its Implications," in *Istituto di Statistica della Facolta di Scienze Statistiche Demografiche ed Attuariali. Studi in onere di Corrado Gini* (Rome, Universita degli Studi di Roma), 2:26 pp.

Gil, B. *See* 1408 and 1410.

Giles, A. K. *See* 874.

970. Gillberg, Jan, and Bengt G. Rundblad

1959 "The Use of the Population Sample Register for Enquiries into the Mobility of Labor. A Study in Method," *Statistik Tidskrift*, 8:32-45 (January).

*971. Gini, Corrado

1955a "International Migrations," *Rivista di Politica Economica*, 45:1-13 (January-February).

*972. Gini, Corrado

1955b "International Migrations," *Rivista di Politica Economica*, 45 (March), pp. 173-186.

973. Gini, Corrado

1958 *On the Extinction of the Norse Settlements in Greenland*, Norwegian School of Economics and Business Administration Paper (Bergen, The Institute of Economics), No. 10, 28 pp.

974. Ginsburgs, G.

1957 "The Soviet Union and the Problem of Refugees and Displaced Persons, 1917-1956," *American Journal of International Law*, pp. 325-361 (April).

975. Gist, Noel P.

1955 "Selective Migration in South India," *Sociological Bulletin*, 4:147-160 (September).

976. Gittus, Elizabeth

1961 "Migration in Lancashire and Cheshire: A Sample Analysis of the National Register," *Town Planning Review*, 32:141-156 (July).

977. Glynn, Jerome

1962 "Some Effects of Migration on Texas Counties, 1950-1960," *Texas Health Bulletin*, pp. 12-17 (April).

978. Glynn, Jerome and Sanford Labovitz

1961 *Population Growth in Texas Counties, 1950-1960*, reprinted from *Texas Business Review*, 35 (May), 6 pp.

979. Goda, Eisaku

1955 "Migration Caused by Marriage in Omishima Ehime Prefecture," *The Geographical Review of Japan*, 28:532-535 (October).

980. Goldberg, David and others

1960 *Estimates of Population Change in Michigan: 1950-1960*, Michigan Population Studies, No. 1 (Ann Arbor: Dept. of Sociology, Institute of Public Administration, University of Michigan), 49 pp.

981. Gonzalez, Nancie L. S. de.

1961 "Family Organization in Five Types of Migratory Wage Labor," *American Anthropologist*, 63:1264-1280 (December).

982. Goodman, Eileen

1957 "Why We Can Take More Immigrants," *Canadian Business*, 30 (June), pp. 90-98.

983. Goodman, Leo A.

1961 "Statistical Methods for the Mover—Stayer Model," *Journal of the American Statistical Association*, 56:841-68 (December).

984. Gottlicher, Erich

1957 "Mobility of Labour in the Common Market," *ICFTU Economic and Social Bulletin*, 5: 6-11 (September).

985. Gottmann, Jean

1957 "Urban Expansion and Population Movements," *R.E.M.P. Bulletin*, 5:53 - 60 (April-June).

*986. Gottman, Jean

  1961 *Megalopolis: The Urbanized Northeastern Seaboard of the United States* (New York, Twentieth Century Fund), 810 pp.

987. Graham, I. C. C.

  1955 "Scottish Emigration to North America, 1707-1783," unpublished doctoral dissertation, University of Illinois, 243 pp.

988. Great Britain. Board of Trade.

  1957 "Revival in Emigration to Canada in 1956: Passenger Movement and Migration to and from United Kingdom," *Board of Trade Journal*, 172:1180-1184 (May 24).

989. Great Britain. Central Office of Information. Reference Division.

  1956 "Ceylon: Progress of Land Colonization Schemes," *Commonwealth Survey*, 20 (20): 825.

990. Great Britain. Colonial Office.

  1955 *Movement of Persons within a British Caribbean Federation*, Report of the conference held in Port of Spain, Trinidad, March 14-17, 1955, Colonial No. 315, 4 pp.

991. Great Britain. Colonial Office. African Studies Branch.

  1958 "Urban Problems in East and Central Africa," report of a conference held at Ndola, Northern Rhodesia, in February, 1958, *Journal of African Administration*, 10:181-251 (October).

992. Great Britain. Commonwealth Relations Office.

  1956 *Child Migration to Australia: Report of a Fact-finding Mission, Presented by the Secretary of State for Commonwealth Relations to Parliament by Command of Her Majesty, August 1956*, Cmd. 9832. (London, H. M. Stationery Office), 14 pp.

993. Great Britain. Ministry of Labour.

  1959 "Age and Regional Analysis of Employees," *Ministry and Labour Gazette*, 67:205-210 (June).

994. Great Britain. Scotland. Department of Health. Regional Research Unit.

  1958 *Depopulation in Rural Scotland*, 88 pp.

995. Greene, Victor R.

  1961 "Pre-World War I Polish Emigration to the United States: Motives and Statistics," *Polish Review*, 6:45-68 (Summer).

*996. Grisero, V.

  1956 "The Industrialization of the Aosta Valley and Its Economic-Agrarian and Demographic Effects," *Rivista di Economia Agraria*, 9: 526-571 (December).

997. Groenman, Sj.

  1958 "The Migration of Agricultural People in Overseas Countries," *R.E.M.P. Bulletin*, 6:61-63 (July-December).

998. Grossman, David A., and Melvin B. Levin

  1961 *The Appalachian Region: A Preliminary Analysis of Economic and Population Trends in An Eleven State Problem Area* (Atlanta, Council of Appalachian Governors), 31 pp.

999. Grove, Robert D.

  1956 "Dimensions of Population Mobility and Change," *American Journal of Public Health and the Nation's Health*, 46:592-596 (May).

Guhl, Ernesto. See 875.

1000. Gulliver, P. H.

  1957 "Nyakyusa Labour Migration," *Journal of the Rhodes-Livingstone Institute*, Problems in British Central Africa, pp. 32-63 (March).

1001. Gupta, T. R.

  1961 "Rural Family Status and Migration: Study of a Punjab Village," *Economic Weekly*, 13: 1597-1603 (October 14).

*1002. Hack, H.

  1960 *The Colonization of Mennonites in the Paraguayan Chaco* (Amsterdam, Konigliches Tropeninstitut), 232 pp.

1003. Hajnal, John

  1955 "The Prospects for Population Forecasts," *Journal of the American Statistical Association*, 50:309-322 (June).

1004. Hall, A. R., and M. R. Hill

  1960 "Housing Demand in Australia, 1959-1974," *Economic Record*, 36(76):550-567.

1005. Hall, Norma E., compiler

  1958 *Bibliography of Settlement in India and Pakistan* (Eugene, Ore. Name of publisher unavailable), 16 pp. (processed).

1006. Hall, Robert B., and Toshio Noh

  1956 *Japanese Geography: A Guide to Japanese Reference and Research Materials*, University of Michigan Center for Japanese Studies, Bibliographical Series, No. 6 (Ann Arbor, University of Michigan Press), 128 pp. (processed).

*1007. Halperin, Haim, and Dan Yaron

  1957 *Moshvei Olim; Survey of Immigrant Villages in Israel* (Rehavot), 147 pp.

*1008. Hama Hidehicko

1959 "Comparative Study of Latest Statistics of Population Migration," in *Annual Reports of the Institute of Population Problems*, No. 4 (Tokyo, Welfare Ministry), pp. 13-28.

1009. Hambro, Edvard

1957 "Chinese Refugees in Hong Kong," *Phylon*, 18(1):69-81.

1010. Hands, J.

1955 "Malay Agricultural Settlements, Kuala Lumpur," *Malayan Historical Journal*, 2:146-161 (December).

1011. Hanizah, Sendut

1961 "Rasah—a Resettlement Village in Malaya," *Asian Survey*, 1:21-26 (November).

1012. Hanna, Margaret

1957 "The Drain of Talent out of Georgia and South Carolina," unpublished master's thesis, Kent State University.

1013. Harewood, Jack

1960 "Overpopulation and Underemployment in the West Indies," *International Labour Review*, 82:103-137 (August).

1014. Harris, B. W.

1956 *Population Changes Among Rural Negroes in Mississippi*, Lorman, Miss., Department of Agricultural Economics, Alcorn A. and M. College, 12 pp.

1015. Harris, George E.

1956 "The Drain of Talent Out of Ohio and Kentucky," unpublished master's thesis, Kent State University.

1016. Harrison, George M.

1959 "U. S. Views on Aid to Palestine Refugees," *Department of State Bulletin*, 40:137-142 (January).

1017. Hart, John F.

1957 "Migration and Population Change in Indiana," *Proceedings of the Indiana Academy of Science*, 66:195-203.

1018. Hartland, Penelope

1955 "Factors in Economic Growth in Canada," *Journal of Economic History*, 15(1):13-22.

1019. Hasan, M. S.

1958 "Growth and Structure of Iraq's Population 1867-1947," *Bulletin of the Oxford University Institute of Statistics*, 20:339-352(November).

1020. Hasan, Riffat Sultana

1956 "Refugee Population and Prospects of Its Resettlement in Urban and Suburban Areas of Karachi," *Pakistan Geographical Review*, 11 (1):33-34.

1021. Hauser, Philip M., ed.

1955 "World Urbanism," *American Journal of Sociology*, 60:427-503 (March).

1022. Hauser, Philip M.

1961 *On the Impact of Population and Community Changes on Local Government*, Seventh annual Wherrett lecture on local government (Pittsburgh: Institute of Local Government, Graduate School of Public and International Affairs, University of Pittsburgh), 27 pp.

1023. Haveman, B. W.

1956 "Planned Emigration—the Solution of Holland's Population Problem," *Progress*, 45:116-122 (Summer).

1024. Hawaii. Department of Planning and Research.

1961 *Migrant and Non-migrant Households in Hawaii, January 1961*, Research Report No. 6, 9 pp.

1025. Hawaii. Department of Planning and Research.

1962 *Hawaiian Migration, 1950-1961*, By Robert C. Schmitt, Research Report No. 21, 20 pp.

1026. Hawaii. State Planning Office.

1960a *Characteristics of Migrant and Non-migrant Households on Oahu, 1959*, Staff Research Memorandum No. 22, 9 pp.

1027. 1960b *Military Personnel and Dependents in Hawaii, 1960*, Staff Research Memorandum No. 29, 8 pp.

1028. 1960c *Provisional Estimates and Projections of the Civilian Population of Hawaii, 1940-1980*, Staff Research Memorandum No. 30, 7 pp.

1029. 1960d *Hawaii's In-migrants, Second Quarter, 1960*, Staff Research Memorandum No. 33, 7 pp.

1030. Hawaii. State Planning Office

1961 *The General Plan of the State of Hawaii. Hawaii's Next Twenty Years, 1960-1980*, 115 pp.

1031. Hawaii, University of. Romanzo Adams Social Research Laboratory.

1962 *Social-Historical Background of the Okinawans in Hawaii*, Report No. 36, By Yukiko Kimura, 22 pp. (processed).

1032. Hawley, Amos H.

1956 *The Changing Shape of Metropolitan Amer-*

ica *Deconcentration since 1920.* (Glencoe, Illinois, The Free Press), 177 pp.

Hawley, Amos H. *See* 2045

1033. Hayden, Albert A.

1959 *Governmental Assistance to Immigration to New South Wales, 1856-1900,* unpublished master's thesis, University of Wisconsin, 284 pp.

1034. Heads, J.

1959 "Urbanization and Economic Progress in Nigeria," *South African Journal of Economics,* 27:229-237 (September).

1035. Heberle, Rudolf

1955 "The Theory of Migration. Sociological Considerations," *Schmollers Jahrbuch für Gestzgebung Verwaltung und Volkswirtschaft,* 75(1): 1-23.

1036. Heberle, Rudolf

1956 "Types of Migration," *R.E.M.P. Bulletin,* 4: 1-5 (January-March).

1037. Heeren, J. J. ed.

1955 *The Urbanisation of Djakarta,* Report on a research project sponsored by UNESCO and carried out by the Institute of the Djakarta School of Economics, University of Indonesia, reprint from *Ekonomi dan Keuangan Indonesia,* 43 pp.

1038. Heffernan, H.

1962 "Migrant Children in California Schools," *California Journal of Elementary Education,* 30:228-36 (May).

1039. Henderson, Sidney

1956 *Labor Force Potentials: Farm Migration Available for Urban Growth, Eight Nebraska Cities, 1940-1950,* Business Research Bulletin No. 60 (Lincoln: College of Business Administration, University of Nebraska), 45 pp.

*1040. Herer, W.

1959 "The Influence of Migration from Agriculture to Industry on the Increase of the National Income," *Ekonomista,* No. 3:574-588.

1041. Heyn, H.

1959 "Psychological and Legal Problems at the Integration of Foreign Refugees in the Federal Republic of Germany," *R.E.M.P. Bulletin,* 7:81-86 (July-September).

1042. Higgins, George C.

1961 "The Migratory Worker in American Agriculture," *Review of Social Economy,* 19:43-56 (March).

1043. Hildebrand, George H.

1955a "The Postwar Italian Migration: Achievements, Problems, Prospects," *World Politics,* 8:46-70 (October).

1044. 1955b "The Italian Parliamentary Survey of Unemployment: A Review Article," *American Economic Review,* 45: 884-899 (December).

Hill, M. R. *See* 1004.

1045. Hill, Polly

1959 "The History of the Migration of Ghana Cocoa Farmers," *Transactions of the Historical Society of Ghana,* 4(1):14-28.

1046. Hill, Polly

1961 "The Migrant Cocoa Farmers of Southern Ghana," *Africa,* 31:209-230 (July).

1047. Hilton, T. E.

1959 "Land Planning and Resettlement in Northern Ghana," *Geography,* 44:227-240 (November).

1048. Hinton, Harold C.

1957 "Colonization as an Instrument of Chinese Communist Policy," *Far Eastern Economic Review,* 23:513-522 (October 24).

*1049. Hissenhoven, Alexandre van

1960 "Italy's Population Problem, An Asset or an Obstacle to European Integration," *Revue du Marché Commun,* No. 28:297-303 (September).

1050. Holborn, Louise W.

1961 "Intergovernmental Partnership for Planned Migration," *Migration,* 1: 5-18 (April-June).

1051. Hollander, A. N. J. den

1960 "The Great Hungarian Plain: A European Frontier Area, Part I," *Comparative Studies in Society and History,* 3:74-88 (October).

1052. Hollander, A. N. J. den

1961 "The Great Hungarian Plain: A European Frontier Area, Part II," *Comparative Studies in Society and History,* 3:155-169 (January).

1053. Holm, Donald S., Jr.

1962 "People—and Area Improvement," *University of Missouri Business and Government Review,* 3:5-14 (March-April).

1054. Holm, Edwin E.

1961 "Virginia Grows Metropolitan," *Virginia Economic Review,* 14:1-8 (January).

1055. Holmstrom, S.

1957 "Population Movement in Sweden from Rural

to Urban Districts—Causes and Effects," *Indian Journal of Agricultural Economics,* 12: 20-24 (July-September).

1056. Hoogenboom, C. J. J.

1962 "The Success of the Dutch Settlement Holambra in Brazil," *Migration News,* 11:1-4 (January-February).

1057. Hook, R. C., Jr., and Paul D. Simpkins

1960 "Recent Migration to Northern Arizona," *Arizona Business Bulletin,* 7:7-12 (March).

1058. Hooper, Antony

1961 "The Migration of Cook Islanders to New Zealand," *Journal of the Polynesian Society,* 70:11-17 (March).

Hormann, Bernard L. *See* 1491.

1059. Horn, R. V.

1962 "Marriages of Migrants in Australia," *Economic Record,* 38:452-461 (December).

1060. Horstmann, K.

1955 "Internal Migration in the Federal Republic of Germany," in *Proceedings of the World Population Conference, Rome 1954,* 2, (New York, United Nations), pp. 557-572.

1061. Houghton, D. Hobart

1960 "Men of Two Worlds: Some Aspects of Migratory Labour in South Africa," *The South African Journal of Economics,* 28:177-190 (September).

1062. House, J. W.

1956 *Northumbrian Tweedside: The Rural Problem* (Newcastle upon Tyne, The Northumberland Rural Community Council), 66 pp.

1063. Houtart, Fr.

1955 "A Sociological Study of the Evolution of the American Catholics," *Social Compass,* 2(5/6): 189-216.

Howland, R. D. *See* 813.

1064. Hu Yueh

1962 "The Problem of the Hong Kong Refugees," *Asian Survey,* 2:28-37 (March).

1065. Hudson, G. F.

1956 "Russian Migration into Asia," *Twentieth Century,* 957:397-408 (November).

Huggins, H. D. *See* 1982.

1066. Hughes, Rufus B.

1959 *Low Incomes in Southern Population Adjust-*

ments, (Chicago: Department of Photoduplication, University of Chicago Library) (Microfilm copy of typescript), 65 pp.

1067. Human Relations Area Files, Inc.

1956a *Algeria,* Subcontractor's Monograph HRAF-54, John Hopkins—1 (New Haven, Human Relations Area Files, Inc.), 562 pp.

1068. 1956b *Indonesia,* Subcontractor's Monograph HRAF-57, Yale—2 (3 vols.) (New Haven, Human Relations Area Files, Inc.), 1222 pp.

1069. 1956c *Iraq,* Subcontractor's Monograph HRAF-58, Johns Hopkins—2 (New Haven, Human Relations Area Files, Inc.), 574 pp.

*1070. Hungary. Hungarian Academy of Sciences. Presidential Committee for Demography.

1961 "Debates of the Presidential Committee for Demography: Agricultural Migration," *Demográfic,* 4(4):494-500.

* 1071. Hungary. Statisztikai Időszaki Közlemények.

1961 *The Population of Hungary 1959* (Budapest, Központi Statisztikai Hivatal), 348 pp.

1072. Hunt, I. L.

1958 "Group Settlement in Western Australia," *University Studies in Western Australia History,* pp. 5-42 (October).

*1073. Hurský, Josef

1957 "On the Question of the Evolution of the Immigration Frontier," *Journal of the Czechoslovak Geographical Society,* 62(2):111-117.

Hurst, H. R. G. *See* 1344.

1074. Hurwitz, Joachim

1955 *Agricultural Resettlement of Javanese Farmers in the Outer Islands of Indonesia Before World War II,* Economic Development Program. Indonesian Project. Working Papers. No. C/55-23, Massachusetts Institute of Technology (Cambridge: Center for International Studies), 52 pp.

1075. Hutchinson, Edward P.

1956 "The Foreign Stock in the United States, 1850 to 1950," *Interpreter Releases,* 33:346-356 (October 24).

1076. Hutchinson, Edward P.

1958 "Notes on Immigration Statistics of the United States," *Journal of the American Statistical Association,* 53: 963-1025 (December).

Hutchinson, Robert S. *See* 1855.

*1077. Hyrenius, Hannes, and others

1959 *Structure and Changes of Income and Population in the Ostersund Region*, Goteborgs Universitet, Skriftserie-5 (Goteborg: Statistiska Institutionen), 142 pp.

Illinois. Commission on Human Relations. *See* 1703.

1078. Illinois. Department of Public Health.

1959 *Health, Housing, and Safety Guide for Employers of Migrant Workers*, 7 pp.

Illinois. Chicago Community Inventory. *See* 905.

1079. India. Assam. Department of Economics and Statistics.

1958 *Statistical Survey of Displaced Persons from East Pakistan in Assam, 1955-56*, Reports on the 1st-2nd phases (Two volumes in one).

1080. India. Cabinet Secretariat.

1961 *Preliminary Estimates of Birth and Death Rates and of the Rate of Growth of Population, Fourteenth Round, July 1958-July 1959*, The National Sample Survey, No. 48, (Calcutta and Delhi, Manager of Publications, Civil Lines), 132 pp.

1081. India. Cabinet Secretariat.

1962 *Tables with Notes on Internal Migration: Ninth, Eleventh, Twelfth and Thirteenth Rounds, May 1955-May 1958*, The National Sample Survey, No. 53, Prepared by the Indian Statistical Institute (Calcutta, Department of Economic Affairs), 86 pp.

1082. India. Controller of Emigrant Labour.

1955 *Annual Report on the Working of the Tea Districts Emigrant Labour Act (XXII of 1932) for the Year Ending the 30th September, 1954* (Shillong: Assam Government Press), 68 pp.

1083. India. Planning Commission.

1961 *Third Five Year Plan*, 774 pp.

1084. Indian Economic Association

1957 *Papers Read at the Thirty-Ninth Annual Conference of the Indian Economic Association, Cuttack, December 26-28, 1956*.

Indian Statistical Institute *See* 1081.

1085. Indiana. State Board of Health.

1961 "Population Changes," *Monthly Bulletin*, 63: 3-19 (April).

1086. Indonesia. Biro Pusat Statistik.

1961 *Statistical Pocketbook of Indonesia 1961*, 273 pp.

Indonesia, University of *See* 1337.

1087. *Industry and Labour*

1955 "Overseas Migration from the United King-
(1) dom: Settlement in Other Parts of the Commonwealth," *Industry and Labour*, 13:26-31 (January 1).

1088. 1955 "Guide to Immigration Laws and Regula-
(2) tions," *Industry and Labour*, 13:97 (January 15).

1089. 1955 "Immigration Laws of Hong Kong," *Industry
(3) and Labour*, 13:97-99 (January 15).

1090. 1955 "Movement to and from Chile in 1953," *In-
(4) dustry and Labour*, 13:99-100 (January 15).

1091. 1955 "Amendments to U. S. Immigration Laws,"
(5) *Industry and Labour*, 13:125-127 (February 1).

1092. 1955 "Migration to and from Malta in 1953," *Indus-
(6) try and Labour*, 13:127-129 (February 1).

1093. 1955 "State Subsidy for Voluntary Organisations
(7) in the Netherlands," *Industry and Labour*, 13:129-130 (February 1).

1094. 1955 "Brazilian National Institute of Immigration
(8) and Land Settlement: New Regulations," *Industry and Labour*, 13:181 (February 15).

1095. 1955 "Emigration from Luxembourg: Control over
(9) Agencies," *Industry and Labour*, 13:228 (March 1).

1096. 1955 "Immigration to the U.S.," *Industry and La-
(10) bour*, 13:225-228 (March 1).

1097. 1955 "Intergovernmental Committee for European
(11) Migration: Eighth Session of the Committee and First Session of the Council," *Industry and Labour*, 13:222-225 (March 1).

1098. 1955 "Extension of the Mandate of the United
(12) Nations Relief and Works Agency for Palestine Refugees in the Near East," *Industry and Labour*, 13:274-76 (March 15).

1099. 1955 "United Nations High Commissioner for Refu-
(13) gees: Fifth Session of the High Commissioner's Advisory Committee," *Industry and Labour*, 13:270-273 (March 15).

1100. 1955 "Council of Europe: Extension of the Man-
(14) date of the Special Representative for National Refugees and Overpopulation," *Industry and Labour*, 13:321-324 (April 1).

1101. 1955 "Co-operative Societies for Emigration in
(15) Italy," *Industry and Labour*, 13:405 (May 1).

1102. 1955 "Legislation to Assist Refugees in Italy,"
(16) *Industry and Labour*, 13:404-405 (May 1).

1103. 1955 "Migration to and from Belgium in 1953,"
(17) *Industry and Labour*, 13:409 (May 1).

1104. 1955 "Migration to and from Ireland since the
(18) War," *Industry and Labour*, 13:405-408 (May
1).

1105. 1955 "Scheme for the Transfer of Expellees and
(19) Refugees within the Federal Republic of Germany," *Industry and Labour*, 13:403-404 (May
1).

1106. 1955 "Convention Relating to the Status of Re-
(20) fugees: Ratifications and Accessions," *Industry and Labour*, 13:457-460 (May 15).

1107. 1955 "Italian Migration in 1952 and 1953," *In-
(21) dustry and Labour*, 13:460-464 (May 15).

1108. 1955 "New Regulations Concerning the Issue of
(22) Portuguese Passports," *Industry and Labour*,
13:464-465 (May 15).

1109. 1955 "Immigration to Canada in 1954," *Industry
(23) and Labour*, 13:513-514 (June 1).

1110. 1955 "Migration to and from the Netherlands in
(24) 1954," *Industry and Labour*, 13:561-562 (June
15).

1111. 1955 "Migrant Workers, Underdeveloped Coun-
(25) tries," 25th Sitting of the 38th Session of the
International Labour Conference, Geneva, June
1-23, 1955, *Industry and Labour*, 14:83-96 (July
1 and 15).

1112. 1955 "Sixth Australian Citizenship Convention,"
(26) *Industry and Labour*, 14:202-205 (August 15).

1113. 1955 "Intergovernmental Committee for European
(27) Migration: Second Session of the Council,"
Industry and Labour, 14:282-286 (September
15).

1114. 1955 "New Emigration Subsidy Regulations in the
(28) Netherlands," *Industry and Labour*, 14:341-
342 (October 1).

1115. 1955 "Recognition and Enforcement Abroad of
(29) Maintenance Obligations: Resolution of the
Economic and Social Council," *Industry and
Labour*, 14:340 (October 1).

1116. 1955 "School for Emigrants in Japan," *Industry
(30) and Labour*, 14:342 (October 1).

1117. 1955 "United Nations High Commissioner for Re-
(31) fugees: First Session of the United Nations
Refugee Fund (U.R.E.F.) Executive Committee," *Industry and Labour*, 14:335-340 (October 1).

1118. 1955 "Fifth Conference of Non-governmental Orga-
(32) nisations Interested in Migration," *Industry
and Labour*, 14:356-362 (October 15).

1119. 1955 "New Legislation Concerning Immigrants and
(33) Aliens in the Federation of Rhodesia and
Nyasaland," *Industry and Labour*, 14:362-
370 (October 15).

1120. 1955 "Migration of Aliens to and from Venezuela
(34) in 1954," *Industry and Labour*, 14:431-433
(November 15).

1121. 1955 "Migration to and from the Union of South
(35) Africa in 1954," *Industry and Labour*, 14:
433-434 (November 15).

1122. 1955 "Resolution Concerning Immigration and Emi-
(36) gration Policies Adopted by the Fifty-fourth
Inter-Parliamentary Conference," *Industry and
Labour*, 14:431 (November 15).

1123. 1955 "Emigration under the Auspices of the Inter-
(37) governmental Committee for European Migration during 1953, 1954 and the First Nine
Months of 1955," *Industry and Labour*, 14:
513-517 (December 15).

1124. *Industry and Labour*

1956 "Establishment of an Immigration Board in
(1) the Dominican Republic," *Industry and Labour*, 15:39 (January 1).

1125. 1956 "Joint Maritime Commission of the I. L. O.:
(2) Adoption of a Resolution Concerning Refugee
Seafarers," *Industry and Labour*, 15:35 (January 1).

1126. 1956 "Migration to and from Israel in 1954," *In-
(3) dustry and Labour*, 15:40-43 (January 1).

1127. 1956 "Settlement of Refugees and Expellees on
(4) the Land in the Federal Republic of Germany," *Industry and Labour*, 15:35-39 (January 1).

1128. 1956 "The Residence of Aliens in Cuba," *Industry
(5) and Labour*, 15:75-77 (January 15).

1129. 1956 "Council of Europe: Resolution of the Com-
(6) mittee of Ministers and Recommendation of
the Consultative Assembly Concerning National Refugees and Overpopulation," *Industry and Labour*, 15:166-168 (February 15).

1130. 1956 "Intergovernmental Committee for European
(7) Migration: Third Session of the Council,"
Industry and Labour, 15:168-172 (February
15).

1131. 1956 "Migration to and from Australia during 1953,
(8) 1954 and the First Six Months of 1955,"
Industry and Labour, 15:211-214 (March 1).

1132. 1956' "Resettlement of Displaced Persons from Pak-
(9) istan in India," *Industry and Labour*, 15:
203-211 (March 1).

1133. 1956 "Bilateral Agreement on Emigration of Italian
(10) Workers to the Federal Republic of Germany,"
Industry and Labour, 15:241-245 (March 15).

1134. 1956 "Immigration to Canada: Extension of Assisted Passage Scheme," *Industry and Labour*, 15:245 (March 15).
(11)

1135. 1956 "Results of the Rural Migration Policy in France from 1949 to 1955," *Industry and Labour*, 15:340-343 (April 15).
(12)

1136. 1956 "Movement to and from the Federal Republic of Germany in 1953 and 1954," *Industry and Labour*, 15:366-370 (May 1).
(13)

1137. 1956 "Portuguese Migration in 1954," *Industry and Labour*, 15:370-371 (May 1).
(14)

1138. 1956 "Migration to Argentina Since 1952," *Industry and Labour*, 15:422-424 (May 15).
(15)

1139. 1956 "Migration to Brazil in 1954," *Industry and Labour*, 15:420-422 (May 15).
(16)

1140. 1956 "United Nations High Commissioner for Refugees: Second Session of the United Nations Refugee Fund Executive Committee," *Industry and Labour*, 15:409-414 (May 15).
(17)

1141. 1956 "United Nations Relief and Works Agency for Palestine Refugees in the Near East: Future Activities of the Agency," *Industry and Labour*, 15:414-420 (May 15).
(18)

1142. 1956 "Emigration under the Auspices of the Intergovernmental Committee for European Migration during 1954 and 1955," *Industry and Labour*, 15:463-465 (June 1).
(19)

1143. 1956 "Immigration to the United States in 1954-55," *Industry and Labour*, 15:466-467 (June 1).
(20)

1144. 1956 "Migration to and from Malta in 1954," *Industry and Labour*, 15:522-524 (June 15).
(21)

1145. 1956 "Migration to and from New Zealand, 1954-55," *Industry and Labour*, 15:520-522 (June 15).
(22)

1146. 1956 "Migration to and from the Netherlands in 1955," *Industry and Labour*, 15:517-520 (June 15).
(23)

1147. 1956 "Immigration of Workers into France in 1954 and 1955," *Industry and Labour*, 16:135-136 (August 1).
(24)

1148. 1956 "Intergovernmental Committee for European Migration: Fourth Session of the Council," *Industry and Labour*, 16:173-176 (August 15).
(25)

1149. 1956 "Permanent Migration of Foreigners to and from Mexico between 1948 and 1954," *Industry and Labour*, 16:213-214 (September 1).
(26)

1150. 1956 "Post-War Migration to and from Canada," *Industry and Labour*, 16:211-213 (September 1).
(27)

1151. 1956 "Council of Europe: Resolutions of the Committee of Ministers Concerning National Refugees and Overpopulation," *Industry and Labour*, 16:263-264 (September 15).
(28)

1152. 1956 "Responsibility for Settling Immigrants in the Dominican Republic," *Industry and Labour*, 16:264 (September 15).
(29)

1153. 1956 "Convention Relating to the Status of Refugees: New Ratifications and Accessions," *Industry and Labour*, 16:338-339 (October 15).
(30)

1154. 1956 "Establishment of a Spanish Emigration Institute," *Industry and Labour*, 16:339-342 (October 15).
(31)

1155. 1956 "Dissolution of the Colombian Land Settlement and Immigration Institute," *Industry and Labour*, 16:379 (November 1).
(32)

1156. 1956 "Emigration Agreement between Spain and the Dominican Republic," *Industry and Labour*, 16:377-79 (November 1).
(33)

1157. 1956 "United Nations Educational, Scientific and Cultural Organisation: Conference on the Cultural Integration of Immigrants," *Industry and Labour*, 16:374-377 (November 1).
(34)

1158. 1956 "Migration of Aliens to and from Venezuela in 1955," *Industry and Labour*, 16:430-431 (November 15).
(35)

1159. 1956 "New Aliens' Act in Norway," *Industry and Labour*, 16:429-430 (November 15).
(36)

1160. 1956 "United Nations Conference on Maintenance Obligations," *Industry and Labour*, 16:423-424 (November 15).
(37)

1161. 1956 "United Nations High Commissioner for Refugees: Third Session of the United Nations Refugee Fund Executive Committee," *Industry and Labour*, 16:424-429 (November 15).
(38)

1162. 1956 "Migration to and from Spain in 1954 and 1955," *Industry and Labour*, 16:463-466 (December 1).
(39)

1163. 1956 "New Assisted Migration Agreement between the Netherlands and Australia," *Industry and Labour*, 16:459-463 (December 1).
(40)

1164. 1956 "Trade Union Conference on International Migration," *Industry and Labour*, 16:457-459 (December 1).
(41)

1165. 1956 "Immigration in the United Kingdom: Establishment of a Welfare Service for West Indian Immigrants," *Industry and Labour*, 16:512-513 (December 15).
(42)

1166. 1956 "Immigration in the United Kingdom: Immigration of Workers in 1954-55," *Industry and Labour*, 16:513-515 (December 15).
(43)

167. *Industry and Labour*

1957 "Italian Emigration Policy and Its Results
(1) in 1955," *Industry and Labour*, 17:22-28 (January 1).

168. 1957 "Migration Situation in Australia: Movements
(2) to and from the Country in 1955," *Industry and Labour*, 17:80-83 (January 15).

169. 1957 "Migration Situation in Australia: Registra-
(3) tion and Naturalisation of Aliens," *Industry and Labour*, 17:83-84 (January 15).

170. 1957 "Migration to and from the Union of South
(4) Africa in 1955," *Industry and Labour*, 17: 84-85 (January 15).

171. 1957 "Japanese-Bolivian Agreement on Migration,"
(5) *Industry and Labour*, 17:114 (February 1).

172. 1957 "Immigration to Peru: Amendments to the
(6) National Legislation," *Industry and Labour*, 17:153-155 (February 15).

173. 1957 "Emigration from Switzerland to Overseas
(7) Countries in 1954 and 1955," *Industry and Labour*, 17:202-203 (March 1).

174. 1957 "Intergovernmental Committee for European
(8) Migration: Fifth Session of the Council," *Industry and Labour*, 17:198-202 (March 1).

175. 1957 "Migration to and from Argentina in 1955
(9) and 1956," *Industry and Labour*, 17:206-208 (March 1).

176. 1957 "Migration to and from New Zealand, 1955-
(10) 56," *Industry and Labour*, 17:203-206 (March 1).

177. 1957 "Migration to Brazil in 1955," *Industry and*
(11) *Labour*, 17:209-210 (March 1).

178. 1957 "Portuguese Migration in 1955," *Industry and*
(12) *Labour*, 17:211-212 (March 1).

179. 1957 "Immigration to the United States in 1955-56,"
(13) *Industry and Labour*, 17:231-233 (March 15).

180. 1957 "Movement to and from the Federal Republic
(14) of Germany in 1954 and 1955," *Industry and Labour*, 17:233-237 (March 15).

181. 1957 "Migration to and from the Netherlands in
(15) 1956," *Industry and Labour*, 17:363-366 (May 1).

182. 1957 "United Nations High Commissioner for Re-
(16) fugees: Fourth Session of the United Nations Refugee Fund Executive Committee," *Industry and Labour*, 17:358-363 (May 1).

183. 1957 "Meeting of the Joint Italo-French Migra-
(17) tion Committee," *Industry and Labour*, 17: 401-403 (May 15).

1184. 1957 "Migration to and from Belgium in 1954 and
(18) 1955," *Industry and Labour*, 17:399-401 (May 15).

1185. 1957 "The Italian Emigration Programme for 1957,"
(19) *Industry and Labour*, 17:403-404 (May 15).

1186. 1957 "Amendment of the Immigration Regulations
(20) in Argentina," *Industry and Labour*, 17:450-454 (June 1).

1187. 1957 "Emigration under the Auspices of the In-
(21) tergovernmental Committee for European Migration in 1956," *Industry and Labour*, 17: 450 (June 1).

1188. 1957 "Temporary Employment of Japanese Miners
(22) in the Federal Republic of Germany," *Industry and Labour*, 17:454-457 (June 1).

1189. 1957 "Agreement Concerning the Repatriation of
(23) Polish Nationals from the U. S. S. R.," *Industry and Labour*, 18:201-202 (September 1).

1190. 1957 "Migration to Canada in 1956," *Industry*
(24) *and Labour*, 18: 199-200 (September 1).

1191. 1957 "Intergovernmental Committee for European
(25) Migration: Sixth Session of the Council," *Industry and Labour*, 18:231-233 (September 15).

1192. 1957 "Establishment of an Interministerial Advisory
(26) Committee on the Settlement of Immigrants in Argentina," *Industry and Labour*, 18:274-275 (October 1).

1193. 1957 "Migration between Spain and Overseas Coun-
(27) tries in 1956," *Industry and Labour*, 18:275-276 (October 1).

1194. 1957 "New Legislation Concerning Migration from
(28) the United Kingdom," *Industry and Labour*, 18:276 (October 1).

1195. 1957 "United Nations High Commissioner for Re-
(29) fugees: Fifth Session and Sixth (Special) Session of the United Nations Refugee Fund Executive Committee," *Industry and Labour*, 18:304-308 (October 15).

1196. 1957 "Immigration into Uruguay during 1956," *In-*
(30) *dustry and Labour*, 18:356 (November 1).

1197. 1957 "United Nations Relief and Works Agency for
(31) Palestine Refugees in the Near East: Resolution of the General Assembly Concerning Future Activities," *Industry and Labour*, 18: 351-355 (November 1).

1198. 1957 "Migration to and from Australia in 1956,"
(32) *Industry and Labour*, 18:377-379 (November 15).

1199. 1957 "Migration to and from Israel in 1955 and
(33) 1956," *Industry and Labour*, 18:379-380 (November 15).

1200. 1957 "Migration to and from Malta in 1955," *Industry and Labour*, 18:380-382 (November 15).
(34)

1201. 1957 "Agricultural Emigration from the Netherlands," *Industry and Labour*, 18:438 (December 1).
(35)

1202. 1957 "Migration to and from New Zealand in 1956-57," *Industry and Labour*, 18:435-438 (December 1).
(36)

1203. 1957 "Portuguese Emigration in 1956," *Industry and Labour*, 18:474-477 (December 15).
(37)

1204. 1957 "Sixth Conference of Non-Governmental Organisations Interested in Migration," *Industry and Labour*, 18:468-473 (December 15).
(38)

1205. *Industry and Labour*
1958 "Amendments to the United States Immigration and Nationality Act," *Industry and Labour*, 19:63-66 (January 15).
(1)

1206. 1958 "Irish Migration from 1954 to 1956," *Industry and Labour*, 19:60-63 (January 15).
(2)

1207. 1958 "Migration to Venezuela During 1956," *Industry and Labour*, 19:66-68 (January 15).
(3)

1208. 1958 "Migration to and from the Union of South Africa in 1956," *Industry and Labour*, 19:99 (February 1).
(4)

1209. 1958 "International Assistance to Refugees: Resolutions of the General Assembly of the United Nations," *Industry and Labour*, 19:134-135 (February 15).
(5)

1210. 1958 "Signing of the European Convention Concerning Social Security for Migrant Workers," *Industry and Labour*, 19:136 (February 15).
(6)

1211. 1958 "United Nations Relief and Works Agency for Palestine Refugees in the Near East: Recent Developments," *Industry and Labour*, 19:224-228 (March 15).
(7)

1212. 1958 "Intergovernmental Committee for European Migration: Seventh Session of the Council," *Industry and Labour*, 19:271-275 (April 1).
(8)

1213. 1958 "Immigration Protocol between Italy and Argentina," *Industry and Labour*, 19:406-407 (May 15).
(9)

1214. 1958 "Migration under the Auspices of the Intergovernmental Committee for European Migration in 1957," *Industry and Labour*, 19:401-404 (May 15).
(10)

1215. 1958 "Status of Refugee Seamen: Agreement between Eight Governments," *Industry and Labour*, 19:405-406 (May 15).
(11)

1216. 1958 "Migration to and from Italy: Agreement on Migration to Luxembourg," *Industry and Labour*, 19:488-490 (June 15).
(12)

1217. 1958 "Migration to and from Italy: Migration Movements in 1956," *Industry and Labour*, 19:492-495 (June 15).
(13)

1218. 1958 "Migration to and from Italy: Recruitment of Workers for Germany and Switzerland," *Industry and Labour*, 19:490-491 (June 15).
(14)

1219. 1958 "Migration to Brazil in 1956," *Industry and Labour*, 19:486-488 (June 15).
(15)

1220. 1958 "United Nations High Commissioner for Refugees: Seventh Session of the United Nations Refugee Fund Executive Committee," *Industry and Labour*, 19:482-486 (June 15).
(16)

1221. 1958 "Migration to and from the Netherlands in 1957," *Industry and Labour*, 20:118-121 (August 1).
(17)

1222. 1958 "Establishment of a National Immigrant Settlement Board in Argentina," *Industry and Labour*, 20:153-154 (August 15).
(18)

1223. 1958 "Migration to and from Malta in 1956," *Industry and Labour*, 20:185-187 (September 1).
(19)

1224. 1958 "Migration to and from the Union of South Africa in 1957," *Industry and Labour*, 20:188-190 (September 1).
(20)

1225. 1958 "Emigration Agreement between Belgium and Spain," *Industry and Labour*, 20:221-224 (September 15).
(21)

1226. 1958 "Immigration into Great Britain," *Industry and Labour*, 20:224-228 (September 15).
(22)

1227. 1958 "Intergovernmental Committee for European Migration: Eighth Session of the Council,: *Industry and Labour*, 20:264-268 (October 1).
(23)

1228. 1958 "Emigration from Greece in 1956 and 1957," *Industry and Labour*, 20:302-304 (October 15).
(24)

1229. 1958 "United Nations High Commissioner for Refugees: Eighth Session of the United Nations Refugee Fund Executive Committee," *Industry and Labour*, 20:298-302 (October 15).
(25)

1230. 1958 "Migration to and from New Zealand in 1957-58," *Industry and Labour*, 20:345-347 (November 1).
(26)

1231. 1958 "Migration to the U. S. in 1956-57," *Industry and Labour*, 20:341-345 (November 1).
(27)

1232. 1958 "Portuguese Emigration in 1957," *Industry and Labour*, 20:381-384 (November 15).
(28)

1233. 1958 "Ammendments to Peruvian Immigration

(29) Laws," *Industry and Labour,* 20:422 (December 1).

1234. 1958 "Migration to and from the United Kingdom
(30) in 1957," *Industry and Labour,* 20:459-461 (December 15).

1235. *Industry and Labour*

1959 "Immigration Policy Changes in Venezuela,"
(1) *Industry and Labour,* 21:68-69 (January 15).

1236. 1959 "Migration Policy in Argentina: Migration to
(2) and from the Republic in 1956 and 1957," *Industry and Labour,* 21:65-66 (January 15).

1237. 1959 "Migration Policy in Argentina: Reorganisation
(3) of the National Immigrant Settlement Board," *Industry and Labour,* 21:67-68 (January 15).

1238. 1959 "Migration Policy in Argentina: Rules for the
(4) Establishment of Foreigners in Argentina," *Industry and Labour,* 21:67 (January 15).

1239. 1959 "United Nations High Commissioner for Re-
(5) fugees: Ninth (Special) Session of the United Nations Refugee Fund Executive Committee," *Industry and Labour,* 21:63-65 (January 15).

1240. 1959 "Migration to and from Ireland in 1957,"
(6) *Industry and Labour,* 21:98-100 (February 1).

1241. 1959 "Migratory Movements between Spain and
(7) Overseas Countries in 1957," *Industry and Labour,* 21:100-101 (February 1).

1242. 1959 Intergovernmental Committee for European
(8) Migration: Ninth Session of the Council," *Industry and Labour,* 21:175-180 (March 1).

1243. 1959 "Regulations of the Council of the European
(9) Economic Community Concerning Social Security for Migrant Workers," *Industry and Labour,* 21:162, 183 (March 1).

1244. 1959 "Italian Migration in 1957," *Industry and*
(10) *Labour,* 21:213-219 (March 15).

1245. 1959 "Migration to Brazil in 1957," *Industry and*
(11) *Labour,* 21:259-260 (April 1).

1246. 1959 "Migration to Venezuela in 1957," *Industry*
(12) *and Labour,* 21:314-315 (April 15).

1247. 1959 "Migration to and from the Netherlands in
(13) 1958," *Industry and Labour,* 21:335-339 (May 1).

1248. 1959 "Migration under the Auspices of the Inter-
(14) governmental Committee for European Migration in 1958," *Industry and Labour,* 21: 334 (May 1).

1249. 1959 "Immigration to Kenya in 1956 and 1957,"
(15) *Industry and Labour,* 21:388 (May 15).

1250. 1959 "Immigration to Uruguay in 1957," *Industry*
(16) *and Labour,* 21:388-390 (May 15).

1251. 1959 "Immigration to Canada in 1957 and 1958,"
(17) *Industry and Labour,* 21:416-419 (June 1).

1252. 1959 "Migration to and from the Federal Repub-
(18) lic of Germany in 1956 and 1957," *Industry and Labour,* 21:420-426 (June 1).

1253. 1959 "United Nations High Commissioner for Re-
(19) fugees: First Session of the Executive Committee of the High Commissioner's Programme," *Industry and Labour,* 21:413-416 (June 1).

1254. 1959 "Emigration and Immigration of Swiss Na-
(20) tionals in 1956, 1957 and 1958," *Industry and Labour,* 21:460-462 (June 15).

1255. 1959 "Lebanese Emigration in 1956 and 1957,"
(21) *Industry and Labour,* 21:459-460 (June 15).

1256. 1959 "Immigration to Singapore in 1957," *Industry*
(22) *and Labour,* 22:125-126 (August 1).

1257. 1959 "New Provisions Regarding Naturalisation in
(23) the United Arab Republic," *Industry and Labour,* 22:158-159 (August 15).

1258. 1959 "Employment of Aliens in Iraq," *Industry*
(24) *and Labour,* 22:193 (September 1).

1259. 1959 "Intergovernmental Committee for European
(25) Migration: Tenth Session of the Council," *Industry and Labour,* 22:189-192 (September 1).

1260. 1959 "Immigration to the U. S. In 1957-58," *In-*
(26) *dustry and Labour,* 22:225-228 (September 15).

1261. 1959 "United Nations High Commissioner for Re-
(27) fugees: First Special Session of the Executive Committee for the High Commissioner's Programme," *Industry and Labour,* 22:222-225 (September 15).

1262. 1959 Immigration into the Federation of Rhodesia
(28) and Nyasaland from 1955 to 1958," *Industry and Labour,* 22:255-259 (October 1).

1263. 1959 "Migration to and from Australia in 1957-
(29) 58," *Industry and Labour,* 22:373-378 (December 1).

1264. 1959 "The World Refugee Year," *Industry and*
(30) *Labour,* 22:357-358 (December 1).

1265. 1959 "Migration to and from New Zealand in
(31) 1958-59," *Industry and Labour,* 22:402-404 (December 15).

1266. *Industry and Labour*

1960 "Japanese-Paraguayan Agreement on Migra-
(1) tion," *Industry and Labour,* 23:23-24 (January 1).

1267.   1960   "Migration from and to Ireland in 1958,"
        (2)   *Industry and Labour*, 23:69-70 (January 15).

1268.   1960   "Migration to and from the Federal Republic
        (3)   of Germany in 1958," *Industry and Labour*,
               23:104-109 (February 1).

1269.   1960   "Migration to and from the Union of South
        (4)   Africa in 1958," *Industry and Labour*, 23:
               126-128 (February 1).

1270.   1960   "United Nations High Commissioner for Re-
        (5)   fugees: Second Session of the Executive Com-
               mittee of the High Commissioner's Pro-
               gramme," *Industry and Labour*, 23:122-126
               (February 15).

1271.   1960   "Migration to and from Belgium in 1956-
        (6)   58," *Industry and Labour*, 23:169-172 (March 1).

1272.   1960   "Seventh Conference of Non-Governmental
        (7)   Organisations Interested in Migration," *In-
               dustry and Labour*, 23:165-169 (March 1).

1273.   1960   "Convention Relating to the Status of Re-
        (8)   fugees: Ratifications and Accessions," *Indus-
               try and Labour*, 23:190-191 (March 15).

1274.   1960   "Employment of Aliens in the Syrian Province
        (9)   of the United Arab Republic," *Industry and
               Labour*, 23:192-193 (March 15).

1275.   1960   "Immigration to Singapore in 1958," *Indus-
        (10)   try and Labour*, 23:278-279 (April 15).

1276.   1960   "Intergovernmental Committee for European
        (11)   Migration: Eleventh Session of the Council,"
               Industry and Labour, 23:273-278 (April 15).

1277.   1960   "Migration under the Auspices of the Inter-
        (12)   governmental Committee for European Migra-
               tion in 1959," *Industry and Labour*, 23:373-
               375 (May 15).

1278.   1960   "Migration to and from the Netherlands in
        (13)   1959," *Industry and Labour*, 23:402-405 (June 1).

1279.   1960   "Immigration to Canada in 1959," *Industry
        (14)   and Labour*, 23:449-452 (June 15).

1280.   1960   "United Nations Relief and Works Agency
        (15)   for Palestine Refugees in the Near East,"
               Industry and Labour, 23:445-449 (June 15).

1281.   1960   "Convention Relating to the Status of State-
        (16)   less Persons: Ratification by France and En-
               try into Force," *Industry and Labour*, 24:
               123 (August 1).

1282.   1960   "Emigration from Greece in 1958 and 1959,"
        (17)   *Industry and Labour*, 24:152-155 (August 15).

1283.   1960   "Immigration to Brazil in 1958," *Industry and
        (18)   Labour*, 24:150-151 (August 15).

1284.   1960   "Immigration to the Federation of Rhodesia
        (19)   and Nyasaland in 1959," *Industry and Labour*,
               24:155-158 (August 15).

1285.   1960   "New Regulations Concerning Aliens in the
        (20)   United Arab Republic," *Industry and Labour*,
               24:158-160 (August 15).

1286.   1960   "Immigration to the United States in 1958-
        (21)   59," *Industry and Labour*, 24:181-184 (Sep-
               tember 1).

1287.   1960   "United Nations High Commissioner for Re-
        (22)   fugees: Third Session of the Executive Com-
               mittee of the High Commissioner's Pro-
               gramme," *Industry and Labour*, 24:178-180
               (September 1).

1288.   1960   "The Movement of Indian Estate Labour
        (23)   to and from Ceylon, 1950-1959," *Industry and
               Labour*, 24:230-231 (September 15).

1289.   1960   "Activities of the Institute for the Provision
        (24)   of Credit to Italian Workers Abroad," *In-
               dustry and Labour*, 24:271-273 (October 1).

1290.   1960   "Immigration of Workers into France in 1956-
        (25)   59," *Industry and Labour*, 24:268-270 (Octo-
               ber 1).

1291.   1960   "Migration to and from Venezuela in 1958,"
        (26)   *Industry and Labour*, 24:273-275 (October 1).

1292.   1960   "Bilateral Agreements Concerning the Emi-
        (27)   gration of Greek and Spanish Workers into
               the Federal Republic of Germany," *Industry
               and Labour*, 24:295-298 (October 15).

1293.   1960   "Migration to and from Malta in 1958," *In-
        (28)   dustry and Labour*, 24:298-302 (October 15).

1294.   1960   "Convention Relating to the Status of Re-
        (29)   fugees: Ratifications and Accessions," *Indus-
               try and Labour*, 24:330-331 (November 1).

1295.   1960   "Placement of Danish Workers in Other Nor-
        (30)   dic Countries under the Common Nordic Em-
               ployment Market Convention," *Industry and
               Labour*, 24:329-330 (November 1).

1296.   1960   "Immigration to Kenya in 1958," *Industry
        (31)   and Labour*, 24:383 (November 15).

1297.   1960   "Intergovernmental Committee for European
        (32)   Migration: Twelfth Session of the Council,"
               Industry and Labour, 24:378-380 (November
               15).

1298.   1960   "Regulations Concerning the Employment of
        (33)   Aliens in Iran," *Industry and Labour*, 24:
               381-383 (November 15).

1299.   1960   "An Act Concerning the Employment and
        (34)   Training of Young Persons in Denmark," *In-
               dustry and Labour*, 24:412-414 (December 1).

1300. 1960 "Migration from and to Morocco in 1958 and
(35) 1959," *Industry and Labour*, 24:417-418 (December 1).

1301. 1960 "Migration to and from Denmark in 1959,"
(36) *Industry and Labour*, 24:414-416 (December 1).

1302. 1960 "Migration to and from New Zealand in
(37) 1959-60," *Industry and Labour*, 24:419-422 (December 1).

1303. 1960 "Immigration to Israel in 1957, 1958 and
(38) 1959," *Industry and Labour*, 24:455-457 (December 15).

1304. 1960 "Immigration to Uruguay in 1958," *Industry
(39) and Labour*, 24:458-460 (December 15).

1305. 1960 "Special Legislation Concerning Immigration
(40) to the U. S.," *Industry and Labour*, 24:457-458 (December 15).

1306. *Industry and Labour*

1961 "Agreement on Engagement and Conditions
(1) of Employment in the Republic of the Ivory
Coast of Workers from the Upper Volta,"
Industry and Labour, 25:26-28 (January 1).

1307. 1961 "Social and Economic Policy in France,"
(2) *Industry and Labour*, 25:84-86 (February 1).

1308. 1961 "United Nations High Commissioner for Re-
(3) fugees: Fourth Session of the Executive Committee of the High Commissioner's Programme," *Industry and Labour*, 25:91-93 (Feb-
uary 1).

1309. 1961 "Migration to and from Belgium in 1959,"
(4) *Industry and Labour*, 25:209-212 (April 1).

1310. 1961 "Migration to and from Italy in 1957, 1958
(5) and 1959," *Industry and Labour*, 25:212-221
(April 1).

1311. 1961 "Migration to and from the Union of South
(6) Africa in 1959," *Industry and Labour*, 25:
271-273 (April 15).

1312. 1961 "Migration under the Auspices of the Inter-
(7) governmental Committee for European Migration in 1960," *Industry and Labour*, 25:306-
308 (May 1).

1313. 1961 "Intergovernmental Committee for European
(8) Migration: Thirteenth Session of the Council,"
Industry and Labour 25:324-325 (May 15).

1314. 1961 "Lebanese Emigration in 1958 and 1959,"
9) *Industry and Labour*, 25:329-331 (May 15).

1315. 1961 "Migration from and to Ireland in 1959,"
(10) *Industry and Labour*, 25:325-329 (May 15).

1316. 1961 "Japanese Emigration from 1952 to 1960,"
(11) *Industry and Labour*, 25:359-360 (June 1).

1317. 1961 "Non-African Migratory Movements to and
(12) from the Federation of Rhodesia and Nyasaland in 1960," *Industry and Labour*, 25:360-
362 (June 1).

1318. 1961 "Extension of the Japanese-Bolivian Migration
(13) Agreement," *Industry and Labour*, 25:393 (June 15).

1319. 1961 "Immigration of Workers into France in 1960,"
(14) *Industry and Labour*, 25:393-395 (June 15).

1320. 1961 "Immigration to the United States in 1959-
(15) 1960," *Industry and Labour*, 25:398-402 (June 15).

1321. 1961 "Migration to and from the Netherlands in
(16) 1960," *Industry and Labour*, 25:395-398 (June 15).

1322. 1961 "Migrant Workers in Spain: Administrative
(17) Rules for Dealing with Offers of Employment
Received from Countries Abroad," *Industry
and Labour*, 26:214-215 (September 15).

1323. 1961 "Migrant Workers in Spain: Regulation of
(18) Emigration Act," *Industry and Labour*, 26:
211-214 (September 15).

1324. 1961 "Rehabilitation in Norway," *Industry and
(19) Labour*, 26:204-205 (September 15).

1325. 1961 "Complementary Agreements and Exchange
(20) on Notes of Migrant Workers between France
and Spain: Complementary Agreement Relating to Permanent Workers," *Industry and
Labour*, 26:265-267 (October 1).

1326. 1961 "Complementary Agreement and Exchange
(21) of Notes on Migrant Workers between France
and Spain: Complementary Agreement Relating to Temporary Workers," *Industry and
Labour*, 26:267-268 (October 1).

1327. 1961 "Complementary Agreement and Exchange
(22) of Notes on Migrant Workers between France
and Spain: Exchange of Notes Between the
French and Spanish Governments on Migrant
Workers," *Industry and Labour*, 26:269 (October 1).

1328. 1961 "Agreement Between the Netherlands and
(23) Spain on the Migration, Engagement and
Placement of Spanish Workers in the Netherlands," *Industry and Labour*, 26:307-309 (October 15).

1329. 1961 "Emigration from Greece in 1960," *Industry
(24) and Labour*, 26:330-332 (November 1).

1330. 1961 "Immigration to Canada in 1960," *Industry
(25) and Labour*, 26:328-330 (November 1).

1331. 1961 "Immigration to Singapore in 1959," *Indus-
(26) try and Labour*, 26:333-334 (November 1).

1332. 1961 "Migration to and from Australia in 1959-
(27) 1960," *Industry and Labour*, 26:364-369 (November 15).

1333. 1961 "Migration to and from Switzerland in 1959
(28) and 1960: Emigration and Return of Swiss
Subjects, *Industry and Labour*, 26:369-371
(November 15).

1334. 1961 "Migration to and from Switzerland in 1959
(29) and 1960: Immigration of Foreign Workers,"
Industry and Labour, 26:371-374 (November 15).

1335. 1961 "Measures to Facilitate Settlement of Euro-
(30) peans from Africa in Argentina," *Industry
and Labour*, 26:407 (December 1 and 15).

[*Industry and Labour* ceased publication at
the end of 1961. Information similar to that
published in this publication is published
after that date in the *International Labour
Review* or in an Official Bulletin of the International Labour Organisation.]

1336. Ingram, James C.

1955 *Economic Change in Thailand since 1850*,
issued under the auspices of the International
Secretariat, Institute of Pacific Relations (Stanford, Stanford University Press), 254 pp.

1337. Institute for Economic and Social Research, Djakarta
School of Economics

1957 "Some Aspects of Spontaneous Immigration."
A report by the Institute for Economic and
Social Research, Djakarta School of Economics, University of Indonesia, ed. Djoko Santoso
and Ali Wardhana, *Ekonomi dan Keuangan
Indonesia*, 10:415-430 (June).

1338. Institute for the Study of the History and Culture of
the U.S.S.R.

1955a "Continuing Settlement in the Far East,"
*Bulletin of the Institute for the Study of the
History and Culture of the U.S.S.R.*, 2:22-25
(March).

1339. 1955b "The Demography of Kazakhstan and the
Cultivation of the New Lands," *Bulletin of
the Institute for the Study of the History
and Culture of the U.S.S.R.*, 2:18-23 (April).

1340. Institute for the Study of the U.S.S.R.

1962 *Handbook Issue on Siberia and the Far East:
Geopolitics, Population, Economics*, Studies
on the Soviet Union, New Series, 1, No. 4
(Munich, Institute for the Study of the
U.S.S.R.), 195 pp.

1341. Institute of Bankers in Ireland

1955 "Commission on Emigration and Population:
Minority Reports," *Journal of the Institute
of Bankers in Ireland*, 57:11-16 (January).

1342. Institute of Jewish Affairs. World Jewish Congress.

1956 *European Jewry Ten Years After the War.
An Account of the Development and Present
Status of the Delineated Jewish Communities
of Europe* (New York, Institute of Jewish Affairs), 294 pp.

1343. Inter-African Labour Institute

1959a "Migrant Labour in Africa South of the Sahara. 4. Organisation of Migrant Labour in
the South-African Mining Industry," by Witwatersrand Native Labour Association Ltd.,
Bulletin of the Inter-African Labour Institute,
6:40-48 (July).

1344. 1959b "Migrant Labour in Africa South of the
Sahara. 5. A Survey of the Development
of Facilities for Migrant Labour in Tanganyika During the Period 1926-1959," by
H.R.G. Hurst, Witwatersrand Native Labour
Association Ltd., *Bulletin of the Inter-African
Labour Institute* 6:50-91 (July).

1345. 1959c "Migrant Labour in Africa South of the
Sahara. 6. The Persistence of Migrant Labour," by Walter Elkan, *Bulletin of the
Inter-African Labour Institute*, 6:36-43 (September).

1346. 1959d "Migrant Labour in Africa South of the
Sahara. 7. Some Aspects of the Labour Migration in the Belgian Congo," by Mme.
P.F. Bouvier, *Bulletin of the Inter-African
Labour Institute*, 6:8-55 (November).

1347. Inter-African Labour Institute

1960a "Labour and Social Problems Associated with
Major Development Projects in Africa. II.
The Kariba Hydroelectric Scheme," *Bulletin of the Inter-African Labour Institute*, 7:
58-85 (January).

*1348. 1960b "Migrant Labour in Africa South of the
Sahara. 8. The Manpower Problems of the
Ivory Coast are the Solutions (the S.I.A.-
M.O.)," by R. Desclercs, *Bulletin of the
Inter-African Labour Institute*, 7:39-54
(March).

1349. Intergovernmental Committee for European Migration

1955a *Draft Report on the First Session of the
Council of Intergovernmental Committee for
European Migration, Geneva, 30 November
1954—4 December 1954*, 43 pp. (processed).

1350. 1955b *Subject Index to the Documents of the Brussels Migration Conference, the Provisional
Intergovernmental Committee for the Movement of Migrants from Europe (PICMME),
and the First to Eighth Sessions of the Intergovernmental Committee for European Migration (ICEM)*, 63 pp. (processed).

1351. Intergovernmental Committee for European Migration

   1957 *Report on the Sixth Session of the Council of the Intergovernmental Committee for European Migration, (adopted at the 56th Meeting on 7 October 1957,) Geneva, 8-12 April 1957*, 58 pp.

1352. Intergovernmental Committee for European Migration

   1958 *Pilot Projects to Increase the Absorptive Capacity of Immigration Countries*, Presented by the Director, Eighth Session MC/287, 29 pp.

1353. Intergovernmental Committee for European Migration

   1961 *Migrants and Refugees: A Bibliography on Legal Matters*. Geneva: 22 p. (processed).

1354. International Bank for Reconstruction and Development

   1957 *The Economic Development of Jordan*, Report of a mission organized by the International Bank for Reconstruction and Development at the request of the Government of Jordan (Baltimore: Johns Hopkins Press, for the International Bank for Reconstruction and Development), 488 pp.

1355. International Catholic Migration Commission

   1957 "Post-war Italian Overseas Migration," *Migration Facts and Figures*, No. 10, supplement to *Migration News*, 6 (July-August).

1356. International Catholic Migration Commission

   1958a "Asian Migration Number," *Migration News*, 7:1-19 (July-August).

1357. 1958b *Asian Migration: Study of Legal Barriers to the Migration of Asiatics* ... Documentary Material No. 12 (Geneva, I.C.M.C.), 47 pp. (processed).

1358. 1958c "African Migration Number," *Migration News*, 7:1-17 (September-October).

1359. International Catholic Migration Commission

   1959a "Overseas Emigration from Europe (1946-1957)," compiled by T. Stark, *Migration Facts and Figures*, No. 16, supplement to *Migration News*, 8 (January-February).

1360. 1959b "Refugee Groups," *Migration News*, 8:6-26 (May-June).

1361. 1959c "The World Refugee Year," *Migration News*, 8:1-48 (May-June) (A special issue).

1362. 1959d "Non-European Refugees," *Migration Facts and Figures*, No. 20, supplement to *Migration News*, 8:1-43 (September-October).

1363. International Catholic Migration Commission

   1961 (A group of articles on the first ten years' operation of the Commission) *Migration News*, 10:1-32 (July-August).

1364. International Catholic Migration Commission

   1962a "Emigration from Portugal," *Migration Facts and Figures*, No. 21, supplement to *Migration News*, 11 (January-February), 4 pp.

1365. 1962b "Fifteen Years of Spanish Emigration (1946-60)." *Migration Facts and Figures*, No. 22, supplement to *Migration News*, 11 (March-April), 4 pp.

1366. 1962c "Comparability of Migration Statistics, 1946-1960," *Migration News*, 11:10-18 (May-June).

1367. 1962d "Gross Overseas Immigration (1946-1960)," *Migration Facts and Figures*, No. 23, supplement to *Migration News*, 11 (May-June), 4 pp.

1368. International Federation of Agriculture Producers

   1959 "Rural-Urban Migration in Under-developed Countries," *World Agriculture*, 8:19-21 (April).

1369. International Institute for Land Reclamation and Improvement

   1960a *Land Reclamation*, by A. E. Brouwn (Wageningen, International Institute for Land Reclamation and Improvement), 37 pp.

1370. 1960b *Bibliography "Land Settlement," July 1960: A Survey of the Literature on Colonization Problems and Planological Aspects in Land Development Projects*, by A. E. Brouwn (Wageningen, International Institute for Land Reclamation and Improvement), 53 pp.

1371. *International Journal of Religious Education*

   1960 "Followers of the Crops," *International Journal of Religious Education*, 36:7-10 (March).

1372. *International Labour Review*

   1955 "The Occupational Selection of Migrants," *International Labour Review*, 72:406-420 (November).

1373. *International Labour Review*

   1956a "Post-War Migration of West Indians to Great Britain," *International Labour Review*, 74:193-209 (August).

1374. 1956b "Rural-Urban Employment Relationship," *International Labour Review*, 74:568-575 (December).

1375. *International Labour Review*

   1957a "Post-War Migration Problems in Japan," *International Labour Review*, 75:53-67 (January).

1376. 1957b "Obstacles to Labour Mobility and Social Problems of Resettlement (A Survey by the

European Coal and Steel Community," *International Labour Review*, 76:72-83 (July).

1377.   1957c   "Inter-territorial Migrations of Africans South of the Sahara," *International Labour Review*, 76:292-310 (September).

1378. *International Labour Review*

1958   "Indian Policy in Latin America," *International Labour Review*, 78:603-604 (December).

1379. *International Labour Review*

1959a   "Recent Developments in the Clearance of Manpower between Western European Countries," *International Labour Review*, 79:173-188 (February).

1380.   1959b   "Labor Mobility in the United States," *International Labour Review*, 79:296-314 (March).

1381. *International Labour Review*

1960   "The Motives of Emigration: Findings of a Recent Study in the Netherlands," *International Labour Review*, 81:74-81 (January).

1382. *International Labour Review*

1961a   "Some Aspects of the International Migration of Families," *International Labour Review*, 83:65-86 (January).

1383.   1961b   "Projections of Population and Labour Force," *International Labour Review*, 83:378-399 (April).

1384. *International Labour Review*

1962a   "Migration to and from New Zealand in 1960-61," *International Labour Review*, 85:63-65 (January).

1385.   1962b   "Free Movement of Workers within the European Economic Community," *International Labour Review*, 85:167-173 (February).

1386.   1962c   "Agreement between Switzerland and Spain on the Engagement of Spanish Workers for Employment in Switzerland," *International Labour Review*, 85:291-293 (March).

1387.   1962d   "Migration to and from the Netherlands in 1961," *International Labour Review*, 86:180-184 (August).

1388.   1962e   "Migration to and from Switzerland in 1961," *International Labour Review*, 86:276-283 (September).

1389.   1962f   "Emigration from Greece in 1961," *International Labour Review*, 86:488-491 (November).

1390.   1962g   "Organisation and Control of Immigration in the Malagasy Republic," *International Labour Review*, 86:578-579 (December).

1391. *International Review Service*

1957   *The Refugee Problem in the Middle East*, ed. A G. Mezerik. *International Review Service*, 3 (March), 70 pp.

1392. International Statistical Institute

1958   *Economic Data of Large Towns 1950-1954*. Tables. International Statistics of Large Towns, Series C, No. 1. (The Hague, International Statistical Institute) 144 pp.

*1393. International Union for the Scientific Study of Population (Union Internationale pour l'Etude Scientifique de la Population)

1960   *Problems in African Demography: A Colloquium, Paris, 20-27 August 1959*, 60 pp.

1394. Inter-Parliamentary Union

1956   "Immigration and Emigration Policies as Related to the Distribution of Manpower and the Fight Against Unemployment," Agenda Paper No. 5 in *Union Inter-Parlementaire Compte Rendu de la XLIV Conference Tenue à Helsinki, 1955* (Geneva, Bureau Interparlementaire), 1174 pp.

1395. *Interpreter Releases*

1960   "Refugee Provisions of Public Law 86-648," *Interpreter Releases*, 37:253-262 (August 22).

1396. Iowa, State University. Agricultural Experiment Station and Department of Economics and Sociology.

1962a   *Geographic and Residential Distribution of Iowa's Population and Change, 1950-1960*, by Jon Doerflinger with assistance of Jeff Robinson, 11 pp.

1397.   1962b   *The Population of Incorporated Places in Iowa, 1900-1960*, 31 pp.

1398. Ipsen, Gunther

1955   "The Population of Central and Western Germany up to 1955," *REMP Bulletin*, 3:57-90 (July-September).

1399. Ireland. Central Statistics Office.

1955   "Irish Born Persons in Britain in 1951," *Irish Trade Journal and Statistical Bulletin*, 30:74-82 (June).

1400. Ireland. Central Statistics Offices.

1956a   *Census of Population, 1956*, Preliminary Report, 9 pp.

1401.   1956b   "Overseas Emigration and Immigration," *Irish Trade Journal and Statistical Bulletin*, 31:89-91 (June).

1402. Ireland. Central Statistics Offices.

1959   "Overseas Emigration and Immigration," *Irish Trade Journal and Statistical Bulletin*, 34:84-86 (June).

1403. Ireland. Central Statistics Offices.

1960 "Overseas Emigration and Immigration," *Irish Trade Journal and Statistical Bulletin*, 35:94-96 (June).

1404. Ireland. Central Statistics Offices.

1961 *Ireland, Census of Population, 1961*, Preliminary Report, 25 pp.

1405. Isaac, J. E.

1960 "Manpower Planning in Australia," *International Labour Review*, 82:403-431 (November).

1406. Isaac, Julius

1955 "Post-War Migration within the Commonwealth," *REMP Bulletin*, 3:15-21 (January).

1407. Isard, Walter, and others

1960 *Methods of Regional Analysis: An Introduction to Regional Science*, (New York, London: Published jointly by the Technology Press of the Massachusetts Institute of Technology and John Wiley and Sons, Inc.), 784 pp.

1408. Israel. Central Bureau of Statistics.

1955 *Jewish Population by Sex, Age and Country of Birth (1931-1954)*, by M. Sicron and B. Gil, Special Series No. 37, XVIII, [iv], 34 and 15 pp.

1409. Israel. Central Bureau of Statistics.

1956a *Jewish Rural Population* (Jerusalem, Study Group on Problems of Individual and Group Settlement, Central Bureau of Statistics), 32 pp.

1410. 1956b *Registration of Population (8 XI 1948). Part B. Characteristics of the Jewish Population and Types of Settlement*, by B. Gil and M. Sicron, Special Series No. 53, (Jerusalem, Government Printer), 64 pp.

1411. Israel. Government Press Office.

1961 *Facts about Israel, 1961: With Supplement, Statistics and Documents*, 168 pp.

*1412. Israel, Arturo

1960 *Labor Mobility* (Santiago, Instituto de Economia, Universidad de Chile), 37 pp.

1413. *Israel Economist*

1957a "The Arab Refugees," *Israel Economist*, 13:67-69 (May).

1414. 1957b "Immigration and the Sinai Campaign," *Israel Economist*, 13:83-84 (June).

1415. *Israel Economist*

1958 "New Hope for the Refugees?" *Israel Economist*, 14:173-174 (November).

1416. Italy. Documentation Centre.

1955 "Italian Emigration during the Period from 1946-1954. An Analysis of the Migratory Movement and Associated Problems," *Italian Affairs*, 4:985-995 (November).

1417. Italy, Documentation Centre.

1956a "Italian Communities Abroad," *Italian Affairs*, Documents and Notes, 5:1129-1136 (March).

1418. 1956b "Italian Emigration in 1955," *Italian Affairs*, Documents and Notes, 5:1463-1470 (November).

1419. Italy. Documentation Centre.

1957 "Remittances of Italian Immigrants. An Important Contribution to the Balance of Payments," *Italian Affairs*, 6:1623-1624 (March).

1420. Italy. Documentation Centre.

1958 "Migration in 1956: Outlines of Migration Activity; International Agreements and Negotiations; Assistance to Migrants," *Italian Affairs*, 7:2029-2040 (January).

1421. Jaatinen, Stig

1960 "Expansion and Retreat of Settlement in the Southwestern Archipelago of Finland," *Fennia*, 84(1):39-65.

1422. Jaatinen, Stig

1962a "The Birthplace Field of Helsinki According to the Census of 1950," *Fennia*, 86(5):17 pp.

*1423. 1962b "The Population of Mariehamn," in *Aland Culture: Twenty-Third Year, Yearbook for 1962*, (Mariehamn, Alands, Tidnings-Tryckeri Ab.), pp. 3-41.

1424. Jackson, Eureal G.

1957 "Some Tendencies in Demographic Trends in Maryland, 1950-1956. Current Trends in Negro Education, and Shorter Papers," Section B, *Journal of Negro Education*, 26:514-519 (Fall).

Jaffe, A. J. *See* 2019.

1425. Japan. Bureau of Statistics.

1962a *Migration, 1960 Population of Japan*, olume 2, Part 2, 209 pp.

1426. 1962b *Population Estimates by Prefecture as of October 1, 1951 to 1954*, Population Estimates Series 21, 70 pp.

*1427. Japan. Institute of Population Problems.

1960 *Annual Reports of the Institute of Population Problems*, Special number in commemoration of the 20th anniversary of the establishment of the Institute, 146 pp.

*1428. Japan. Institute of Population Problems.

    1962 *Annual Reports of the Institute of Population Problems, No. 7,* 103 pp.

1429. Jay, Florence E.

    1956 "Those Who Stay: A Sociological Study of the Stability of a Community," unpublished doctoral dissertation, University of Pittsburgh, 224 pp.

1430. Jay, L. J.

    1957 "Pioneer Settlement on the Darling Downs; A Scottish Contribution to Australian Colonisation," *The Scottish Geographical Magazine,* 7:35-49 (April).

*1431. Jelínkova, R.

    1957 "The Growth of Czechoslovak Towns in 1921-1957," *Statistický Obzor,* 47:485-496 (October).

1432. Jelínkova, R., and Vladimir Srb

    1956 "Internal Migration in Czechoslovak Republic," *Statistický Obzor,* 36:354-363 (August).

Johnson, Helen. *See* 1939.

1433. Jones, Roger W.

    1961 "Department Supports Continuation of Refugee and Migration Programs," *Department of State Bulletin,* 45(1157):380-385.

Jong, Gordon F. de. *See* 890.

1434. Joshi, V. R.

    1957 "Patterns of Rural Mobility," *Indian Journal of Agricultural Economics,* 12:32-46 (October-December).

1435. Journalist's Co-operative (Zachodnia Agencja Prasowa)

    1960 *Western and Northern Territories of Poland. Demographic Problems, Part II,* Studies and Monographs, Pamphlet 5 (Poznaw, Warsaw: Wydawnictwo Zachodnic), 108 pp.

Jugoslovenskog Statističkog Društva. *See* 2039 and 2040.

* 1436. Kahanpää, K. H.

    1960 "Vital Statistics in 1959," *Tilastokatsauksia,* 35(8):40-43.

1437. Kaigl, Vl., ed.

    1959 *Czechoslovak Economic Papers,* (Prague, Nakladatelst vi Ceskoslovenske Akademie Ved), 332 pp.

1438. Karcha, R.

    1957 "The Restoration of the Liquidated Republics and the Rehabilitation of the Deported Peoples," *Caucasian Review,* No. 5:41-46.

Kasahara, Y. *See* 1487.

* 1439. Kawabe, Hiroshi

    1961 "Migration to Cities in Japan: 1950-1955," *Journal of Geography,* 70(4):16-30.

Kay, Georbe. *See* 1727.

Keate, D. M. R. *See* 925.

Kennedy, Ruby J. R. *See* 884.

Kimura, Yukiko. *See* 1031.

1440. King, Morton B., Jr., Harold A. Pedersen, and John N. Burrus

    1955 *Mississippi's People, 1950,* Sociological Study Series, No. 5, (University of Mississippi, Bureau of Business Administration), 98 pp.

1441. Kinvig, R. H.

    1955 *Manx Settlement in the U. S. of America,* reprinted from *Proceedings of the Isle of Man Natural History and Antiquarian Society,* 5(4):20 pp.

1442. Kirk, Dudley

    1957 *The Character and Implications of Population Trends in the U. S.,* in *A Look to the Future,* presented at a conference held at the W. K. Kellogg Foundation, June, 1955 (Battle Creek, W. K. Kellogg Foundation), 20 pp.

1443. Kirk-Greene, A. H. M.

    1962 "America in the Niger Valley: A Colonization Centenary," *Phylon,* 23(3):225-239.

1444. Kiser, Clyde V.

    1957 "Population Research," in *Review of Sociology: Analysis of a Decade,* ed. Joseph B. Gittler, (New York: John Wiley) pp. 56-86.

1445. Kiser, Clyde V.

    1959 "Fertility Rates by Residence and Migration," in *International Population Conference, Vienna, 1959* (Vienna, International Union for the Scientific Study of Population), pp. 273-286.

1446. Kiiskinen, Auvo

    1961 "Regional Economic Growth in Finland, 1880-1952," *Scandinavian Economic History Review,* 9(1):83-104.

1447. Klausner, Samuel Z.

    1955 "Immigrant Absorption and Social Tension in Israel: A Case Study of Iraqi Jewish Immigrants," *Middle East Journal,* 9:281-294 (Summer).

*1448. Klinger, Andras

    1958 "Hungary's Vital Statistics in Recent Years," *Demográfia,* 1(1):95-108.

* 1449. Klinger, Andras, and others

1960 "Population and Tourism in the Balaton Region," *Demográfia*, 3(1):76-107.

1450. Kluckhohn, Clyde

1956 "Aspects of the Demographic History of a Small Population," in *Estudios Antropologicos Publicados on Homenaje al Doctor Manual Gamio* (México, D. F.),pp. 359-381.

1451. Kmenta, J.

1961 "Economic Mobility of Immigrants in Australia," *Economic Record*, 37:456-469 (December).

1452. Knicely, Howard

1960 *Characteristics of Mobile Workers in a Rural Industrialized Community*, unpublished master's thesis, University of West Virginia.

*1453. Kobayashi, Kazumasa

1959 "A Study on Population Distribution in India by States of Birth and States of Residence," in *Annual Reports of the Institute of Population Problems, No. 4* (Tokyo, Welfare Ministry) pp. 63-69 (English summary, pp. 90-91).

1454. Koehl, R

1956 "The Deutsche Volksliste in Poland 1939-1945," *Journal of Central European Affairs*, 15:354-366 (January).

1455. Kornrumpf, Martin

1955 "Enforced and Directed Mass Migration in Europe, 1912-1954," *I.C.M.C. News*, 2:1-3 (February).

* 1456. Kosínski, Leszek

1960a "Resettlement Problems of the Western Territories of Poland," *Demográfia*, 2(3):257-266.

1457. 1960b "Problems of Settling the Polish Western and Northern Territories," *Przeglad Geograficzny*, Vol. 32, Supplement, pp. 193-209.

1458. Kostanick, Huey L.

1955 "Turkish Resettlement of Refugees from Bulgaria 1950-1953," *The Middle East Journal*, 9:41-52 (Winter).

1459. Kostanik, Huey L.

1957 "Turkish Resettlement of Bulgarian Turks 1950-1953," *University of California Publications in Geography*, 8(2):65-146.

1460. Kraak, J. H.

1957 "The Repatriation of Netherlands Citizens and Ambonese Soldiers from Indonesia," *Integration*, 4(4):348-355.

1461. Kraak, J. H.

1958 "The Repatriation of the Dutch from Indonesia," *R.E.M.P. Bulletin*, 6:27-40 (April-June).

*1462. Kučera, M.

1958 "The Population Point of View and the Location of the Socialist Production," *Statistický Obzor*, 38:300-307 (July).

*1463. Kulcsár, Kálmán, and Millosné Nozdroviczky

1958 "Problems of Social Transformation and Migration at the Village Bélapátfalva," *Demográfia*, 1(2-3):281-288.

1464. Kulkarni, M. G.

1960 "Spatial Distribution of Migrants and Marriage-Connections in Gokak Taluka," *Artha Vijñána*, 2:287-306 (December).

1465. Kung, S. W.

1962 "Chinese Immigration into North America, with Special Reference to the Problem of Illegal Entry," *Queen's Quarterly*, 68:610-620 (Winter).

*1466. Kuroda, Toshio

1961 "Analysis of Recent Trends in Internal Migration in Japan," in *Annual Reports of the Institute of Population Problems, No. 36* (Tokyo, Institute of Population Problems), pp. 19-23.

1467. Kuznets, Simon

1955 "Economic Growth and Income Inequality," *American Economic Review*, 45:1-28 (March).

1468. Laan, H. L. van der

1957 "The Geizira Scheme: Results of an Irrigation-project in the Sudan," *Tijdschrift voor Economische en Sociale Geografie*, 48:183-187 (July-August).

Labovitz, Sanford. *See 978.*

1469. Lal, Amrit

1961 "Pattern of In-migration in India's Cities," *Geographical Review of India*, 23:16-23 (September).

1470. Lalwani, Kastur C., ed.

n.d. *Recent Population Movements in India*, Monographs on Indian Economic Problems, 157 (Calcutta, Artha Vanijya Gabesania Mandir), 16 pp.

1471. Lannes, Xavier

1956a "International Mobility of Manpower in Western Europe: I," *International Labour Review*, 73:1-24 (January).

1472.   1956b "International Mobility of Manpower in Western Europe: II," *International Labour Review,* 73:135-151 (February).

*1473. Lannes, Xavier, and Roland Pressat

    1955 "Some Results of the 1954 Census," *Population,* 10:135-142 (January-March).

1474. Lao Kan

    1956 "Population and Geography in the Two Han Dynasties," in *Chinese Social History: Translations of Selected Studies,* ed. Sun E tu Zen, and John De Francis, Studies in Chinese and Related Civilizations, No. 7, (Washington, American Council of Learned Societies), pp. 83-102.

1475. Larnaud, Jean

    1959 "The Work of UNESCO Concerning Migration and Social Development," *Migration News,* 8:6-12 (July-August).

1476. Latham, John D.

    1957 "Towards A Study of Andalusian Immigration and Its Place in Tunisian History," *Les Cahiers de Tunisie,* 5 (19-20):203-248.

1477. Lawton, R.

    1958 "Population Movements in the West Midlands 1841-61," *Geographical Journal,* 124:164-176 (September).

1478. Lawton, R.

    1959 "Irish Immigration to England and Wales in the Mid-Nineteenth Century," *Irish Geography,* 4(1):35-54.

1479. Lebergott, Stanley

    1960 "Population Change and the Supply of Labour," comment by James N. Morgan and John Durand in *Demographic and Economic Change of Developed Countries,* (Princeton, Princeton University Press), pp. 377-422.

1480. Lebeuf, J. P.

    1958 "Recent Research on Migration in West Africa," *Migration News,* 7(5):13-17.

1481. LeBlanc, Robert G.

    1962 "The Acadian Migrations," *Minnesota Academy of Science, Proceedings,* 30 (1):55-59.

1482. Lee, John F.

    1956 "Statutory Provision for Admission of Mexican Agricultural Workers—An Exception to the Immigration and Nationality Act of 1952," *George Washington Law Review,* 24:464-477 (March).

Lee, Lung-hsiung *See* 2038.

1483. Lee, Rose Hum,

    1956 "The Chinese Abroad," *Phylon,* 17(3):257-270.

1484. Lee, Y. L.

    1961 "Land Settlement for Agriculture in North Borneo," *Tijdshrift von Economische en Sociale Geografie,* 52:184-191 (July).

1485. Lee, Y. L.

    1962 "The Population of British Borneo," *Population Studies,* 15:226-243 (March).

Leedy, Frederick A. *See* 1744.

1486. Legendre, Pierre

    1960 "The European Common Market and Agricultural Migration in France," *Migration News,* 9:12-19 (January-February).

1487. LeNeveu, A. H., and Y. Kasahara

    1958 "Demographic Trends in Canada, 1941-56, and Some of Their Implications," *Canadian Journal of Economics and Political Science,* 24:9-20 (February).

1488. Leser, C.E.V.

    1959 "Migration and the Australian Work Force," *Economic Record,* 35:264-266 (August).

1489. Lerner, Daniel, and A. J. Weiner eds.

    1958 "A Special Issue on: Attitude Research in Modernizing Areas," *Public Opinion Quarterly,* 22:217-420 (Fall).

Levin, Melvin B. *See* 998.

Levine, Selma M. *See* 1682.

1490. Lewis, R.

    1956 "Commonwealth Migration 1946-56," *Investor's Chronicle, Annual Commonwealth Survey, August 25, 1956,* pp. 13-17.

1491. Lind, Andres W., and Bernard L. Hormann, eds.

    n.d. *Papers Presented at the Tenth Pacific Science Congress, Honolulu, Hawaii, 1961, Sponsored by the National Academy of Sciences, Bernice Pauahi Bishop Museum, University of Hawaii. Social Process,* 25, 84 pp.

1492. Lindt, Gillian N.

    1955 "The Cultural Assimilation of Immigrants," unpublished master's thesis, Columbia University.

1493. Little, Kenneth

    1960 "West African Urbanization as a Social Process," *Cahiers d'Etudes Africaines,* No. 3: 90-102.

1494. Livingston, William S.

    1957 "Emigration as a Theoretical Doctrine during the American Revolution," *Journal of Politics*, 19:591-615 (November).

1495. London, University of. School of Oriental and African Studies.

    1962 "Third Conference on African History and Archaeology, Held at the School of Oriental and African Studies, University of London, 3-7 July, 1961," *Journal of African History*, 3(2):171-374.

1496. Louisiana. Interdepartmental Committee on Health, Education, and Services.

    1960 *Report on the Louisiana Migrant Labour Problem*, 51 pp.

1497. Lövgren, Esse

    1956 "The Geographical Mobility of Labor; A Study of Migrations," *Geografisker Annaler*, 38(4): 344-394.

1498. Lowenthal, David

    1957 "The Population of Barbados," *Social and Economic Studies*, 6:445-501 (December).

1499. Lowenthal, David

    1960 "Population Contrasts in the Guianas," *Geographical Review*, 50:41-58 (January).

1500. Lowenthal, David, and Lambros Comitas

    1962 "Emigration and Depopulation: Some Neglected Aspects of Population Geography," *Geographical Review*, 52:195-210 (April).

1501. Ludlow, James M.

    1958 "The Arab Refugees: A Decade of Dilemma for the United Nations," *Department of State Bulletin*, 39(1012):775-782.

1502. Lupori, Nello

    1956 "Emigration and Incomes in Agriculture," *Rivista di Economia Agraria*, 11:30-85 (March).

1503. Lutovac, M.

    1958 "Migrations and Settlements in Yugoslavia in the Past and in the Present," *Glasnik*, No. 7:13-24.

1504. Lutz, Vera C.

    1961 "Some Structural Aspects of the Southern Problem: The Complementarity of 'Emigration' and Industrialization," *Banca Nazionale del Lavoro Quarterly Review*, 59:367-403 (December).

1505. Lyon, A. V.

    1955 "Group Settlement at Trentham Cliffs, New South Wales," *R.E.M.P. Bulletin*, 3:101-106 (October-December).

1506. Lyubovny, V. Ya

    1961 "Some Questions Relating to the Formation of Urban Population," *Soviet Geography*, 2: 51-57 (December).

1507. McCollum, R. S.

    1957 "Relation of the United States to World Migration," *Department of State Bulletin*, 37: 65-67 (July 8).

1508. McArthur, Neil, and Martin E. Gerland

    1961 "The Spread and Migration of French Canadians," *Tijdschrift voor Economische en Sociale Geografie*, 52:141-147 (June).

1509. McDermott, George L.

    1959 "Advancing and Retreating Frontiers of Agricultural Settlement in the Great Clay Belt of Ontario and Quebec," unpublished master's thesis, University of Wisconsin, 160 pp.

1510. McDermott, George L.

    1961 "Frontiers of Settlement in the Great Clay Belt, Ontario and Quebec," *Annals of the Association of American Geographers*, 51: 261-273 (September).

1511. McDonald, J. S.

    1958 "Some Socio-Economic Emigration Differentials in Rural Italy, 1902-1913," *Economic Development and Cultural Change*, 7:55-72 (October).

1512. McDougall, Duncan M.

    1961 "Immigration into Canada, 1851-1920," *Canadian Journal of Economics and Political Science*, 27:162-175 (May).

1513. McGee, T. G.

    1960 "Aspects of the Political Geography of South-East Asia: A Study of a Period of Nation-building," *Pacific Viewpoint*, 1:39-58 (March).

1514. McGee, T. G.

    1962 "Indian Settlement in New Zealand: 1900-1956," *New Zealand Geographer*, 18:203-223 (October).

1515. Mabogunje, Akin

    1962 "The Growth of Residential Districts in Ibadan," *Geographical Review*, 52:56-77 (January).

1516. Maccotta, Giuseppe W.

    1962 "European Multilateral Organizations Concerned with the Movement of Workers," *Migration*, 2:9-20 (January-March).

1517. MacDonagh, Oliver

    1955 "Emigration and the State, 1833-55: An Essay in Administrative History," *Royal Historical Society Transactions*, 5th Series, 5:133-159.

MacDonald, Gordon D. *See* 1878.

1518. MacKaye, Benton

    1962 *The New Exploration: A Philosophy of Regional Planning* (Urbana, University of Illinois Press) 243 pp.

1519. Mahavir

    1959 "Agricultural Resettlement of the Refugees in (East) Punjab," *Uttar a Bharati*, 6:101-106 (March).

1520. Mahhouk, Adnan

    1956 "Recent Agricultural Development and Bedouin Settlement in Syria," *Middle East Journal*, 10:165-176 (Spring).

1521. Maitland, Sheridan T.

    1958 *The Hired Farm Working Force of 1956*, Agricultural Information Bulletin No. 187 (Washington, U. S. Agricultural Marketing Service), 50 pp.

1522. Malaya. Federation of Malaya. Department of Statistics.

    1958- *1957 Population Census of the Federation of*
    1960 *Malaya*, Reports 1-14, 15 publications.

1523. Malta. Central Office of Statistics.

    1958 *Population, Housing and Employment Census of the Maltese Islands, November, 1957. Preliminary Report*, 37 pp.

1524. Malta. Department of Emigration, Labour and Social Welfare.

    1958 *Report on the Working of the Department of Emigration, Labour and Social Welfare for the Year 1957*, 38 pp.

1525. Malenbaum, Wilfred

    1957 "Urban Unemployment in India," *Pacific Affairs*, 30:138-150 (July).

1526. Malzberg, Benjamin

    1956 "Migration and Mental Disease in New York State, 1939-1941," *Human Biology*, 28:350-364 (September).

1527. Malzberg, Benjamin

    1962 "Migration and Mental Disease Among the White Population of New York State, 1949-1951," *Human Biology*, 34:89-98 (May).

1528. Mamer, John W.

    1961 "The Use of Foreign Labour for Seasonal Farm Work in the United States: Issues Involved and Interest Groups in Conflict," *Journal of Farm Economics*, 43:1204-1210 (December).

1529. Mangin, William P.

    1959 "The Role of Regional Associations in the Adaptation of Rural Population in Peru," *Sociologus*, No. 1:23-36.

1530. Mangrum, Claude Thomas, Jr.

    1958 "The Drain of Talent Out of North Carolina and Tennessee," unpublished master's thesis, Kent State University.

Manley, Douglas *See* 1788.

1531. Manshard, W.

    1951 "Land Use Patterns and Agricultural Migration in Central Ghana (Western Gonja)," *Tijdschrift voor Economische en Sociale Geografie*, 52:225-230 (September).

1532. Marks, Edward B.

    1957a "Internationally Assisted Migration: I.C.E.M. (Intergovernmental Committee for European Migration) Rounds out Five Years of Resettlement," *International Organization*," 11(3):481-494.

1533.   1957b "Planned Migration, 1956-1957: A Report Based on the Sixth Session of the Intergovernmental Committee for European Migration Geneva, Switzerland," *Interpreter Releases*, 34:100-114 (May 22).

1534. Marsal, Juan F.

    1961 "Argentina as an Immigration Country," *Migration*, 1:17-36 (October-December).

1535. Marshall, Douglas G.

    1957 *Selected Population Data by Countries: Wisconsin, 1950-1957. How Wisconsin's Population Is Changing* (Madison: Department of Sociology, College of Agriculture, University of Wisconsin), unpaged.

1536. Martin, J. A.

    1957 "Off-farm Migration and a Changing Agriculture in Tennessee," *Tennessee Farm and Home Science Progress Report*, No. 24:10-11 (October-December).

*1537. Martín de la Escalera, Carmen

    1955 "Algerian Economy, Demography, and Emigration," *Cuadernos Africanos y Orientales*, 29:39-51.

1538. Maryland. Governor's Committee for the Regulation and Study of Migratory Labour.

    1960 *Progress in Meeting Problems of Migratory*

Labour in Maryland, A report (College Park, University of Maryland).

Marx, Sue. *See 1547.*

1539. Mather, D. B.

1956 "Migration in the Sudan," in *Geographical Essays on British Tropical Lands*, ed. R. W. Steel and C. A. Fisher (London: G. Philip and Son), pp. 115-143.

1540. Matousek, V.

1958 "Problems of Insufficient Agricultural Resettlement," *Sbornik, Ceskoslovenska Spolecnost Zemepisna*, 63(4):323-328.

1541. Maude, H. E.

1959 "Tahitian Interlude; the Migration of the Pitcairn Islanders to the Motherland in 1831," *Journal of the Polynesian Society*, 58:115-140 (June).

1542. Maugini, Armado

1956 "Toward a Better Knowledge of Overseas Emigration and Colonization," *Rivista di Agricoltura Subtropicale e Tropicale*, 50:5-21 (January-March).

1543. Maugini, Armado

1957 "Reclamation and Rural Population with Immigrants as Factors of Progress in the Underdeveloped Territories of Latin America," *Rivista di Agricoltura Subtropicale e Tropicale*, 51:385-392 (October-December).

1544. Maugini, Armado

1958 "Efforts of CIME in increasing European Agricultural Emigration to Latin America," *Rivista di Agricoltura Subtropicale e Tropicale*, 52:337-354 (July-September).

1545. Maunder, W. F.

1955 "The New Jamaican Emigration," *Social and Economic Studies*, 4:38-63 (March).

1546. Mauro, F.

1961 "Towards an 'Intercontinental Model': European Overseas Expansion Between 1500 and 1800," *Economic History Review*, 3rd Series, 14:1-17 (August).

1547. Mayer, Albert J., and Sue Marx

1957 "Social Change, Religion, and Birth Rates," *American Journal of Sociology*, 62(4):383-390.

1548. Mayer, H. M.

1955 "Current and Prospective Population Trends," *Appraisal Journal*, 23:212-224 (April).

1549. Mead, W. R.

1957 "The Margin of Transference in Finland's

Rural Resettlement," *Tijdschrift voor Economische en Sociale Geografie*, 48:178-183 (July-August).

1550. Meerdink, J.

1962 "Internal Migration in Amsterdam," *Bulletin de l'Institut International de Statistique*, 39(4): 183-193.

1551. Meissner, F.

1960 "Australia's Postwar Immigrants," *American Journal of Economics and Sociology*, 19:169-176 (January).

1552. Mellor, George R.

1955 "Emigration from the British Isles to the New World, 1765-1775," *History*, 40:68-83 (February/June).

1553. Mellor, Roy E. H.

1957 "The German Refugee Problem: Ten Years Retrospect," *The Scottish Geographical Magazine*, 73:1-18 (April).

1554. Mendoza-Pascual, Elvira

1962 "Reinvestigation of Birth and Death Statistics in the Philippines," *Philippine Statistician*, 11:171-189 (December).

1555. Mendras, Henri

1960 "The Rural Exodus and Industrialization," *Diogenes*, No. 30:104-119 (Summer).

Merwe, M. F. van der *See 2027.*

1556. Metraux, Alfred

1959 "The Social and Economic Structure of the Indian Communities of the Andean Region," *International Labour Review*, 79:225-243 (March).

1557. Metropolitan Life Insurance Company

1955 "Population Still Moving Westward," *Statistical Bulletin*, 36:6-8 (June).

1558. Metropolitan Life Insurance Company

1957 "Current Patterns of Immigration," *Statistical Bulletin*, 38:6-8 (April).

1559. Metzler, William H.

1955 *Migratory Farm Workers in the Atlantic Coast Stream. A Study in the Belle Glade Area of Florida*, Department of Agriculture Circular No. 966 (Washington, Government Printing Office), 79 pp.

Mezerik, A. G. *See 1391.*

1560. Michigan. Bay County Board of Education.

1956 *Bay County School for Migrant Children* (mimeographed).

1561. Michigan. State University of Agriculture and Applied Science, East Lansing. Vietnam Advisory Group, Saigon. Field Administration Division.

    1955 *Research Report, Field Study of Refugee Commission*, Ralph Smuckler, Research Coordinator (East Lansing, Michigan State University of Agriculture and Applied Science), 9 pp.

1562. Migrator

    1962 "The Free Movement of Workers in EEC Countries," *Migration*, 2:3-19 (April-June).

*1563. Mikoalj, L.

    1959 "Present External Migration of the Population of Poland," *Zeszyty Naukowe*, No. 11: 159-230.

Miller, Vincent A. *See* 1770.

1564. Miller, W. L.

    1961 "Slavery and the Population of the South," *Southern Economic Journal*, 38:46-54 (July).

Mills, D. O. *See* 1737.

1565. Minnesota. Governor's Human Rights Commission.

    1958 *The Migrant Worker in Minnesota*, Report of the Governor's Human Rights Commission on Migrant Workers.

1566. Mintz, Sidney W.

    1955 "Puerto Rican Emigration: A Threefold Comparison," *Social and Economic Studies*, 4: 311-325 (December).

1567. Mirengoff, William, and Albert Shostack

    1958 *Housing for Florida's Migrants: A Survey of Migratory Farm Labor Housing in Dade County, Florida* (Washington, Government Printing Office), 46 pp.

1568. Mironenko, V. P.

    1955 "Population Growth and Movement Within the R.S.F.S.R. between 1947 and 1955," *Bulletin of the Institute for the Study of the History and Culture of the U.S.S.R.*, pp. 15-18 (November).

1569. Mitchell, C.

    1956 "Labour Migration and the Tribe," *Listener*, 56:646-647 (October).

1570. Mitchell, J. Clyde

    1957 "Africans in Industrial Towns in Northern Rhodesia," in *Report of the Duke of Edinburgh's Study Conference*, Volume II, (London: Oxford University Press), p. 3.

1571. Mitchell, J. Clyde

    1959 "Migrant Labour in Africa South of the Sahara. 1. The Causes of Labour Migration," *Inter-African Labour Institute Bulletin*, 6:8-47 (January).

Mohammed, Azizali F. *See* 709.

1572. Mol, Johannis J.

    1959 "Theoretical Frame of Reference for the Interactional Patterns of Religion and the Adjustment of Immigrants," *REMP Bulletin*, 7 (April-June).

1573. Molinari, Alessandro

    1958 "Manpower and the Common Market," *Banca Nazionale del Lavoro, Quarterly Review*, No. 47:484-510 (December).

*1574. Möller, Gustav

    1955 "Aliens in Sweden by Sex and Age Groups," *Sociala Meddelanden*, No. 6:321-326.

1575. Montgomery, Robert

    1959 *Regulation of Migrant Farm Worker Transportation in North Carolina* (Chapel Hill: Institute of Government, University of North Carolina).

1576. Monticello, L.

    1961 "A Century of Italian Emigration," *Migration News*, 10:1-4 (March-April).

1577. Mookerjee, Sudhansubimal

    1958 "Early Years of Indian Immigration to Mauritius (1837-1842)," *The Calcutta Review*, 149: 275-284 (December).

1578. Moorthy, K. Krishna

    1961 "India's Third Five-Year Plan," *Far Eastern Economic Review*, 33:356-361 (August).

1579. Morgen, W. B.

    1955 "Farming Practice, Settlement Plans and Population Density in South-Eastern Nigeria," *Geographical Journal*, 121, Pt. 3:320-334 (September).

*1580. Mori, Alberto

    1961 "Observations on Lifelong Emigration from Southern Italy," *Bollettino della Società Geografica Italiana*, Ser. 9, 2:224-235 (April-June).

*1581. Mörner, Magnus

    1960 "Immigration and the Rise of Modern Latin America," *Ymer*, 80(4):260-274.

1582. Morrill, Richard L.

    1961 *Local Migration and Urbanization in Sweden*, Paper presented at the 57th annual meeting of the Association of American Geographers, East Lansing, Michigan, August 28-September 1, 1961, abstracted in *Annals of Association of American Geographers*, 51:417-418 (December).

583. Morse, Richard M.

1962 "Latin American Cities: Aspects of Function and Structure," *America Latina*, 5:35-64 (July-September).

584. Mugge, Robert H.

1957 *Negro Migrants in Atlanta*, Microfilm 5337 F, Library, University of Chicago (Chicago, Department of Photographic Reproduction), 188 pp.

585. Muhsam, H. V.

1961 "Labour Force Characteristics and Economic Absorption of Immigrants in Israel," *Integration*, 8:71-86 (Also separately reprinted).

586. Mulder, William

1956 "Immigration and the 'Mormon Question': An International Episode," *Western Political Quarterly*, 9:416-433 (June).

587. Mullaly, Harry F.

1960 *United States Refugee Policy, 1789-1956: A Study of the Traditional Policy of Asylum for Political, Racial or Religious Refugees*, microfilm copy of typescript, (Ann Arbor, Michigan: University Microfilms), 363 pp.

588. Myrdal, Gunnar

1956 *An International Economy: Problems and Prospects* (New York, Harper), 382 pp.

Nagi, Saad Z. *See* 708.

589. Nairn, N. B.

1956 "A Survey of the History of the White Australia Policy in the Nineteenth Century," *Australian Quarterly*, 28:16-31 (September).

590. Narain, Iqbal

1955 "Beginning of Emigration to Natal," *India Quarterly*, 11:31-55 (January-March).

591. Narain, Iqbal

1957 "Indians in the Orange Free State and the Cape," *Uttara Bharati*, 4:83-96 (December).

592. National Bureau of Economic Research

1960 *Demographic and Economic Change of Developed Countries*, A Conference of the Universities-National Bureau Committee for Economic Research, Special Conference Series, No. 11 (Princeton, Princeton University Press), 536 pp.

593. National Council of the Churches of Christ in the U.S.A. Division of Home Missions.

1957a *An Experiment in Homemaking with the Children of Migrant Farm Workers* (New York, National Council of the Churches of Christ in the U.S.A.) (July-August).

1594. 1957b *Excerpts from the Findings of a Pilot Project in Parent Education with a Crew of Migratory Negro Farm Workers in the Atlantic Coast Stream* (New York, National Council of the Churches of Christ in the U.S.A.) (mimeographed).

1595. Nederlandse Vereniging voor Economische en Sociale Geografie

1960 "Special Issue on the Occasion of the XIXth International Geographical Congress at Stockholm, Sweden, 5-13 August 1960," *Tijdschrift voor Economische en Sociale Geografie*, 51: 161-200 (July).

1596. Neiva, Arthur H.

1961 "The Importance of Immigration in the Development of Brazil," *Migration*, 1:41-52 (January-March).

Nellner, Werner *See* 962.

*1597. Nelson, Helge

1957 "The Immigrants into the U.S.A. and Their Children," *Statistik Tidskrift*, 6:126-134 (March).

*1598. Netherlands. Centraal Bureau voor de Statistiek.

1961a "Estimates of the Future Course of the Population of the Netherlands," *Maandschrift van het Centraal Bureau voor de Statistiek* 56:657-662 (July).

*1599. 1961b "Special Data. Vital Statistics, Migration and Age Distribution 1960," *Maandstatistiek van de Bevolking en de Volksgezondheid*, 9:216-152 (July).

*1600. 1961c *Statistics of Internal Migration, 1958-1959* (Zeist, Uitgeversmaatschappij W. de Haan N. V.), 56 pp.

*1601. Netherlands. Centraal Bureau voor de Statistiek.

1962a *Statistics of External Migration, 1959-1960* (The Hague and Zeist, W. de Haan N. V.), 124 pp.

*1602. 1962b "Special Data. Vital Statistics, Migration and Age Distribution 1961," *Maandstatistiek van de Bevolking en de Volksgezondheid*, 10: 135-164 (July).

*1603. Netherlands. Ministerie van Sociale Zaken en Volksgezondheid.

1957 *Emigratie 1956* (The Hague, Staatsdrukkerij-en Vitgeverijbedriff), 212 pp.

1604. Neumark, S. Daniel

1957 *Economic Influences on the South African Frontier, 1652-1836* (Stanford, Stanford University Press), 196 pp.

1605. *New Commonwealth*

1956 "Pakistan; Refugee Resettlement," *New Commonwealth*, 32(9):452.

1606. New Jersey. Department of Labor and Industry.

1958 *Thirteenth Annual Bureau of Migrant Labor Report.*

1607. New York. Department of Social Welfare.

1958 *The Movement of Population and Public Welfare in New York State: A Report on America's Mobile Labour Force and Its Economic Contributions and Public Welfare Costs to New York State*, 35 pp.

New York. Interdepartmental Committee on Low Incomes. *See* 852.

1608. New York. State Legislature. Joint Legislative Committee on Migrant Labor.

1956 *Report of the Joint Legislative Committee on Migrant Labor Legislative Document*, 21 pp.

1609. New York. New York City Department of City Planning.

1957 *Puerto Rican Migration to New York City*, 9 pp. (processed).

New York. State Education Department. *See* 752.

1610. New York. State Education Department. University of the State of New York.

1957 *A Report on the State Education Department Pilot Project: Summer School Education of Migrant Children* (mimeographed).

1611. *New Outlook*

1961 "The Refugee Problem in Facts and Figures," *New Outlook*, 4:23-30 (February).

1612. New Zealand. Census and Statistics Department.

1956 *Population Census, 1951*, Vol. VIII. General Report (Wellington, Government Printer), 196 pp.

1613. New Zealand. Department of Labour.

1959 "Survey of Post-war Migration to New Zealand; With Brief Account of Earlier Settlement, and Some Comparisons of Australia, Canada, New Zealand in Their Participation in Migration from Europe," *Labour and Employment Gazette*, 9:24-28 (August).

1614. New Zealand. Department of Labour.

1960 "Immigration and the Labour Force," A background paper presented to the Industrial Development Conference, June 1960, by N. S. Woods, *Labour and Employment Gazette*, 10: 44-49 (August).

1615. New Zealand. Department of Statistics.

1957 *Population Census, 1956*, Vol. I. *Increase and Location of Population* (Wellington, Government Printer), 124 pp.

1616. Newman, Jeremiah

1958 "The Future of Rural Ireland," *Studies*, 47: 388-409 (Winter).

*1617. Neymark, E.

1961 *Selective Mobility. Migratory Tendencies and Tendencies in Vocational Choice in Relation to Education, Intelligence and Social Background* (Stockholm, Council of Personnel Administration, University of Stockholm), 526 pp.

1618. Niddrie, David L.

1959 "Land Utilization and Settlement in Tobago, the West Indies" (Research Note), *Social and Economic Studies*, 8:219-221 (June).

1619. Nixon, Richard

1957 "Providing for the Needs of the Hungarian Refugees: Report to President Eisenhower by Vice President Nixon, January 1, 1957," *Department of State Bulletin* 36:94-99.

Noh, Toshio. *See* 1006.

Noring, Gunnar. *See* 924.

1620. North Carolina. Board of Health. Public Health Statistics Section.

1961 *Net Migration by Color, Sex and Age for North Carolina and for Each County by Color: 1950 to 1960*, 22 pp.

*1621. Norway. Statistisk Sentralbyrå.

1955 *Vital Statistics and Migration Statistics 1952, Norges Offisielle Statistikk XI: 191*, 60 pp.

*1622. Norway. Statistisk Sentralbyrå.

1957 *Vital Statistics and Migration Statistics 1955 with Survey Tables 1951-1955 and Life Tables 1951-1955, Norges Offisielle Statistikk XI:282*, 112 pp.

*1623. Norway. Statistisk Sentralbyrå.

1958 *Vital Statistics and Migration Statistics 1956*, 70 pp.

*1624. Norway. Statistisk Sentralbyra.

1960 *Vital Statistics and Migration Statistics 1958, Norges Officielle Statistikk XII: 123.*

625. Norway. Statistisk Sentralbyrå.

1961 *Vital Statistics and Migration Statistics 1959, Norges Offisielle Statistikk XII: 49*, 60 pp.

626. Norway. Statistisk Sentralbyrå.

1962 *Statistical Yearbook of Norway, 1962, 81st Issue, Norges Offisielle Statistikk XII: 87*, 369 pp.

627. Nozdroviczky, Miklósné

1959 "Influence of Migration on Population Growth in the County of Szabolcs-Szatmár," *Demográfia*, 2(1):134-138.

Nozdroviczky, Millósné. *See* 1463.

628. Ohio. Governor's Committee on Migrant Labor.

1960 *Migratory Labor in Ohio Agriculture; A Report*, ed. Sally Bingham (Columbus, Division of Labor Statistics), 37 pp.

629. Ohio. Governor's Committee on Migrant Labor.

1962 *Migratory Labor in Ohio Agriculture: A Report*, ed. Sally Bingham (Columbus, Division of Labor Statistics), 38 pp.

630. Ohio. Legislative Service Commission.

1961 *Migrant Workers in Ohio*, Staff Research Report 49, 61 pp.

Ohio. Ottawa County. *See* 927.

631. Ohio. State Bureau of Unemployment Compensation. Division of Research and Statistics.

1962 *The Mobile, Unemployed Worker: A Labor Mobility Study of Unemployed Workers Who Migrated to Columbus, Ohio, from Other States*, 91 pp.

632. Okada, Shigekiyo

1955 "Migration and Religion," *Jinrui Kagaku* [Science of Mankind], No. 7:62-76 (March).

633. Okun, Bernard, and Richard W. Richardson

1961 "Regional Income Inequality and Internal Population Migration," *Economic Development and Cultural Change*, 9:128-143 (January).

634. Ono, Kazuichiro

1958 "The Problem of Japanese Emigration," *Kyoto University Economic Review*, 28:40-54 (April).

635. Oregon Bureau of Labor.

1958 *We Talk to the Migrants* ..... Preliminary report to the Governor's Inter-Agency Committee on Agricultural Labor and to the Legislative Interim Committee on Migratory Labor, unpaged.

636. Oregon. Bureau of Labor.

1959 ..... *And Migrant Problems Demand Attention*, The final report of the 1958-59 farm studies in Oregon, 218 pp.

637. Oregon, Legislative Assembly. Interim Committee on Migratory Labor.

1958 *Migratory Labor in Oregon. Report of Findings and Recommendations*, 72 pp.

638. Oregon. State Board of Census.

1961 "Components of Population Growth, State of Oregon, 1940-1960," *Population Bulletin*, Release No. P. 3., Portland State College, 8 pp.

639. Oregon. State Department of Education in Cooperation with the Governor's Inter-Agency Committee on Migratory Labor.

1959 *Study of Seasonal Workers' Children in Oregon Schools*, mimeographed.

640. Organski, A. F. K.

1961 "Population and Politics in Europe," *Science*, 133:1803-1807 (June 9).

Organski, A. F. K. *See* 1641.

641. Organski, Katherine F., and A. F. K. Organski

1961 *Population and World Power* (New York, Knopf), 263 pp.

642. *Oriental Economist*

1961 "Exodus of Agricultural Population," *Oriental Economist*, 29:416 (July).

643. Orleans, Leo A.

1958 "The Volume of Migration in Relation to Land Reclamation in Communist China," *R.E.M.P. Bulletin*, 6:25-26 (April-June).

644. Orleans, Leo A.

1959 "The Recent Growth of China's Urban Population," *Geographical Review*, 49:43-57 (January).

645. Orleans, Leo A.

1960 "Population Redistribution in Communist China," in *Population Trends in Eastern Europe, the USSR and Mainland China*, (New York, Milbank Memorial Fund), pp. 141-150.

646. Osborne, E.

1955 "Inter-county Migration in South-eastern England," *Geography*, 40(187):47-48.

647. Osborne, Richard H.

1956 "Internal Migration in England and Wales, 1951," *Advancement of Science*, 12:424-34 (March).

1648. Osborne, Richard H.

1958   *The Movements of People in Scotland, 1851-1951*, reprinted from *Scottish Studies*, 2, Part I, 45 pp.

1649. Osborne, Richard H.

1960   "The 'Drift South' in Britain Countinues," *Tijdschrift voor Economische en Sociale Geografie*, 51:286-289 (November).

1650. Osman, Omer M.

1958   "The Social and Economic Development of the Sudan," *International Labour Review*, 78:329-347 (October).

Oyama, Misako. *See* 1840.

*1651. Pan American Union

1955   *Causes and Effects of the Rural Exodus in Venezuela* (Washington: Consejo Interamericano Economico y Social, Organización de los Estados Americanos), 272 pp.

1652. Panofsky, Hans E.

1961   *A Bibliography of Labor Migration in Africa South of the Sahara* (Evanston: University Library, Northwestern University), 28 pp. (processed).

*1653. Pápai, Béla

1961   "Development of the Districts of Settlement of Budapest; Demographic Structure of the Last Decade by Areas," *Demográfia*, 4(3): 325-342.

1654. Parnaby, Owen W.

1956   "The Regulation of Indentured Labour to Fiji, 1864-1888," *The Journal of the Polynesian Society*, 65:55-65 (March).

1655. Parsons, Kenneth H., and others

1956   *Land Tenure*, Proceedings of the International Conference on Land Tenure and Related Problems in World Agriculture held at Madison, Wisconsin, 1951 (Madison, University of Wisconsin Press), 740 pp.

1656. Patterson, David

1960   "The First Fifty Years of Collective Settlement in Israel," *Jewish Journal of Sociology*, 2:42-55 (June).

1657. Patterson, Sheila

1961   "The Polish Exile Community in Britain," *Polish Review*, 6:69-97 (Summer).

*1658. Pavlik, Z.

1959   "Recent Data on Migration in Czechoslovakia," *Journal of the Czechoslovak Geographical Society*, 64(4):324-337.

1659. Pedersen, Harald A.

1956   "The Costs of Migration," in *The Church in the Changing Community*, Sociology and Rural Life Conference Series 2 (State College, Mississippi State College), pp. 16-18.

Pedersen, Harald A. *See* 1440.

1660. Peking Jen-min Jih-pao

1958   "A Million Migrants Settle in Border Regions," *Survey of China Mainland Press*, No. 1920 1-2 (December 23).

1661. Pennsylvania.   Governor's Committee on Migratory Labor.

1959   *Final Report, 1958: Pennsylvania Migratory Labor Program*, mimeographed.

Pennsylvania. Urban League of Philadelphia. *See* 757.

1662. Pennsylvania. State University. College of Education

1958   *Report on the Pennsylvania State University School for Migrant Children* (University Park: College of Education, Pennsylvania State University).

1663. Pentland, H. C.

1959   "The Development of a Capitalistic Labour Market in Canada," *Canadian Journal of Economics and Political Science*, 25:450-461 (November).

1664. Peretz, Don

1955   "Israel and the Arab Refugees," unpublished doctoral dissertation, Columbia University, 438 pp.

1665. Peretz, Don

1961   "Detente in the Arab Refugee Dilemma," *Orbis*, 5:306-319 (Fall).

*1666. Perevedentsev, V.

1962   "Problems on Territorial Redistribution of Labor Resources," *Voprosy Ekonomiki*, No. 5:48-56 (May); English translation: U. S. Joint Publications Research Service, Translations on U.S.S.R. Labor, No. 23, JPRS, 15,000, pp. 1-24.

1667. Perloff, Harvey S., and others

1960   *Regions, Resources, and Economic Growth* (Baltimore: The Johns Hopkins Press, published for Resources for the Future, Inc.), 716 pp.

1668. Petersen, William

1956   "The Study of Man: Immigration and Acculturation in Israel and in Australia," *Commentary*, 22:463-470 (November).

1669. Peterson, William

    1958   "Internal Migration and Economic Development in Northern America," *The Annals of the American Academy of Political and Social Science*, 316:52-59 (March).

1670. Petty, Julian J.

    1961   "South Carolina Population Redistribution," *University of South Carolina Business and Economic Review*, 7:1-4 (May).

1671. Petty, Julian J.

    1962   *20th Century Changes in South Carolina Population*, A study prepared for the State Organization for Associated Research, SOAR Report 5A-USC 1962 (Columbia: Bureau of Business and Economic Research, University of South Carolina), 209 pp.

1672. Petz, Rudolf

    1959   "Experiment in Cooperation: Japanese Miners in Germany," *Migration News*, 8:3-6 (January-February).

1673. Phillips, Doris G.

    1959   "Rural-to-Urban Migration in Iraq," *Economic Development and Cultural Change*, 7: 405-421 (July).

1674. Piault, M. P.

    1961   "The Migration of Workers in West Africa. Migrant Labour in Africa South of the Sahara, XI," *Bulletin of the Inter-African Labour Institute*, 8:98-123 (February).

1675. Piccardi, Silvio

    1958   "Essay on the Study of the Depopulation of the Mountains in the Aosta Valley," *L'Universo*, 38:985-990 (November-December).

Pinard, Maurice. *See* 778.

1676. Piotrow, P. T.

    1958   "Palestine Arab Refugees," *Editorial Research Reports*, pp. 23-40 (January 8).

1677. Pipes, Richard

    1959   "Demographic and Ethnographic Changes in Transcaucasia, 1897-1956," *The Middle East Journal*, 13(1):41-63.

1678. Pitcher, June Dickerson

    1955   "Occupational Status and Reasons for Leaving the State of West Virginia: Graduates of Division of Home Economics, West Virginia University, 1932-1952," unpublished master's thesis, West Virginia University.

*1679. Poland. Szkoła Glowna Planowania i Statystyki.

    1960   *Population Problems Zeszyty Naukowe*, Szkoły Glownej Planowania i Statystyki 21, 102 pp.

1680. Political and Economic Planning (P.E.P.)

    1957   "Britain and Commonwealth Migration," *Planning*, 23:70-83 (April).

1681. Political and Economic Planning (P.E.P.)

    1958   "Refugees in Britain. Hungarians and Anglo-Egyptians," *Planning*, 24:18-35 (February 17).

1682. Pollitt, Daniel H., and Selma M. Levine

    1960   *The Migrant Farm Worker in America: Background Data on the Migrant Worker Situation in the United States Today*, Prepared for the Subcommittee on Migratory Labor of the Committee on Labor and Public Welfare, U. S. Senate, 86th Congress, 2nd Session, Committee Print (Washington, Government Printing Office), 79 pp.

1683. Porter, R.

    1956   "Approach to Migration through its Mechanism," *Geografiska Annaler*, 38(4):317-343.

1684. Pounds, Norman J. G., ed.

    1961   *Geographical Essays on Eastern Europe*, Indiana University Publications, Russia and East European Series, Volume 24 (Bloomington, Indiana University; The Hague, Mouton), 159 pp.

1685. Prabhu, Pandari Nath

    1956   *A Study of the Social Effects of Urbanization of Industrial Workers Migrating from Rural Areas to the City of Bombay* (Calcutta, UNESCO).

1686. Prain, R. L.

    1956   "The Stabilization of Labour in the Rhodesian Copperbelt," *African Affairs*, pp. 305-312 (October).

1687. Pramanik, Paramanada

    1957   "Study of Family Structure among East Pakistan Refugees," *Modern Review*, 101:233-238 (March).

Pressat, Roland. *See* 1473.

1688. Price, C. A.

    1957   "The Effects of Post-war Immigration on the Growth of Population, Ethnic Composition and Religious Structure of Australia," *Australian Quarterly*, 29:28-40 (December).

1689. Price, C. A.

    1960   *Is It Possible or Desirable to Maintain Closed and Homogeneous Immigrant Church Communities?* (Geneva: Migration Conference on the World Council of Churches, Preparatory Commission), Document 9.

1690. Price, C. A.

1962 "Overseas Migration to and from Australia, 1947-1961," *Australian Outlook* 16:160-174 (August).

1691. Price, C. A., ed.

1960 *The Study of Immigrants in Australia* (Canberra, The Australian National University) (mimeographed).

1692. Prothero, R. Mansell

1957a "Labour Migration in British West Africa," *Corona* (London), 9:169-171 (May).

1693. 1957b "Migratory Labour from North-western Nigeria," *Africa*, 27:251-261 (July).

1694. Prothero, R. Mansell

1961a "Migrants and Malaria. Migrant Labour in Africa South of the Sahara, X," *Bulletin of the Inter-African Labour Institute*, 8:87-97 (February).

1695. 1961b "Population Movements and Problems of Malaria Eradication in Africa," *Bulletin of the World Health Organization*, 24 (4-5): 405-425.

Prothero, R. M. *See* 734.

1696. Prudenskii, G.

1962 "Problems in Utilizing the Manpower of Siberia and the Far East," *Problems of Economics*, 5:25-31 (October).

1697. Puerto Rico. Department of Labor, Bureau of Labor Standards.

1955 *Migration and Population Growth for Puerto Rico, 1954. Preliminary Estimates*, Report on Population, No. 3, 4 pp.

1698. Puerto Rico. Department of Labor. Migration Division.

1955 "Implications of Puerto Rican Migration to the Continent Outside New York City," by Arthur C. Gernes, Address before the Ninth Annual Convention on Social Orientation, December 10, 1955, P.A.I.S. 43 (20).

1699. Puerto Rico. Department of Labor. Migration Division.

1956 "A Summary in Facts and Figures: Progress in Puerto Rico; Puerto Rican Migration, 1940-1955," 17 pp. (processed).

1700. Puerto Rico. Department of Labor. Migration Division.

1959 *Bibliography on Puerto Ricans in the United States*, annotated by Clarence Senior, chief, Migration Division, 37 pp. (processed).

1701. Raimon, Robert L.

1962 "Interstate Migration and Wage Theory," *Review of Economics and Statistics*, 44:428-438 (November).

*1702. Rajaković, Z.

1957 "Migratory Movements of the Croatian Population According to the Population Censuses of 1948 and 1953," *Ekonomski Pregled*, 8 (1/2):94-113.

1703. Ramanow, Mirro

1959 *Nonwhite Population Changes in Chicago's Suburbs* (Chicago, Illinois Commission on Human Relations), 14 pp.

1704. Ramsay, A. B.

1956 "Indonesians in Malaya," *Journal of the Malayan Branch of the Royal Asiatic Society*, 29:119-124 (May).

Ramsey, Ralph J. *See* 785.

1705. Randall, Laura

1962 "Labour Migration and Mexican Economic Development," *Social and Economic Studies*, 11:73-81 (March).

1706. Rao, G. Raghava

1956 "Indian Immigrants in Kenya—A Survey," *Indian Economic Journal*, 4:33-42 (July).

1707. Rao, G. Raghava

1957 "Indian Immigrants in Kenya—A Final Rejoinder," *Indian Economic Journal*, 5:204-206 (October).

1708. Rao, P. K.

1955 "Indians Abroad," in *Indian Year Book of International Affairs*, No. 4:42-54.

1709. Rao, V. K. R. V.

1961 "The Problem of India's Increasing Numbers: A Plea for an Inter-State Approach," *AICC Economic Review*, 13:10-12 (August 7).

*1710. Raptschinsky, B.

1957a "The Arab Refugees," *Tijdschrift voor Economische en Sociale Geografie*, 48:133-141 (June).

*1711. 1957b "Israel: The Growth of a Nation," *Tijdschrift voor Economische en Sociale Geografie*, 48:248-258 (November).

1712. Rasmussen, Tor Fr.

1960 "Population and Land Utilization in the Assam

Valley," *Journal of Tropical Geography*, 14: 51-76 (July).

1713. Rawlyk, G. A.

1962 "Canada's Immigration Policy, 1945-1962," *Dalhousie Review*, 42:287-300 (Autumn).

1714. Read, James M.

1957 "International Action for Hungarian Refugees," *Migration News*, No. 2:1-8.

1715. Rees, Elfan

1957 *Century of the Homeless Man*, International Conciliation, No. 515 (New York, Carnegie Endowment for International Peace), 62 pp.

1716. Rees, Elfan

1960 "The Refugee Problem: Joint Responsibility," *Annals of the American Academy of Political and Social Science*, 329:15-22 (May).

1717. Reid, George W., and others

1957 "Population Estimates for the State of Oklahoma," *American Society of Civil Engineers Proceedings*, 83 (January), *Journal of City Plan Division*, No. C.P. 1.: pp. 1136-1—1136-2.

1718. *Review of the River Plate*

1955 "Bigger Migratory Balance," *Review of the River Plate*, No. 3230:24 (September 9).

1719. *Review of the River Plate*

1958 "Rising Migratory Movements," *Review of the River Plate*, 123:18-19 (April 29).

1720. *Review of the River Plate*

1959 "Immigration and Land Settlement," *Review of the River Plate*, 125:9 (April 10).

1721. *Review of the River Plate*

1960 "Population Exodus from the 'Camp'," *Review of the River Plate*, 128:11-12 (November 30).

1722. *Review of the River Plate*

1961a "The Immigration Trickle," *Review of the River Plate*, 129:17 (May 23).

1723. 1961b "Shifting and Drifting: Urban and Rural Populations," *Review of the River Plate*, 130:15-16 (November 21).

1724. 1961c "National Census Results: 90 Years of Top-heavy Growth," *Review of the River Plate*, 130:23-24 (November).

1725. 1961d "An Underdeveloped Province: Economic Plight of La Pampa," *Review of the River Plate*, 130:33-34 (December 30).

1726. *Review of the River Plate*

1962 "The Flight to the Cities: In Buenos Aires and in Entre Rios," *Review of the River Plate*, 131:141-142 (April 30).

1727. Rhodes-Livingstone Institute

1962 A Population Map (1:500,000) of the Laupula-Bangweulu Region of Northern Rhodesia, with Notes on the Population, by George Kay, Rhodes-Livingstone Communication 26 (Lusaka, Rhodes Livingstone Institute), 17 pp.

1728. Ribeiro, Darcy

1962a "The Social Integration of Indigenous Populations in Brazil," *International Labour Review*, 85:325-346 (April).

1729. 1962b "The Social Integration of Indigenous Populations in Brazil: II. The Indian Problem in Brazil," *International Labour Review*, 85:459-477 (May).

Richardson, Richard W. *See* 1633.

1730. Richmond, Anthony H.

1956 "Immigration as a Social Process: The Case of Coloured Colonials in the United Kingdom," *Social and Economic Studies*, 5:185-201 (June).

1731. Ripley, Josephine

1955 *Peoples on the Move; A Selection from the Series of Articles Written for the Christian Science Monitor* (Geneva: Office of Public Information, Intergovernmental Committee for European Migration), 46 pp.

1732. Robbins, Richard

1958 "Myth and Realities of International Migration into Latin America," *The Annals of the American Academy of Political and Social Science*, 316:102-110 (March).

1733. Roberts, D. F., and R. E. S. Tanner

1959 "A Demographic Study in an Area of Low Fertility in North-East Tanganyika," *Population Studies*, 13:61-80 (July).

1734. Roberts, G. W.

1955 "Emigration from the Island of Barbados," *Social and Economic Studies*, 4:245-288 (September).

1735. Roberts, G. W.

1956 "Recent Demographic Trends in Cuba, Haiti and the British Caribbean," in *Population Bulletin of the United Nations*, No. 5 (ST/SOA/Ser. N/5. 15 July 1956. Sales No.: 1956. XIII. 4.) (New York: United Nations, Department of Economic and Social Affairs), pp. 42-50.

1736. Roberts, G. W.

    1962 "Prospects for Population Growth in the West Indies," *Social and Economic Studies*, 11: 339-350 (December).

1737. Roberts, G. W., and D. O. Mills

    1958 *Study of External Migration Affecting Jamaica: 1953-55*, Supplement to *Social and Economic Studies*, 7, No. 2:126 pp. (June).

1738. Robinson, J. B. Perry

    1956 *Transformation in Malaya* (London, Secker), 232 pp.

Robinson, Jeff. *See* 1396.

*1739. Rocchetti, Giuseppe

    1958 "Agricultural Emigration from Italy to Brazil in the Last Decade," *Rivista di Agricoltura Subtropicale e Tropicale*, 52:183-222 (April-June).

1740. Rochau, Georges de

    1959 "Immigration into France in 1957," *Migration News*, 8:16-19 (January-February).

Rodgers, Ruth. *See* 766.

1741. Rohrer, Wayne C.

    1961 *A Century of Migration of the Kansas Population*, Kansas State University Economics and Sociology Report 1, 21 pp.

1742. Rolland, Charlotte

    1962 "The Demographic and Social Situation of French Jewry," *Alliance Review*, 16:40-42 (Winter).

*1743. Rompietti, Attilio

    1961 "Agricultural Colonization in Tripolitania," *Rivista di Agricoltura Subtropicale e Tropicale*, 55:30-34 (January-March).

1744. Roof, Michael K. and Frederick A. Leedy

    1959 "Population Redistribution in the Soviet Union," *Geographical Review*, 49:208-221 (April).

1745. Rose, A. J.

    1959 "Irish Migration to Australia in the 20th Century," *Irish Geography*, 4(1):79-84.

1746. *Round Table*

    1962 "Migration in the Commonwealth: The United Kingdom Bill," *Round Table*, 52:119-130 (March).

Rowley, Diana. *See* 714.

1747. Rowntree, John A.

1957 *Internal Migration: A Study of the Frequency of Movement of Migrants*, General Register Office Studies No. 11 (London, H. M. Stationery Office), 12 pp.

1748. Rubin, Ernest

    1959 "Immigration and the Economic Growth of the U. S.: 1790-1914," *R.E.M.P. Bulletin*, 7: 87-95 (October-December).

Rundblad, Bengt G. *See* 970.

*1749. Ruocco, Domenico

    1961 "The Recent Emigration of Italians to Sweden," *Rivista Geografica Italiana*, 68:162-168 (June).

Russell, Amy. *See* 739 and 2001.

1750. Ryder, Norman B.

    1956 "The Interpretation of Origin Statistics," *Estadística*, 14:651-666 (December).

1751. Saharouni, Suren

    1960 "On the Origin of the Armenians," *Armenian Review*, 13:55-78 (May).

1752. Saldanha, P. H.

    1962 "Race Mixture Among the Northeastern Brazilian Populations," *American Anthropologist*, 64:751-759 (August).

1753. Salzano, Francisco M.

    1961 "Studies on the Caingang Indians," *Human Biology*, 33:110-130 (May).

1754. Samuel, Edwin

    1956 "The Immigration Cycle in Palestine and Israel, 1919-1954," *South African Journal of Economics*, 24:29-36 (March).

1755. Sanders, Irwin T., and Robert E. Galloway

    1956 *Rural Families in the Purchase Area of Western Kentucky (A Study of Economic Area 1)*, University of Kentucky Agricultural Experiment Station Bulletin 647, 28 pp.

1756. Sanderson, F. E.

    1961 "The Development of Labour Migration from Nyasaland, 1891-1914," *Journal of African History*, 2(2):259-271.

1757. Sandhu, Kernial S.

    1961 "Chinese Colonization of Malacca: A Study in Population Change, 1500 to 1957 A. D.," *Journal of Tropical Geography*, 15:1-26 (June).

1758. Sansonetti, Luigi

    1955 "An Italian Experiment in Organized Colonization in Costa Rica," *I.C.M.C. News*, 4: 6-7 (April).

Santoso, Djoko. *See* 1337.

1759. Sarafian, Vahe A.

1956 "Turkish Armenian and Expatriate Population Statistics," *Armenian Review,* pp. 118-128 (September).

Sardi, Endre. *See* 933.

1760. Sas, Anthony

1957a "Dutch Migration to and Settlement in Canada: 1945-1955," unpublished doctoral dissertation, Clark University, 194 pp.

1761. 1957b "Some Aspects of Dutch Immigration to Canada Since 1945," *Tijdschrift voor Economische en Sociale Geografie,* 48:189-190 (July-August).

1762. Sas, Anthony

1958 "Dutch Concentrations in Rural Southwestern Ontario during the Postwar Decade," *Annals of the Association of American Geographers,* 48:185-194 (September).

1763. Sauvy, A.

1956 *Socio-Psychological Aspects of Migration,* Paper submitted to the UNESCO Conference on the Cultural Integration of Immigrants in Havana (UNESCO/SS/Conf. Mig/11) (Paris, UNESCO).

*1764. Scarpa, G.

1957 "Depopulation of Mountain Areas and Economic Development," *Rivista di Economia Agraria,* 12:157-171 (June).

1765. Schaffer, Helen B.

1959 "Migratory Farm Workers," *Editorial Research Reports,* pp. 105-122 (February 11).

1766. Schapera, I.

1955 "An Anthropologist's Approach to Population Growth; Studies in the Bechuanaland Protectorate," in *The Numbers of Man and Animals,* by J. B. Cragg and N. W. Pirie, (London and Edinburgh, Oliver and Boyd) pp. 23-29.

*1767. Schätzel, W.

1955 "The Citizenship of Political Refugees," *Archiv des Völkerrechts,* pp. 63-69 (March).

1768. Schauff, J. and others

1955 *The Land Settlements of Immigrants in Latin America, Migration Digest,* Volume 2, 46 pp.

1769. Schechtman, Joseph B.

1961 *Star in Eclipse: Russian Jewry Revisited* (New York and London: Thomas Yoseloff), 255 pp.

1770. Schmid, Calvin F., Sanford M. Dornbusch, and Vincent A. Miller

1955 *Population Growth and Distribution: State of Washington* (Seattle, Washington State Census Board).

1771. Schmitt, Robert C.

1956 "A Century of Hawaiian Out-migration," *Social Process in Hawaii,* 20:38-46.

1772. Schmitt, Robert C.

1958 "Differential Mobility in Honolulu," *Sociology and Social Research,* 42:332-335 (May-June).

Schmitt, Robert C. *See* 1025.

1773. Schnore, Leo F.

1962 Municipal Annexations and the Growth of Metropolitan Suburbs, 1950-60," *American Journal of Sociology,* 67:406-417 (January).

Schnore, Leo F. *See* 1790.

1774. Scholes, W. E.

1956a "Who Are These Migrants?" *International Journal of Religious Education,* 32:6-7 (April).

1775. 1956b "Our Migrant Neighbors," *International Journal of Religious Education,* 32:4-6 (May).

1776. Schultz, Theodore W., ed.

1962 *Investment in Human Beings,* Papers presented at a conference called by the Universities-National Bureau Committee for Economic Research, *Journal of Political Economy,* 70 Part 2, Supplement:1-157 (October).

1777. Schwartz, Bella

1958 *Immigration of Professional Workers to the United States, 1953-1956,* Scientific Manpower Bulletin 8, NSF-58-4 (Washington, National Science Foundation), 11 pp.

1778. Schwartz, C. P., Jr.

1955 "American Immigration Policy," *Columbia Law Review,* 55:311-341 (March).

1779. Schwartz, K.

1961 *Migration in the Federal Republic of Germany by Town and Country* (New York, International Population Conference 1961, Paper 97), 10 pp. (mimeographed).

1780. Scott, Frances G.

1958 "Intrastate Migration of the Pre-aged and the Aged in Texas, 1935-1940," *Journal of Gerontology,* 13:296-304 (July).

1781. Sears, William P., Jr.

1957 "Indentured Servants in Colonial America," *Dalhousie Review*, 37:121-140 (Summer).

1782. Segal, Martin

1960 *Wages in the Metropolis: Their Influence on the Location of Industries in the New York Region*, New York Metropolitan Region Study Series (Cambridge, Harvard University Press), 211 pp.

1783. Selegen, Galina V.

1960 "The First Report on the Recent Population Census in the Soviet Union," *Population Studies*, 14:17-27 (July).

Selvaratnam, S. *See* 822.

1784. Semmingsen, Ingrid

1960 "Norwegian Emigration in the Nineteenth Century," *Scandinavian Economic History Review*, 8(2):150-160.

1785. Sendut, Hamzah

1962 "The Resettlement Villages in Malaya," *Geography*, 47:41-46 (January).

1786. Senior, Clarence

1957 "Race Relations and Labor Supply in Great Britain," *Social Problems*, 4:302-312 (April).

1787. Senior, Clarence

1962 "Migration as a Process and Migrant as a Person," *Population Review*, 6:30-41 (January).

Senior, Clarence *See* 1700.

1788. Senior, Clarence and Douglas Manley

1956 "British Experience of Immigration," *I.C.M.C. Migration News*, 5:3-9 (March).

1789. Seychelles. Central Civil Status Office.

1961 *Vital Statistics and Annual Report of the Civil Status Department, 1961—.*

1790. Sharp, Harry, and Leo F. Schnore

1962 "The Changing Color Composition of Metropolitan Areas," *Land Economics*, 38:169-185 (May).

1791. Shibata, Ginjiro

1960 "Japanese Emigration and Its Effect on International Payments," *Kobe Economic and Business Review*, No. 7:1-13.

*1792. Shimamura, Toshihiko

1959 "Changes in Vocational Composition of Emigrants from the United Kingdom," in *Annual Reports of the Institute of Population Problems, No. 4*, (Tokyo, Welfare Ministry), pp. 70-74.

1793. Shimkin, Demitri B.

1960 "Demographic Changes and Socio-Economic Forces within the Soviet Union, 1939-1959," in *Population Trends in Eastern Europe, the USSR and Mainland China*, (New York, Milbank Memorial Fund) pp. 224-258.

Shostack, Albert. *See* 1567.

1794. Shotwell, Louisa Rossiter

1958 *This is the Migrant* (New York, Friendship Press), 24 pp.

1795. Shrikant, L. M.

1956 "The Integration of the Aboriginal Population of India," *International Labour Review*, 73:241-251 (March).

1796. Shrinavasan, K. N.

1961 "Growth of Population in India during 1941-1961 and Thereafter," *AICC Economic Review*, 13:11-13 (June).

1797. Siam. Central Statistical Office. Office of the National Economic Development Board.

1959 *Final Report of the Demographic and Economic Survey, 1954*, Volume 1 (ii), 20, 26, iii, 532 pp.

Sicron, M. *See* 1408 and 1410.

1798. Sydney, University of. Department Tutorial Classes.

1959 "British Emigration: End of an Era?" *Current Affairs Bulletin*, pp. 82-96 (July 20).

*1799. Šifrer, Ž.

1957 "Some Data Taken from Migration Statistics of Slovenia," *Statistička Revija*, 7:68-72 (March).

1800. Silva, Nimalasiri

1960 "The Problem of Indian Immigration to Ceylon," in *South Asian Affairs Number One*. [Oxford University, St. Anthony's College], *St. Anthony's Papers, No. 8*, ed. Raghavan Iyer (London, Chatto and Windus), pp. 141-153.

*1801. Simoes, Nuno

n.d. "Numbers and Suggestions on Colonizing Emigration," *Boletim Geral do Ultramar*, 34(395):105-138.

1802. Simoniya, N. A.

1960 *Overseas Chinese in Southeast Asia: A Russian Study* J. P. R. S.:3442 (Washington, U. S. Joint Publications Research), 160 pp. (processed).

Simpkins, Paul D. *See* 1057.

1803. Singh, Chanan

1957a "Indian Immigrants in Kenya—A Survey," *Indian Economic Journal*, 4:295-299 (January).

1804. 1957b "Indian Immigrants in Kenya—A Reply to the Rejoinder," *Indian Economic Journal*, 5:202-204 (October).

1805. Sizer, Leonard M.

1959 *Population Estimates for the Counties of West Virginia, July 1, 1957*, West Virginia University Agricultural Experiment Station Current Report 19, 5 pp.

1806. Skinner, Elliot P.

1960 "Labour Migration and Its Relationship to Socio-cultural Change in Mossi Society," *Africa*, 30:274-400.

1807. Skone, J. F.

1957 "The Coloured Worker," *Royal Society for the Promotion of Health Journal*, 77:170-178 (April).

1808. Slater, David W.

1961 "Decentralization of Urban Peoples and Manufacturing Activity in Canada," *Canadian Journal of Economics and Political Science*, 27:72-84 (February).

Slesinger, Doris P. *See* 948.

1809. Slocum, Walter L.

1962 *Agricultural Sociology. A Study of Sociological Aspects of American Farm Life*, Harper's Social Science Series (New York, Harper), 522 pp.

1810. Smith, Bulkeley, Jr.

1959 "The Reshuffling Phenomenon: A Pattern of Residence of Unsegregated Negroes," *American Sociological Review*, 24:77-79 (February).

1811. Smith, Louis P. F.

1960 "Observations on a Declining Population," *Christus Rex: An Irish Quarterly Journal of Sociology*, 14:23-34 (January).

1812. Smith, T. Lynn

1958a "The Changing Number and Distribution of the Aged Negro Population of the United States," *Phylon*, 18(4):339-354.

*1813. 1958b "A Comparative Analysis of Rural-Urban Migration in Latin America," *Estadistica*, 16:436-453 (December).

Smuckler, Ralph. *See* 1561.

*1814. Sobajic, P.

1957 "Migratory Currents, Active and Passive, in Migratory Areas," *Glasnik*, 4-6:321-323.

1815. *Sociology and Social Research*

1959 "Areas for Sociological Research," *Sociology and Social Research*, 42:395-472 (July-August).

*1816. Somogyi, Stefano

1956 "Social and Demographic Repercussions of Italian Emigration," *Previdenza Sociale*, 12: 1273-1300 (September-October).

1817. Soper, Tom

1959 "Labour Migration in Africa," *Journal of African Administration*, 11:93-99 (April).

South Africa, Union of *See* 1890.

1818. Sovani, N. V.

1961 "The Urban Social Situation in India," *Artha Vijñāna*, 3:195-224 (September).

1819. Spaulding, Irving A.

1958a *Rhode Island Population: Selected County Data—1940-1950*, Rhode Island Agricultural Experiment Station Miscellaneous Publication 54, 29 pp.

1820. 1958b *Rhode Island Population: Selected Characteristics of Migration, 1950*, Rhode Island Agricultural Experiment Station Miscellaneous Publication 55, 14 pp.

Spaventa, L. *See* 683.

1821. Spengler, Joseph J.

1962 "Population Movements and Economic Development in Nigeria," in *The Nigerian Political Scene*, ed. by Robert O. Tilman and Taylor Cole (Durham, Duke University Press; London, Cambridge University Press, published for the Duke University Commonwealth Studies Center), pp. 147-197.

1822. Spradlin, T. Richard

1961 "The Mexican Farm Labor Importation Program: Review and Reform," *George Washington Law Review*, 30:84-122 (October), 311-327 (December).

1823. Spuhler, J. N., and Philip J. Clark

1961 "Migration into the Human Breeding Population of Ann Arbor, Michigan, 1900-1950," *Human Biology*, 33:223-236 (September).

1824. Stanbery, Van Beuren

1959 *Some New Techniques for Area Population Projections with Illustrative Projections of California's Population* (Los Angeles, John Randolph Haynes and Dora Haynes Foundation), 98 pp.

Starbird, Irving R. See 852.

1825. Steigenga, W.

1960 "The Urbanization of the Netherlands; An Analysis of the Development of a Decentralized Urbanization Pattern from 1880-1950," *Tijdschrift van het Koninklijk Nederlandsch Aardrijkskundig Genootschap,* 2nd series, 77: 324-331 (July).

Stein, J. L. See 767.

1826. Stenning, Derrick J.

1957 "Transhumance, Migration Drift, Migration; Patterns of Pastoral Fulani Nomadism," *Journal of the Royal Anthropological Institute of Great Britain and Ireland,* 87:57-73 (January-June).

Stewart, C. M. See 942.

1827. Stone, Kirk H.

1958 *High Latitude Frontier Settlement. Annual Report for First Year of Project,* Report to U.S. Office of Naval Research, Geography Branch, under Contract No. N. R. 388:042 (Madison, University of Wisconsin), 17 pp.

1828. Storey, Merle

1957 "Hungarians in Canada," *Canadian Geographical Journal,* 55:46-53 (August).

1829. Strömmer, A.

1956 "Recent Demographic Development and Population Policies in Finland," *Population Index,* 22(1):3-22.

*1830. Strömmer, A.

1960 *A Report on Regional Differences in the Growth of the Population of Finland during the Period 1951-1955,* Publications of the National Planning Bureau, Series A:1 (Helsinki), 50 pp.

1831. Sundrum, R. M.

1957 *Population Statistics of Burma,* Economics Research Project, Statistical Paper No. 3 (Rangoon: Economics, Statistics and Commerce Departments, University of Rangoon), 54 pp.

1832. Sung, Sui Lieng

1956 "Japanese Migration," *Far Eastern Economic Review,* 20:750-753 (June).

1833. Sutton, Elizabeth

1959 *Children on the Move,* (Washington, Department of Labor) Migratory Labor Notes, No. 10.

*1834. Sweden. Socialstyrelsen.

1957 "The Refugee Question: An International So-

cial Problem," [A group of articles], *Sociala Meddelanden,* No. 4:217-252.

*1835. Sweden. Statistiska Centralbyrån

1957 "Swedish Immigrants to Canada in 1946-1955," *Statistik Tidskrift,* 6 (August), pp. 441-442.

1836. Sykes, J.

1959 "Location of Industry and Population," *Journal of the Town Planning Institute,* 45:126-130 (May).

Szabady, Egon. See 687.

1837. Szajkowski, Zosa

1956 "Jewish Emigration from Bordeaux during the 18th and 19th Centuries," *Jewish Social Studies,* 18:118-124 (April).

1838. Szczepanik, Edward F.

1955 "The Fate of Hambro Report on Hong Kong Refugees," *Far Eastern Economic Review,* 19:132-135 (August 4).

*1839. Tachi, Minoru, ed.

1961 *Internal Migration in Japan* (Tokyo, Kokon Shoin Book Publishing Company), 214 pp.

*1840. Tachi, Minoru, and Misako Oyama

1961 "Migration Potential and Actual Migration of Population in Japan," in *Annual Reports of the Institute of Population Problems,* No. 36 (Tokyo, Institute of Population Problems), pp. 14-18.

1841. Taeuber, Irene B.

1958 "Migration, Mobility, and the Assimilation of the Negro," *Population Bulletin,* 14:127-151 (November).

1842. Taeuber, Irene B.

1959a "The Population of the Forty-ninth State," *Population Index,* 25:93-113 (April).

1843.   1959b "Western Expansion and Ethnic Convergence in the Population of the United States," reprinted from *American Statistical Association, Social Statistics Section,* pp. 104-109.

1844. Taeuber, Irene B.

1962 "Hawaii," *Population Index,* 28:97-125 (April).

1845. Taeuber, Karl E., and others

1961 "Residence Histories and Exposure Residences for the United States Population," *Journal of the American Statistical Association,* 56: 824-834 (December).

1846. Talbert, R. H.

1955 *Spanish-name People in the Southwest and*

West. (Fort Worth, Texas Christian University).

1847. Tanaka, Kosaku

1957 "Japanese Immigrants in Amazonia and Their Future," *Kobe University Economic Review*, No. 3.

1848. Tang, Anthony M.

1958 *Economic Development in the Southern Piedmont 1860-1950* (Chapel Hill, University of North Carolina Press), 256 pp.

1849. Tanganyika. Labour Department.

1957 *Annual Report of the Labour Department, 1957* (Dar es Salaam, Government Printer), 105 pp.

1850. Tanner, R. E. S.

1961 "Population Changes, 1955-1959, in Musoma District, Tanganyika, and Their Effect on Land Usage," *East African Agriculture and Forestry Journal*, 26(3):164-169.

Tanner, R. E. S. *See* 1733.

1851. Tanoglu, Ali

1955 "The Recent Emigration of the Bulgarian Turks," *Review of the Geographical Institute of the University of Istanbul, International Edition*, 2:3-35.

1852. Tarver, James D.

1955 *A Study of Rural Manpower in Southeastern Oklahoma*, Oklahoma Agricultural and Mechanical College Experiment Station Technical Bulletin, No. T-56, prepared in cooperation with the U. S. Agricultural Marketing Service, 27 pp.

1853. Tarver, James D.

1962 "Evaluation of Census Survival Rates in Estimating Intercensal State Net Migration," *Journal of the American Statistical Association*, 57:841-862 (December).

1854. Taylor, P. A. M., and L. J. Arrington

1958 "Religion and Planning in the Far West: The First Generation of Mormons in Utah," *Economic History Review*, 11:71-86 (August).

1855. Tennessee. General Assembly. Legislative Council Committee.

1958 *Migration and Industrial Development in Tennessee; A Report to the Industrial Development and Migration Subcommittee of the Tennessee Legislative Council*, submitted October 1, 1958 by Robert S. Hutchinson, direc-

1856. Texas. Legislative Council.

1956 *Transportation of Migrant Labor in Texas*, 82 pp.

1857. Thailand. Central Statistical Office.

n.d. *Statistical Yearbook, Thailand*, No. 22 (Vol. I), B. E. 2488 (1945) to 2498 (1955), 283 pp.

1858. Thistlethwaite, F.

1961 "Migration from Europe Overseas in the Nineteenth and Twentieth Centuries," paper in Volume 5 of the *International Congress in History, Eleventh, Stockholm, 1960*, the Reports and Papers of the Congress (Stockholm, Almquist).

1959. Thomas, Brinley

1959 "Wales and the Atlantic Economy," *Scottish Journal of Political Economy*, 6:169-192 (November).

1860. Thomas, Brinley

1960 "Changing Determinants of International Migration," *Current Economic Comment* (A review note), 22:51-57 (November).

1861. Thomas, Brinley

1961a "International Factor Movements and Unequal Rates of Growth," *Manchester School of Economic and Social Studies*, 29:1-21 (January).

1862. 1961b "Trends in the International Migration of Skilled Manpower," *Migration*, 1:5-20 (July-September).

1863. Thomas, Brinley

1962 "The Economic Resurgence of Western Europe and Its Bearing on Oversea Emigration," *Migration*, 2:79-83 (July-December).

1864. Thomas, Dorothy S.

1959 "Age and Economic Differentials in Internal Migration in the United States: Structure and Distance," in *International Population Conference, Vienna, 1959* (Vienna, *International Union for the Scientific Study of Population*), pp. 714-721.

1865. Thomlinson, Ralph

1961 "A Model for Migration Analysis," *Journal of the American Statistical Association*, 56:675-686 (September).

1866. Thomlinson, Ralph

1962 "Methodological Needs in Migration Research," *Population Review*, 6:59-64 (January).

1867. Thompson, Raymond H., ed.

1958 *Migrations in New World Culture History,*

University of Arizona Bulletin, 29(2), Social Science Bulletin No. 27, (Tucson, University of Arizona Press), 68 pp.

1868. Thompson, Richard A.

1957 "The Yellow Peril, 1890-1924," unpublished master's thesis, University of Wisconsin (In 2 volumes), 501 pp.

1869. Thompson, Robert A.

1958 "Social Dynamics in Demographic Trends and the Housing of Minority Groups," *Phylon*, 19(1):31-43.

1870. Thompson, S. P.

1955 "The Relocation of Population and Its Problems," *Royal Sanitary Institute Journal*, 75: 24-33 (January).

1871. Thompson, Virginia, and Richard Adloff

1960 *The Emerging States of French Equatorial Africa* (Stanford, Stanford University Press; London, Oxford University Press), 595 pp.

1872. Thrupp, Sylvia L.

1957 "A Survey of the Alien Population of England in 1440," *Speculum*, 32:262-273 (April).

1873. Timlin, Mabel F.

1955 "Recent Changes in Government Attitudes Towards Immigration," *Transactions of the Royal Society of Canada*, 49:95-105.

1874. Timlin, Mabel F.

1960 "Canada's Immigration Policy, 1896-1910," *Canadian Journal of Economics and Political Science*, 26:517-532 (November).

1875. Tobata, Seiichi

1960 "Japan's Farming Population," *Asian Review*, 56:71-80 (January).

1876. Tomasek, R. D.

1961 "The Migrant Problem and Pressure Group Politics," *Journal of Politics*, 23:295-319 (May).

1877. Topley, K. W. J.

1961 "Hong Kong's Immigrant Problem in 1960," *I.U.L.A.* (International Union of Local Authorities) *Quarterly*, 13:122-125 (Spring-Summer).

1878. Tough, Rosalind, and Gordon D. MacDonald

1961 "The New York Metropolitan Region: Social Forces and the Flight to Suburbia," *Land Economics*, 37:327-336 (November).

1879. Trager, Frank N., and Janet Welsh

1956 "Comments on the Chinese Diaspora," *Jewish Frontier*, pp. 17-21 (September).

1880. Traho, R.

1957 "Literature on Checheno-Ingushes and Karachay-Balkars," *Caucasian Review*, No. 5:76-96.

1881. Treadgold, Donald W.

1956 "Siberian Colonization and the Future of Asiatic Russia," *Pacific Historical Review*, 25: 47-54 (February).

1882. Trewartha, Glenn T., and Wilbur Zelinsky

1955 "Population Distribution and Change in Korea, 1925-1949," *Geographical Review*, 45:1-26 (January).

*1883. Trigona, G.

1958 "Directions in the Organization and Administration of Overseas Settlement Projects," *Rivista di Agricoltura Subtropicale e Tropicale*, 52:380-399 (July-September).

1884. Tuinman, A. S.

1956 "The Netherlands-Canadian Migration," *Tijdschrift voor Economische en Sociale Geografie*, 47:181-188 (August).

1885. Tümertekin, Erol

1958 "The Distribution of Sex Ratios with Special Reference to Internal Migration in Turkey," *Review of the Geographical Institute of the University of Istanbul, International Edition*, No. 4: 9-16.

*1886. Tuncdilek, Necdet, and Erol Tümertekin

1959 *The Population of Turkey; Population Density, Population Increase, Internal Migration and Urbanization*, publications of Istanbul University, No. 802; Geographical Institute, No. 25; Geographical Institute, Monograph Series, 2 (Istanbul, Istanbul Matbaasi), 77 pp.

*1887. Turbani, M.

1955 "The Development of Rhodesia in Relation to European Immigration," *Italiani nel Mondo*, pp. 13-16 (March 25).

1888. Uchida, Naosaku

1960 "Overseas Chinese Problems in Southeast Asia Nations," *Asian Affairs*, 5:1-71 (October).

*1889. Ueda, Masao

1961 "Differential Net Migration by Age and Sex in Prefectures, 1930-1935 and 1950-1955," in *Annual Reports of the Institute of Population Problems*, No. 36 (Tokyo Institute of Population Problems), pp. 24-29.

Union Internationale pour L'Etude Scientifique de la Population. *See* 1393.

1890. Union of South Africa. Natives Resettlement Board.

1956 *Annual Report 1955/56* (Pretoria, Government Printer), 16 pp.

1891. United Nations. Economic Commission for Asia and the Far East.

1962 "Evaluation of the Population Census Data of Malaya," *Economic Bulletin for Asia and the Far East*, 13:23-44 (September).

1892. UNESCO

1956 "Cultural Assimilation and Tensions in a Country of Large-Scale Immigration: Israel," *International Social Science Bulletin*, 8(1): 5-123.

1893. UNESCO

1959 "Nomads and Nomadism in the Arid Zone," *International Social Science Journal*, 11(4): 481-585.

U. S. Agricultural Marketing Service

1955 *See* 1852.
1958 *See* 1521.
1960 *See* 772.

1894. U. S. Bureau of the Census

1955 *Current Population Reports, Series P-20. Population Characteristics.* No. 57: *Mobility of the Population of the U. S.: April, 1953 to April, 1954,* 12 pp.

1895. U. S. Bureau of the Census

1956 *U. S. Census of Population: 1950, Volume IV, Special Reports,* Part 4, Chapter B, *Population Mobility—States and State Economic Areas.*

1896. U. S. Bureau of the Census.

1957a *U. S. Census of Population: 1950. Volume IV, Special Reports,* Part 4 Chapter C, *Population Mobility—Farm-Nonfarm Movers,* 244 pp.

1897. 1957b *U.S. Census of Population: 1950. Volume IV, Special Reports,* Part 4, Chapter D, *Population Mobility—Characteristics of Migrants,* 335 pp.

1898. U. S. Bureau of the Census

1958a *Current Population Reports. Series P-20. Population Characteristics.* No. 82: *Mobility of the Population of the United States: April 1956 to 1957,* 17 pp.

1899. 1958b *Current Population Reports. Series P-20, Population Characteristics.* No. 85: *Mobility of the Population of the United States: March 1957 to 1958,* 15 pp.

U. S. Bureau of the Census
1959 *See* 736.

1900. U. S. Bureau of the Census.

1960 *Current Population Reports. Series P-20. Population Characteristics.* No. 104: *Mobility of the Population of the United States: April 1958 to 1959,* 28 pp.

1901. U. S. Bureau of the Census

1961a *Statistical Abstract of the United States 1961,* 82nd annual edition, 1037 pp.

1902. 1961b *Current Population Reports, Series P-25, Population Estimates.* No. 227: *Preliminary Estimates of the Components of Population Change, by States:1950 to 1960,* 8 pp.

1903. U. S. Bureau of the Census

1962a *Current Population Reports, Series P-20, Population Characteristics,* No. 113: *Mobility of the Population of the United States: March 1959 to 1960,* 29 pp.

1904. 1962b *Current Population Reports, Series P-20, Population Characteristics,* No. 118: *Mobility of the Population of the United States: March 1960 to March 1961,* 30 pp.

1905. 1962c *1960 Census of Population. Series PC(SI). Supplementary Reports.* No. 16: *Annexations and the Growth of Population in Standard Metropolitan Statistical Areas: 1950 to 1960,* 14 pp.

1906. 1962d *Census of Population 1960, Final Reports, Series PC(1)-D, Detailed Characteristics.* No. 19: *Geographic Mobility of the Population of the United States, April 1960.*

1907. 1962e *Census of Population 1960. Final Reports. Series PC(1)-D. Detailed Characteristics.* No. 22:*Place of Work and Means of Transportation to Work for the United States: 1960.*

1908. 1962f *Census of Population 1960. Supplementary Reports. Series PC(SI).* No. 30: *Mobility of the Population, by Age: 1960,* 6 pp.

1909. 1962g *County and City Data Book, 1962: A Statistical Abstract Supplement,* 669 pp.

1910. 1962h *Statistical Abstract of the United States 1962,* 83rd annual edition, 1036 pp.

1911. U. S. Bureau of Old-Age and Survivors Insurance

1960 *Interstate Mobility of Aged Beneficiaries under OASI in 1958,* Analytical Note, No. 107, 4 pp.

1912. U. S. Congress. House.

1961 *Mexican Farm Labor Program: Conference Report* (to accompany H. R. 2010) (Washington: 87th Congress, 1st Session, House Report 1198), 5 pp.

1913. U. S. Congress. House. Committee on Agriculture. Subcommittee on Equipment, Supplies and Manpower.

    1958 *Farm Labor: Hearings, on Problems in the Southwest, held in Riverside, California, February 28, 1958, El Centro, California, March 1, 1958, and Phoenix, Arizona, March 3, 1958: and Mexican Labor on June 9-July 2, 1958.* Serial CCC (Washington: 85th Congress, 2nd Session), 633 pp.

1914. U. S. Congress. House. Committee on Agriculture. Subcommittee on Equipment, Supplies and Manpower.

    1961 *Extension of Mexican Farm Labor Program: Hearings before Subcommittee on Equipment, Supplies, and Manpower, 87th Congress, 1st Session, on H. R. 2010, March 6-17, 1961.* (Committee Hearings) (Washington, 87th Congress), 370 pp.

1915. U. S. Congress. House. Committee on Agriculture. Subcommittee on Equipment, Supplies and Manpower.

    1962 *Mexican Farm Labor Program, Hearing before the Subcommittee on Equipment, Supplies and Manpower, 87th Congress, 2nd Session, January 19, 1962,* 46 pp.

1916. U. S. Congress. House. Committee on Education and Labor. Select Subcommittee on Labor.

    1961 *Migratory Labor. Hearings before the Select Subcommittee on Labor. 87th Congress, 1st Session, on H. R. 5288 (and other) Related Bills . . . ,* 366 pp.

1917. U. S. Congress. House. Committee on Interstate and Foreign Commerce

    1956 *Transportation of Migrant Farm Workers. Hearing before a subcommittee of the Committee on Interstate and Foreign Commerce, House of Representatives, 84th Congress, 2nd Session, on HR 9836 and S 3391, to provide for the regulation of the interstate transportation of migrant farm workers,* 54 pp.

1918. U. S. Congress. House. Committee on the Judiciary.

    1955 *Report on the Administration of the Immigration and Nationality Act,* 137 pp.

1919. U. S. Congress. House. Committee on the Judiciary

    1957 *ICEM and Land Resettlement; Resettlement of European Migrants in Latin America. Report of Subcommittee No. 1 pursuant to H. Res. 107, 85th Congress (85th Congress, 1st Session, House Report No. 203),* 79 pp.

1920. U. S. Congress, House. Committee on the Judiciary.

    1960 *Admission of Refugees on Parole. Hearings before Subcommittee No. 1 on H. J. Res. 397, joint resolution enabling the United States to participate in the resettlement of certain refugees. July 15, 1959, March 24, 1960,* 68 pp.

1921. U. S. Congress, House. Committee on the Judiciary

    1961 *Migration and Refugee Assistance: Hearing, August 3, 1961, on H. R. 8291, a bill to amend the act of July 14, 1960, enabling the United States to participate in the resettlement of certain refugees and for other purposes,* 49 pp.

1922. U. S. Congress, House. Committee on the Judiciary.

    1962 *Refugee Problem in Hong Kong. Report of a special subcommittee of the Committee on the Judiciary pursuant to H. Res. 56, 87th Congress (87th Congress, 2nd Session, House Report 1284),* 49 pp.

1923. U. S. Congress. Senate.

    1956 *Study of Immigration and Naturalization. Report to accompany S. Res. 172, 84th Congress, 2nd Session. Senate Report 1384,* 5 pp.

1924. U. S. Congress. Senate. Committee on Agriculture and Forestry.

    1961 *Extension of Mexican Farm Labor Program. Hearings before a subcommittee of the Committee on Agriculture and Forestry, United States Senate, 87th Congress, 1st Session on S. 1466, S. 1945, and H. R. 2010, bills to 111 June 12 and 13, 1961,* 364 pp.

1925. U. S. Congress. Senate. Committee on the Judiciary.

    1956 *Amendments to Refugee Relief Act of 1953. Hearing before the subcommittee on S. 3570 and other bills to amend the Refugee Relief Act of 1953, so as to increase the number of orphan visas and raise the age; extend the life of the Act . . . provide for the reallocation of visas, and change the conditions under which visas may be issued to refugees in the Far East. May 3, 1956,* 106 pp.

1926. U. S. Congress. Senate. Committee on the Judiciary.

    1957a *Emigration on Refugees and Escapees. Report of the Committee on the Judiciary, U. S. Senate, made by its Subcommittee to Investigate Problems Connected with the Emigration of Refugees and Escapees, pursuant to S. Res. 168, 84th Congress, 2nd Session, as extended by S. Res. 84, 85th Congress (85th Congress, 1st Session, Senate Report No. 129),* 10 pp.

1927. 1957b *Hungarian Refugee Resettlement in Latin America. A report by Senator William Langer to the Subcommittee to Investigate Problems Connected with Emigration of Refugees and Escapees, of the Committee on the Judiciary, U. S. Senate, 85th Congress, 1st Session, October 23, 1957,* 10 pp.

1928. U. S. Congress. Senate. Committee on the Judiciary.

    1958 *Emigration of Refugees and Escapees. Report of the Committee on the Judiciary, U. S. Senate, made by its Subcommittee to Investigate Problems Connected With the Emigration of Refu-*

gees and Escapees, pursuant to S. Res. 53, 85 Congress, 1st Session, as extended, 85th Congress, 2nd Session, Senate, Report No. 1493, 4 pp.

1929. U. S. Congress. Senate. Committee on the Judiciary.

1961 *World Refugee Problems. Hearings before the Subcommittee to Investigate Problems Connected with Refugees and Escapees, 87th Congress, 1st Session, July 12-14, 1961,* 159 pp.

1930. U. S. Congress. Senate. Committee on the Judiciary.

1962 *Cuban Refugee Problems. Hearings before the Subcommittee to Investigate Problems Connected with Refugees and Escapees, United States Senate, 87th Congress, 1st Session, December 6, 7, 13, 1961,* 304 pp.

1931. U. S. Congress. Senate. Committee on Labor and Public Welfare.

1960- *Migratory Labor. Hearings before the Subcom-*
1961 *mittee on Migratory Labor of the Committee on Labor and Public Welfare, United States Senate, 86th Congress, 1st and 2nd Session, on S. 1085 (and other) bills (in two parts),* 1853 pp.

1932. U. S. Congress. Senate. Committee on Labor and Public Welfare.

1961 *The Migratory Farm Labor Problem in the United States. A report ... to the Committee on Labor and Public Welfare made by its Subcommittee on Migratory Labor September 20, 1961. 87th Congress, 1st Session, Report 1098,* 56 pp.

1933. U. S. Congress. Senate Committee on Labor and Public Welfare.

1962 *The Migratory Farm Labor Problem in the United States. Second report to the Committee on Labor and Public Welfare pursuant to S. Res. 86, 87th Congress, 1st Session. A resolution authorizing a study of the problems of migratory labor. 87th Congress, 2nd Session, Senate Report 1225,* 79 pp.

U. S. Congress. Senate. Committee on Labor and Public Welfare. Subcommittee on Migratory Labor. See 1682.

1934. U. S. Congress. Senate. Committee on Rules and Administration.

1962 *Study of Migratory Labor: Report to Accompany S. Res. 273, 87th Congress, 2nd Session, Senate Report 1159,* 13 pp.

1935. U. S. Department of Agriculture

1955a *Development of Agriculture's Human Resources. A Report on Problems of Low-Income Farmers.* 44 pp.

1955b *See* 1559.

1936. 1955c *Low-Income Farm People: A Selected List of References,* compiled by Elizabeth Gould Davis (Washington: U. S. Department of Agriculture, Library List No. 62), 42 pp. (processed).

U. S. Department of Agriculture
1958 *See* 953.

U. S. Department of Agriculture
1962 *See* 773.

1937. U. S. Department of Health, Education and Welfare. Public Health Service.

1955 *Domestic Agricultural Migrants in Ten East Coast States,* Publication 478 (Washington: Superintendent of Documents).

1938. U. S. Department of Health, Education and Welfare. Public Health Service.

1956 *Health Services in Major Migrant Work Areas; East Coast Guide* (Washington: U. S. Department of Health, Education and Welfare, Public Health Service and Children's Bureau), 70 pp.

1939. U. S. Department of Health, Education and Welfare. Public Health Service.

1961a *Agricultural Migrants,* Selected films compiled by William Yanniello and Helen Johnston (Washington: U. S. Department of Health, Education and Welfare, Public Health Service, Divisions of Community Health Practice), 12 pp.

1940. 1961b *Children in Migrant Families. A report to the Committee on Appropriations, U. S. Senate* (Washington: Government Printing Office, U. S. Department of Health, Education and Welfare, Children's Bureau), 61 pp.

1961c *See* 779.

1941. U. S. Department of Health, Education and Welfare. Departmental Committee on Migratory Labor.

1955 *Program Directions in Migrant Labor of the U. S. Department of Health, Education and Welfare* (Washington, Office of Program Analysis).

1942. U. S. Department of Labor. Bureau of Employment Security.

1955a *Estimating the Need and Supply of Hired Seasonal Farm Workers, Baldwin County, Alabama,* 57 pp.

1943. 1955b *Puerto Rican Farm Workers in Florida: Highlights of a Study* (Washington: Department of Labor, Division of Reports and Analysis), 7 pp. (processed).

1944. U. S. Department of Labor. Bureau of Employment Security.

  1956 *Report to the President on Domestic Migratory Labor* (Washington: Department of Labor, Bureau of Employment Security The President's Commission on Migratory Labor).

1945. U. S. Department of Labor. Bureau of Employment Security.

  1957 *Proceedings of Consultation on Migratory Labor.* (Washington: Department of Labor, Bureau of Employment Security, Office of Program Review and Analysis), 107 pp.

  U. S. Department of Labor. Bureau of Employment Security.

  1958a *See* 1567.

1946. 1958b *Report on Operations of the Domestic Migratory Labor Program*, 12 pp.

1947. U. S. Department of Labor. Bureau of Employment Security.

  1961 *Hired Farm Workers in the U. S.* (Washington: Department of Labor, Bureau of Employment Security), 46 pp.

1948. U. S. Department of Labor. Bureau of Labor Standards.

  1956 *Selected References on Migratory Workers and Their Families: Problems and Programs, 1950-56*, 16 pp.

1949. U. S. Department of Labor. Bureau of Labor Standards.

  1959 *State Migratory Labor Committees: Their Organization and Problems* (Washington: Department of Labor, Bureau of Labor Standards, Field Services Branch, State Services Division), 74 pp.

  U. S. Department of Labor. Bureau of Labor Standards.

  1960a *See* 756.
  1960b *See* 959.

1950. U. S. Department of Labor. Bureau of Labor Standards.

  1961 *Selected References on Domestic Migratory Agricultural Workers, Their Families, Problems and Programs 1955-1960*, Bulletin 225, 38 pp.

1951. U. S. Department of Labor. Bureau of Labor Statistics.

  1959 "Labor and Labor Relations on the West Coast" (A group of 15 articles) *Monthly Labor Review*, 82:489-582 (May).

1952. U. S. Department of Labor. Bureau of Labor Statistics.

  1960a *Labor Supply and Mobility in a Newly Industrialized Area*, BLS Bulletin No. 1261, 47 pp.

1953. 1960b "The Social Science Annual Meetings" (A group of papers), *Monthly Labor Review*, 83:133-149 (February).

1954. U. S. Department of Labor. Farm Placement Service.

  1954- *Service to Agricultural Migrants; What Some
  1955 Communities Are Doing.*

1955. U. S. Department of Labor

  1958 *Migratory Labor Notes, No. 7* (September-December).

1956. U. S. Department of Labor

  1959a *Migratory Labor Notes*, No. 10 (July-September).

  1959b *See* 1833.

1957. U. S. Department of State

  1956 *Immigration to Latin America, 1940-1954.* Intelligence Report No. 7257 (Washington: Department of State, Office of Intelligence Research), 12 pp. (processed).

1958. U. S. Department of State

  1957a "Question of Financing Aid to Palestine Refugees," (statement by Genoa S. Washington and text of United Nations resolution), *Department of State Bulletin*, 38 (967): 34-40 (January 6).

  1957b *See* 1619.

  1957c *See* 2007.

1959. 1957d "Committee for Hungarian Relief Submits Final Report," *Department of State Bulletin*, 36:984-985 (June 17).

  1957e *See* 1507.

  U. S. Department of State

  1958 *See* 1501.

  U. S. Department of State

  1959a *See* 1016.

  1959b *See* 2008.

1960. 1959c "The United States Role in the World Refugee Year," (proclamation and statement by President Eisenhower and address by John W. Hanes Jr.), *Department of State Bulletin*, 40 (1042):872-879 (June 15).

  1959d *See* 2009.

1961. 1959e "Refugees. Eleventh Session of ICEM Council (Delegation)," *Department of State Bulletin*, 41 (1065):770 (November 23).

U. S. Department of State

1960a *See* 2010.

1960b *See* 2011.

1962. 1960c "Immigration Quotas Established for Fourteen New Nations: White House Announcement," *Department of State Bulletin*, 43 (1113):654-655 (October 24).

1963. 1960d *World Refugee Year, July 1959-June 1960. Report on participation of the United States Government*, Department of State Publication 7095, General Foreign Policy Series, 158, 17 pp.

U. S. Department of State

1961a *See* 1998.

1964. 1961b "Mr. Voorhees Submits Final Report on Cuban Refugee Problem," *Department of State Bulletin*, 44 (1129):219-225 (February 13).

1961c *See* 2012.

1965. 1961d "President Submits New Legislation on Refugee Aid Programs," *Department of State Bulletin*, 45 (1154):255-257 (August 7).

1961e *See* 1433.

1961f *See* 2013.

1966. U. S. Federal Interdepartmental Committee on Children and Youth

1955 *When the Migrant Families Come Again: A Guide for Better Community Living.*

1967. U. S. Immigration and Naturalization Service

1955 *Administrative Decisions under Immigration and Nationality Laws*, Volume XV, 842 pp.

1968. U. S. Immigration and Naturalization Service

1957 *Annual Report of the U. S. Immigration and Naturalization Service for the Fiscal Year Ended June 30, 1956*, 122 pp.

1969. U. S. Immigration and Naturalization Service

1960 *Annual Report of the U. S. Immigration and Naturalization Service 1960*, 99 pp.

1970. U. S. Immigration and Naturalization Service

1961 *Annual Report of the Immigration and Naturalization Service for the Year Ended June 30, 1961*, 102 pp.

1971. U. S. Immigration and Naturalization Service

1962 *Report of the Commissioner of Immigration and Naturalization, 1962*, 107 pp.

U. S. Joint Publication Research

1960a *See* 1802.

1972. 1960b *Resettlement Efforts in Indonesia*, JPRS,6197, 2 pp. (processed).

1973. U. S. Joint Publication Research

1962 *Translations on USSR Labor, No. 15*, JPRS, 12,000.

1974. U. S. Laws, Statutes, etc.

1960 *Immigration and Nationality Act, with Amendments and Notes on Amendments and Related Laws*, Committee print for the use of the Committee on the Judiciary, House of Representatives, United States, 2nd edition, revised through September 1, 1960, 197 pp.

1975. U. S. Library of Congress. Slavic and Central European Division.

1959 *East Germany: A Selected Bibliography*, Compiled by Fritz T. Epstein, 55 pp.

1976. U. S. National Archives

1955 *Preliminary Inventory of the Records of the President's Commission on Migratory Labor*, Publication No. 56-4.

U. S. Office of Education

1957 *See* 755.

1977. U. S. Office of Education.

1958a *Excerpts from "The Education of the Migrant Child,"* (Report of the Oregon State Bureau of Labor to the Interim Committee on Migratory Labor and the Governor's Inter-agency Committee on Agricultural Labor).

1978. 1958b *Pennsylvania Migratory Labor Program: A Summary.*

U. S. Office of Naval Research

1958 *See* 1827.

1979. U. S. Treaties, etc.

1959 *Mexican Agricultural Workers. Agreements between the United States of America and Mexico, extending agreement of August 11, 1951, as amended and extended, effected by exchange of notes signed at Mexico August 31, 1959, and exchange of notes signed at Mexico July 28 and 30, 1959, and exchange of notes signed at Mexico June 24 and 27, 1959*, Treaties and Other International Acts Series, 4310, 8 pp.

1980. U. S. Treaties, etc.

1962 *Migratory Workers: Mexican Agricultural Work-*

ers. *Agreement between the United States of America and Mexico, amending and extending the agreement of August 11, 1951, as amended and extended; and including joint interpretations of 1961 effected by exchange of notes signed at Mexico, December 29, 1961,* U. S. Department of State, Treaties and Other International Acts Series 5160, 43 pp.

1981. U. S. Trust Territory of the Pacific Islands

    1961 *Trust Territory of the Pacific Islands, 1960: Thirteenth Annual Report to the United Nations on the Administration of the Trust Territory of the Pacific Islands, July 1, 1959-June 30, 1960,* 258 pp.

1982. University College of the West Indies. Institute of Social and Economic Research.

    1958 *Study Conference on Economic Development in Underdeveloped Countries,* Special Number, ed. H. D. Huggins, *Social and Economic Studies,* 7:139 pp. (September).

1983. Urban, C. Stanley

    1957 "The Africanization of Cuba Scare, 1853-1855," *The Hispanic American Historical Review,* 37:29-45 (February).

1984. VanAbbe, D.

    1956 "The Germans in South Australia," *Australian Quarterly,* 28(3):69-79.

1985. VanAs, J. B.

    1959 *Financial Aspects of Land Settlement as Illustrated by Experience in Surinam,* Conference on the Financing of Agriculture (Port-of-Spain, Caribbean Commission), 9 pp.

1986. Vanderhill, Burke G.

    1959 "Post-war Agricultural Settlement in Manitoba," *Economic Geography,* 35:259-268 (July).

1987. Vanderhill, Burke G.

    1962a "The Farming Frontier of Western Canada, 1950-1960," *Journal of Geography,* 61:13-20 (January).

1988.   1962b "The Decline of Land Settlement in Manitoba and Saskatchewan," *Economic Geography,* 38:270-278 (July).

1989.   1962c "The Success of Government-Sponsored Settlement in Manitoba," *Journal of Geography,* 61:152-161 (April).

1990. VanVelsen, J.

    1960 "Labor Migration as a Positive Factor in the Continuity of Tonga Tribal Society," *Economic Development and Cultural Change,* 8: 265-278 (April).

*1991. Vanni, Manfredo

    1957 "Immigration into Turin from the South of Italy," *Rivista Geografica Italiana,* 64:1-8 (March).

*1992. Vasconcelos, Luiz L.

    1956 "Internal Migration in Brazil," *Revista Brasileira de Economia,* 10:83-114 (September).

*1993. Velho, Fernanda

    1962 "Population Change and Use of the Land in Continental Portugal, 1940-1960," *Boletim do Centro de Estudos Geograficos,* 3 (19):21-29.

1994. Velikonja, Joseph

    1958 "Postwar Population Movements in Europe," *Annals of the Association of American Geographers,* 48:458-472 (December).

*1995. Verstappen, Herman T.

    1957 *The Physiographic Basis of Pioneer Settlement in Southern Sumatra* (Djakarta), 25 pp.

Vladimir, Srb. *See* 1432.

*1996. Vogelnik, Dolfe

    1961 *Urbanization in Yugoslavia as Expression of Its Economic Development* (Belgrade, Ekonomska Biblioteka No. 13, 311 pp.

1997. Volacic, Mikota

    1956 "The Population of Western Belorussia and Its Resettlement in Poland and the U.S.S.R.," *Belorussian Review,* No. 3:5-30.

1998. Vorrhees, Tracy S.

    1961 "Cuba: Interim Report on Cuban Refugees to President Eisenhower, December 19th, 1960," *Department of State Bulletin,* 44 (1124): 45-48 (January 9).

*1999. Votrubec, C.

    1960 "Migration to Larger Towns in Central and Northern Bohemia during the Years 1954-1958," *Ceskoslovenska Spolecnost Zemepisna, Sbornik,* 65(1):21-28.

2000. *Vox Guyanae*

    1959 "Surinam: Present Demographic Position," *Vox Guyanae,* 3(3):97-128.

Wakeley, Ray E. *See* 739.

2001. Wakeley, Ray E., and Amy Russell

    1960 *Migration and Changes of Population in Iowa, 1960,* A & HEES Project No. 1225 (Ames, Iowa State University), 44 pp.

2002. Walraven, Karnelis J.

    1962 *Impact of New Plants on Local Labor Sup-*

ply: *Northwest Arkansas: A Regional Case Study of Labor Force Flexibility* (University of Arkansas, College of Business Administration, Industrial Research and Extension Center, n. p.), 51 pp.

2003. Ward, R. Gerard

1959 "The Population of Fiji," *Geographical Review*, 49:322-341 (July).

2004. Ward, R. Gerard

1961a "Internal Migration in Fiji," *Journal of the Polynesian Society*, 70:257-271 (September).

2005. 1961b "A Note on Population Movements in the Cook Islands," *Journal of the Polynesian Society*, 70:1-10 (March).

Wardhana, Ali. *See* 1337.

2006. Warkentin, John

1959 "Mennonite Agricultural Settlements of Southern Manitoba," *Geographical Review*, 49:342-368 (July).

2007. Warren, George L.

1957 "Meeting the Challenge of Moving Hungarian Refugees," *Department of State Bulletin*, 36 (932):743-745 (May).

2008. Warren, George L.

1959a "Migration from Europe in 1958: 11th session of the Executive Committee and 9th session of the Council of the Intergovernmental Committee for European Migration," *Department of State Bulletin*, 40 (1029):384-388 (March 16).

2009. 1959b "Prospects of Migration from Europe in 1959-60," *Department of State Bulletin*, 41 (1046): 58-62 (July 13).

2010. Warren, George L.

1960a "Progress and Prospects for European Migration, 1959-1960," *Department of State Bulletin*, 42 (1076):218-221 (February 8).

2011. 1960b "Migration from Europe in 1960," *Department of State Bulletin*, 43 (1103):254-258 (August 15).

2012. Warren, George L.

1961a "Migration from Europe in 1961: 16th Session of the Executive Committee and 13th Session of the Council of the Intergovernmental Committee for European Migration," *Department of State Bulletin*, 44 (1133):386-389 (March 13).

2013. 1961b "Pressure for Migration from Europe Slacker in 1961: 14th Session of Council and 17th Session of Executive Committee of Intergovernmental Committee for European Migra-

tion," *Department of State Bulletin*, 45(1162): pp. 565-569 (October 2).

Washington, Genoa S. *See* 1958.

Washington. State Census Board. *See* 1770.

2014. Watson, William

1958 "Migrant Labour in Africa South of the Sahara 2. Migrant Labour and Detribalisation," *Inter-African Labour and Institute Bulletin*, 6:8-33 (March).

2015. Waughray, Vernon

1960 "The French Racial Scene: North African Immigrants in France," *Race*, 2:60-70 (November).

2016. Weaver, D. A.

1957 "Migrant Children in Vocation Schools," *International Journal of Religious Education*, 33:20-21 (April).

2017. Weinryb, Bernard D.

1957 "The Impact of Urbanization in Israel," *Middle East Journal*, 11:23-36 (Winter).

2018. Weisbrod, Burton A.

1962 "An Expected-income Measure of Economic Welfare," *Journal of Political Economy*, 70: 355-367 (August).

2019. Weiss, Samuel, and A. J. Jaffe

1955 "Puerto Rico: The Labor Force and Level of Living," *Monthly Labor Review*, 78:1347-1353 (December).

Weldon, J. C. *See* 737.

2020. Welfare Council of Metropolitan Chicago

1956 "In-Migrants: Number, Location, and Selected Characteristics," *Statistics*, 23:107 (November-December).

Welsh, Janet. *See* 1879.

West Indies, University College of the. *See* 1983.

2021. Wichienchareen, A.

1959 "Movements of Population within Thailand," *Public Welfare*, pp. 3-8 (February).

*2022. Widstam, Ture

1962 "Immigration into Sweden and Re-Emigration during the 1950's," *Statistik Tidskrift*, 11:267-272 (May).

Wiener, A. J. *See* 1489.

2023. Wikkramatileke, Rudolf

1962 "Trends in Settlement and Economic Development in Eastern Malaya," *Pacific Viewpoint*, pp. 27-50 (March).

2024. Willms, A. M.

1958 "The Brethren Known As Hutterians," *Canadian Journal of Economics and Political Science*, 24:391-405 (August).

2025. Wills, C.

1958 "Families on the Move," *International Journal of Religious Education*, 35:20-21 (October).

2026. Wilson, Peter J., and John Buettner-Janusch

1961 "Demography and Evolution on Providencia Island, Colombia," *American Anthropologist*, 63:940-954 (October).

2027. Winkle, F. F., and M. F. vander Merwe

1956 "Economic Expansion of the Union as Reflected by the Shift of White Population (1936-1951)," *Finance and Trade Review*, 2:93-101 (October-November).

2028. Wisconsin. State Employment Service. Farm Labor Service.

1962 *Migratory Labor in Wisconsin Agriculture, 1961*, 10 pp.

2029. Wiskemann, Elizabeth

1961 "Too Many Foreigners in Switzerland," *World Today*, 17:355-363 (August).

2030. Witcover, Jules

1958 "The Role of the Intergovernmental Committee for European Migration in the Resettlement of Hungarian Refugees, 1956-57," *R.E.M.P. Bulletin*, 6:1-23 (January-March).

2031. Witkamp, F. Th.

1957 "The Refugee Problem in the Middle East," *R.E.M.P. Bulletin*, 5:3-51 (January-March).

Woods, N. S. *See* 1614.

2032. Woolmington, E. R.

1958 "Post-war Immigration and Industrial Development in Australia," *Australian Quarterly*, 30:77-88 (March).

2033. Woolmington, E. R.

1959 "Australian Immigration Since the War," *India Quarterly*, 15:109-120 (April-June).

2034. World Council of Churches

1961 *In a Strange Land* (Geneva, World Council of Churches), 96 pp.

*2035. Yanagida, Kunio

1955 "On the Migration by Sea," *Jinrui-Kagaka* [Anthropological Science], No. 7:88-101 (March).

Yaniello, William. *See* 1939.

Yaron, Dan. *See* 1007.

2036. Yarwood, A. T.

1961 "The 'White Australia' Policy: Some Administrative Problems, 1901-1920," *Australian Journal of Politics and History*, 7:245-260 (November).

*2037. Yokoyama, Ryoichi, and others

1955 "Migration and Industry in a City: A Research in Yokkaichi-City, Mie Pref.," *Shakaigaku Hyôron* [Japanese Sociological Review] 5:73-95 (January).

2038. Yu Lai-chien and Lee Lung-hsiung

1960 *The Village Leaving of the Farmers in Suburban Taipei: Originally Surveyed in the Period from September 1953 to May 1954*, Final Analysis and Summary by Hsiao Chipei, in *Occasional Abstracts from Fu-Min Institute of Economic Development*, 3, 16 pp.

*2039. Yugoslav Statistical Society (Jugoslovenskog Statističkog Društva)

1956 *Third Annual Meeting of the Jugoslovenskog Statičkog Društva, Zagreb, 17-21 November, 1955*, 503 pp.

2040. Yugoslav Statistical Society (Jugoslovenskog Statističkog Društva)

1958 "Papers on Regional Statistics Presented at the Fifth Meeting, September 18-21, 1958," *Sastanak* (Referati), pp. 5-232, n.d.

2041. Zachariah, K. C.

1962 "A Note on the Census Survival Ratio Method of Estimating Net Migration," *American Statistical Association Journal*, 57:175-183 (March).

Zachodnia Agencja Prasowa. *See* 1435.

2042. Zasloff, Joseph J.

1962-63 "Rural Resettlement in South Vietnam: The Agroville Program," *Pacific Affairs*, 35:327-340 (Winter).

2043. Zeff, Stephen

1957 "The Movement of Manufacturing Workers to Denver," *Colorado Business Review*, 30:1-2 (June).

2044. Zelinsky, Wilbur

1962 "Changes in the Geographic Patterns of Rural Population in the United States 1790-1960," *Geographical Review*, 52:492-524 (October).

Zelinsky, Wilbur. *See* 1882.

2045. Zimmer, Basil G., and Amos H. Hawley

1961 "Suburbanization and Some of Its Consequences," *Land Economics*, 37:88-93 (February).

2046. Zimmerman, Carle C.

1955 *American Roots in an Italian Village*, reprinted from *Genus*, 11 (1-4), 63 pp.

2047. Ziolwski, Janusz

1959 "The Population of the Western Territories," in *Polish Western Territories*, by Gruchman, Bohdan, and others (Poznan, Instytut Zachodni) 276 pp.

2048. Zubrzycki, Jerzy

1956 "Patterns of Peasant Migration with Special Reference to Eastern Europe," *R.E.M.P. Bulletin*, 4:73-87 (October-December).

2049. Zubrzycki, Jerzy

1958 "The Geographical Distribution of Australia's Immigrant Population: Statistical Tables," Presented at 33rd Congress of the Australian and New Zealand Association for the Advancement of Science, Adelaide, 19 pp.

2050. Zubrzycki, Jerzy

1961a "Greek Immigrants in Australia. A Demographic Survey," *Migration*, 1:45-54 (April-June).

2051. 1961b "Sociological Methods for the Study of Immigrant Adjustment," *Migration*, 1:51-62 (October-December).

SOURCES OF MIGRATION LITERATURE

Acta Genetica et Statistica Medica, Arnold Böcklin, Strasse 25, Basel, Switzerland.

Advancement of Science, British Association for the Advancement of Science, Sanctuary Buildings, Great Smith Street, London S.W.I, England.

Africa, International African Institute, 10-11 Fetter Lane, London E.C. 4, England.

African Affairs, Royal African Society, 18 Northumberland Avenue, London W.C.2, England.

Agra University Journal of Research, Agra University, Agra, India.

Agricultural Economics Bulletin for Africa, Addis Ababa, Ethiopia.

Agricultural Index, The H. W. Wilson Company, 950 University Avenue, Bronx, New York 10452.

Agriculture Marketing Service, Superintendent of Documents, U. S. Government Printing Office, Washington, D. C. 20402.

A.I.C.C. Economic Review, Economic and Political Research Department, All India Congress Committee, 7 Jantar Mantar Road, New Delhi, India.

Alliance Review - No address available.

América Indígena, Mexico, D. F.

America Latina, Rio de Janeiro, Brazil.

American Anthropologist, American Anthropological Association, 1530 P Street, N. W., Washington, D. C. 20005.

American Bar Association Journal, 1155 E. Sixtieth Street, Chicago, Illinois 60637.

American Economic Review, The American Economic Association, Curtis Reed Plaza, Menasha, Wisconsin 54952.

American Federationist, AFL-CIO Building, 815 Sixteenth St., N. W., Washington, D. C. 20006.

American Historical Review, American Historical Association, Macmillan Co., 2901 Byrdhill Road, Richmond, Virginia 23205.

The American Journal of Economics and Sociology, 50 East 69th Street, New York, New York 10021.

American Journal of International Law, American Society of International Law, 2223 Massachusetts Avenue, N. W., Washington, D. C. 20008.

American Journal of Public Health and the Nation's Health, American Public Health Association, Inc., 1790 Broadway, New York, New York 10019.

The American Journal of Sociology, The University of Chicago Press, 5750 Ellis Avenue, Chicago, Illinois 60637.

The American Philosophical Society (Memoirs), The American Philosophical Society, 104 South Fifth St., Philadelphia, Pennsylvania 19106.

American Quarterly, Box 46, College Hall, University of Pennsylvania, Philadelphia, Pennsylvania 19104.

American Slavic and East European Review, American Association for the Advancement of Slavic Studies, Inc., 508 Thomson Hall, University of Washington, Seattle, Washington 98105.

American Society of Civil Engineers. Proceedings, 345 E. 47th Street, New York, New York 10017.

American Sociological Review, American Sociological Association, Suite 215, 1755 Massachusetts Avenue, N. W., Washington, D. C. 20036.

American Statistical Association, Journal of the, Eighteenth Street, N. W., Washington, D. C. 20006.

The Americas, Academy of American Franciscan History, Box 5850, Washington, D. C. 20014.

Annals of the American Academy of Political and Social Science, 3937 Chestnut Street, Philadelphia, Pennsylvania 19104.

Annals of the Association of American Geographers, Association of American Geographers, 1146 Sixteenth Street, N.W., Washington, D. C. 20036.

The Appraisal Journal, American Institute of Real Estate Appraisers of the National Association of Real Estate Boards, 36 South Wabash Avenue, Chicago, Illinois 60603.

Archiv des Völkerrechts, JV. C. B. Mohr (Paul Siebeck), Tübingen, Germany.

Arctic, Arctic Institute of North America, 3458 Redpath Street, Montreal 25, Canada.

Arizona Business Bulletin, Bureau of Business Research and Services, College of Business Administration, Arizona State University, Fayetteville, Arkansas 72701.

Arkansas Economist, Industrial Research and Extension Center, College of Business Administration, University of Arkansas, P.O. Box 3017, Little Rock, Arkansas 72203.

Armenian Review, Hairenik Association, Inc., 212 Stuart Street, Boston, Massachusetts 02116.

Artha Vijñána, Gokhale Institute of Politics and Economics, Poona 4, India.

Asian Affairs (Asia Kyokai), Maruzen Company, Ltd., Box 605 Tokyo Central, Tokyo, Japan.

Asian Review, East and West Ltd., 2 Temple Chambers, Temple Avenue, London E. C. 4, England.

Asian Survey (Supersedes: *Far Eastern Survey*), Institute for International Studies, University of California, 2538 Channing Way, Berkeley, California 94720.

Atlanta Economic Review, School of Business Administration, Georgia State College, 33 Gilmer Street, S.E., Atlanta, Georgia 30303.

The Australian Geographer - No address available.

Australian Journal of Politics and History, University of Queensland Press, St. Lucia S. W. 6, Queensland, Brisbane, Australia.

Australian Journal of Psychology, Australian Branch, British Psychological Society, Melbourne University Press, Parkville N.2, Victoria, Australia.

Australian Outlook (Journal of the Australian Institute of International Affairs), 124 Jolimont Road, East Melbourne, C. 2, Victoria, Australia.

Australian Quarterly, Australian Institute of Political Science, 34 Elizabeth Street, Sydney, Australia.

Banca Nazionale del Lavoro Quarterly Review, Ufficio Studi, Via Vittorio Veneto 119, Rome, Italy.

Belorussian Review, Munich, Germany.

Board of Trade Journal (of London), H. M. Stationery Office, York House, Kingsway, London W. C. 2, England.

Boletim do Centro de Estudos Geograficos, Coimbra, Portugal.

Boletim Geral do Ultramar, Agencia Geral do Ultramar, Rua de São Ledrode Alcantara 81, Lisbon, Portugal.

Bollettino della Societá Geografica Italiana, Villa Celimontana, Rome, Italy.

Bulletin de L'Institut International de Statistique - No address available.

Bulletin of the Institute for the Study of the History and Culture of the U.S.S.R. (Institut zur Erforschung der U.S.S.R), Mannhardtstrasse 6, 8 Munich 22, Germany.

Bulletin of the Inter-African Labour Institute (Bulletin, Inter-African Labour Institute) Commission for Technical Co-Operation of Africa South of the Sahara, Publications Bureau, Watergate House, York Buildings, London W. C. 2, England.

Bulletin of the Oxford University Institute of Statistics, Basil Blackwell, 49 Broad Street, Oxford, England.

Bulletin of the World Health Organization, World Health Organization, Sales Section, Palais des Nations, Geneva, Switzerland; Columbia University Press, International Document Service, 2960 Broadway, New York, New York 10027.

Cahiers d'Études Africaines (École Partique des Hautes Études-Sorbonne), 20 rue de la Baume, Paris (8e), France.

Les Cahiers de Tunisie, Faculté des Lettres et des Sciences Humaines, Université de Tunis, Place de l'Ecole Israelite, Tunis, Africa.

The Calcutta Review, Calcutta University Press, 48 Hazra Road, Calcutta 19, India.

The California Citrograph, California Citrograph Printing Co., Ltd., 5380 Poplar Boulevard, Los Angeles , California 90032.

Canadian Business, The Canadian Chamber of Commerce, 300 St. Sacrament St., Montreal, Quebec, Canada.

Canadian Geographical Journal, Royal Canadian Geographical Society, 488 Wilbrod Street, Ottawa 2, Canada.

Canadian Journal of Economics and Political Science, Canadian Political Science Association, 100 St. George Street, Toronto 5, Canada.

Caribbean Quarterly, Department of Extra-Mural Studies, University of the West Indies, Mona, Kingston 7, Jamaica.

Caucasian Review, Augustenstrasse 46, Munich, Germany.

Central America and Mexico, Houston, Texas 77001.

Ceskoslovenská Spolecnost Zemepisna, *Sbornik*, Prague, Czechoslovakia.

Chigaki Zasshi, See Journal of Geography (Japan).

Children, Superintendent of Documents, U. S. Government Printing Office, Washington, D. C. 20402.

Christus Rex: An Irish Quarterly Journal of Sociology, Christus Rex Publications, Main Street, Naas, Ireland.

Civilisations, International Institute of Differing Civilisations, 11 boulevard de Waterloo, Brussels, Belgium.

Colorado Business Review, Bureau of Business Research, University of Colorado, Boulder, Colorado 80302.

Columbia Law Review, Columbia Law Students, Kent Hall, Columbia University, New York, New York 10027.

Commentary, American Jewish Committee, 165 E. 56th Street, New York, New York 10022.

Commonwealth Survey, Reference Division, Central Office of Information, Hercules Road, Westminster Bridge Road, London, S. E. 1, England.

Comparative Studies in Society and History, Mouton and Co., Herderstraat 5, The Hague, Netherlands; Editorial Office, Department of History, University of Michigan, Ann Arbor, Michigan 48104.

Co-Op Grain Quarterly, Co-Op Grain Publishing Company, 1667 North Snelling Avenue, St. Paul, Minnesota 55101.

Corona, H. M. Stationery Office, York House, Kingsway, London W. C. 2, England.

Cuadernos Africanos y Orientales - No address available.

Current Affairs Bulletin, University of Sydney, Department of Tutorial Classes, Sydney, Australia.

Current Economic Comment, Bureau of Economic and Business Research, Box 658, Station A, Champaign, Illinois 61820.

Current Population Reports, Superintendent of Documents, U.S. Government Printing Office, Washington, D.C. 20402.

Dalhousie Review, Review Publishing Company, Ltd., Dalhousie University, Halifax, N. S., Canada.

Demográfia, Statistical Publishing Company, Keleti K. U. 18/b., Budapest II, Hungary.

Demografie, Prague, Czechoslovakia.

Demographe (International Union for the Scientific Study of Population), M. Croze, 20 Quai Branly, Paris (7e), France.

Department of State Bulletin, U. S. Department of State, Washington, D. C. 20520.

Diogenes, Mario Casalini, Ltd., 1519 Pine Avenue West, Montreal 25, P. Q., Canada.

Dissertation Abstracts, University Microfilms, Inc., 313 North First Street, Ann Arbor, Michigan 48103.

East Africa and Rhodesia, East Africa Ltd., 66 Great Russell Street, London W. C. 1, England.

East African Agriculture and Forestry Journal, Kenya, Africa.

East Turkic Review, Munich, Germany.

Econometrica, Box 1264 Yale Station, New Haven, Conn. 06520; North-Holland Publishing Company, P. O. Box 103, Amsterdam-C, The Netherlands.

Economic Bulletin for Asia and the Far East, U. N. Economic Commission for Asia and the Far East, Sales and Circulation Section, United Nations, New York, New York 10017.

Economic Development and Cultural Change, Research Center in Economic Development and Cultural Change, University of Chicago Press, 5750 Ellis Avenue, Chicago, Illinois 60637.

Economic Geography, 950 Main Street, Worchester, Massachusetts 01610.

Economic History Review, N. V. A. Oosthoek's Uitgevers Mij, Domstraat 11-13, Utrecht, Holland.

Economic Opinion, Netherlands Bank of South Africa Ltd., Box 1144, Johannesburg, S. A.

Economic Record, Economic Society of Australia and New Zealand, Melbourne University Press, The University, Parkville N. 2, Victoria, Australia; London: Cambridge University Press, Bentley House, 200 Euston Road, London N. W. 1, England.

Economic Weekly, Co-operative Insurance Building, Sir P M Road, Bombay 1, India.

The Economist, 25 St. James Street, London S. W. 1, England.

Editorial Research Reports, 1735 K Street, Washington, D. C. 20006.

Educational Index, The H. W. Wilson Company, 950 University Avenue, Bronx, New York 10452.

Educational Leadership, Association for Supervision and Curriculum Development, National Education Association, 1201 Sixteenth Street, N. W., Washington, D. C. 20036.

Ekonomi dan Keuangan Indonesia, Baden Penerbit, Pembangunan P.T., Gunung Sahari no. 84, Djakarta, Indonesia.

Ekonomista (Polska Akademia Nauk, Komitet Nauk Ekonomicznych i Polskie Towarzystwo Ekonomiczne), Panstwowe Wysawnictwo Naukowe, Nowy Swiat 49, Warsaw, Poland.

Ekonomska Biblioteka, Belgrade, Yugoslavia.

Ekonomski Preglad, Zagreb, Yugoslavia.

Estadistica, Inter-American Statistical Institute, Pan American Union, Washington, D. C. 20006.

Eugenics Quarterly, American Eugenics Society, 230 Park Avenue, New York, New York 10017.

Eugenics Review, Eugenics Society, Oliver and Boyd Ltd., Tweedale Court, 14 High Street, Edinburgh 1, Scotland.

Far Eastern Economic Review, Windsor House, Hong-Kong, China; U. S.: Stechert-Hafner Inc., 31 E. Tenth Street, New York, New York 10003; England: Arthur H. Wheeler 6 Co., St. Stephen's House, Victoria Embankment, London S.W. 1, England.

Far Eastern Survey (Discontinued November, 1960. See *Asian Survey*), American IPR, 333 Sixth Avenue, New York, New York 10014.

Farm and Home Science, Agricultural Experiment Station, Utah State University, Logan, Utah 84321.

Farm Policy Forum, The Iowa State University Press, Ames, Iowa 50010.

Fennia, Helsinki, Finland.

Finance and Trade Review, Volkskas Ltd., Box 578, Pretoria, S. A.

Foreign Affairs, Council on Foreign Relations, 58 E. 68th Street, New York, New York 10021.

French Affairs, Ambassade de France, Service de Presse et d'Information, Paris, France.

Genus, Segreteria del Comitato Italiano per lo Studio del Problemi della Popolazione, via delle Terme di Diocleziano 10 Rome, Italy.

Geografiska Annaler (Sevenska Sallskapet for Anthropologi och Geografi), Drottninggatan, Stockholm, Sweden.

Geographical Journal (Royal Geographical Society), Kensington Gore, London S.W. 7, England.

Geographical Review, The American Geographical Society of New York, Broadway at 156th Street, New York, New York 10032.

Geographical Review of India, Calcutta University, 35 Ballygunge, Circular Road, Calcutta 19, India.

The Geographical Review of Japan (Chirigaku Hyoron), The Association of Japanese Geographers, Institute of Geography, Faculty of Science, University of Tokyo, Tokyo, Japan.

Geography, The Geographical Association, 343 Fulwood Road, Sheffield 10, England; G. Philip & Son, Ltd., Victoria Road, London N.W. 10, England.

George Washington Law Review, Students of George Washington University Law School, George Washington University, Washington, D. C. 20006.

Glasnik (Glasnik Srpskog Geografskog Drushtua), Studentskiftrg 3, Belgrade, Yugoslavia.

Harvard Educational Review, Graduate School of Education, Harvard University, Cambridge, Massachusetts 02138.

The Hispanic American Historical Review, Duke University Press, Box 6697, College Station, Durham, N. C. 27708.

History, The Historical Association, 59A Kennington Park Road, London S. E. 11, England.

Human Biology, Wayne State University Press, Detroit, Michigan 48202.

Human Organization, Society for Applied Anthropology, New York State School of Industrial and Labor Relations, Cornell University, Ithaca, New York 14850.

Human Relations, Tavistock Publications, Ltd., 11 New Fetter Lane, London, E. C. 4, England; United States and Canada: Fred B. Rothman & Co., 57 Leuning Street, South Hackensack, New Jersey 07606.

ICFTU Economic and Social Bulletin, Brussels, Belgium.

ICMC News, The Hague, Netherlands.

ICMC Migration News, International Catholic Migration Commission, 65 rue de Lausanne, Geneva, Switzerland.

I.U.L.A. Quarterly, International Union of Local Authorities, Paleisstraat 5, The Hague, Netherlands.

India Quarterly (A Journal of International Affairs), Asia Publishing House for Indian Council of World Affairs, Bombay 1, India; 447 Strand, London W. C. 2, England; 119 W. 57th Street, New York, New York 10019.

Indian Economic Journal, Indian Economic Association, Department of Economics, University of Bombay, Bombay 1, India.

Indian Economic Review, Asia Publishing House for Delhi School of Economics, Calicut Street, Ballard Estate, Bombay 1, India.

Indian Journal of Agricultural Economics, 46-48 Esplanade Mansions, Mahatma Gandhi Road, Fort, Bombay 1, India.

Indian Journal of Economics, Departments of Economics and Commerce, University of Allahabad, Allahabad, India.

Industrial and Labor Relations Review, New York State School of Industrial and Labor Relations, Cornell University, Ithaca, New York 14850.

Industrial Bulletin (New York State Department of Labor), Office of Public Information, Gov. Smith State Office Building, Albany, New York 12207.

Industry and Labour (Ceased publication at end of 1961), The International Labour Office (Sales Section), Geneva, Switzerland; United States: Mr. Ralph Wright, 917 Fifteenth Street, N. W., Washington, D. C. 20005.

Integration - No address available.

Inter-African Labour Institute, Bulletin, See *Bulletin of the Inter-African Labour Institute*.

International Index (A Quarterly Guide to Periodical Literature in the Social Sciences and Humanities), The H. W. Wilson Company, 950 University Avenue, Bronx, New York 10452.

International Journal, Canadian Institute of International Affairs, 230 Bloor Street West, Toronto 5, Canada.

International Journal of Comparative Sociology, Department of Social Anthropology, Karnatak University, Dharwar, India.

International Journal of Religious Education, National Council of Churches, 475 Riverside Drive, New York, New York 10027.

International Labour Review, International Labour Office, (Sales Section), Geneva, Switzerland.

International Organization, World Peace Foundation, 40 Mount Vernon Street, Boston, Mass. 02108; United Kingdom:

Stevens & Sons, Ltd., 11 New Fetter Lane, London E. C. 4, England; Netherlands: N.V. Matrinus Nijhoff, Lange Voorhout 9, The Hague, Netherlands; Switzerland: La Librairie Payet, S. A., Lausanne, Switzerland.

International Review Service - No address available.

International Social Science Bulletin (to 1959), See *International Social Science Journal*.

International Social Science Journal (1959-), UNESCO, place de Fontenoy, Paris (7e), France.

Interpreter Releases, American Council for Nationalities Service, 20 W. 49th Street, New York, New York 10018.

Iowa Farm Science, Morrill Hall, Iowa State University, Ames, Iowa 50010.

Iowa Journal of History, The State Historical Society, Iowa City, Iowa 52240.

Irish Geography - No address available.

Irish Trade Journal and Statistical Bulletin (Central Statistics Office), Government Publications Sales Office. Arcade, Henry Street, Dublin, Ireland.

Israel Economist, 16 King George Avenue, Box 7052, Jerusalem, Israel.

Italian Affairs, The Italian Society of Authors and Publishers, Via Po 14, Rome, Italy.

Italiani nel Mondo, Ministero Affari Esteri, Rome, Italy.

Jewish Frontier, Jewish Frontier Publishing Association, 45E, 17th Street, New York, New York 10003.

Jewish Journal of Sociology (World Jewish Congress), William Heinemann Ltd., 15-16 Queen Street, London W. 1, England.

Jewish Social Studies, Conference on Jewish Social Studies, 1841 Broadway, New York, New York 10023.

Jinrui Kagaku, Tokyo, Japan.

John Rylands Library, John Rylands Library and Manchester University Press, 316 Oxford Road, Manchester 13, England.

Journal of African Administration, Colonial Office, London, England.

Journal of African History, School of Oriental and African Studies, University of London, London, W.C. 1, England.

Journal of Central European Affairs, University of Colorado, Boulder, Col. 80301; B. H. Blackwell Ltd., 51 Broad Street, Oxford, England.

Journal of City Plan Division (Oklahoma) - No address available.

Journal of Economic History (Economic History Association), 100 Trinity Place, New York, New York 10006.

Journal of Farm Economics, James Nielson, American Farm Economic Association, Department of Agricultural Economics, Michigan State University, East Lansing, Michigan 48823.

Journal of Geography (U.S.), A. J. Nystrom and Company, 3333 Elston Avenue, Chicago, Illinois 60618.

Journal of Geography (Chigaku Zasshi) (Japan), Charles E. Tuttle Co., Tokyo, Japan.

Journal of Gerontology, Gerontological Society, Inc., 660 South Euclid Avenue, St. Louis, Missouri 63110.

Journal of Heredity, American Genetic Association, 32nd Street and Elm Avenue, Baltimore, Maryland 21211.

Journal of Negro Education, Bureau of Educational Research, Howard University, Washington, D. C. 20001.

Journal of Osteopathy, Kirksville College of Osteopathy and Surgery, Kirksville, Missouri 63501.

Journal of Political Economy, The University of Chicago Press, 5750 Ellis Avenue, Chicago, Illinois 60637.

Journal of Politics, Peabody Hall, Southern Political Science Association, University of Florida, Gainesville, Florida 32603.

Journal of Social Psychology, The Journal Press, 2 Commercial Street, Provincetown, Massachusetts 02657.

Journal of Social Sciences, Institute of Social Sciences, Agra University, Agra, India.

Journal of Tropical Geography, Department of Geography, University of Singapore, Singapore 10.

Journal of the American Statistical Association, See *American Statistical Association, Journal of*.

Journal of the Czechoslovak Geographical Society, Prague, Czechoslovakia.

Journal of the Institute of Bankers in Ireland, 20 College Green, Dublin 2, Ireland.

Journal of the Malayan Branch of the Royal Asiatic Society, Singapore; London office: Journal of the Royal Asiatic Society of Great Britain and Ireland, 56 Queen Anne Street, London W. 1, England.

Journal of the Polynesian Society, Polynesian Society, Wellington, New Zealand.

Journal of the Rhodes-Livingstone Institute, Lusaka, Rhodesia.

Journal of the Royal Anthropological Institute of Great Britain and Ireland, 21 Bedford Square, London W.C. 1, England.

Journal of the Royal Society of Arts, 6-8 John Adam Street, Adelphi, London W.C. 2, England.

Journal of the Royal Statistical Society, 21 Bentinck Street, London W. 1, England.

Journal of the Town Planning Institute, Town Planning Institute, 26 Portland Place, London W. 1, England.

Kobe Economic and Business Review, Kobe, Japan.

Kobe University Economic Review, Kobe University, Kobe, Japan.

Kulturgeografi, Vanløsevej 15, Arhus, Denmark.

Kyoto University Economic Review, Faculty of Economics, Kyoto University, Kyoto, Japan.

Labour and Employment Gazette, New Zealand Department of Labour, Box 6310, Wellington C. 2, New Zealand.

Labour Gazette, S. R. Ceylon.

Ladies Home Journal, Curtis Publishing Company, Independence Square, Philadelphia, Pennsylvania 19105.

Land Economics, Journals Department, The University of Wisconsin Press, Box 1379, Madison, Wisconsin 53701.

Law and Contemporary Problems, Duke University School of Law, Duke Station, Durham, North Carolina 21706.

Listener, British Broadcasting Corporation, 35 Marylebone High Street, London W. 1, England, British Publications, Inc., 30 East 60th Street, New York, New York 10022.

Maandschrift van het Centraal Bureau voor de Statistick, W de Haan N. V., Von Zinzendorflaan 3, Zeist, Netherlands.

Maandstatistick van de Bevolking en de Volksgezondheid- No address available.

Malayan Historical Journal, Kuala Lumpur, Malaya.

Manchester School of Economic and Social Studies, Department of Economics, University of Manchester, Dover Street, Manchester 13, England.

Marché Commun, See *Revue du Marché Commun*.

Mexican-American Review, Nazar 45-B, Mexico 1, D. F.

Michigan Education Journal, Michigan Education Association, Box 673, East Lansing, Michigan 48824.

Michigan Farm Economics, Michigan State University, Department of Agricultural Economics, East Lansing, Michigan 48824.

Middle East Journal, Middle East Institute, 1761 N St., N.W., Washington, D. C. 20036.

Midwest Journal of Political Science (Midwest Conference of Political Scientists), Wayne State University Press, 4841 Cass Avenue, Detroit, Michigan 48202.

Migration, Inter-Governmental Committee for European Migration, 63 rue des Paquis, Geneva, Switzerland.

Migration Digest - No address available.

Migration News, International Catholic Migration Commission, 65 rue des Lausanne, Geneva, Switzerland.

Milbank Memorial Fund Quarterly, 40 Wall Street, New York, New York 10005.

Ministry of Labour Gazette, H. M. Stationery Office, York House, Kingsway, London W.C. 2, England.

Minnesota Academy of Science, Proceedings - No address available.

Mississippi Farm Research, Mississippi Agricultural Experiment Station, State College, Mississippi 39762.

Mississippi Quarterly, Social Science Research Center, Box 23, State College, Mississippi 39762.

Modern Review, Modern Review Office, 120-2 Upper Circular Road, Calcutta 9, India.

Monthly Bulletin, Indiana State Board of Health, State Board of Health Building, 1098 W. Michigan Street, Indianapolis, Indiana 46202.

Monthly Bulletin of Agricultural Economics and Statistics, Food and Agriculture Organization, Vialle della Termedi Caracalla, Rome, Italy.

Monthly Digest of Statistics, Central African Statistical Office, Box 8063, Causeway, Salisbury, S. Rhodesia.

Monthly Labor Review, Superintendent of Documents, U. S. Government Printing Office, Washington, D. C. 20402.

National Association Secondary School Principals Bulletin, National Education Association, 1201 Sixteenth Street, N.W., Washington, D. C. 20036.

National Education Association Journal, National Education Association, 1201 Sixteenth Street, N.W., Washington, D. C. 20036.

National Geographical Journal of India, National Geographical Society of India, Banaras Hindu University, Varanasi-5, India.

Nebraska Agricultural Experiment Station Quarterly, Nebraska Agricultural Experiment Station, University of Nebraska, Lincoln, Nebraska 68503.

Nebraska History, Nebraska State Historical Society, 1500 R Street, Lincoln, Nebraska 68508.

New Commonwealth, Tothill Press Ltd., 33 Tothill Street, London S. W. 1, England.

New Mexico Business, University of New Mexico, 1821 Roma Avenue, N.E., Albuquerque, New Mexico 87106.

New Outlook, Trazpoit Ltd., Karl Netter 8, Tel Aviv, Israel.

New York History, New York State Historical Association, Cooperstown, New York 13326.

New Zealand Geographer, New Zealand Geographical Society,

Department of Geography, University of Canterbury, Christchurch 1, New Zealand.

La Nouvelle Revue Francaise d'Outre-Mer, (Now Communantés et Continents), Comité Central Francais pour l'Outre-Mer, 41 rue de la Bienfaisance, Paris (8e), France.

Nyasaland Journal, The Nyasaland Society, P.O. Box 125, Blantyre, Nyasaland.

Orbis, Foreign Policy Research Institute, University of Pennsylvania, 133 S. 36th Street, Room 102, Philadelphia, Pennsylvania 19104.

Oriental Economist, Nihonbashi, Tokyo, Japan.

Oxford Economic Papers, Geoffery Cumberlege, Oxford University Press, Amen House, London E. C. 4, England.

Pacific Affairs, University of British Columbia, Vancouver 8, Canada.

Pacific Historical Review (Pacific Coast Branch, American Historical Association), University of California Press, Berkeley, California 94720.

Pacific Viewpoint, Geography Department, Victoria University of Wellington, Box 196, Wellington, New Zealand.

Pakistan Geographical Review, University of Panjab, Lahore, West Pakistan.

Philippine Statistician, Philippine Statistical Association, Box 3223, Manila, Philippines.

Phylon, Atlanta University, 223 Chestnut Street. S.W., Atlanta, Georgia 31714.

Planning, Political and Economic Planning, 16 Queen Anne's Gate, London S.W. 1, England.

Polish Review, Polish Institute of Arts and Sciences in America, 59 East 66th Street, New York, New York 10021.

Population, Institut National D'Etudes Démographiques, 23 avenue Franklin-Roosevelt, Paris (8e), France.

Population Bulletin, The Population Reference Bureau, Inc., 1755 Massachusetts Avenue N.W., Washington, D. C. 20036.

Population Index, Office of Population Research, Princeton University, Princeton, New Jersey 08540.

Population Review, Indian Institute for Population Studies, Gandhinagar, Madras-20, India.

Population Studies, Population Investigation Committee, London School of Economics, Houghton Street, Aldwych, London W.C. 2, England.

Previdenza Sociale (Instituto Nazionale della Previdenza Sociale), Via Marco Minghetti 22, Rome, Italy.

La Previdenza Sociale nell-Agricoltura, Via Marco Minghetti 22, Rome, Italy.

Problems of Economics, International Arts and Sciences Press, 108 Grand Street, White Plains, New York 10601.

Proceedings of the Indian Academy of Science - No address available.

Proceedings of the Isle of Man Natural History and Antiquarian Society - No address available.

Progress, Unilever Ltd., Unilever House, Blackfriars, London E. C. 4, England.

Przeglad Geograficzny (Polska Akademia Nauk, Instytut Geografii), Pánstwowe Wydownietwo Naukowe,ul Miodowa 10, Warsaw, Poland.

Public Health (Society of Medical Officers of Health), Bailliere, Tindall and Cox, 7 Henrietta Street, London W.C. 2, England.

Public Opinion Quarterly, Princeton University Press, P.O. Box 231, Princeton, New Jersey 08540.

Public Welfare, American Public Welfare Association, 1313 E. 60th Street, Chicago, Illinois 60637.

Queen's Quarterly, Quarterly Committee of Queen's University, Kingston, Canada.

Race (Institute of Race Relations), Oxford University Press, Amen House, Warwick Square, London E.C. 2, England.

R.E.M.P. Bulletin (Research Group for European Migration Problems), 17 Pauwenlaan, The Hague, Netherlands.

Research and Farming, North Carolina Agricultural Experiment Station, North Carolina State College, Raleigh, North Carolina 27607.

Review of Economics and Statistics, Harvard University Press, Cambridge, Massachusetts 02138.

Review of Politics, The University of Notre Dame, Notre Dame, Indiana 46556.

Review of Social Economy (Catholic Economic Association), Boston College, Chestnut Hill, Massachusetts 02167.

Review of the Economic Conditions in Italy, Banco Di Roma, Direzione Cantrale, Ufficio Studi, Via del Corso 307, Rome, Italy.

Review of the Economic Situation (of Mexico), Mexico, D. F.

Review of the Geographical Institute of the University of Istanbul, International Edition, University of Istanbul, Istanbul, Turkey.

Review of the River Plate, Robert Dalziel, Austria 1828, Buenos Aires, Argentina.

Revista Brasileira de Economia (Funda çaõ Getulio Vargas), Praia de Bota fogo 186, Rio de Janeiro, Brazil.

Revista de História de América (Instituto Panamericano de

Geografia e Historia), Ex Arzobispado 29,   Tacubaya, Mexico 18, D.F.

Revue de l'Institut International de Statistique - No address available.

Revue du Marché Commun (now Marché Commun), Éditions Techniques et Economiques, 3 rue Soufflot, Paris (5e), France.

Riso, Milan, Italy.

Rivista di Agricoltura Subtropicale e Tropicale, Instituto Agronomico per l'Oltremare, Via Antonio Cocchi 4, Florence, Italy.

Rivista di Economia Agraria, Feltrinelli, Via Andegari 6, Milan, Italy.

Rivista di Politica Economica, Confederazion e General dell' Industria Italiana, Corso Vittorio Emanuele 21, Rome, Italy.

Rivista Geografica Italiana (Società di Studi Geografici), Nuova Itali Editrice S.P.A., Piazza Indipendenza 29, Florence, Italy.

Round Table, The Round Table, Ltd., 166 Piccadilly, London W. 1, England; H. W. Macdonnell, 188 Steeles Avenue East, Willowdale, Ontario; Angus & Robertson, Ltd., 89-95 Castlereagh Street, Sydney, Australia; The Round Table, P.O. Box 2440, Wellington, New Zealand.

Royal Historical Society Transactions, Offices of the Royal Historical Society, 96 Cheyne Walk, London S.W. 10, England.

Royal Sanitary Institute Journal (through July 1955; called Royal Society for the Promotion of Health, August 1955 through December 1957; Royal Society of Health Journal; 1958 to date), 90 Buckingham Palace Road, London S.W. 1, England.

Royal Society for the Promotion of Health Journal (formerly Royal Sanitary Institute Journal; from 1958 called Royal Society of Health Journal), 90 Buckingham Palace Road, London S.W. 1, England.

Rural Sociology, Rural Sociological Society, Michigan State University, East Lansing, Michigan 48823.

Sastanak (Referati), Belgrade, Yugoslavia.

Sbornik, Ceskoslavenska Spolecnost Zemepisna - No address available.

Scandinavian Economic History Review (Scandinavian Society for Economic History and Historical Geography), Institute of Economic History, Tegnerlunden 10, Stockholm Va., Sweden.

Schmollers Jahrbuck für Gesetzgebung, Verwaltung und Volkswirtschaft, Duncker and Humblot, Berlin-München, Germany.

Schweizerische Zeitschrift für Volkswirtschaft und Statistik, Schweizerische Gesellschaft für Statistik und Volkswirtschaft, Hallwylstrasse 15, Bern, Switzerland.

Science, American Association for the Advancement of Science, 1515 Massachusetts Avenue, N.W., Washington, D. C. 20005.

The Scientific Monthly (absorbed by Science in 1957), American Association for the Advancement of Science, 1515 Massachusetts Avenue, N.W., Washington D.C. 20005.

The Scottish Geographical Magazine, Royal Scottish Geographical Society, 10 Randolph Crescent, Edinburgh 3, Scotland.

Scottish Studies (School of Scottish Studies), Oliver and Boyd Ltd., Tweeddale Court, 14 High Street, Edinburgh, Scotland.

Shakaigaku Hyôron (Japanese Sociological Review), Charles E. Tuttle Co., Tokyo, Japan.

Sinologica, Verlag für Rechtund Gesellschaft AG, Bundesstrasse 15, Basel, Switzerland.

Slovakia, Middletown, Pennsylvania 17057.

Social and Economic Studies, Institute of Social and Economic Research, University College of the West Indies, Mona, Jamaica.

Social Casework, Family Service Association of America, 44 East 23rd Street, New York, N. Y. 10010.

Social Compass, Paul Gabriëlstraat 28-30, La Haye, Pays-Bas, The Hague, Netherlands.

Social Education, 1201 Sixteenth Street, N.W., Washington, D. C. 20036.

Social Forces, University of North Carolina Press, Box 510, Chapel Hill, North Carolina 27515.

Social Problems, Society for the Study of Social Problems, 35B New Street, Worchester, Massachusetts 01605.

Social Process - No address available.

Social Process in Hawaii - No address available.

Social Service Review, University of Chicago Press, 5750 Ellis Avenue, Chicago, Illinois 60637.

Sociala Meddelanden, Socialstyrelsen, Stockholm, Sweden.

Sociological Abstracts, Sociological Abstracts, Inc., 2315 Broadway, New York, New York 10024.

Sociological Bulletin, Indian Sociological Society, Rajsi Mansion, 3rd Pasta Lane, Colaba, Bombay-5, India.

Sociological Quarterly, Department of Sociology, Southern Illinois University, Carbondale, Illinois 62901.

The Sociological Review, University of Keele, Keele, Staffordshire, England.

Sociologus, Verlag Duncker and Humbolt, Berlin 41 (Steglitz), Germany.

Sociology and Social Research, University of Southern California, University Park, Los Angeles, California 90007.

Sociology of Rural Life, Minnesota Agricultural Experiment Station, Minneapolis, Minnesota 55455.

Sociometry, The American Sociological Association, Suite 215, 1755 Massachusetts Avenue, N.W., Washington, D. C. 20036.

South African Journal of Economics, P.O. Box 5316, Johannesburg, South Africa.

South Pacific, Sydney, Australia.

The Southwestern Social Science Quarterly, University of Texas, Austin, Texas 78712.

The Southern Economic Journal, Carrol Hall, Chapel Hill, N. C. 27514.

Soviet Geography, American Geographical Society, Broadway at 156th Street, New York, New York 10032.

State Government, Council of State Governments, 1313 East 60th Street, Chicago, Illinois 60637.

Speculum, The Mediaeval Academy of America, 1430 Massachusetts Avenue, Cambridge, Massachusetts 02138.

Statistical Bulletin, Metropolitan Life Insurance Co., 1 Madison Avenue, New York, New York 10038.

Statistička Revija, Jugoslovensko Statisticko Drustvo, Kneza Milosa 20, Belgrade, Yugoslavia.

Statistický Obzor, Prague, Czechoslovakia.

Statistics - No address available.

Statistik Tidskrift, A B Nordiska Bokhandel, Fack, Stockholm 1, Sweden.

Statisztikai Szemle, Hungarian Central Statistical Office, Keleti Karoly u. 5-7, Budapest 2, Hungary.

Studies, 35 Lower Lesson Street, Dublin 2, Ireland.

Survey of China Mainland Press, Hong Kong, China.

Teachers College Record, Teachers College, Columbia University, 525 West 120th Street, New York, New York 10027.

Tennessee Farm and Home Science Progress Report - No address available.

Terra (Geografiska Sallskapets i Finland Tidskrift), Lautturink 8, Kulosaari, Helsinki, Finland.

Texas Business Review, Bureau of Business Research, University of Texas, Austin, Texas 78712.

Texas Health Bulletin - No address available.

Tijdschrift van het Koninklijk Nederlandsch Aardrijkskundig Genootschap, Amsterdam, Netherlands.

Tijdschrift voor Economische en Sociale Geografie, Van Waesberge, Hoogewerff en Richards n.v., Banierstraat 1, Rotterdam-1, Netherlands.

Tilastokatsauksia - No address available.

The Times Educational Supplement, G. Bell and Sons, Ltd., Portugal Street, London W.C. 2, England.

Town and Country Planning, The Planning Centre, 28 King Street, London W.C. 2, England.

Town Planning Review (Department of Civic Design, Liverpool School of Architecture), Liverpool University Press, Liverpool 3, England.

Transactions of the Historical Society of Ghana - No address available.

Transactions of the Royal Society of Canada, Royal Society of Canada, Ottawa, Canada.

Tropical Agriculture (Imperial College of Tropical Agriculture), Butterworths Scientific Publications, 88 Kingsway, London W.C. 2, England.

Twentieth Century, The Garden City Press Ltd., Letchworth, Hertfordshire, England.

University Microfilms, 313 North First Street, Ann Arbor, Mich. 48103. (Source for microfilms of Ph.D. dissertations done in the U.S.A.)

University of California Publications in Geography, University of California, Berkeley, California 94720.

University of Missouri Business and Government Review, University of Missouri, Columbia, Missouri 65201.

University of South Carolina Business and Economic Review, University of South Carolina, Columbia, South Carolina 29208.

University Studies in History and Economics, Freemantle, Western Australia.

University Studies in Western Australia, Freemantle, Western Australia.

L'Universo, Instituto Geografico Militare, Via Cesare Battisti 10, Florence, Italy.

Uttara Bharati, University of Agra, Uttar Pradesh, India.

Virginia Economic Review, Virginia Department of Conservation and Economic Development, State Office Building, Richmond, Virginia 23219.

Voprosy Ekonomiki, Moscow, Russia.

Vox Guyanae - No address available.

Weltwirtschaftliches Archiv (Institute für Weltwirtschaft an der Universitat Kiel), Hoffmann und Campe Verlag, Hamburg, Germany.

Western Political Quarterly, University of Utah, Salt Lake City, Utah 84112.

Wirtschaft und Statistik, W. Kohlhammer GmbH., Bahnhofsplatz 2, Mainz, Germany.

World Agriculture, International Federation of Agricultural Producers, 1624 Eye Street, N.W., Washington, D. C. 20006.

World Politics, Princeton University Press, Princeton, New Jersey 08540.

World Today, Royal Institute of International Affairs, Chatham House, 10 St. James's Square, London S.W. 1, England.

Ymer (Svenska Sallskapet for Anthropologi och Geografi), Geografiska Institutionen, Drottninggaten 120, Stockholm, Sweden.

Yorkshire Bulletin of Economic and Social Research (Departments of Economics of the Universities of Hull, Leeds, and Sheffield), Department of Economics, The University, Leeds, Yorkshire, England.

Zeszyty Naukowe, Warsaw, Poland.

SUBJECT INDEX

[183]

distance (*continued*)
204, 207, 230, 245, 246, 250, 253, 262, 273, 276, 285, 292, 310, 322, 323, 325, 330, 336, 343, 345, 352, 358, 366, 369, 374, 383, 486, 551, 794, 1864.

Dominican Republic — 717, 1124, 1152, 1156.

drouth, effects of — 165.

ecological dispersion — 90, 433, 462, 576.

economic changes — 177, 199, 320, 330, 339, 343, 378, 389, 447, 461, 528, 530, 546, 609, 616, 622, 636, 661, 692, 921, 1336, 1446, 1451, 1467, 1592, 2027.

economic characteristics — 214, 233, 291, 317, 335, 382, 395, 471, 491, 512, 646, 650, 1907.

economic costs — 54, 69, 204, 241, 311, 319, 369, 1659.

economic development — (See under "development, economic.")

economic differentials — 89, 177, 295, 343, 546, 1511, 1864.

economic factors — 8, 13, 14, 15, 16, 18, 19, 21, 23, 24, 40, 44, 45, 52, 53, 55, 60, 66, 67, 73, 75, 78, 79, 81, 82, 83, 87, 88, 89, 92, 94, 98, 100, 101, 102, 105, 113, 114, 119, 125, 126, 129, 130, 132, 137, 146, 156, 159, 163, 164, 166, 170, 171, 175, 177, 178, 179, 186, 188, 194, 195, 196, 197, 198, 199, 200, 202, 203, 205, 207, 208, 209, 213, 214, 215, 216, 220, 222, 223, 227, 229, 233, 235, 236, 237, 240, 241, 242, 246, 250, 251, 255, 256, 264, 266, 267, 269, 270, 271, 272, 273, 277, 279, 280, 281, 282, 283, 284, 285, 288, 291, 292, 294, 295, 296, 297, 299, 305, 306, 208, 310, 311, 312, 317, 318, 319, 320, 322, 323, 324, 325, 327, 329, 330, 333, 335, 336, 337, 338, 339, 340, 341, 343, 344, 347, 348, 349, 351, 352, 356, 358, 360, 363, 364, 368, 369, 370, 372, 373, 378, 382, 385, 389, 395, 396, 407, 413, 417, 419, 427, 428, 440, 445, 447, 455, 461, 471, 473, 474, 476, 480, 484, 487, 493, 496, 502, 504, 505, 508, 511, 512, 521, 528, 530, 533, 534, 537, 538, 541, 543, 544, 546, 547, 567, 581, 582, 585, 591, 592, 594, 595, 605, 609, 611, 616, 617, 619, 623, 624, 628, 629, 636, 650, 651, 655, 672, 709, 731, 736, 738, 764, 796, 813, 852, 859, 862, 958, 984, 996, 1018, 1289, 1295, 1340, 1385,

1392, 1419, 1437, 1462, 1468, 1537, 1585, 1604, 1607, 1659, 1725, 1776, 1786, 1793, 1797, 1849, 1859, 1861, 1862, 1863, 1907, 1935, 1936, 1985, 2018, 2019, 2027.

economic implications — 16, 18, 31, 35, 173, 177, 223, 270, 271, 279, 280, 317, 319, 325, 329, 349, 351, 369, 385, 413, 428, 511, 629, 926, 1604.

economic level — 98, 132, 170, 369.

economic opportunity — 18, 52, 53, 60, 78, 102, 105, 113, 119, 125, 129, 137, 159, 163, 164, 170, 177, 179, 202, 203, 213, 241, 242, 246, 266, 269, 273, 280, 281, 283, 284, 285, 291, 296, 305, 306, 312, 318, 319, 325, 333, 337, 338, 343, 344, 347, 352, 360, 364, 370, 378, 385, 546, 679, 862, 1588. (Also see "non-farm opportunity.")

economic problems — 58, 60, 126, 146, 159, 164, 166, 304, 344, 348, 385, 440, 441, 445, 497, 512, 670, 931, 937, 1347, 1496, 1588, 1666, 1696, 1932, 1935. 2036.

economic status — 98, 125, 186, 191, 325, 344, 361, 368, 372, 378, 379, 428, 440, 445, 447, 570, 632, 655, 660, 1342. (Also see "socio-economic status.")

economic structure — 126, 127, 139, 150, 159, 170, 173, 177, 270, 271, 282, 330, 340, 351, 363, 370, 372, 428, 440, 461, 494, 511, 512, 516, 521, 528, 544, 546, 609, 672, 762, 1556, 1792, 1864.

education — 3, 9, 26, 28, 39, 40, 43, 48, 49, 53, 55, 56, 63, 71, 72, 78, 83, 84, 87, 95, 98, 102, 103, 114, 117, 119, 124, 132, 133, 137, 138, 141, 143, 153, 158, 165, 170, 172, 182, 191, 193, 194, 198, 204, 210, 211, 212, 213, 214, 219, 220, 225, 235, 236, 237, 241, 242, 262, 263, 269, 273, 275, 277, 278, 289, 306, 308, 315, 326, 336, 355, 357, 366, 369, 371, 372, 378, 380, 381, 382, 383, 407, 409, 447, 464, 511, 540, 558, 622, 625, 630, 650, 796, 801, 817, 1038, 1560, 1617, 1977.

academic grades — 337.

achievement — 118, 183, 224, 297, 328.

distribution — 121, 171.

expectations — 240.

level — 19, 22, 24, 25, 46, 47, 51, 121, 123, 127, 129, 163, 171, 187, 190, 226, 297, 302, 377.

needs — 376, 755.

parents' — 29, 64, 96, 104, 122, 187, 224, 337, 1594.

pattern — 121.

problems — 327, 341, 376, 621, 779.

programs — 179, 377, 755, 800, 817, 844, 845, 1116, 1560, 1610.

selectivity — 121, 123.

system — 257.

trends — 1424.

vocational — 79, 282, 288. (Also see "school.")

Egypt — 1, 1414, 1681.

El Salvador — 313.

emigration — (See under "out-migration.")

emigration cycle — 172. (Also see "migration pattern.")

employment — 5, 9, 36, 39, 52, 54, 62, 69, 82, 111, 112, 137, 145, 147, 160, 163, 173, 202, 206, 214, 252, 254, 271, 282, 285, 288, 291, 292, 295, 296, 297, 304, 310, 320, 333, 337, 347, 375, 429, 495, 496, 508, 510, 513, 583, 605, 609, 620, 632, 650, 729, 880, 1188, 1258, 1274, 1298, 1299, 1306, 1322, 1374, 1386, 1523.

background — 179.

opportunities — 14, 27, 164, 165, 242, 283, 1322, 1386.

status — 261, 378, 440, 442.

structure — 255, 405, 461, 511, 609.

environment — 118, 155, 158, 272, 284, 299, 310, 315, 321, 326, 342, 381, 382, 388, 406, 485, 512, 660.

Equador — 313.

equalization, man-land — 15.

ethnic background, group, composition, or convergence — 31, 34, 80, 88, 141, 143, 146, 166, 168, 174, 185, 186, 189, 198, 201, 207, 257, 258, 259, 275, 284, 289, 318, 328, 352, 389, 395, 400, 402, 403, 416, 421, 429, 433, 453, 456, 492, 516, 526, 527, 543, 569, 570, 587, 602, 604, 627, 631, 669, 675, 730, 808, 943, 1341, 1688, 1753, 1806, 1843, 1854, 1869, 2006, 2014. Also see "race."

Europe (in general) — 12, 73, 146, 147, 159, 208, 209, 226, 227, 257, 272, 321, 323, 407, 428, 442, 466, 468, 481, 504, 527, 550, 557, 579, 590, 624, 629, 646, 647, 652, 677, 683, 835, 854, 871, 902, 918, 984, 1097, 1108, 1137, 1142, 1148, 1174, 1178, 1191, 1203, 1212, 1227, 1232, 1242, 1248, 1259, 1276, 1277, 1297, 1312, 1313, 1335, 1342, 1355, 1359, 1364, 1379, 1385, 1455,

1471, 1472, 1473, 1516, 1544, 1546, 1562, 1573, 1577, 1613, 1640, 1858, 1863, 1887, 1919, 1993, 1994, 2008, 2009, 2010, 2011, 2012, 2013, 2046, 2048. (Also see under respective countries.)

evolution — 180, 2026.

expectations — 50, 96, 107, 112, 221, 237, 240, 267. (Also see "aspirations.")

extent of migration — 48, 83, 184, 191, 263, 369, 999, 1420, 1840. (Also see "volume.")

factor analysis — 5, 106.

family life and relations — 1, 53, 72, 77, 117, 179, 203, 207, 210, 212, 220, 221, 289, 294, 314, 315, 342, 359, 403, 405, 407, 409, 451, 485, 487, 492, 543, 547, 556, 562, 606, 608, 614, 617, 622, 660, 671, 674, 898, 911, 1001, 1382, 1593, 1755, 1948, 2025. (Also see "kin-related behavior.")

family planning — 363, 394, 650.

family size — 22, 72, 73, 74, 84, 140, 174, 187, 203, 267, 335, 383, 396, 512, 650, 1753.

family solidarity — 30, 88, 143, 171, 352, 353, 359, 547, 556, 614.

family structure — 1, 9, 28, 48, 102, 104, 142, 179, 192, 314, 371, 394, 396, 403, 487, 492, 543, 544, 551, 608, 981, 1001, 1024, 1025, 1687.

Far East — 22, 72, 143, 162, 289, 306, 330, 339, 390, 421, 451, 457, 475, 623, 631, 638, 669, 682, 825, 831, 832, 833, 867, 886, 887, 911, 929, 930, 947, 979, 1006, 1008, 1009, 1048, 1064, 1089, 1116, 1171, 1188, 1266, 1316, 1318, 1338, 1340, 1375, 1425, 1426, 1427, 1428, 1439, 1465, 1466, 1474, 1483, 1634, 1643, 1644, 1645, 1660, 1672, 1696, 1757, 1791, 1802, 1832, 1838, 1839, 1840, 1847, 1875, 1877, 1879, 1882, 1888, 1889, 1922, 2037, 2038. (Also see under respective countries.)

Faran Act — 442.

farmers — 3, 4, 13, 14, 15, 16, 17, 19, 20, 23, 24, 28, 37, 38, 40, 42, 45, 46, 47, 52, 56, 58, 61, 66, 69, 75, 78, 79, 84, 85, 87, 89, 91, 92, 98, 100, 101, 115, 116, 117, 118, 119, 122, 125, 126, 129, 132, 136, 137, 145, 149, 160, 163, 165, 171, 173, 178, 179, 190, 195, 198, 199, 202, 204,

Intergovt. Comm. (*continued*) 1533, 1919, 1961, 2008, 2012, 2013, 2030.
intergovernmental partnership — (See under "programs.")
intermarriage — 138, 168, 173, 189, 257, 258, 259, 284, 352, 359, 583, 633, 695, 824, 1059.
International Population Conference — 156, 233, 289, 302, 313.
International Refugee Organization — 385, 490, 618, 628.
intervening opportunities — 7, 144, 148.
investment — 13, 26, 534.
Iowa Test of Basic Skills — 224.
Iowa Test of Education Development — 357.
Iran — 1298.
Iraq — 387, 1019, 1069, 1258, 1447, 1673.
Ireland — 20, 100, 231, 311, 385, 438, 444, 513, 518, 592, 628, 769, 873, 931, 1104, 1206, 1240, 1267, 1315, 1341, 1399, 1400, 1401, 1402, 1403, 1404, 1441, 1478, 1616, 1745.
isolation — 18, 180, 189, 274, 341, 348.
Israel — 146, 147, 234, 303, 407, 439, 456, 492, 493, 497, 505, 582, 587, 602, 624, 663, 762, 920, 951, 969, 1007, 1126, 1199, 1303, 1408, 1409, 1410, 1411, 1415, 1447, 1585, 1656, 1664, 1668, 1711, 1754, 1892, 2017.
Italy — 20, 259, 351, 385, 461, 485, 487, 537, 565, 621, 683, 711, 726, 732, 733, 754, 818, 830, 971, 996, 1043, 1044, 1049, 1101, 1102, 1107, 1133, 1167, 1183, 1185, 1213, 1216, 1217, 1218, 1244, 1289, 1310, 1365, 1416, 1417, 1418, 1419, 1511, 1576, 1580, 1675, 1739, 1749, 1758, 1816, 1991, 2046.

Jansen's Family Solidarity Scale — 221.
Japan — 22, 72, 143, 162, 289, 330, 390, 451, 623, 682, 929, 930, 979, 1006, 1008, 1116, 1171, 1188, 1266, 1316, 1318, 1375, 1425, 1426, 1427, 1428, 1439, 1466, 1634, 1672, 1791, 1832, 1839, 1840, 1847, 1875, 1889, 2037.
Jews or Jewish — (See under "race.")
Jordan — 1354.

Kenya — 1249, 1296, 1706, 1707, 1803, 1804.
kin marriages — 695.

kin-related behavior — 30, 68, 77, 112, 171, 179, 192, 203, 237, 239, 274, 280, 281, 322, 337, 369, 405, 608, 695.
Klineberg Hypothesis — 181.
Korea — 1882.
Kruder Preference Record — 215.
Kulischer, population theory of — 150.

Labor Attitude Scale — 194.
labor conditions — 4, 13, 17, 53, 60, 61, 67, 69, 83, 89, 173, 195, 206, 207, 209, 210, 214, 223, 227, 230, 235, 256, 270, 271, 285, 291, 305, 319, 320, 339, 373, 385, 401, 440, 442, 496, 655, 907, 1686, 1951.
labor force, industrial — 8, 35, 61, 83, 108, 115, 117, 145, 163, 177, 214, 219, 254, 262, 292, 296, 334, 348, 401, 405, 426, 428, 442, 485, 493, 496, 510, 511, 513, 514, 528, 530, 531, 533, 538, 541, 563, 581, 602, 619, 620, 632, 672, 720, 724, 736, 744, 864, 879, 901, 907, 936, 937, 993, 1039, 1218, 1289, 1290, 1292, 1295, 1306, 1319, 1325, 1328, 1343, 1344, 1345, 1346, 1348, 1379, 1383, 1385, 1386, 1394, 1405, 1471, 1472, 1479, 1488, 1516, 1538, 1562, 1573, 1585, 1607, 1614, 1663, 1666, 1674, 1685, 1686, 1696, 1777, 1786, 1807, 1849, 1862, 1951, 1952, 1973, 2002, 2019, 2043.
farm — 206, 212, 296, 297, 394, 412, 424, 437, 443, 444, 488, 826, 1039, 1243, 1288, 1325, 1521, 1538, 1852, 1913, 1914, 1915, 1924, 1932, 1935. (Also see "migrant labor.")
labor mobility — (See under "occupational mobility.")
land resources — 16, 31, 163, 178, 214, 316, 387, 400, 623, 753, 1667.
land settlement — (See under "settlement.")
language — 72, 168, 171, 174, 189, 198, 201, 220, 226, 234, 257, 265, 304, 328, 333, 352, 377, 384, 394, 400, 553, 559.
Latin America — (See under "America, Latin.")
Latvia — 174, 355.
Laws, regulations — 11, 17, 208, 270, 279, 295, 296, 339, 344, 349, 585, 776, 804, 903, 1041, 1082, 1088, 1089, 1091, 1098, 1100, 1102, 1108, 1114, 1119, 1125, 1129, 1151, 1153, 1159, 1171, 1172, 1183, 1186, 1189, 1194, 1197, 1205,

1210, 1213, 1233, 1235, 1236, 1237, 1238, 1243, 1257, 1273, 1281, 1285, 1289, 1294, 1298, 1299, 1305, 1322, 1323, 1335, 1353, 1357, 1390, 1395, 1420, 1433, 1465, 1482, 1575, 1608, 1714, 1746, 1912, 1913, 1914, 1915, 1916, 1917, 1918, 1919, 1920, 1921, 1922, 1923, 1924, 1925, 1926, 1927, 1928, 1929, 1930, 1931, 1932, 1933, 1934, 1935, 1936, 1962, 1965, 1967, 1974. (Also see "policies.")
leaders, leadership — 56, 76, 90.
leaving-order of households — 375.
Lebanon — 170, 1255, 1314.
legislation — (See under "policy" and "laws, regulations.")
level of living — 18, 31, 39, 44, 48, 125, 195, 237, 246, 277, 280, 291, 308, 310, 319, 324, 348, 356, 360, 378, 417, 484, 609, 611, 2019.
life-cycle — 187, 359, 378, 795.
Likert-type word list — 265.
location of industries — 330, 360, 528, 710, 1782, 1836.
longitudinal design — 158.
loyalty as a factor in migration — 355, 359, 746.
Luxembourg — 1095, 1216.

"M" factor — 248.
M. S. U. Work Belief Check list — 118.
Madagascar (Malagasy Republic) — 892, 957, 1390.
Malaya — 306, 318, 356, 397, 514, 928, 946, 947, 1010, 1011, 1256, 1275, 1331, 1522, 1704, 1738, 1757, 1785, 1891, 2023.
Malta — 261, 272, 896, 1092, 1144, 1200, 1223, 1293, 1523, 1524.
manufacturing — 113, 348, 360, 447, 486, 528, 530, 533, 546, 655, 1808, 2043. (Also see "industrialization.")
marital status — 9, 10, 22, 34, 43, 46, 47, 48, 49, 73, 81, 85, 137, 145, 170, 171, 179, 189, 192, 194, 211, 214, 258, 259, 261, 266, 304, 311, 314, 315, 342, 357, 371, 378, 380, 381, 405, 543, 610, 613, 617, 622, 632, 652, 660, 695, 824, 951, 979, 1059, 1464, 1753.
mass communication — 48, 84, 407, 461.
mass migration — 20, 145, 197, 253, 505, 539, 679, 1455.
matrifocal family structure — 142.
matrimonial selection — 138. (Also see "marital status.")

Mauritius — 67, 1577.
McCarran-Walter Immigration Act — 339, 430, 637.
measures or tests for
assimilation — 72, 80, 385.
birth control attitude — 194.
centralization — 80.
community satisfaction — 96, 221.
economic welfare — 2018.
ethnicity — 198, 328.
farm operator level of living index — 110.
general achievement — 328.
home satisfaction — 221.
integration attitude — 328.
intelligence — 224, 268, 303.
knowledge of Israel — 303.
labor and labor union attitude — 194, 328.
migration — 33, 182, 795.
mobility potential — 187.
neighborliness of women — 193.
personal adjustment — 328.
personality — 43, 55, 118, 133, 215, 267.
racial attitudes — 194, 328.
social distance — 80, 304.
social participation — 193, 372.
Southern identification — 194.
values — 315.
Zionism — 303.
mechanism of internal migration — 117. (Also see "causes of," "consequences of," and "reasons for" migration.)
mechanization of industry — 110, 111, 119, 125, 179, 202, 442. (Also see "industrialization.")
meetings — (See under "conferences.")
mental illness — 5, 99, 143, 169, 183, 203, 268, 290, 328, 342, 542, 554, 663, 674, 1526, 1527.
methods and techniques (general) — 8, 25, 26, 32, 72, 80, 93, 96, 120, 124, 134, 152, 153, 177, 182, 184, 187, 189, 233, 249, 258, 260, 261, 288, 331, 332, 335, 336, 340, 345, 346, 354, 355, 356, 367, 370, 372, 379, 385, 404, 406, 462, 471, 481, 528, 580, 598, 649, 663, 664, 689, 758, 784, 795, 967, 970, 983, 1003, 1366, 1407, 1683, 1824, 1853, 1865, 1866, 2041, 2051.
Metropolitan Achievement Tests — 328.
metropolitan and metropolises — 6, 8, 25, 31, 60, 62, 76, 106, 144, 189, 191, 269, 292, 293, 298, 300, 301, 329, 330, 360, 361, 371, 378, 383, 404, 405, 462, 479, 486, 491, 613, 622, 632, 659, 662, 727, 917, 946, 1032, 1054, 1392, 1469,

social participation — 1, 22, 50, 53, 55, 72, 76, 98, 104, 149, 157, 158, 174, 176, 192, 193, 194, 215, 218, 237, 262, 266, 274, 280, 328, 352, 359, 369, 371, 372, 380, 381, 383, 547, 556, 652.

social pressures — 149.

social problems — 28, 35, 58, 126, 154, 164, 170, 172, 268, 284, 310, 348, 409, 414, 441, 445, 447, 497, 523, 608, 628, 652, 667, 674, 1347, 1376, 1834, 2036.

social relationships — 18, 58, 1786.

Social Security — (See under "programs.")

social situation — 22, 133, 284, 319, 512, 1742, 1818.

social status — 55, 80, 84, 90, 95, 96, 98, 103, 104, 138, 139, 140, 158, 183, 190, 191, 193, 215, 226, 235, 240, 263, 273, 275, 277, 284, 325, 352, 366, 371, 372, 378, 382, 445, 570. (Also see "economic status.")

social stratification — 226, 284.

social structure — 30, 60, 76, 77, 80, 81, 85, 90, 91, 95, 98, 115, 126, 127, 128, 133, 138, 139, 140, 141, 143, 147, 149, 165, 170, 173, 187, 193, 226, 229, 246, 257, 271, 284, 286, 293, 299, 300, 306, 312, 314, 315, 317, 337, 349, 351, 355, 367, 372, 373, 378, 380, 441, 481, 576, 604, 652, 1556.

social system — 154, 356.

social work — (See under "programs.")

socio-economic status — 2, 3, 9, 13, 18, 21, 25, 30, 40, 44, 45, 55, 68, 74, 78, 81, 85, 89, 96, 98, 119, 125, 126, 133, 139, 140, 141, 163, 164, 170, 175, 177, 179, 186, 187, 190, 191, 193, 194, 200, 202, 203, 204, 213, 215, 216, 230, 235, 237, 246, 249, 251, 255, 273, 276, 277, 282, 312, 316, 320, 326, 328, 331, 335, 336, 343, 344, 358, 363, 366, 368, 369, 371, 373, 375, 378, 382, 613, 661. (Also see "economic status" and "social status.")

South America — (See under "America, South.")

Southern Identification Scale — 195.

Spain — 20, 351, 385, 612, 1154, 1156, 1162, 1193, 1225, 1241, 1292, 1322, 1323, 1325, 1326, 1327, 1328, 1365, 1386, 1476.

specification level — 107.

spontaneous migration — 363.

S. R. A. Junior Inventory — 328.

Stanford-Binet Test — 268.

statistical techniques — 5, 13, 73, 82, 83, 102, 110, 120, 182, 184, 228, 237, 258, 260, 261, 301, 315, 345, 346, 351, 784, 2041. (Also see "measures or tests" and "methods and techniques.")

statistics — 288, 301, 340, 345, 346, 401, 404, 406, 413, 426, 464, 467, 486, 495, 499, 513, 527, 528, 530, 546, 552, 554, 564, 566, 570, 595, 596, 598, 607, 614, 620, 629, 641, 646, 649, 655, 666, 675, 681, 686, 694, 699, 718, 737, 759, 785, 821, 831, 881, 882, 891, 908, 932, 956, 965, 966, 995, 1003, 1008, 1076, 1079, 1086, 1366, 1392, 1400, 1404, 1408, 1411, 1422, 1423, 1425, 1426, 1436, 1448, 1473, 1522, 1535, 1554, 1599, 1600, 1601, 1602, 1611, 1612, 1621, 1622, 1623, 1624, 1625, 1626, 1658, 1699, 1724, 1750, 1759, 1783, 1789, 1799, 1819, 1831, 1853, 1857, 1891, 1894, 1895, 1896, 1897, 1898, 1899, 1900, 1901, 1902, 1903, 1904, 1905, 1906, 1907, 1908, 1909, 1910, 2040, 2049.

Story Completion Test — 133.

Stouffer's Theory — 7, 93, 144, 148, 323.

subsidization — 15.

suburb and suburbanization — 75, 76, 78, 175, 176, 188, 202, 330, 360, 374, 383, 428, 481, 796, 1020, 1703, 1773, 1878, 2038, 2045.

suburban fringe — 24, 75, 76, 175, 176, 225, 269, 293, 361, 374, 383.

Sudan — 201, 563, 965, 1468, 1539, 1650.

Surinam — 397, 1985, 2000.

Sweden — 111, 116, 117, 148, 149, 246, 252, 351, 370, 444, 481, 695, 923, 963, 964, 1055, 1077, 1574, 1582, 1749, 1835, 2022.

Switzerland — 385, 1173, 1218, 1254, 1333, 1334, 1386, 1388, 2029.

Syria — 170, 1274, 1520.

Tahiti — 1541.

Tanganyika — 112, 471, 1344, 1733, 1849, 1850.

T. A. T. — 133.

technological
changes — 60, 177, 461, 654, 1824.
conditions — 324.
development — 655.
improvements — 125, 173, 177, 192, 283, 305, 318.
techniques — (See under "methods and techniques.")

technology — 150, 611.

tenancy — 125, 129, 187, 368, 495, 666, 1655.

test scores — 181, 190, 337, 357.

Thailand — 306, 421, 626, 675, 867, 1336, 1797, 1857, 2021.

theory and theoretical — 5, 7, 15, 22, 24, 44, 53, 65, 75, 81, 84, 93, 101, 106, 113, 128, 144, 148, 150, 154, 156, 161, 177, 180, 192, 203, 208, 228, 232, 243, 244, 245, 257, 273, 294, 299, 319, 321, 323, 325, 332, 367, 371, 611, 629, 663, 759, 763, 791, 1035, 1494, 1572, 1701. (Also see "concepts.")

Tobago — 894.

Togoland — 864.

tourist — (See under "migration-temporary.")

trailer households — 74.

transference — 1549.

transhumance — 1826.

transmigration — 363, 496.

transportation — 44, 84, 114, 188, 198, 219, 285, 296, 330, 358, 461, 481, 635, 655, 1575, 1856, 1907, 1917, 2035.

treaties — (See under "agreements.")

Tree test — 133.

trends — 10, 77, 79, 118, 125, 162, 166, 167, 184, 262, 283, 302, 313, 319, 350, 405, 484, 535, 646, 756, 998, 1466, 1862. (Also see "patterns.")

tribal — (See under "ethnic.")

Trinidad — 67, 520, 894.

Trust Territory of the Pacific Islands — 1981.

Tunisia (Tunis) — 1476.

Turkey — 351, 780, 827, 1458, 1459, 1759, 1851, 1885, 1886.

types of migration — 1, 12, 24, 112, 113, 235, 243, 244, 257, 276, 363, 366, 1036.

typology — 161, 176, 193, 355.

U.S.S.R. — (See under "Russia.")

Uganda — 440, 567, 907.

underemployment — 27, 1013.

unemployment — 8, 25, 27, 230, 291, 339, 360, 405, 513, 620, 672, 731, 1044, 1394, 1525, 1631. (Also see "employment.")

Union of South Africa — 20, 218, 607, 1170, 1208, 1224, 1269, 1311, 1890.

unions — 60, 109, 195, 270, 328, 347, 511, 1164.

United Kingdom — 1, 2, 10, 20, 35, 42, 49, 50, 60, 97, 197, 238, 254, 255, 259, 265, 267, 285, 304, 318, 351, 385, 391, 392, 416, 418, 422, 427, 431, 438, 444, 449, 453, 458, 465, 470, 480, 485, 531, 539, 552, 583, 588, 598, 600, 628, 651, 679, 777, 786, 806, 816, 838, 874, 879, 895, 898, 925, 934, 942, 956, 958, 976, 987, 988, 993, 994, 1033, 1062, 1087, 1165, 1166, 1194, 1226, 1234, 1373, 1399, 1406, 1430, 1441, 1477, 1490, 1498, 1505, 1517, 1552, 1646, 1647, 1648, 1649, 1657, 1680, 1681, 1730, 1746, 1786, 1788, 1792, 1798, 1859, 1872.

United Nations — 573, 639, 640, 641, 642, 644, 645, 646, 647, 648, 1098, 1099, 1117, 1140, 1141, 1160, 1161, 1182, 1195, 1197, 1209, 1211, 1220, 1229, 1239, 1253, 1261, 1270, 1280, 1287, 1308, 1501, 1981.

United States (general) — 396, 401, 406, 409, 418, 420, 424, 431, 437, 438, 441, 452, 455, 464, 465, 470, 476, 478, 480, 485, 486, 489, 494, 515, 528, 529, 530, 536, 548, 550, 555, 557, 560, 565, 566, 592, 597, 599, 600, 612, 621, 622, 624, 628, 634, 635, 637, 651, 655, 662, 665, 690, 767, 768, 772, 784, 799, 808, 812, 855, 858, 885, 948, 953, 959, 988, 995, 1016, 1032, 1042, 1075, 1076, 1091, 1096, 1143, 1179, 1205, 1231, 1260, 1286, 1305, 1320, 1380, 1441, 1442, 1465, 1507, 1528, 1559, 1587, 1597, 1619, 1669, 1682, 1698, 1700, 1748, 1777, 1778, 1781, 1809, 1812, 1843, 1845, 1864, 1894, 1895, 1896, 1897, 1898, 1899, 1900, 1901, 1902, 1903, 1904, 1905, 1906, 1907, 1908, 1909, 1910, 1911, 1912, 1913, 1914, 1915, 1916, 1917, 1918, 1920, 1921, 1923, 1924, 1925, 1926, 1928, 1929, 1930, 1931, 1932, 1933, 1934, 1935, 1936, 1937, 1938, 1939, 1940, 1941, 1942, 1943, 1944, 1945, 1946, 1947, 1948, 1949, 1950, 1951, 1952, 1953, 1954, 1955, 1956, 1960, 1962, 1963, 1964, 1965, 1966, 1967, 1968, 1969, 1970, 1971, 1974, 1976, 1979, 1980, 1981, 1998, 2007, 2044, 2046.

United States (regional)
Atlantic Coast — 523, 1594, 1937, 1938.
Atlantic metropolitan belt — 360.
Great Plains — 773, 839, 840.
inter-regional — 62, 131.
Lake states — 171, 360.